VERBAL REVIEW

P9-CRQ-384

The only study guide with 300 real GMAT® questions —and their answers— by the creators of the test.

- The -
OFFICIAL
Guide

THE OFFICIAL GUIDE FOR
GMAT® VERBAL REVIEW

- Real questions from past GMAT® tests
- 300 real questions, answers, and explanations in:
  Reading Comprehension · Critical Reasoning ·
  Sentence Correction · Analytical Writing Assessment
- NEW organization of questions in order of difficulty saves study time

From the Graduate Management Admission Council®

THE OFFICIAL GUIDE FOR GMAT® VERBAL REVIEW

For additional information contact:
Graduate Management Admission Council
1600 Tysons Blvd., Ste. 1400
McLean, VA 22102 USA
www.gmac.com

ISBN: 0-9765709-1-2

10 9 8 7 6 5 4 3 2 1

Produced by Blanche Brann LP, Lawrenceville, NJ
Charles Forster, Designer
Mike Wilson, Production Designer

Printed in the United States of America

Table of Contents

1.0 What Is the GMAT®?

1.0 What Is the GMAT®?

The Graduate Management Admission Test® (GMAT®) is a standardized, three-part exam delivered in English. The test was designed to help admissions officers evaluate how suitable individual applicants are for their graduate business and management programs. It measures basic verbal, mathematical, and analytical writing skills that a test taker has developed over a long period of time through education and work.

The GMAT® exam does not a measure a person's knowledge of specific fields of study. Graduate business and management programs enroll people from many different undergraduate and work backgrounds, so rather than test your mastery of any particular subject area, the GMAT® exam will assess your acquired skills. Your GMAT® score will give admissions officers a statistically reliable measure of how well you are likely to perform academically in the core curriculum of a graduate business program.

Of course, there are many other qualifications that can help people succeed in business school and in their careers—for instance, job experience, leadership ability, motivation, and interpersonal skills. The GMAT® exam does not gauge these qualities. That is why your GMAT® score is intended to be used as one standard admissions criterion among other, more subjective, criteria, such as admission's essays and interviews.

1.1 Why Take the GMAT® Test?

GMAT® scores are used by admissions officers in roughly 1,800 graduate business and management programs worldwide. Schools that require prospective students to submit GMAT® scores in the application process are generally interested in admitting the best-qualified applicants for their programs, which means that you may find a more beneficial learning environment at schools that require GMAT® scores as part of your application.

Because the GMAT® test gauges skills that are important to successful study of business and management at the graduate level, your scores will give you a good indication of how well prepared you are to succeed academically in a graduate management program; how well you do on the test may also help you choose the business schools to which you apply. Furthermore, the percentile table you receive with your scores will tell you how your performance on the test compares to the performance of other test takers, giving you one way to gauge your competition for admission to business school.

Schools consider many different aspects of an application before making an admissions decision, so even if you score well on the GMAT® exam, you

Myth -vs- **FACT**

M – **If I don't score in the 90th percentile, I won't get into any school I choose.**

F – **Very few people get super-high scores.**

Less than 50 of the more than 200,000 people taking the GMAT® exam each year get a perfect score of 800. Thus, while you may be exceptionally capable, the odds are against your achieving a perfect score. Also, the GMAT® exam is just one piece of your application packet. Admissions officers use GMAT® scores in conjunction with undergraduate record, application essays, interviews, letters of recommendation, and other information when deciding whom to accept into their programs.

should contact the schools that interest you to learn more about them and to ask about how they use GMAT® scores and other admissions criteria (such as your undergraduate grades, essays, and letters of recommendation) to evaluate candidates for admission. School admissions offices, school Web sites, and materials published by the school are the best sources for you to tap when you are doing research about where you might want to go to business school.

For more information about how schools should use GMAT® scores in admissions decisions, please read the Appendix A of this book. For more information on the GMAT®, registering to take the test, sending your scores to schools, and applying to business school, please visit our Web site at www.mba.com.

1.2 GMAT® Test Format

The GMAT® exam consists of four separately timed sections (see the table on the next page). You start the test with two 30-minute Analytical Writing Assessment (AWA) questions that require you to type your responses using the computer keyboard. The writing section is followed by two 75-minute, multiple-choice sections: the Quantitative and Verbal sections of the test.

The GMAT® is a computer-adaptive test (CAT), which means that in the multiple-choice sections of the test, the computer constantly gauges how well you are doing on the test and presents you with questions that are appropriate to your ability level. These questions are drawn from a huge pool of possible test questions. So, although we talk about the GMAT® as one test, the GMAT® exam you take may be completely different from the test the person sitting next to you.

Here's how it works. At the start of each GMAT® multiple-choice section (Verbal and Quantitative), you will be presented with a question of moderate difficulty. The computer uses your response to that first question to determine which question to present next. If you respond correctly, the test usually will give you questions of increasing difficulty. If you respond incorrectly, the next question you see usually will be easier than the one you answered incorrectly. As you continue to respond to the questions presented, the computer will narrow your score to the number that best characterizes your ability. When you complete each section, the computer will have an accurate assessment of your ability.

Myth -vs- FACT

M – **Getting an easier question means I answered the last one wrong.**

F – **Getting an easier question does not necessarily mean you got the previous question wrong.**

To ensure that everyone receives the same content, the test selects a specific number of questions of each type. The test may call for your next question to be a relatively hard problem solving item involving arithmetic operations. But, if there are no more relatively difficult problem solving items involving arithmetic, you might be given an easier item.

Most people are not skilled at estimating item difficulty, so don't worry when taking the test or waste valuable time trying to determine the difficulty of the questions you are answering.

Because each question is presented on the basis of your answers to all previous questions, you must answer each question as it appears. You may not skip, return to, or change your responses to previous questions. Random guessing can significantly lower your scores. If you do not know the answer to a question, you should try to eliminate as many choices as possible, then select the answer you think is best. If you answer a question incorrectly by mistake—or correctly by lucky guess—your answers to subsequent questions will lead you back to questions that are at the appropriate level of difficulty for you.

Each multiple-choice question used in the GMAT® exam has been thoroughly reviewed by professional test developers. New multiple-choice questions are tested each time the exam is administered. Answers to trial questions are not counted in the scoring of your test, but the trial questions are not identified and could appear anywhere in the test. Therefore, you should try to do your best on every question.

The test includes the types of questions found in this *Guide*, but the format and presentation of the questions are different on the computer. When you take the exam:

- Only one question at a time is presented on the computer screen.

- The answer choices for the multiple-choice questions will be preceded by circles, rather than by letters.

- Different question types appear in random order in the multiple-choice sections of the test.

- You must select your answer using the computer.

- You must choose an answer and confirm your choice before moving on to the next question.

- You may not go back to change answers to previous questions.

Format of the GMAT®		
	Questions	Timing

Analytical Writing
   Analysis of an Issue
   Analysis of an Argument
	
	1
	1
		
		30 min.
		30 min.

Optional break		5 min.

Quantitative
   Problem Solving
   Data Sufficiency
	37	75 min.

Optional break		5 min.

Verbal
   Reading Comprehension
   Critical Reasoning
   Sentence Correction
	41	75 min.

	Total Time:	210-220 min.

1.3 What Is the Content of the Test Like?

It is important to recognize that the GMAT® test evaluates skills and abilities developed over a relatively long period of time. Although the sections contain questions that are basically verbal and mathematical, the complete test provides one method of measuring overall ability.

Keep in mind that although the questions in this *Guide* are arranged by question type and ordered from easy to difficult, the test is organized differently. When you take the test, you may see different types of questions in any order.

1.4 Quantitative Section

The GMAT® Quantitative section measures your ability to reason quantitatively, solve quantitative problems, and interpret graphic data.

Two types of multiple-choice questions are used in the Quantitative section:

- Problem solving

- Data sufficiency

Problem solving and data sufficiency questions are intermingled throughout the Quantitative section. Both types of questions require basic knowledge of:

- Arithmetic

- Elementary algebra

- Commonly known concepts of geometry

To review the basic mathematical concepts that will be tested in the GMAT® Quantitative questions, see the math review in chapter 4. For test-taking tips specific to the question types in the Quantitative section of the GMAT® exam, sample questions, and answer explanations, see chapters 5 and 6.

1.5 Verbal Section

The GMAT® Verbal section measures your ability to read and comprehend written material, to reason and evaluate arguments, and to correct written material to conform to standard written English. Because the Verbal section includes reading sections from several different content areas, you may be generally familiar with some of the material; however, neither the reading passages nor the questions assume detailed knowledge of the topics discussed.

Three types of multiple-choice questions are used in the Verbal section:

- Reading comprehension

- Critical reasoning

- Sentence correction

These question types are intermingled throughout the Verbal section.

1.6 What Computer Skills Will I Need?

You only need minimal computer skills to take the GMAT® Computer-Adaptive Test (CAT). You will be required to type your essays on the computer keyboard using standard word–processing keystrokes. In the multiple-choice sections, you will select your responses using either your mouse or the keyboard.

To learn more about the specific skills required to take the GMAT CAT®, download the free test-preparation software available at www.mba.com.

1.7 What Are The Test Centers Like?

The GMAT® test is administered at a test center providing the quiet and privacy of individual computer workstations. You will have the opportunity to take two five-minute breaks—one after completing the essays and another between the Quantitative and Verbal sections. An erasable notepad will be provided for your use during the test.

1.8 How Are Scores Calculated?

Your GMAT® scores are determined by:

- the number of questions you answer
- whether you answer correctly or incorrectly
- the level of difficulty and other statistical characteristics of each question

Your Verbal, Quantitative, and Total GMAT® scores are determined by a complex mathematical procedure that takes into account the difficulty of the questions that were presented to you and how you answered them. When you answer the easier questions correctly, you get a chance to answer harder questions—making it possible to earn a higher score. After you have completed all the questions on the test—or when your time is up—the computer will calculate your scores. Your scores on the Verbal and Quantitative sections are combined to produce your Total score. If you have not responded to all the questions in a section (37 Quantitative questions or 41 Verbal questions), your score is adjusted, using the proportion of questions answered.

Appendix A contains the 2005 percentile ranking tables that explain how your GMAT® scores compare with scores of other GMAT® test takers.

1.9 Analytical Writing Assessment Scores

The Analytical Writing Assessment consists of two writing tasks: Analysis of an Issue and Analysis of an Argument. The responses to each of these tasks are scored on a 6-point scale, with 6 being the highest score and 1, the lowest. A score of zero (0) is given to responses that are off-topic, are in a foreign language, merely attempt to copy the topic, consist only of keystroke characters, or are blank.

The readers who evaluate the responses are college and university faculty members from various subject matter areas, including management education. These readers read holistically—that is, they respond to the overall quality of your critical thinking and writing. (For details on how readers are qualified, visit www.mba.com.) In addition, responses may be scored by an automated scoring program designed to reflect the judgment of expert readers.

Each response is given two independent ratings. If the ratings differ by more than a point, a third reader adjudicates. (Because of ongoing training and monitoring, discrepant ratings are rare.)

Your final score is the average (rounded to the nearest half point) of the four scores independently assigned to your responses—two scores for the Analysis of an Issue and two for the Analysis of an Argument. For example, if you earned scores of 6 and 5 on the Analysis of an Issue and 4 and 4 on the Analysis of an Argument, your final score would be 5: $(6 + 5 + 4 + 4) \div 4 = 4.75$, which rounds up to 5.

Your Analytical Writing Assessment scores are computed and reported separately from the multiple-choice sections of the test and have no effect on your Verbal, Quantitative, or Total scores. The schools that you have designated to receive your scores may receive your responses to the Analytical Writing Assessment with your score report. Your own copy of your score report will not include copies of your responses.

1.10 Test Development Process

The GMAT® exam is developed by experts who use standardized procedures to ensure high-quality, widely appropriate test material. All questions are subjected to independent reviews and are revised or discarded as necessary. Multiple-choice questions are tested during GMAT® test administrations. Analytical Writing Assessment tasks are tried out on first-year business school students and then assessed for their fairness and reliability. For more information on test development, see www.mba.com.

2.0 How To Prepare

2.0 How To Prepare

2.1 How Can I Best Prepare to Take the Test?

We at the Graduate Management Admission Council® (GMAC®) firmly believe that the test-taking skills you can develop by using this book—and *The Official Guide for GMAT® Review, 11th Edition*, if you want additional practice—are all you need to perform your best when you take the GMAT® test. By answering questions that have appeared on the GMAT® exam before, you will gain experience with the types of questions you may see on the test when you take it. As you practice with this book, you will develop confidence in your ability to reason through the test questions. No additional techniques or strategies are needed to do well on the standardized test if you develop a practical familiarity with the abilities it requires. Simply by practicing and understanding the concepts that are assessed on the exam, you will learn what you need to know to answer the questions correctly.

2.2 What About Practice Tests?

Because a computer-adaptive test cannot be presented in paper form, we have created GMATPrep® software to help you prepare for the exam. The software is available for download at no charge for those who have created a user profile on www.mba.com. It is also provided on a disk, by request, to anyone who has registered for the GMAT® test. The software includes two practice GMAT® tests plus additional practice questions, information about the test, and tutorials to help you become familiar with how the GMAT® test will appear on the computer screen at the test center.

We recommend that you download the software as you start to prepare for the exam. Take one practice test to better familiarize yourself with the test and to get an idea of how you might score. After you have studied, using this book, and as your test date approaches, take the second practice test to determine whether you need to shift your focus to other areas you need to strengthen.

Myth -vs- **FACT**

M – **You need very advanced math skills to get a high GMAT® score.**

F – **The math skills tested on the GMAT® test are quite basic.**

The GMAT® exam only requires basic quantitative analytic skills. You should review the underlying math skills (algebra, geometry, basic arithmetic) presented in this book, but the required skill level is low. The difficulty of GMAT® Quantitative questions stems from the logic and analysis used to solve the problems and not the underlying math skills.

2.3 Where Can I Get Additional Practice?

If you complete all the questions in this book and would like additional practice, you may purchase *The Official Guide for GMAT® Review, 11th Edition*, or *The Official Guide for GMAT® Quantitative Review* at www.mba.com.

Note: There may be some overlap between this book and the review sections of the GMATPrep® software.

2.4 General Test-Taking Suggestions

Specific test-taking strategies for individual question types are presented later in this book. The following are general suggestions to help you perform your best on the test.

Use your time wisely.

Although the GMAT® exam stresses accuracy more than speed, it is important to use your time wisely. On average, you will have about 1¾ minutes for each verbal question and about 2 minutes for each quantitative question. Once you start the test, an onscreen clock will continuously count the time you have left. You can hide this display if you want, but it is a good idea to check the clock periodically to monitor your progress. The clock will automatically alert you when five minutes remain in the allotted time for the section you are working on.

Answer practice questions ahead of time.

After you become generally familiar with all question types, use the sample questions in this book to prepare for the actual test. It may be useful to time yourself as you answer the practice questions to get an idea of how long you will have for each question during the actual GMAT® test as well as to determine whether you are answering quickly enough to complete the test in the time allotted.

Read all test directions carefully.

The directions explain exactly what is required to answer each question type. If you read hastily, you may miss important instructions and lower your scores. To review directions during the test, click on the Help icon. But be aware that the time you spend reviewing directions will count against the time allotted for that section of the test.

Read each question carefully and thoroughly.

Before you answer a multiple-choice question, determine exactly what is being asked, then eliminate the wrong answers and select the best choice. Never skim a question or the possible answers; skimming may cause you to miss important information or nuances.

Do not spend too much time on any one question.

If you do not know the correct answer, or if the question is too time-consuming, try to eliminate choices you know are wrong, select the best of the

Myth -vs- FACT

M – **It is more important to respond correctly to the test questions than it is to finish the test.**

F – **There is a severe penalty for not completing the GMAT® test.**

If you are stumped by a question, give it your best guess and move on. If you guess incorrectly, the computer program will likely give you an easier question, which you are likely to answer correctly, and the computer will rapidly return to giving you questions matched to your ability. If you don't finish the test, your score will be reduced greatly. Failing to answer five verbal questions, for example, could reduce a person's score from the 91st percentile to the 77th percentile. Pacing is important.

remaining answer choices, and move on to the next question. Try not to worry about the impact on your score—guessing may lower your score, but not finishing the section will lower your score more.

Bear in mind that if you do not finish a section in the allotted time, you will still receive a score.

Confirm your answers ONLY when you are ready to move on.

Once you have selected your answer to a multiple-choice question, you will be asked to confirm it. Once you confirm your response, you cannot go back and change it. You may not skip questions, because the computer selects each question on the basis of your responses to preceding questions.

Plan your essay answers before you begin to write.

The best way to approach the two writing tasks comprised in the Analytical Writing Assessment is to read the directions carefully, take a few minutes to think about the question, and plan a response before you begin writing.

Take care to organize your ideas and develop them fully, but leave time to reread your response and make any revisions that you think would improve it.

Myth -vs- **FACT**

𝓜 – The first 10 questions are critical and you should invest the most time on those.

F – All questions count.

It is true that the computer-adaptive testing algorithm uses the first 10 questions to obtain an initial estimate of your ability; however, that is only an *initial* estimate. As you continue to answer questions, the algorithm self-corrects by computing an updated estimate on the basis of all the questions you have taken, and then administers items that are closely matched to this new estimate of your ability. Your final score is based on all your responses and considers the difficulty of all the questions you answered. Taking additional time on the first 10 questions will not game the system and can hurt your ability to finish the test.

3.0 Reading Comprehension

3.0 Reading Comprehension

Reading comprehension questions appear in the Verbal section of the GMAT® exam. The Verbal section uses multiple-choice questions to measure your ability to read and comprehend written material, to reason and evaluate arguments, and to correct written material to conform to standard written English. Because the Verbal section includes content from a variety of topics, you may be generally familiar with some of the material; however, neither the passages nor the questions assume knowledge of the topics discussed. Reading comprehension questions are intermingled with critical reasoning and sentence correction questions throughout the Verbal section of the exam.

You will have 75 minutes to complete the Verbal section, or an average of about 1¾ minutes to answer each question. Keep in mind, however, that you will need time to read the written passages—and that time is not factored into the 1¾ -minute average. You should therefore plan to proceed more quickly through the reading comprehension questions to give yourself enough time to read the passages thoroughly.

Reading comprehension questions begin with written passages up to 350 words long. The passages discuss topics from the social sciences, humanities, physical or biological sciences, and such business-related fields as marketing, economics, and human resource management. The passages are accompanied by questions that will ask you to interpret the passage, apply the information you gather from the reading, and make inferences (or informed assumptions) based on the reading. For these questions, you will see a split computer screen. The written passage will remain visible on the left side as each question associated with that passage appears in turn on the right side. You will see only one question at a time, however. The number of questions associated with each passage may vary.

As you move through the reading comprehension practice questions, try to determine a process that works best for you. You might begin by reading a passage carefully and thoroughly, though some test takers prefer to skim the passages the first time through, or even to read the first question before reading the passage. You may want to reread any sentences that present complicated ideas or introduce terms that are new to you. Read each question and series of answers carefully. Make sure you understand exactly what the question is asking and what the answer choices are.

If you need to, you may go back to the passage and read any parts that are relevant to answering the question. Specific portions of the passages may be highlighted in related questions.

The following pages describe what reading comprehension questions are designed to measure, present the directions that will precede questions of this type, and describe the various question types. This chapter also provides test-taking strategies, sample questions, and detailed explanations of all the questions. The explanations further illustrate how reading comprehension questions evaluate basic reading skills.

3.1 What Is Measured

Reading comprehension questions measure your ability to understand, analyze, and apply information and concepts presented in written form. All questions are to be answered on the basis of what is stated or implied in the reading material, and no specific prior knowledge of the material is required.

The GMAT® reading comprehension questions evaluate your ability to do the following:

- **Understand words and statements.**
  Although the questions do not test your vocabulary (they will not ask you to define terms), they do test your ability to interpret special meanings of terms as they are used in the passages. The questions will also test your understanding of the English language. These questions may ask about the overall meaning of a passage.

- **Understand logical relationships between points and concepts.**
  This type of question may ask you to determine the strong and weak points of an argument or evaluate the relative importance of arguments and ideas in a passage.

- **Draw inferences from facts and statements.**
  The inference questions will ask you to consider factual statements or information presented in a reading passage and, on the basis of that information, reach conclusions.

- **Understand and follow the development of quantitative concepts as they are presented in written material.**
  This may involve the interpretation of numerical data or the use of simple arithmetic to reach conclusions about material in a passage.

There are six kinds of reading comprehension questions, each of which tests a different skill. The reading comprehension questions ask about the following areas.

Main idea

Each passage is a unified whole—that is, the individual sentences and paragraphs support and develop one main idea or central point. Sometimes you will be told the central point in the passage itself, and sometimes it will be necessary for you to determine the central point from the overall organization or development of the passage. You may be asked in this kind of question to—

- recognize a correct restatement, or paraphrasing, of the main idea of a passage;

- identify the author's primary purpose or objective in writing the passage; or

- assign a title that summarizes, briefly and pointedly, the main idea developed in the passage.

Supporting ideas

These questions measure your ability to comprehend the supporting ideas in a passage and differentiate them from the main idea. The questions also measure your ability to differentiate ideas that are *explicitly stated* in a passage from ideas that are *implied* by the author but that are not explicitly stated. You may be asked about—

- facts cited in a passage;

- the specific content of arguments presented by the author in support of his or her views; or

- descriptive details used to support or elaborate on the main idea.

Whereas questions about the main idea ask you to determine the meaning of a passage *as a whole*, questions about supporting ideas ask you to determine the meanings of individual sentences and paragraphs that *contribute* to the meaning of the passage as a whole. In other words, these questions ask for the main point of *one small part* of the passage.

Inferences

These questions ask about ideas that are not explicitly stated in a passage but are *implied* by the author. Unlike questions about supporting details, which ask about information that is directly stated in a passage, inference questions ask about ideas or meanings that must be inferred from information that is directly stated. Authors can make their points in indirect ways, suggesting ideas without actually stating them. Inference questions measure your ability to understand an author's intended meaning in parts of a passage where the meaning is only suggested. These questions do not ask about meanings or implications that are remote from the passage; rather, they ask about meanings that are developed indirectly or implications that are specifically suggested by the author.

To answer these questions, you may have to—

- logically take statements made by the author one step beyond their literal meanings;

- recognize an alternative interpretation of a statement made by the author; or

- identify the intended meaning of a word used figuratively in a passage.

If a passage explicitly states an effect, for example, you may be asked to infer its cause. If the author compares two phenomena, you may be asked to infer the basis for the comparison. You may be asked to infer the characteristics of an old policy from an explicit description of a new one. When you read a passage, therefore, you should concentrate not only on the explicit meaning of the author's words, but also on the more subtle meaning implied by those words.

Applying information to a context outside the passage itself

These questions measure your ability to discern the relationships between situations or ideas presented by the author and other situations or ideas that might parallel those in the passage. In this kind of question, you may be asked to—

- identify a hypothetical situation that is comparable to a situation presented in the passage;

- select an example that is similar to an example provided in the passage;

- apply ideas given in the passage to a situation not mentioned by the author; or

- recognize ideas that the author would probably agree or disagree with on the basis of statements made in the passage.

Unlike inference questions, application questions use ideas or situations *not* taken from the passage. Ideas and situations given in a question are *like* those given in the passage, and they parallel ideas and situations in the passage; therefore, to answer the question, you must do more than recall what you read. You must recognize the essential attributes of ideas and situations presented in the passage when they appear in different words and in an entirely new context.

Logical structure

These questions require you to analyze and evaluate the organization and logic of a passage. They may ask you—

- how a passage is constructed—for instance, does it define, compare or contrast, present a new idea, or refute an idea?

- how the author persuades readers to accept his or her assertions;

- the reason behind the author's use of any particular supporting detail;

- to identify assumptions that the author is making;

- to assess the strengths and weaknesses of the author's arguments; or

- to recognize appropriate counterarguments.

These questions measure your ability not only to comprehend a passage but also to evaluate it critically. However, it is important for you to realize that logical structure questions do not rely on any kind of formal logic, nor do they require you to be familiar with specific terms of logic or argumentation. You can answer these questions using only the information in the passage and careful reasoning.

About the style and tone

Style and tone questions ask about the expression of a passage and about the ideas in a passage that may be expressed through its diction—the author's choice of words. You may be asked to deduce the author's attitude to an idea, a fact, or a situation from the words that he or she uses to describe it. You may also be asked to select a word that accurately describes the tone of a passage—for instance, "critical," "questioning," "objective," or "enthusiastic."

To answer this type of question, you will have to consider the language of the passage as a whole: It takes more than one pointed, critical word to make the tone of an entire passage "critical." Sometimes, style and tone questions ask what audience the passage was probably intended for or what type of publication it probably appeared in. Style and tone questions may apply to one small part of the passage or to the passage as a whole. To answer them, you must ask yourself what meanings are contained in the words of a passage beyond the literal meanings. Did the author use certain words because of their emotional content, or because a particular audience would expect to hear them? Remember, these questions measure your ability to discern meaning expressed by the author through his or her choice of words.

3.2 Test-Taking Strategies for Reading Comprehension Questions

1. **Do not expect to be completely familiar with any of the material presented in reading comprehension passages.**

   You may find some passages easier to understand than others, but all passages are designed to present a challenge. If you have some familiarity with the material presented in a passage, do not let this knowledge influence your choice of answers to the questions. Answer all questions on the basis of what is *stated or implied* in the passage itself.

2. **Analyze each passage carefully, because the questions require you to have a specific and detailed understanding of the material.**
    You may find it easier to do the analysis first, before moving to the questions. Or, you may find that you prefer to skim the passage the first time and read more carefully once you understand what a question asks. You may even want to read the question before reading the passage. You should choose the method most suitable for you.

3. **Focus on key words and phrases, and make every effort to avoid losing the sense of what is discussed in the passage.**
    Keep the following in mind:

    *   Note how each fact relates to an idea or an argument.

    *   Note where the passage moves from one idea to the next.

    *   Separate main ideas from supporting ideas.

    *   Determine what conclusions are reached and why.

4. **Read the questions carefully, making sure that you understand what is asked.**
    An answer choice that accurately restates information in the passage may be incorrect if it does not answer the question. If you need to, refer back to the passage for clarification.

5. **Read all the choices carefully.**
    Never assume that you have selected the best answer without first reading all the choices.

6. **Select the choice that answers the question best in terms of the information given in the passage.**
    Do not rely on outside knowledge of the material to help you answer the questions.

7. **Remember that comprehension—not speed—is the critical success factor when it comes to reading comprehension questions.**

3.3 The Directions

These are the directions that you will see for reading comprehension questions when you take the GMAT® test. If you read them carefully and understand them clearly before going to sit for the exam, you will not need to spend too much time reviewing them once you are at the test center and the exam is under way.

The questions in this group are based on the content of a passage. After reading the passage, choose the best answer to each question. Answer all questions following the passage on the basis of what is *stated or implied in the passage.*

3.4 Reading Comprehension Sample Questions

The questions in this group are based on the content of a passage. After reading the passage, choose the best answer to each question. Answer all questions following the passage on the basis of what is <u>stated</u> or <u>implied</u> in the passage.

Line   Coral reefs are one of the most fragile, biologically complex, and diverse marine ecosystems on Earth. This ecosystem is one of the fascinating paradoxes of the biosphere: how

(5)   do clear, and thus nutrient-poor, waters support such prolific and productive communities? Part of the answer lies within the tissues of the corals themselves. Symbiotic cells of algae known as zooxanthellae carry out photosynthesis using the

(10)   metabolic wastes of the corals, thereby producing food for themselves, for their coral hosts, and even for other members of the reef community. This symbiotic process allows organisms in the reef community to use sparse nutrient resources

(15)   efficiently.

    Unfortunately for coral reefs, however, a variety of human activities are causing worldwide degradation of shallow marine habitats by adding nutrients to the water. Agriculture, slash-and-burn

(20)   land clearing, sewage disposal, and manufacturing that creates waste by-products all increase nutrient loads in these waters. Typical symptoms of reef decline are destabilized herbivore populations and an increasing abundance of algae and filter-

(25)   feeding animals. Declines in reef communities are consistent with observations that nutrient input is increasing in direct proportion to growing human populations, thereby threatening reef communities sensitive to subtle changes in nutrient input to their

(30)   waters.

Questions 1–5 refer to the passage above.

1.   The passage is primarily concerned with

    (A)   describing the effects of human activities on algae in coral reefs

    (B)   explaining how human activities are posing a threat to coral reef communities

    (C)   discussing the process by which coral reefs deteriorate in nutrient-poor waters

    (D)   explaining how coral reefs produce food for themselves

    (E)   describing the abundance of algae and filter-feeding animals in coral reef areas

2.   The passage suggests which of the following about coral reef communities?

    (A)   Coral reef communities may actually be more likely to thrive in waters that are relatively low in nutrients.

    (B)   The nutrients on which coral reef communities thrive are only found in shallow waters.

    (C)   Human population growth has led to changing ocean temperatures, which threatens coral reef communities.

    (D)   The growth of coral reef communities tends to destabilize underwater herbivore populations.

    (E)   Coral reef communities are more complex and diverse than most ecosystems located on dry land.

3. The author refers to "filter-feeding animals" (lines 24–25) in order to

(A) provide an example of a characteristic sign of reef deterioration

(B) explain how reef communities acquire sustenance for survival

(C) identify a factor that helps herbivore populations thrive

(D) indicate a cause of decreasing nutrient input in waters that reefs inhabit

(E) identify members of coral reef communities that rely on coral reefs for nutrients

4. According to the passage, which of the following is a factor that is threatening the survival of coral reef communities?

(A) The waters they inhabit contain few nutrient resources.

(B) A decline in nutrient input is disrupting their symbiotic relationship with zooxanthellae.

(C) The degraded waters of their marine habitats have reduced their ability to carry out photosynthesis.

(D) They are too biologically complex to survive in habitats with minimal nutrient input.

(E) Waste by-products result in an increase in nutrient input to reef communities.

5. It can be inferred from the passage that the author describes coral reef communities as paradoxical most likely for which of the following reasons?

(A) They are thriving even though human activities have depleted the nutrients in their environment.

(B) They are able to survive in spite of an over-abundance of algae inhabiting their waters.

(C) They are able to survive in an environment with limited food resources.

(D) Their metabolic wastes contribute to the degradation of the waters that they inhabit.

(E) They are declining even when the water surrounding them remains clear.

Line   Although genetic mutations in bacteria and viruses can lead to epidemics, some epidemics are caused by bacteria and viruses that have undergone no significant genetic change. In analyzing the
(5)   latter, scientists have discovered the importance of social and ecological factors to epidemics. Poliomyelitis, for example, emerged as an epidemic in the United States in the twentieth century; by then, modern sanitation was able to delay
(10)   exposure to polio until adolescence or adulthood, at which time polio infection produced paralysis. Previously, infection had occurred during infancy, when it typically provided lifelong immunity without paralysis. Thus, the hygiene that helped prevent
(15)   typhoid epidemics indirectly fostered a paralytic polio epidemic. Another example is Lyme disease, which is caused by bacteria that are transmitted by deer ticks. It occurred only sporadically during the late nineteenth century but has recently become
(20)   prevalent in parts of the United States, largely due to an increase in the deer population that occurred simultaneously with the growth of the suburbs and increased outdoor recreational activities in the deer's habitat. Similarly, an outbreak of dengue
(25)   hemorrhagic fever became an epidemic in Asia in the 1950's because of ecological changes that caused Aedes aegypti, the mosquito that transmits the dengue virus, to proliferate. The stage is now set in the United States for a dengue epidemic
(30)   because of the inadvertent introduction and wide dissemination of another mosquito, *Aedes albopictus*.

Questions 6–11 refer to the passage above.

6.   The passage suggests that a lack of modern sanitation would make which of the following most likely to occur?

(A)   An outbreak of Lyme disease
(B)   An outbreak of dengue hemorrhagic fever
(C)   An epidemic of typhoid
(D)   An epidemic of paralytic polio among infants
(E)   An epidemic of paralytic polio among adolescents and adults

7.   According to the passage, the outbreak of dengue hemorrhagic fever in the 1950's occurred for which of the following reasons?

(A)   The mosquito *Aedes aegypti* was newly introduced into Asia.
(B)   The mosquito *Aedes aegypti* became more numerous.
(C)   The mosquito *Aedes albopictus* became infected with the dengue virus.
(D)   Individuals who would normally acquire immunity to the dengue virus as infants were not infected until later in life.
(E)   More people began to visit and inhabit areas in which mosquitoes live and breed.

8. It can be inferred from the passage that Lyme disease has become prevalent in parts of the United States because of which of the following?

    (A) The inadvertent introduction of Lyme disease bacteria to the United States
    (B) The inability of modern sanitation methods to eradicate Lyme disease bacteria
    (C) A genetic mutation in Lyme disease bacteria that makes them more virulent
    (D) The spread of Lyme disease bacteria from infected humans to noninfected humans
    (E) An increase in the number of humans who encounter deer ticks

9. Which of the following can most reasonably be concluded about the mosquito *Aedes albopictus* on the basis of information given in the passage?

    (A) It is native to the United States.
    (B) It can proliferate only in Asia.
    (C) It transmits the dengue virus.
    (D) It caused an epidemic of dengue hemorrhagic fever in the 1950's.
    (E) It replaced *Aedes aegypti* in Asia when ecological changes altered *Aedes aegypti's* habitat.

10. Which of the following best describes the organization of the passage?

    (A) A paradox is stated, discussed, and left unresolved.
    (B) Two opposing explanations are presented, argued, and reconciled.
    (C) A theory is proposed and is then followed by descriptions of three experiments that support the theory.
    (D) A generalization is stated and is then followed by three instances that support the generalization.
    (E) An argument is described and is then followed by three counterexamples that refute the argument.

11. Which of the following, if true, would most strengthen the author's assertion about the cause of the Lyme disease outbreak in the United States?

    (A) The deer population was smaller in the late nineteenth century than in the mid twentieth century.
    (B) Interest in outdoor recreation began to grow in the late nineteenth century.
    (C) In recent years the suburbs have stopped growing.
    (D) Outdoor recreation enthusiasts routinely take measures to protect themselves against Lyme disease.
    (E) Scientists have not yet developed a vaccine that can prevent Lyme disease.

Line   Homeostasis, an animal's maintenance of
      certain internal variables within an acceptable
      range, particularly in extreme physical
      environments, has long interested biologists.
(5)   The desert rat and the camel in the most water-
      deprived environments, and marine vertebrates
      in an all-water environment, encounter the same
      regulatory problem: maintaining adequate internal
      fluid balance.
(10)   For desert rats and camels, the problem is
      conservation of water in an environment where
      standing water is nonexistent, temperature is high,
      and humidity is low. Despite these handicaps,
      desert rats are able to maintain the osmotic
(15) pressure of their blood, as well as their total body-
      water content, at approximately the same levels
      as other rats. One countermeasure is behavioral:
      these rats stay in burrows during the hot part of
      the day, thus avoiding loss of fluid through panting
(20) or sweating, which are regulatory mechanisms
      for maintaining internal body temperature by
      evaporative cooling. Also, desert rats' kidneys can
      excrete a urine having twice as high a salt content
      as sea water.
(25)   Camels, on the other hand, rely more on
      simple endurance. They cannot store water,
      and their reliance on an entirely unexceptional
      kidney results in a rate of water loss through renal
      function significantly higher than that of desert
(30) rats. As a result, camels must tolerate losses in
      body water of up to thirty percent of their body
      weight. Nevertheless, camels do rely on a special
      mechanism to keep water loss within a tolerable
      range: by sweating and panting only when their
(35) body temperature exceeds that which would kill a
      human, they conserve internal water.
         Marine vertebrates experience difficulty with
      their water balance because though there is no
      shortage of seawater to drink, they must drink a lot
(40) of it to maintain their internal fluid balance. But the
      excess salts from the seawater must be discharged
      somehow, and the kidneys of most marine vertebrates
      are unable to excrete a urine in which the salts are
      more concentrated than in seawater. Most of these
(45) animals have special salt-secreting organs outside the
      kidney that enable them to eliminate excess salt.

Questions 12–15 refer to the passage above.

12. Which of the following most accurately states the
     purpose of the passage?

     (A) To compare two different approaches to the
          study of homeostasis
     (B) To summarize the findings of several studies
          regarding organisms' maintenance of
          internal variables in extreme environments
     (C) To argue for a particular hypothesis regarding
          various organisms' conservation of water in
          desert environments
     (D) To cite examples of how homeostasis is
          achieved by various organisms
     (E) To defend a new theory regarding the
          maintenance of adequate fluid balance

13. According to the passage, the camel maintains
     internal fluid balance in which of the following
     ways?

     I.   By behavioral avoidance of exposure to
           conditions that lead to fluid loss
     II.   By an ability to tolerate high body
           temperatures
     III. By reliance on stored internal fluid supplies

     (A) I only
     (B) II only
     (C) I and II only
     (D) II and III only
     (E) I, II, and III

14. It can be inferred from the passage that some mechanisms that regulate internal body temperature, like sweating and panting, can lead to which of the following?

    (A)   A rise in the external body temperature
    (B)   A drop in the body's internal fluid level
    (C)   A decrease in the osmotic pressure of the blood
    (D)   A decrease in the amount of renal water loss
    (E)   A decrease in the urine's salt content

15. It can be inferred from the passage that the author characterizes the camel's kidney as "entirely unexceptional" (line 27) primarily to emphasize that it

    (A)   functions much as the kidney of a rat functions
    (B)   does not aid the camel in coping with the exceptional water loss resulting from the extreme conditions of its environment
    (C)   does not enable the camel to excrete as much salt as do the kidneys of marine vertebrates
    (D)   is similar in structure to the kidneys of most mammals living in water-deprived environments
    (E)   requires the help of other organs in eliminating excess salt

Line   The new school of political history that emerged in the 1960's and 1970's sought to go beyond the traditional focus of political historians on leaders and government institutions by examining directly
(5)   the political practices of ordinary citizens. Like the old approach, however, this new approach excluded women. The very techniques these historians used to uncover mass political behavior in the nineteenth century United States—quantitative analyses of
(10)   election returns, for example—were useless in analyzing the political activities of women, who were denied the vote until 1920.

By redefining "political activity," historian Paula Baker has developed a political history
(15)   that includes women. She concludes that among ordinary citizens, political activism by women in the nineteenth century prefigured trends in twentieth century politics. Defining "politics" as "any action taken to affect the course of behavior
(20)   of government or of the community," Baker concludes that, while voting and holding office were restricted to men, women in the nineteenth century organized themselves into societies committed to social issues such as temperance and poverty. In
(25)   other words, Baker contends, women activists were early practitioners of nonpartisan, issue oriented politics and thus were more interested in enlisting lawmakers, regardless of their party affiliation, on behalf of certain issues than in ensuring that one
(30)   party or another won an election. In the twentieth century, more men drew closer to women's ideas about politics and took up modes of issue oriented politics that Baker sees women as having pioneered.

Questions 16–21 refer to the passage above.

16.   The primary purpose of the passage is to

(A)   enumerate reasons why both traditional scholarly methods and newer scholarly methods have limitations

(B)   identify a shortcoming in a scholarly approach and describe an alternative approach

(C)   provide empirical data to support a long-held scholarly assumption

(D)   compare two scholarly publications on the basis of their authors' backgrounds

(E)   attempt to provide a partial answer to a long-standing scholarly dilemma

17.   The passage suggests which of the following concerning the techniques used by the new political historians described in the first paragraph of the passage?

(A)   They involved the extensive use of the biographies of political party leaders and political theoreticians.

(B)   They were conceived by political historians who were reacting against the political climates of the 1960's and 1970's.

(C)   They were of more use in analyzing the positions of United States political parties in the nineteenth century than in analyzing the positions of those in the twentieth century.

(D)   They were of more use in analyzing the political behavior of nineteenth-century voters than in analyzing the political activities of those who could not vote during that period.

(E)   They were devised as a means of tracing the influence of nineteenth-century political trends on twentieth-century political trends.

18. It can be inferred that the author of the passage quotes Baker directly in the second paragraph primarily in order to

    (A) clarify a position before providing an alternative to that position
    (B) differentiate between a novel definition and traditional definitions
    (C) provide an example of a point agreed on by different generations of scholars
    (D) provide an example of the prose style of an important historian
    (E) amplify a definition given in the first paragraph

19. According to the passage, Paula Baker and the new political historians of the 1960's and 1970's shared which of the following?

    (A) A commitment to interest group politics
    (B) A disregard for political theory and ideology
    (C) An interest in the ways in which nineteenth-century politics prefigured contemporary politics
    (D) A reliance on such quantitative techniques as the analysis of election returns
    (E) An emphasis on the political involvement of ordinary citizens

20. Which of the following best describes the structure of the first paragraph of the passage?

    (A) Two scholarly approaches are compared, and a shortcoming common to both is identified.
    (B) Two rival schools of thought are contrasted, and a third is alluded to.
    (C) An outmoded scholarly approach is described, and a corrective approach is called for.
    (D) An argument is outlined, and counterarguments are mentioned.
    (E) A historical era is described in terms of its political trends.

21. The information in the passage suggests that a pre-1960's political historian would have been most likely to undertake which of the following studies?

    (A) An analysis of voting trends among women voters of the 1920's
    (B) A study of male voters' gradual ideological shift from party politics to issue-oriented politics
    (C) A biography of an influential nineteenth-century minister of foreign affairs
    (D) An analysis of narratives written by previously unrecognized women activists
    (E) A study of voting trends among naturalized immigrant laborers in a nineteenth-century logging camp

Line   Two recent publications offer different
assessments of the career of the famous British nurse
Florence Nightingale. A book by Anne Summers seeks
to debunk the idealizations and present a reality at
(5)   odds with Nightingale's heroic reputation. According
to Summers, Nightingale's importance during the
Crimean War has been exaggerated: not until near
the war's end did she become supervisor of the
female nurses. Additionally, Summers writes that the
(10)   contribution of the nurses to the relief of the wounded
was at best marginal. The prevailing problems of
military medicine were caused by army organizational
practices, and the addition of a few nurses to the
medical staff could be no more than symbolic.
(15)   Nightingale's place in the national pantheon, Summers
asserts, is largely due to the propagandistic efforts of
contemporary newspaper reporters.
   By contrast, the editors of a new volume of
Nightingale's letters view Nightingale as a person
(20)   who significantly influenced not only her own age
but also subsequent generations. They highlight
her ongoing efforts to reform sanitary conditions
after the war. For example, when she learned that
peacetime living conditions in British barracks were
(25)   so horrible that the death rate of enlisted men far
exceeded that of neighboring civilian populations, she
succeeded in persuading the government to establish
a Royal Commission on the Health of the Army. She
used sums raised through public contributions to
(30)   found a nurses' training hospital in London. Even in
administrative matters, the editors assert, her practical
intelligence was formidable: as recently as 1947 the
British Army's medical services were still using the
cost-accounting system she had devised in the 1860's.
(35)   I believe that the evidence of her letters
supports continued respect for Nightingale's
brilliance and creativity. When counseling a village
schoolmaster to encourage children to use their
faculties of observation, she sounds like a modern
(40)   educator. Her insistence on classifying the problems
of the needy in order to devise appropriate
treatments is similar to the approach of modern
social workers. In sum, although Nightingale may
not have achieved all of her goals during the
(45)   Crimean War, her breadth of vision and ability
to realize ambitious projects have earned her an
eminent place among the ranks of social pioneers.

Questions 22–28 refer to the passage above.

22. The passage is primarily concerned with evaluating

(A) the importance of Florence Nightingale's
     innovations in the field of nursing
(B) contrasting approaches to the writing of
     historical biography
(C) contradictory accounts of Florence
     Nightingale's historical significance
(D) the quality of health care in nineteenth
     century England
(E) the effect of the Crimean War on
     developments in the field of health care

23. According to the passage, the editors of
Nightingale's letters credit her with contributing to
which of the following?

(A) Improvement of the survival rate for soldiers
     in British Army hospitals during the
     Crimean War
(B) The development of a nurses' training
     curriculum that was far in advance of its day
(C) The increase in the number of women
     doctors practicing in British Army hospitals
(D) Establishment of the first facility for training
     nurses at a major British university
(E) The creation of an organization for
     monitoring the peacetime living conditions
     of British soldiers

24. The passage suggests which of the following about
Nightingale's relationship with the British public of
her day?

(A) She was highly respected, her projects
     receiving popular and governmental
     support.
(B) She encountered resistance both from the
     army establishment and the general public.
(C) She was supported by the working classes
     and opposed by the wealthier classes.
(D) She was supported by the military
     establishment but had to fight the
     governmental bureaucracy.
(E) After initially being received with enthusiasm,
     she was quickly forgotten.

25. The passage suggests which of the following about sanitary conditions in Britain after the Crimean War?

(A) While not ideal, they were superior to those in other parts of the world.
(B) Compared with conditions before the war, they had deteriorated.
(C) They were more advanced in rural areas than in the urban centers.
(D) They were worse in military camps than in the neighboring civilian populations.
(E) They were uniformly crude and unsatisfactory throughout England.

26. With which of the following statements regarding the differing interpretations of Nightingale's importance would the author most likely agree?

(A) Summers misunderstood both the importance of Nightingale's achievements during the Crimean War and her subsequent influence on British policy.
(B) The editors of Nightingale's letters made some valid points about her practical achievements, but they still exaggerated her influence on subsequent generations.
(C) Although Summers' account of Nightingale's role in the Crimean War may be accurate, she ignored evidence of Nightingale's subsequent achievement that suggests that her reputation as an eminent social reformer is well deserved.
(D) The editors of Nightingale's letters mistakenly propagated the outdated idealization of Nightingale that only impedes attempts to arrive at a balanced assessment of her true role.
(E) The evidence of Nightingale's letters supports Summers' conclusions both about Nightingale's activities and about her influence.

27. Which of the following is an assumption underlying the author's assessment of Nightingale's creativity?

(A) Educational philosophy in Nightingale's day did not normally emphasize developing children's ability to observe.
(B) Nightingale was the first to notice the poor living conditions in British military barracks in peacetime.
(C) No educator before Nightingale had thought to enlist the help of village schoolmasters in introducing new teaching techniques.
(D) Until Nightingale began her work, there was no concept of organized help for the needy in nineteenth-century Britain.
(E) The British Army's medical services had no cost-accounting system until Nightingale devised one in the 1860's.

28. In the last paragraph, the author is primarily concerned with

(A) summarizing the arguments about Nightingale presented in the first two paragraphs
(B) refuting the view of Nightingale's career presented in the preceding paragraph
(C) analyzing the weaknesses of the evidence presented elsewhere in the passage
(D) citing evidence to support a view of Nightingale's career
(E) correcting a factual error occurring in one of the works under review

Line   At the end of the nineteenth century, a rising
interest in Native American customs and an
increasing desire to understand Native American
culture prompted ethnologists to begin recording
(5)   the life stories of Native Americans. Ethnologists
had a distinct reason for wanting to hear the
stories: they were after linguistic or anthropological
data that would supplement their own field
observations, and they believed that the personal
(10)   stories, even of a single individual, could increase
their understanding of the cultures that they had
been observing from without. In addition many
ethnologists at the turn of the century believed
that Native American manners and customs were
(15)   rapidly disappearing, and that it was important
to preserve for posterity as much information as
could be adequately recorded before the cultures
disappeared forever.

There were, however, arguments against
(20)   this method as a way of acquiring accurate and
complete information. Franz Boas, for example,
described autobiographies as being "of limited
value, and useful chiefly for the study of the
perversion of truth by memory," while Paul
(25)   Radin contended that investigators rarely spent
enough time with the tribes they were observing,
and inevitably derived results too tinged by the
investigator's own emotional tone to be reliable.

Even more importantly, as these life stories
(30)   moved from the traditional oral mode to recorded
written form, much was inevitably lost. Editors
often decided what elements were significant to the
field research on a given tribe. Native Americans
recognized that the essence of their lives could
(35)   not be communicated in English and that events
that they thought significant were often deemed
unimportant by their interviewers. Indeed, the
very act of telling their stories could force Native
American narrators to distort their cultures, as
(40)   taboos had to be broken to speak the names of
dead relatives crucial to their family stories.

Despite all of this, autobiography remains a
useful tool for ethnological research: such personal
reminiscences and impressions, incomplete as
(45)   they may be, are likely to throw more light on the
working of the mind and emotions than any amount
of speculation from an ethnologist or ethnological
theorist from another culture.

Questions 29–34 refer to the passage above.

29.   Which of the following best describes the
organization of the passage?

(A)   The historical backgrounds of two currently
used research methods are chronicled.

(B)   The validity of the data collected by using
two different research methods is
compared.

(C)   The usefulness of a research method is
questioned and then a new method is
proposed.

(D)   The use of a research method is described
and the limitations of the results obtained
are discussed.

(E)   A research method is evaluated and the
changes necessary for its adaptation to
other subject areas are discussed.

30.   Which of the following is most similar to the actions
of nineteenth-century ethnologists in their editing of
the life stories of Native Americans?

(A)   A witness in a jury trial invokes the Fifth
Amendment in order to avoid relating
personally incriminating evidence.

(B)   A stockbroker refuses to divulge the source
of her information on the possible future
increase in a stock's value.

(C)   A sports announcer describes the action in a
team sport with which he is unfamiliar.

(D)   A chef purposely excludes the special
ingredient from the recipe of his
prizewinning dessert.

(E)   A politician fails to mention in a campaign
speech the similarities in the positions held
by her opponent for political office and by
herself.

31. According to the passage, collecting life stories can be a useful methodology because

    (A) life stories provide deeper insights into a culture than the hypothesizing of academics who are not members of that culture
    (B) life stories can be collected easily and they are not subject to invalid interpretations
    (C) ethnologists have a limited number of research methods from which to choose
    (D) life stories make it easy to distinguish between the important and unimportant features of a culture
    (E) the collection of life stories does not require a culturally knowledgeable investigator

32. Information in the passage suggests that which of the following may be a possible way to eliminate bias in the editing of life stories?

    (A) Basing all inferences made about the culture on an ethnological theory
    (B) Eliminating all of the emotion laden information reported by the informant
    (C) Translating the informant's words into the researcher's language
    (D) Reducing the number of questions and carefully specifying the content of the questions that the investigator can ask the informant
    (E) Reporting all of the information that the informant provides regardless of the investigator's personal opinion about its intrinsic value

33. The primary purpose of the passage as a whole is to

    (A) question an explanation
    (B) correct a misconception
    (C) critique a methodology
    (D) discredit an idea
    (E) clarify an ambiguity

34. It can be inferred from the passage that a characteristic of the ethnological research on Native Americans conducted during the nineteenth century was the use of which of the following?

    (A) Investigators familiar with the culture under study
    (B) A language other than the informant's for recording life stories
    (C) Life stories as the ethnologist's primary source of information
    (D) Complete transcriptions of informants' descriptions of tribal beliefs
    (E) Stringent guidelines for the preservation of cultural data

Line   Seeking a competitive advantage, some
professional service firms (for example, firms
providing advertising, accounting, or health care
services) have considered offering unconditional
(5)   guarantees of satisfaction. Such guarantees specify
what clients can expect and what the firm will do
if it fails to fulfill these expectations. Particularly
with first-time clients, an unconditional guarantee
can be an effective marketing tool if the client is
(10)   very cautious, the firm's fees are high, the negative
consequences of bad service are grave, or business
is difficult to obtain through referrals and word-of-
mouth.
　　　However, an unconditional guarantee can
(15)   sometimes hinder marketing efforts. With its
implication that failure is possible, the guarantee
may, paradoxically, cause clients to doubt the
service firm's ability to deliver the promised level
of service. It may conflict with a firm's desire to
(20)   appear sophisticated, or may even suggest that
a firm is begging for business. In legal and health
care services, it may mislead clients by suggesting
that lawsuits or medical procedures will have
guaranteed outcomes. Indeed, professional service
(25)   firms with outstanding reputations and performance
to match have little to gain from offering
unconditional guarantees. And any firm that
implements an unconditional guarantee without
undertaking a commensurate commitment to
(30)   quality of service is merely employing a potentially
costly marketing gimmick.

Questions 35–40 refer to the passage above.

35.   The primary function of the passage as a whole is
to

(A)   account for the popularity of a practice
(B)   evaluate the utility of a practice
(C)   demonstrate how to institute a practice
(D)   weigh the ethics of using a strategy
(E)   explain the reasons for pursuing a strategy

36.   All of the following are mentioned in the passage
as circumstances in which professional service
firms can benefit from offering an unconditional
guarantee EXCEPT:

(A)   The firm is having difficulty retaining its
clients of long standing.
(B)   The firm is having difficulty getting business
through client recommendations.
(C)   The firm charges substantial fees for its
services.
(D)   The adverse effects of poor performance by
the firm are significant for the client.
(E)   The client is reluctant to incur risk.

37.   Which of the following is cited in the passage as a
goal of some professional service firms in offering
unconditional guarantees of satisfaction?

(A)   A limit on the firm's liability
(B)   Successful competition against other firms
(C)   Ability to justify fee increases
(D)   Attainment of an outstanding reputation in a
field
(E)   Improvement in the quality of the firm's
service

38. The passage's description of the issue raised by unconditional guarantees for health care or legal services most clearly implies that which of the following is true?

    (A) The legal and medical professions have standards of practice that would be violated by attempts to fulfill such unconditional guarantees.

    (B) The result of a lawsuit or medical procedure cannot necessarily be determined in advance by the professionals handling a client's case.

    (C) The dignity of the legal and medical professions is undermined by any attempts at marketing of professional services, including unconditional guarantees.

    (D) Clients whose lawsuits or medical procedures have unsatisfactory outcomes cannot be adequately compensated by financial settlements alone.

    (E) Predicting the monetary cost of legal or health care services is more difficult than predicting the monetary cost of other types of professional services.

39. Which of the following hypothetical situations best exemplifies the potential problem noted in the second sentence of the second paragraph (lines 15–19)?

    (A) A physician's unconditional guarantee of satisfaction encourages patients to sue for malpractice if they are unhappy with the treatment they receive.

    (B) A lawyer's unconditional guarantee of satisfaction makes clients suspect that the lawyer needs to find new clients quickly to increase the firm's income.

    (C) A business consultant's unconditional guarantee of satisfaction is undermined when the consultant fails to provide all of the services that are promised.

    (D) An architect's unconditional guarantee of satisfaction makes clients wonder how often the architect's buildings fail to please clients.

    (E) An accountant's unconditional guarantee of satisfaction leads clients to believe that tax returns prepared by the accountant are certain to be accurate.

40. The passage most clearly implies which of the following about the professional service firms mentioned in lines 24–25.

    (A) They are unlikely to have offered unconditional guarantees of satisfaction in the past.

    (B) They are usually profitable enough to be able to compensate clients according to the terms of an unconditional guarantee.

    (C) They usually practice in fields in which the outcomes are predictable.

    (D) Their fees are usually more affordable than those charged by other professional service firms.

    (E) Their clients are usually already satisfied with the quality of service that is delivered.

Line   The fact that superior service can generate
a competitive advantage for a company does not
mean that every attempt at improving service will
create such an advantage. Investments in service,
(5)   like those in production and distribution, must be
balanced against other types of investments on
the basis of direct, tangible benefits such as cost
reduction and increased revenues. If a company
is already effectively on a par with its competitors
(10)   because it provides service that avoids a damaging
reputation and keeps customers from leaving at
an unacceptable rate, then investment in higher
service levels may be wasted, since service is a
deciding factor for customers only in extreme
(15)   situations.
         This truth was not apparent to managers of
one regional bank, which failed to improve its
competitive position despite its investment in
reducing the time a customer had to wait for a
(20)   teller. The bank managers did not recognize the
level of customer inertia in the consumer banking
industry that arises from the inconvenience of
switching banks. Nor did they analyze their service
improvement to determine whether it would attract
(25)   new customers by producing a new standard of
service that would excite customers or by proving
difficult for competitors to copy. The only merit
of the improvement was that it could easily be
described to customers.

Questions 41–46 refer to the passage above.

41.   The primary purpose of the passage is to

(A)   contrast possible outcomes of a type of
      business investment
(B)   suggest more careful evaluation of a type of
      business investment
(C)   illustrate various ways in which a type of
      business investment could fail to enhance
      revenues
(D)   trace the general problems of a company to a
      certain type of business investment
(E)   criticize the way in which managers tend to
      analyze the costs and benefits of business
      investments

42.   According to the passage, investments in service
      are comparable to investments in production and
      distribution in terms of the

(A)   tangibility of the benefits that they tend to
      confer
(B)   increased revenues that they ultimately
      produce
(C)   basis on which they need to be weighed
(D)   insufficient analysis that managers devote to
      them
(E)   degree of competitive advantage that they
      are likely to provide

43. The passage suggests which of the following about service provided by the regional bank prior to its investment in enhancing that service?

  (A) It enabled the bank to retain customers at an acceptable rate.
  (B) It threatened to weaken the bank's competitive position with respect to other regional banks.
  (C) It had already been improved after having caused damage to the bank's reputation in the past.
  (D) It was slightly superior to that of the bank's regional competitors.
  (E) It needed to be improved to attain parity with the service provided by competing banks.

44. The passage suggests that bank managers failed to consider whether or not the service improvement mentioned in line 19

  (A) was too complicated to be easily described to prospective customers
  (B) made a measurable change in the experiences of customers in the bank's offices
  (C) could be sustained if the number of customers increased significantly
  (D) was an innovation that competing banks could have imitated
  (E) was adequate to bring the bank's general level of service to a level that was comparable with that of its competitors

45. The discussion of the regional bank (lines 16-27) serves which of the following functions within the passage as a whole?

  (A) It describes an exceptional case in which investment in service actually failed to produce a competitive advantage.
  (B) It illustrates the pitfalls of choosing to invest in service at a time when investment is needed more urgently in another area.
  (C) It demonstrates the kind of analysis that managers apply when they choose one kind of service investment over another.
  (D) It supports the argument that investments in certain aspects of service are more advantageous than investments in other aspects of service.
  (E) It provides an example of the point about investment in service made in the first paragraph.

46. The author uses the word "only" in line 27 most likely in order to

  (A) highlight the oddity of the service improvement
  (B) emphasize the relatively low value of the investment in service improvement
  (C) distinguish the primary attribute of the service improvement from secondary attributes
  (D) single out a certain merit of the service improvement from other merits
  (E) point out the limited duration of the actual service improvement

Line   In an attempt to improve the overall
performance of clerical workers, many companies
have introduced computerized performance
monitoring and control systems (CPMCS) that
(5)   record and report a worker's computer-driven
activities. However, at least one study has shown
that such monitoring may not be having the
desired effect. In the study, researchers asked
monitored clerical workers and their supervisors
(10) how assessments of productivity affected
supervisors' ratings of workers' performance. In
contrast to unmonitored workers doing the same
work, who without exception identified the most
important element in their jobs as customer service,
(15) the monitored workers and their supervisors
all responded that productivity was the critical
factor in assigning ratings. This finding suggested
that there should have been a strong correlation
between a monitored worker's productivity and
(20) the overall rating the worker received. However,
measures of the relationship between overall rating
and individual elements of performance clearly
supported the conclusion that supervisors gave
considerable weight to criteria such as attendance,
(25) accuracy, and indications of customer satisfaction.
     It is possible that productivity may be a
"hygiene factor"; that is, if it is too low, it will hurt
the overall rating. But the evidence suggests that
beyond the point at which productivity becomes
(30) "good enough," higher productivity per se is unlikely
to improve a rating.

Questions 47–51 refer to the passage above.

47.   According to the passage, before the final results
of the study were known, which of the following
seemed likely?

(A)   That workers with the highest productivity
would also be the most accurate
(B)   That workers who initially achieved high
productivity ratings would continue to do
so consistently
(C)   That the highest performance ratings would
be achieved by workers with the highest
productivity
(D)   That the most productive workers would be
those whose supervisors claimed to value
productivity
(E)   That supervisors who claimed to value
productivity would place equal value on
customer satisfaction

48.   It can be inferred that the author of the passage
discusses "unmonitored workers" (line 12) primarily
in order to

(A)   compare the ratings of these workers with
the ratings of monitored workers
(B)   provide an example of a case in which
monitoring might be effective
(C)   provide evidence of an inappropriate use of
CPMCS
(D)   emphasize the effect that CPMCS may have
on workers' perceptions of their jobs
(E)   illustrate the effect that CPMCS may have on
workers' ratings

49. Which of the following, if true, would most clearly have supported the conclusion referred to in lines 23–25?

    (A) Ratings of productivity correlated highly with ratings of both accuracy and attendance.
    (B) Electronic monitoring greatly increased productivity.
    (C) Most supervisors based overall ratings of performance on measures of productivity alone.
    (D) Overall ratings of performance correlated more highly with measures of productivity than the researchers expected.
    (E) Overall ratings of performance correlated more highly with measures of accuracy than with measures of productivity.

50. According to the passage, a "hygiene factor" (line 27) is an aspect of a worker's performance that

    (A) has no effect on the rating of a worker's performance
    (B) is so basic to performance that it is assumed to be adequate for all workers
    (C) is given less importance than it deserves in rating a worker's performance
    (D) is not likely to affect a worker's rating unless it is judged to be inadequate
    (E) is important primarily because of the effect it has on a worker's rating

51 The primary purpose of the passage is to

    (A) explain the need for the introduction of an innovative strategy
    (B) discuss a study of the use of a particular method
    (C) recommend a course of action
    (D) resolve a difference of opinion
    (E) suggest an alternative approach

Line   Neotropical coastal mangrove forests are
usually "zonal," with certain mangrove species
found predominantly in the seaward portion of
the habitat and other mangrove species on the
(5)   more landward portions of the coast. The earliest
research on mangrove forests produced descriptions
of species distribution from shore to land, without
exploring the causes of the distributions.
        The idea that zonation is caused by plant
(10)   succession was first expressed by J. H. Davis in a
study of Florida mangrove forests. According to
Davis' scheme, the shoreline is being extended in
a seaward direction because of the "land-building"
role of mangroves, which, by trapping sediments
(15)   over time, extend the shore. As a habitat gradually
becomes more inland as the shore extends, the
"land-building" species are replaced. This
continuous process of accretion and succession
would be interrupted only by hurricanes or storm
(20)   flushings.
        Recently the universal application of Davis'
succession paradigm has been challenged. It
appears that in areas where weak currents and
weak tidal energies allow the accumulation of
(25)   sediments, mangroves will follow land formation
and accelerate the rate of soil accretion; succession
will proceed according to Davis' scheme. But on
stable coastlines, the distribution of mangrove
species results in other patterns of zonation; "land
(30)   building" does not occur.
        To find a principle that explains the various
distribution patterns, several researchers have
looked to salinity and its effects on mangroves.
While mangroves can develop in fresh water, they
(35)   can also thrive in salinities as high as 2.5 times that
of seawater. However, those mangrove species
found in freshwater habitats do well only in the
absence of competition, thus suggesting that
salinity tolerance is a critical factor in competitive
(40)   success among mangrove species. Research
suggests that mangroves will normally dominate
highly saline regions, although not because
they require salt. Rather, they are metabolically
efficient (and hence grow well) in portions of
(45)   an environment whose high salinity excludes
plants adapted to lower salinities. Tides create
different degrees of salinity along a coastline. The
characteristic mangrove species of each zone

should exhibit a higher metabolic efficiency at that
(50)   salinity than will any potential invader, including
other species of mangrove.

Questions 52–55 refer to the passage above.

52.   The primary purpose of the passage is to

(A)   refute the idea that the zonation exhibited in
        mangrove forests is caused by adaptation
        to salinity
(B)   describe the pattern of zonation typically
        found in Florida mangrove forests
(C)   argue that Davis' succession paradigm cannot
        be successfully applied to Florida mangrove
        forests
(D)   discuss hypotheses that attempt to explain
        the zonation of coastal mangrove forests
(E)   establish that plants that do well in saline
        forest environments require salt to achieve
        maximum metabolic efficiency

53.   According to the passage, the earliest research on
mangrove forests produced which of the following?

(A)   Data that implied random patterns of
        mangrove species distribution
(B)   Descriptions of species distributions
        suggesting zonation
(C)   Descriptions of the development of mangrove
        forests over time
(D)   Reclassification of species formerly thought to
        be identical
(E)   Data that confirmed the "land-building" role
        of mangroves

54.   It can be inferred from the passage that Davis'
paradigm does NOT apply to which of the following?

(A)   The shoreline of Florida mangrove forests
        first studied by Davis
(B)   A shoreline in an area with weak currents
(C)   A shoreline in an area with weak tidal energy
(D)   A shoreline extended by "land-building"
        species of mangroves
(E)   A shoreline in which few sediments can
        accumulate

55. Information in the passage indicates that the author would most probably regard which of the following statements as INCORRECT?

(A) Coastal mangrove forests are usually zonal.

(B) Hurricanes interrupt the process of accretion and succession that extends existing shorelines.

(C) Species of plants that thrive in a saline habitat require salt to flourish.

(D) Plants with the highest metabolic efficiency in a given habitat tend to exclude other plants from that habitat.

(E) Shorelines in areas with weak currents and tides are more likely to be extended through the process of accumulation of sediment than are shorelines with strong currents and tides.

Line   A meteor stream is composed of dust particles that have been ejected from a parent comet at a variety of velocities. These particles follow the same orbit as the parent comet, but due to their differing velocities they

(5) slowly gain on or fall behind the disintegrating comet until a shroud of dust surrounds the entire cometary orbit. Astronomers have hypothesized that a meteor stream should broaden with time as the dust particles' individual orbits are perturbed by planetary gravita-

(10) tional fields. A recent computer-modeling experiment tested this hypothesis by tracking the influence of planetary gravitation over a projected 5,000-year period on the positions of a group of hypothetical dust particles. In the model, the particles were randomly

(15) distributed throughout a computer simulation of the orbit of an actual meteor stream, the Geminid. The researcher found, as expected, that the computer-model stream broadened with time. Conventional theories, however, predicted that the distribution

(20) of particles would be increasingly dense toward the center of a meteor stream. Surprisingly, the computer-model meteor stream gradually came to resemble a thick walled, hollow pipe.

Whenever the Earth passes through a meteor

(25) stream, a meteor shower occurs. Moving at a little over 1,500,000 miles per day around its orbit, the Earth would take, on average, just over a day to cross the hollow, computer-model Geminid stream if the stream were 5,000 years old. Two brief periods

(30) of peak meteor activity during the shower would be observed, one as the Earth entered the thick-walled "pipe" and one as it exited. There is no reason why the Earth should always pass through the stream's exact center, so the time interval between the two bursts of

(35) activity would vary from one year to the next.

Has the predicted twin-peaked activity been observed for the actual yearly Geminid meteor shower? The Geminid data between 1970 and 1979 show just such a bifurcation, a secondary burst of

(40) meteor activity being clearly visible at an average of 19 hours (1,200,000 miles) after the first burst. The time intervals between the bursts suggest the actual Geminid stream is about 3,000 years old.

Questions 56–63 refer to the passage on page 41.

56.   The primary focus of the passage is on which of the following?

(A)   Comparing two scientific theories and contrasting the predictions that each would make concerning a natural phenomenon

(B)   Describing a new theoretical model and noting that it explains the nature of observations made of a particular natural phenomenon

(C)   Evaluating the results of a particular scientific experiment and suggesting further areas for research

(D)   Explaining how two different natural phenomena are related and demonstrating a way to measure them

(E)   Analyzing recent data derived from observations of an actual phenomenon and constructing a model to explain the data

57.   According to the passage, which of the following is an accurate statement concerning meteor streams?

(A)   Meteor streams and comets start out with similar orbits, but only those of meteor streams are perturbed by planetary gravitation.

(B)   Meteor streams grow as dust particles are attracted by the gravitational fields of comets.

(C)   Meteor streams are composed of dust particles derived from comets.

(D)   Comets may be composed of several kinds of materials, while meteor streams consist only of large dust particles.

(E)   Once formed, meteor streams hasten the further disintegration of comets.

58.   The author states that the research described in the first paragraph was undertaken in order to

(A)   determine the age of an actual meteor stream

(B)   identify the various structural features of meteor streams

(C)   explore the nature of a particularly interesting meteor stream

(D)   test the hypothesis that meteor streams become broader as they age

(E)   show that a computer model could help in explaining actual astronomical data

59.   It can be inferred from the passage that which of the following would most probably be observed during the Earth's passage through a meteor stream if the conventional theories mentioned in lines 18–19 were correct?

(A)   Meteor activity would gradually increase to a single, intense peak, and then gradually decline.

(B)   Meteor activity would be steady throughout the period of the meteor shower.

(C)   Meteor activity would rise to a peak at the beginning and at the end of the meteor shower.

(D)   Random bursts of very high meteor activity would be interspersed with periods of very little activity.

(E)   In years in which the Earth passed through only the outer areas of a meteor stream, meteor activity would be absent.

60. According to the passage, why do the dust particles in a meteor stream eventually surround a comet's original orbit?

    (A) They are ejected by the comet at differing velocities.
    (B) Their orbits are uncontrolled by planetary gravitational fields.
    (C) They become part of the meteor stream at different times.
    (D) Their velocity slows over time.
    (E) Their ejection velocity is slower than that of the comet.

61. The passage suggests that which of the following is a prediction concerning meteor streams that can be derived from both the conventional theories mentioned in lines 18–19 and the new computer-derived theory?

    (A) Dust particles in a meteor stream will usually be distributed evenly throughout any cross section of the stream.
    (B) The orbits of most meteor streams should cross the orbit of the Earth at some point and give rise to a meteor shower.
    (C) Over time the distribution of dust in a meteor stream will usually become denser at the outside edges of the stream than at the center.
    (D) Meteor showers caused by older meteor streams should be, on average, longer in duration than those caused by very young meteor streams.
    (E) The individual dust particles in older meteor streams should be, on average, smaller than those that compose younger meteor streams.

62. It can be inferred from the last paragraph of the passage that which of the following must be true of the Earth as it orbits the Sun?

    (A) Most meteor streams it encounters are more than 2,000 years old.
    (B) When passing through a meteor stream, it usually passes near to the stream's center.
    (C) It crosses the Geminid meteor stream once every year.
    (D) It usually takes over a day to cross the actual Geminid meteor stream.
    (E) It accounts for most of the gravitational perturbation affecting the Geminid meteor stream.

63. Which of the following is an assumption underlying the last sentence of the passage?

    (A) In each of the years between 1970 and 1979, the Earth took exactly 19 hours to cross the Geminid meteor stream.
    (B) The comet associated with the Geminid meteor stream has totally disintegrated.
    (C) The Geminid meteor stream should continue to exist for at least 5,000 years.
    (D) The Geminid meteor stream has not broadened as rapidly as the conventional theories would have predicted.
    (E) The computer-model Geminid meteor stream provides an accurate representation of the development of the actual Geminid stream.

Line   Caffeine, the stimulant in coffee, has been called "the most widely used psychoactive substance on Earth." Snyder, Daly, and Bruns have recently proposed that caffeine affects behavior
(5)   by countering the activity in the human brain of a naturally occurring chemical called adenosine. Adenosine normally depresses neuron firing in many areas of the brain. It apparently does this by inhibiting the release of neurotransmitters,
(10)   chemicals that carry nerve impulses from one neuron to the next.

       Like many other agents that affect neuron firing, adenosine must first bind to specific receptors on neuronal membranes. There are
(15)   at least two classes of these receptors, which have been designated A_1 and A_2. Snyder et al. propose that caffeine, which is structurally similar to adenosine, is able to bind to both types of receptors, which prevents adenosine from attaching there and allows the neurons to fire more readily
(20)   than they otherwise would.

       For many years, caffeine's effects have been attributed to its inhibition of the production of phosphodiesterase, an enzyme that breaks
(25)   down the chemical called cyclic AMP. A number of neurotransmitters exert their effects by first increasing cyclic AMP concentrations in target neurons. Therefore, prolonged periods at the elevated concentrations, as might be brought about
(30)   by a phosphodiesterase inhibitor, could lead to a greater amount of neuron firing and, consequently, to behavioral stimulation. But Snyder et al point out that the caffeine concentrations needed to inhibit the production of phosphodiesterase in the
(35)   brain are much higher than those that produce stimulation. Moreover, other compounds that block phosphodiesterase's activity are not stimulants.

       To buttress their case that caffeine acts instead by preventing adenosine binding, Snyder et al
(40)   compared the stimulatory effects of a series of caffeine derivatives with their ability to dislodge adenosine from its receptors in the brains of mice. "In general," they reported, "the ability of the compounds to compete at the receptors correlates
(45)   with their ability to stimulate locomotion in the mouse; i.e., the higher their capacity to bind at the receptors, the higher their ability to stimulate locomotion." Theophylline, a close structural relative of caffeine and the major stimulant in tea, was one

(50)   of the most effective compounds in both regards.
       There were some apparent exceptions to the general correlation observed between adenosine-receptor binding and stimulation. One of these was a compound called 3-isobutyl-1-methylxanthine
(55)   (IBMX), which bound very well but actually depressed mouse locomotion. Snyder et al suggest that this is not a major stumbling block to their hypothesis. The problem is that the compound has mixed effects in the brain, a not unusual occurrence
(60)   with psychoactive drugs. Even caffeine, which is generally known only for its stimulatory effects, displays this property, depressing mouse locomotion at very low concentrations and stimulating it at higher ones.

Questions 64–69 refer to the passage above.

64.   The primary purpose of the passage is to

(A)   discuss a plan for investigation of a phenomenon that is not yet fully understood

(B)   present two explanations of a phenomenon and reconcile the differences between them

(C)   summarize two theories and suggest a third theory that overcomes the problems encountered in the first two

(D)   describe an alternative hypothesis and provide evidence and arguments that support it

(E)   challenge the validity of a theory by exposing the inconsistencies and contradictions in it

65. According to Snyder et al, caffeine differs from adenosine in that caffeine

    (A) stimulates behavior in the mice and in humans, whereas adenosine stimulates behavior in humans only
    (B) has mixed effects in the brain, whereas adenosine has only a stimulatory effect
    (C) increases cyclic AMP concentrations in target neurons, whereas adenosine decreases such concentrations
    (D) permits release of neurotransmitters when it is bound to adenosine receptors, whereas adenosine inhibits such release
    (E) inhibits both neuron firing and the production of phosphodiesterase when there is a sufficient concentration in the brain, whereas adenosine inhibits only neuron firing

66. In response to experimental results concerning IBMX, Snyder et al contended that it is not uncommon for psychoactive drugs to have

    (A) mixed effects in the brain
    (B) inhibitory effects on enzymes in the brain
    (C) close structural relationships with caffeine
    (D) depressive effects on mouse locomotion
    (E) the ability to dislodge caffeine from receptors in the brain

67. According to Snyder et al, all of the following compounds can bind to specific receptors in the brain EXCEPT

    (A) IBMX
    (B) caffeine
    (C) adenosine
    (D) theophylline
    (E) phosphodiesterase

68. Snyder et al suggest that caffeine's ability to bind to A_1 and A_2 receptors can be at least partially attributed to which of the following?

    (A) The chemical relationship between caffeine and phosphodiesterase
    (B) The structural relationship between caffeine and adenosine
    (C) The structural similarity between caffeine and neurotransmitters
    (D) The ability of caffeine to stimulate behavior
    (E) The natural occurrence of caffeine and adenosine in the brain

69. The author quotes Snyder et al. in lines 43–48 most probably in order to

    (A) reveal some of the assumptions underlying their theory
    (B) summarize a major finding of their experiments
    (C) point out that their experiments were limited to the mice
    (D) indicate that their experiments resulted only in general correlations
    (E) refute the objections made by supporters of the older theory

Line   Historians of women's labor in the United States
          at first largely disregarded the story of female service
          workers — women earning wages in occupations
          such as salesclerk, domestic servant, and office
(5)   secretary. These historians focused instead on factory
          work, primarily because it seemed so different from
          traditional, unpaid "women's work" in the home,
          and because the underlying economic forces of
          industrialism were presumed to be gender-blind
(10)   and hence emancipatory in effect. Unfortunately,
          emancipation has been less profound than expected,
          for not even industrial wage labor has escaped
          continued sex segregation in the workplace.
                To explain this unfinished revolution in the
(15)   status of women, historians have recently begun
          to emphasize the way a prevailing definition of
          femininity often determines the kinds of work
          allocated to women, even when such allocation is
          inappropriate to new conditions. For instance, early
(20)   textile-mill entrepreneurs, in justifying women's
          employment in wage labor, made much of the
          assumption that women were by nature skillful at
          detailed tasks and patient in carrying out repetitive
          chores; the mill owners thus imported into the
(25)   new industrial order hoary stereotypes associated
          with the homemaking activities they presumed to
          have been the purview of women. Because women
          accepted the more unattractive new industrial tasks
          more readily than did men, such jobs came to
(30)   be regarded as female jobs. And employers, who
          assumed that women's "real" aspirations were for
          marriage and family life, declined to pay women
          wages commensurate with those of men. Thus many
          lower-skilled, lower-paid, less secure jobs came to be
(35)   perceived as "female."
                More remarkable than the original has been the
          persistence of such sex segregation in twentieth-
          century industry. Once an occupation came to be
          perceived as "female," employers showed surprisingly
(40)   little interest in changing that perception, even when
          higher profits beckoned. And despite the urgent need
          of the United States during the Second World War to
          mobilize its human resources fully, job segregation
          by sex characterized even the most important war
(45)   industries. Moreover, once the war ended, employers
          quickly returned to men most of the "male" jobs that
          women had been permitted to master.

Questions 70–77 refer to the passage above.

70. According to the passage, job segregation by sex in the United States was

(A) greatly diminished by labor mobilization during the Second World War

(B) perpetuated by those textile-mill owners who argued in favor of women's employment in wage labor

(C) one means by which women achieved greater job security

(D) reluctantly challenged by employers except when the economic advantages were obvious

(E) a constant source of labor unrest in the young textile industry

71. According to the passage, historians of women's labor focused on factory work as a more promising area of research than service-sector work because factory work

(A) involved the payment of higher wages

(B) required skill in detailed tasks

(C) was assumed to be less characterized by sex segregation

(D) was more readily accepted by women than by men

(E) fitted the economic dynamic of industrialism better

72. It can be inferred from the passage that early historians of women's labor in the United States paid little attention to women's employment in the service sector of the economy because

(A) the extreme variety of these occupations made it very difficult to assemble meaningful statistics about them

(B) fewer women found employment in the service sector than in factory work

(C) the wages paid to workers in the service sector were much lower than those paid in the industrial sector

(D) women's employment in the service sector tended to be much more short-term than in factory work

(E) employment in the service sector seemed to have much in common with the unpaid work associated with homemaking

73. The passage supports which of the following statements about the early mill owners mentioned in the second paragraph?

    (A) They hoped that by creating relatively unattractive "female" jobs they would discourage women from losing interest in marriage and family life.
    (B) They sought to increase the size of the available labor force as a means to keep men's wages low.
    (C) They argued that women were inherently suited to do well in particular kinds of factory work.
    (D) They thought that factory work bettered the condition of women by emancipating them from dependence on income earned by men.
    (E) They felt guilty about disturbing the traditional division of labor in the family.

74. It can be inferred from the passage that the "unfinished revolution" the author mentions in line 14 refers to the

    (A) entry of women into the industrial labor market
    (B) recognition that work done by women as homemakers should be compensated at rates comparable to those prevailing in the service sector of the economy
    (C) development of a new definition of femininity unrelated to the economic forces of industrialism
    (D) introduction of equal pay for equal work in all professions
    (E) emancipation of women wage earners from gender-determined job allocation

75. The passage supports which of the following statements about hiring policies in the United States?

    (A) After a crisis many formerly "male" jobs are reclassified as "female" jobs.
    (B) Industrial employers generally prefer to hire women with previous experience as homemakers.
    (C) Post-Second World War hiring policies caused women to lose many of their wartime gains in employment opportunity.
    (D) Even war industries during the Second World War were reluctant to hire women for factory work.
    (E) The service sector of the economy has proved more nearly gender-blind in its hiring policies than has the manufacturing sector.

76. Which of the following words best expresses the opinion of the author of the passage concerning the notion that women are more skillful than men in carrying out detailed tasks?

    (A) "patient" (line 23)
    (B) "repetitive" (line 23)
    (C) "hoary" (line 25)
    (D) "homemaking" (line 26)
    (E) "purview" (line 27)

77. Which of the following best describes the relationship of the final paragraph to the passage as a whole?

    (A) The central idea is reinforced by the citation of evidence drawn from twentieth-century history.
    (B) The central idea is restated in such a way as to form a transition to a new topic for discussion.
    (C) The central idea is restated and juxtaposed with evidence that might appear to contradict it.
    (D) A partial exception to the generalizations of the central idea is dismissed as unimportant.
    (E) Recent history is cited to suggest that the central idea's validity is gradually diminishing.

Line   Two modes of argumentation have been used on behalf of women's emancipation in Western societies. Arguments in what could be called the "relational" feminist tradition maintain the doctrine of "equality in
(5)   difference," or equity as distinct from equality. They posit that biological distinctions between the sexes result in a necessary sexual division of labor in the family and throughout society and that women's pro-creative labor is currently undervalued by society,
(10)   to the disadvantage of women. By contrast, the individualist feminist tradition emphasizes individual human rights and celebrates women's quest for personal autonomy, while downplaying the importance of gender roles and minimizing discussion of
(15)   childbearing and its attendant responsibilities.
    Before the late nineteenth century, these views coexisted within the feminist movement, often within the writings of the same individual. Between 1890 and 1920, however, relational feminism, which had
(20)   been the dominant strain in feminist thought, and which still predominates among European and non-Western feminists, lost ground in England and the United States. Because the concept of individual rights was already well established in the Anglo-Saxon legal
(25)   and political tradition, individualist feminism came to predominate in English-speaking countries. At the same time, the goals of the two approaches began to seem increasingly irreconcilable. Individualist feminists began to advocate a totally gender-blind system with equal
(30)   rights for all. Relational feminists, while agreeing that equal educational and economic opportunities outside the home should be available for all women, continued to emphasize women's special contributions to society as homemakers and mothers; they demanded special
(35)   treatment for women, including protective legislation for women workers, state-sponsored maternity benefits, and paid compensation for housework.
    Relational arguments have a major pitfall: because they underline women's physiological and psychological
(40)   distinctiveness, they are often appropriated by political adversaries and used to endorse male privilege. But the individualist approach, by attacking gender roles, denying the significance of physiological difference, and condemning existing familial institutions as hopelessly
(45)   patriarchal, has often simply treated as irrelevant the family roles important to many women. If the individualist framework, with its claim for women's autonomy, could be harmonized with the family-oriented concerns of relational feminists, a more fruitful
(50)   model for contemporary feminist politics could emerge.

Questions 78–83 refer to the passage above.

78. The author of the passage alludes to the well-established nature of the concept of individual rights in the Anglo-Saxon legal and political tradition in order to

(A) illustrate the influence of individualist feminist thought on more general intellectual trends in English history
(B) argue that feminism was already a part of the larger Anglo-Saxon intellectual tradition, even though this has often gone unnoticed by critics of women's emancipation
(C) explain the decline in individualist thinking among feminists in non-English speaking countries
(D) help account for an increasing shift toward individualist feminism among feminists in English-speaking countries
(E) account for the philosophical differences between individualist and relational feminists in English-speaking countries

79. The passage suggests that the author of the passage believes which of the following?

(A) The predominance of individualist feminism in English-speaking countries is a historical phenomenon, the causes of which have not yet been investigated.
(B) The individualist and relational feminist views are irreconcilable, given their theoretical differences concerning the foundations of society.
(C) A consensus concerning the direction of future feminist politics will probably soon emerge, given the awareness among feminists of the need for cooperation among women.
(D) Political adversaries of feminism often misuse arguments predicated on differences between the sexes to argue that the existing social system should be maintained.

(E)   Relational feminism provides the best theoretical framework for contemporary feminist politics, but individualist feminism could contribute much toward refining and strengthening modern feminist thought.

80.   It can be inferred from the passage that the individualist feminist tradition denies the validity of which of the following causal statements?

(A)   A division of labor in a social group can result in increased efficiency with regard to the performance of group tasks.

(B)   A division of labor in a social group causes inequities in the distribution of opportunities and benefits among group members.

(C)   A division of labor on the basis of gender in a social group is necessitated by the existence of sex-linked biological differences between male and female members of the group.

(D)   Culturally determined distinctions based on gender in a social group foster the existence of differing attitudes and opinions among group members.

(E)   Educational programs aimed at reducing inequalities based on gender among members of a social group can result in a sense of greater well-being for all members of the group.

81.   According to the passage, relational feminists and individualist feminists agree that

(A)   individual human rights take precedence over most other social claims

(B)   the gender-based division of labor in society should be eliminated

(C)   laws guaranteeing equal treatment for all citizens regardless of gender should be passed

(D)   a greater degree of social awareness concerning the importance of motherhood would be beneficial to society

(E)   the same educational and economic opportunities should be available to both sexes

82.   According to the author, which of the following was true of feminist thought in Western societies before 1890?

(A)   Individualist feminist arguments were not found in the thought or writing of non-English-speaking feminists.

(B)   Individualist feminism was a strain in feminist thought, but another strain, relational feminism, predominated.

(C)   Relational and individualist approaches were equally prevalent in feminist thought and writing.

(D)   The predominant view among feminists held that the welfare of women was ultimately less important than the welfare of children.

(E)   The predominant view among feminists held that the sexes should receive equal treatment under the law.

83.   The author implies that which of the following was true of most feminist thinkers in England and the United States after 1920?

(A)   They were less concerned with politics than with intellectual issues.

(B)   They began to reach a broader audience and their programs began to be adopted by main-stream political parties.

(C)   They called repeatedly for international cooperation among women's groups to achieve their goals.

(D)   They moderated their initial criticism of the economic systems that characterized their societies.

(E)   They did not attempt to unite the two different feminist approaches in their thought.

Line   While there is no blueprint for transforming
a largely government-controlled economy into a
free one, the experience of the United Kingdom
since 1979 clearly shows one approach that works:
(5)   privatization, in which state-owned industries
are sold to private companies. By 1979, the total
borrowings and losses of state-owned industries
were running at about £3 billion a year. By selling
many of these industries, the government has
(10)   decreased these borrowings and losses, gained
over £34 billion from the sales, and now receives
tax revenues from the newly privatized companies.
Along with a dramatically improved overall
economy, the government has been able to repay
(15)   12.5 percent of the net national debt over a two-
year period.
        In fact, privatization has not only rescued
individual industries and a whole economy headed
for disaster, but has also raised the level of
(20)   performance in every area. At British Airways and
British Gas, for example, productivity per employee
has risen by 20 percent. At Associated British Ports,
labor disruptions common in the 1970's and early
1980's have now virtually disappeared. At British
(25)   Telecom, there is no longer a waiting list — as
there always was before privatization — to have a
telephone installed.
        Part of this improved productivity has come
about because the employees of privatized
(30)   industries were given the opportunity to buy
shares in their own companies. They responded
enthusiastically to the offer of shares: at British
Aerospace, 89 percent of the eligible work force
bought shares; at Associated British Ports, 90
(35)   percent; and at British Telecom, 92 percent.
When people have a personal stake in something,
they think about it, care about it, work to make
it prosper. At the National Freight Consortium,
the new employee-owners grew so concerned
(40)   about their company's profits that during wage
negotiations they actually pressed their union to
lower its wage demands.
        Some economists have suggested that
giving away free shares would provide a needed
(45)   acceleration of the privatization process. Yet they
miss Thomas Paine's point that "what we obtain
too cheap we esteem too lightly." In order for the
far-ranging benefits of individual ownership to be

achieved by owners, companies, and countries,
(50)   employees and other individuals must make their
own decisions to buy, and they must commit some
of their own resources to the choice.

Questions 84–90 refer to the passage above.

84. According to the passage, all of the following were
benefits of privatizing state-owned industries in the
United Kingdom EXCEPT:

(A) Privatized industries paid taxes to the
government.
(B) The government gained revenue from selling
state-owned industries.
(C) The government repaid some of its national
debt.
(D) Profits from industries that were still state-
owned increased.
(E) Total borrowings and losses of state-owned
industries decreased.

85. According to the passage, which of the following
resulted in increased productivity in companies that
have been privatized?

(A) A large number of employees chose to
purchase shares in their companies.
(B) Free shares were widely distributed to
individual shareholders.
(C) The government ceased to regulate major
industries.
(D) Unions conducted wage negotiations for
employees.
(E) Employee-owners agreed to have their wages
lowered.

86. It can be inferred from the passage that the author considers labor disruptions to be

(A) an inevitable problem in a weak national economy

(B) a positive sign of employee concern about a company

(C) a predictor of employee reactions to a company's offer to sell shares to them

(D) a phenomenon found more often in state-owned industries than in private companies

(E) a deterrence to high performance levels in an industry

87. The passage supports which of the following statements about employees buying shares in their own companies?

(A) At three different companies, approximately nine out of ten of the workers were eligible to buy shares in their companies.

(B) Approximately 90 percent of the eligible workers at three different companies chose to buy shares in their companies.

(C) The opportunity to buy shares was discouraged by at least some labor unions.

(D) Companies that demonstrated the highest productivity were the first to allow their employees the opportunity to buy shares.

(E) Eligibility to buy shares was contingent on employees' agreeing to increased work loads.

88. Which of the following statements is most consistent with the principle described in lines 36–38?

(A) A democratic government that decides it is inappropriate to own a particular industry has in no way abdicated its responsibilities as guardian of the public interest.

(B) The ideal way for a government to protect employee interests is to force companies to maintain their share of a competitive market without government subsidies.

(C) The failure to harness the power of self-interest is an important reason that state-owned industries perform poorly.

(D) Governments that want to implement privatization programs must try to eliminate all resistance to the free-market system.

(E) The individual shareholder will reap only a minute share of the gains from whatever sacrifices he or she makes to achieve these gains.

89. Which of the following can be inferred from the passage about the privatization process in the United Kingdom?

(A) It depends to a potentially dangerous degree on individual ownership of shares.

(B) It conforms in its most general outlines to Thomas Paine's prescription for business ownership.

(C) It was originally conceived to include some giving away of free shares.

(D) It has been successful, even though privatization has failed in other countries.

(E) It is taking place more slowly than some economists suggest is necessary.

90. The quotation in lines 46–47 is most probably used to

(A) counter a position that the author of the passage believes is incorrect

(B) state a solution to a problem described in the previous sentence

(C) show how opponents of the viewpoint of the author of the passage have supported their arguments

(D) point out a paradox contained in a controversial viewpoint

(E) present a historical maxim to challenge the principle introduced in the third paragraph

Line   Most large corporations in the United States
were once run by individual capitalists who owned
enough stock to dominate the board of directors
and dictate company policy. Because putting such
(5)   large amounts of stock on the market would only
depress its value, they could not sell out for a quick
profit and instead had to concentrate on improving
the long-term productivity of their companies.
Today, with few exceptions, the stock of large
(10)   United States corporations is held by large institutions—pension funds, for example—and because
these institutions are prohibited by antitrust
laws from owning a majority of a company's
stock and from actively influencing a company's
(15)   decision-making, they can enhance their wealth
only by buying and selling stock in anticipation of
fluctuations in its value. A minority shareholder is
necessarily a short-term trader. As a result, United
States productivity is unlikely to improve unless
(20)   shareholders and the managers of the companies
in which they invest are encouraged to enhance
long-term productivity (and hence long-term
profitability), rather than simply to maximize short-
term profits.
(25)   Since the return of the old-style capitalist is
unlikely, today's short-term traders must be remade
into tomorrow's long-term capitalistic investors. The
legal limits that now prevent financial institutions
from acquiring a dominant shareholding position
(30)   in a corporation should be removed, and such
institutions encouraged to take a more active role
in the operations of the companies in which they
invest. In addition, any institution that holds 20
percent or more of a company's stock should be
(35)   forced to give the public one day's notice of the
intent to sell those shares. Unless the announced
sale could be explained to the public on grounds
other than anticipated future losses, the value
of the stock would plummet and, like the old-
(40)   time capitalists, major investors could cut their
losses only by helping to restore their companies'
productivity. Such measures would force financial
institutions to become capitalists whose success
depends not on trading shares at the propitious
(45)   moment, but on increasing the productivity of the
companies in which they invest.

Questions 91–97 refer to the passage above.

91. In the passage, the author is primarily concerned with doing which of the following?

(A) Comparing two different approaches to a problem
(B) Describing a problem and proposing a solution
(C) Defending an established method
(D) Presenting data and drawing conclusions from the data
(E) Comparing two different analyses of a current situation

92. It can be inferred from the passage that which of the following is true of majority shareholders in a corporation?

(A) They make the corporation's operational management decisions.
(B) They are not allowed to own more than 50 percent of the corporation's stock.
(C) They cannot make quick profits by selling off large amounts of their stock in the corporation.
(D) They are more interested in profits than in productivity.
(E) They cannot sell any of their stock in the corporation without giving the public advance notice.

93. According to the passage, the purpose of the requirement suggested in lines 33–36 would be which of the following?

(A) To encourage institutional stockholders to sell stock that they believe will decrease in value
(B) To discourage institutional stockholders from intervening in the operation of a company whose stock they own
(C) To discourage short-term profit taking by institutional stockholders
(D) To encourage a company's employees to take an active role in the ownership of stock in the company
(E) To encourage investors to diversify their stock holdings

94. The author suggests that which of the following is a true statement about people who typify the "old-style capitalist" referred to in line 25?

    (A) They now rely on outdated management techniques.
    (B) They seldom engaged in short-term trading of the stock they owned.
    (C) They did not influence the investment policies of the corporations in which they invested.
    (D) They now play a very small role in the stock market as a result of antitrust legislation.
    (E) They were primarily concerned with maximizing the short-term profitability of the corporations in which they owned stock.

95. It can be inferred that the author makes which of the following assumptions about the businesses once controlled by individual capitalists?

    (A) These businesses were less profitable than are businesses today.
    (B) Improving long-term productivity led to increased profits.
    (C) Each business had only a few stockholders.
    (D) There was no short-term trading in the stock of these businesses.
    (E) Institutions owned no stock in these companies.

96. The author suggests that the role of large institutions as stockholders differs from that of the "old-style capitalist" in part because large institutions

    (A) invest in the stock of so many companies that they cannot focus attention on the affairs of any single corporation
    (B) are prohibited by law from owning a majority of a corporation's stock
    (C) are influenced by brokers who advise against long-term ownership of stocks
    (D) are able to put large amounts of stock on the market without depressing the stock's value
    (E) are attracted to the stocks of corporations that demonstrate long-term gains in productivity

97. The primary function of the second paragraph of the passage is to

    (A) identify problems
    (B) warn of consequences
    (C) explain effects
    (D) evaluate solutions
    (E) recommend actions

Line The modern multinational corporation is
described as having originated when the owner-
managers of nineteenth-century British firms
carrying on international trade were replaced
(5) by teams of salaried managers organized
into hierarchies. Increases in the volume of
transactions in such firms are commonly believed
to have necessitated this structural change.
Nineteenth-century inventions like the steamship
(10) and the telegraph, by facilitating coordination of
managerial activities, are described as key factors.
Sixteenth- and seventeenth-century chartered
trading companies, despite the international
scope of their activities, are usually considered
(15) irrelevant to this discussion: the volume of their
transactions is assumed to have been too low and
the communications and transport of their day
too primitive to make comparisons with modern
multinationals interesting.
(20) In reality, however, early trading companies
successfully purchased and outfitted ships, built and
operated offices and warehouses, manufactured
trade goods for use abroad, maintained trading posts
and production facilities overseas, procured goods
(25) for import, and sold those goods both at home and
in other countries. The large volume of transactions
associated with these activities seems to have
necessitated hierarchical management structures
well before the advent of modern communications
(30) and transportation. For example, in the Hudson's
Bay Company, each far-flung trading outpost was
managed by a salaried agent, who carried out the
trade with the Native Americans, managed day-to-
day operations, and oversaw the post's workers and
(35) servants. One chief agent, answerable to the Court
of Directors in London through the correspondence
committee, was appointed with control over all of the
agents on the bay.
The early trading companies did differ
(40) strikingly from modern multinationals in many
respects. They depended heavily on the national
governments of their home countries and thus
characteristically acted abroad to promote national
interests. Their top managers were typically owners
(45) with a substantial minority share, whereas senior
managers' holdings in modern multinationals
are usually insignificant. They operated in a
preindustrial world, grafting a system of capitalist

international trade onto a premodern system of
(50) artisan and peasant production. Despite these
differences, however, early trading companies
organized effectively in remarkably modern ways
and merit further study as analogues of more
modern structures.

Questions 98–105 refer to the passage above.

98. The author's main point is that

(A) modern multinationals originated in the sixteenth and seventeenth centuries with the establishment of chartered trading companies
(B) the success of early chartered trading companies, like that of modern multinationals, depended primarily on their ability to carry out complex operations
(C) early chartered trading companies should be more seriously considered by scholars studying the origins of modern multinationals
(D) scholars are quite mistaken concerning the origins of modern multinationals
(E) the management structures of early chartered trading companies are fundamentally the same as those of modern multinationals

99. According to the passage, early chartered trading companies are usually described as

(A) irrelevant to a discussion of the origins of the modern multinational corporation
(B) interesting but ultimately too unusual to be good subjects for economic study
(C) analogues of nineteenth-century British trading firms
(D) rudimentary and very early forms of the modern multinational corporation
(E) important national institutions because they existed to further the political aims of the governments of their home countries

100. It can be inferred from the passage that the author would characterize the activities engaged in by early chartered trading companies as being

   (A) complex enough in scope to require a substantial amount of planning and coordination on the part of management
   (B) too simple to be considered similar to those of a modern multinational corporation
   (C) as intricate as those carried out by the largest multinational corporations today
   (D) often unprofitable due to slow communications and unreliable means of transportation
   (E) hampered by the political demands imposed on them by the governments of their home countries

101. The author lists the various activities of early chartered trading companies in order to

   (A) analyze the various ways in which these activities contributed to changes in management structure in such companies
   (B) demonstrate that the volume of business transactions of such companies exceeded that of earlier firms
   (C) refute the view that the volume of business undertaken by such companies was relatively low
   (D) emphasize the international scope of these companies' operations
   (E) support the argument that such firms coordinated such activities by using available means of communication and transport

102. With which of the following generalizations regarding management structures would the author of the passage most probably agree?

   (A) Hierarchical management structures are the most efficient management structures possible in a modern context.
   (B) Firms that routinely have a high volume of business transactions find it necessary to adopt hierarchical management structures.
   (C) Hierarchical management structures cannot be successfully implemented without modern communications and transportation.
   (D) Modern multinational firms with a relatively small volume of business transactions usually do not have hierarchically organized management structures.
   (E) Companies that adopt hierarchical management structures usually do so in order to facilitate expansion into foreign trade.

103. The passage suggests that modern multinationals differ from early chartered trading companies in that

   (A) the top managers of modern multinationals own stock in their own companies rather than simply receiving a salary
   (B) modern multinationals depend on a system of capitalist international trade rather than on less modern trading systems
   (C) modern multinationals have operations in a number of different foreign countries rather than merely in one or two
   (D) the operations of modern multinationals are highly profitable despite the more stringent environmental and safety regulations of modern governments
   (E) the overseas operations of modern multi-nationals are not governed by the national interests of their home countries

104. The author mentions the artisan and peasant production systems of early chartered trading companies as an example of

    (A) an area of operations of these companies that was unhampered by rudimentary systems of communications and transport
    (B) a similarity that allows fruitful comparison of these companies with modern multinationals
    (C) a positive achievement of these companies in the face of various difficulties
    (D) a system that could not have emerged in the absence of management hierarchies
    (E) a characteristic that distinguishes these companies from modern multinationals

105. The passage suggests that one of the reasons that early chartered trading companies deserve comparison with early modern multinationals is

    (A) the degree to which they both depended on new technology
    (B) the similar nature of their management structures
    (C) similarities in their top managements' degree of ownership in the company
    (D) their common dependence on political stability abroad in order to carry on foreign operations
    (E) their common tendency to revolutionize systems of production

3.5 Reading Comprehension Answer Key

1.	B	32.	E	63.	E	94.	B
2.	A	33.	C	64.	D	95.	B
3.	A	34.	B	65.	D	96.	B
4.	E	35.	B	66.	A	97.	E
5.	C	36.	A	67.	E	98.	C
6.	C	37.	B	68.	B	99.	A
7.	B	38.	B	69.	B	100.	A
8.	E	39.	D	70.	B	101.	C
9.	C	40.	E	71.	C	102.	B
10.	D	41.	B	72.	E	103.	E
11.	A	42.	C	73.	C	104.	E
12.	D	43.	A	74.	E	105.	B
13.	B	44.	D	75.	C		
14.	B	45.	E	76.	C		
15.	B	46.	B	77.	A		
16.	B	47.	C	78.	D		
17.	D	48.	D	79.	D		
18.	B	49.	E	80.	C		
19.	E	50.	D	81.	E		
20.	A	51.	B	82.	B		
21.	C	52.	D	83.	E		
22.	C	53.	B	84.	D		
23.	E	54.	E	85.	A		
24.	A	55.	C	86.	E		
25.	D	56.	B	87.	B		
26.	C	57.	C	88.	C		
27.	A	58.	D	89.	E		
28.	D	59.	A	90.	A		
29.	D	60.	A	91.	B		
30.	C	61.	D	92.	C		
31.	A	62.	C	93.	C		

3.6 Reading Comprehension Answer Explanations

The following discussion of reading comprehension is intended to familiarize you with the most efficient and effective approaches to the kinds of problems common to reading comprehension. The particular questions in this chapter are generally representative of the kinds of reading comprehension questions you will encounter on the GMAT®. Remember that it is the problem solving strategy that is important, not the specific details of a particular question.

Questions 1–5 refer to the passage on page 22.

1. The passage is primarily concerned with

    (A) describing the effects of human activities on algae in coral reefs
    (B) explaining how human activities are posing a threat to coral reef communities
    (C) discussing the process by which coral reefs deteriorate in nutrient-poor waters
    (D) explaining how coral reefs produce food for themselves
    (E) describing the abundance of algae and filter-feeding animals in coral reef areas

Main idea

This question concerns the author's main point, the focus of the passage as a whole. The first paragraph describes the symbiosis of the coral reef so that readers will understand how human activities are degrading this fragile ecosystem, as explained in the second paragraph. The author focuses on how harmful these human activities are to coral reefs.

A The growth of algae (lines 23–26) is a detail supporting the main point.
B **Correct.** Human activities are threatening complex coral reef communities.
C The first paragraph explains how coral reefs thrive in nutrient-poor waters.
D The zooxanthellae cells of algae feed the coral reefs (lines 8–12); this point is a detail.
E This abundance is a detail supporting the main idea, not the main idea itself.

The correct answer is B.

2. The passage suggests which of the following about coral reef communities?

    (A) Coral reef communities may actually be more likely to thrive in waters that are relatively low in nutrients.
    (B) The nutrients on which coral reef communities thrive are only found in shallow waters.
    (C) Human population growth has led to changing ocean temperatures, which threatens coral reef communities.
    (D) The growth of coral reef communities tends to destabilize underwater herbivore populations.
    (E) Coral reef communities are more complex and diverse than most ecosystems located on dry land.

Inference

The word *suggests* in the question indicates that the answer will be an inference based on what the passage says about coral reef communities. The beginning of the passage states that *nutrient-poor* waters (line 5) sustain the thriving life of a coral reef. Lines 21–23 show that *nutrient input is increasing* because of human activities, with consequent *declines in reef communities*. Given this information, it is reasonable to conclude that coral reefs thrive in nutrient-poor, rather than nutrient-rich, waters.

A **Correct.** Coral reefs flourish in clear, nutrient-poor waters.
B Shallow waters are mentioned only in the context of deteriorating marine habitats (line 18), not as a source of nutrients.
C Ocean temperatures are not mentioned in the passage.
D Reef decline, not reef growth, leads to destabilized herbivore populations (line 23).
E No comparisons are made between ecosystems in water and on land.

The correct answer is A.

3. The author refers to "filter-feeding animals" (lines 24–25) in order to

(A) provide an example of a characteristic sign of reef deterioration
(B) explain how reef communities acquire sustenance for survival
(C) identify a factor that helps herbivore populations thrive
(D) indicate a cause of decreasing nutrient input in waters that reefs inhabit
(E) identify members of coral reef communities that rely on coral reefs for nutrients

Logical structure

This question concerns why the author has included a particular detail. Look at the context for the phrase *filter-feeding animals*. The complete sentence (lines 22–25) shows that a higher population of filter-feeding animals is a symptom of reef decline.

A **Correct.** An *increasing abundance* of these animals is a *typical* sign of reef decline.
B Zooxanthellae cells of algae, not filter-feeding animals, provide sustenance for reef communities (lines 8–12).
C An increase in filter-feeding animals is associated with *destabilized*, not thriving, herbivore populations.
D An increase in nutrients, rather than a decrease, causes reef decline, when the population of filter-feeding animals then grows.
E The author includes filter-feeding animals in the context of the decline of coral reefs, not their symbiosis.

The correct answer is A.

4. According to the passage, which of the following is a factor that is threatening the survival of coral reef communities?

(A) The waters they inhabit contain few nutrient resources.
(B) A decline in nutrient input is disrupting their symbiotic relationship with zooxanthellae.
(C) The degraded waters of their marine habitats have reduced their ability to carry out photosynthesis.
(D) They are too biologically complex to survive in habitats with minimal nutrient input.
(E) Waste by-products result in an increase in nutrient input to reef communities.

Supporting ideas

The phrase *according to the passage* indicates that the necessary information is explicitly stated in the passage. Look at the threats to coral reefs listed in lines 19–22 and match them against the possible answers. Waste by-products increase nutrients in the water, and reefs decline as nutrients grow more plentiful (lines 21–25).

A Coral reefs thrive in nutrient-poor waters, as the first paragraph explains.
B Nutrient input is increasing, not decreasing (lines 21–22).
C The passage does not say that the degraded waters inhibit photosynthesis.
D The complex ecosystem of coral reefs thrives in nutrient-poor waters.
E **Correct.** Waste by-products contribute to increased nutrient input, which causes reef decline.

The correct answer is E.

5. It can be inferred from the passage that the author describes coral reef communities as paradoxical most likely for which of the following reasons?

    (A) They are thriving even though human activities have depleted the nutrients in their environment.
    (B) They are able to survive in spite of an over-abundance of algae inhabiting their waters.
    (C) They are able to survive in an environment with limited food resources.
    (D) Their metabolic wastes contribute to the degradation of the waters that they inhabit.
    (E) They are declining even when the water surrounding them remains clear.

Inference

A paradox is a puzzling statement that seems to contradict itself. To answer this question, look for information that appears puzzling. The author calls coral reefs *one of the fascinating paradoxes of the biosphere* because the reefs are *prolific and productive* despite inhabiting clear waters with few nutrients. The paradox is that the reefs seem to flourish with little food.

A   Human activities have harmed coral reefs by increasing nutrient input (lines 26–28).
B   An increase in algae is a sign of reef decline, not reef survival (lines 22–24).
C   **Correct.** Coral reefs thrive in waters that provide little food.
D   Algae cells use the metabolic wastes of the corals to carry out photosynthesis; the result is sustenance for the reef community, not a degradation of waters (lines 8–10).
E   Coral reefs thrive in clear, nutrient-poor water and decline in nutrient-rich water.

The correct answer is C.

Questions 6–11 refer to the passage on page 24.

6. The passage suggests that a lack of modern sanitation would make which of the following most likely to occur?

    (A) An outbreak of Lyme disease
    (B) An outbreak of dengue hemorrhagic fever
    (C) An epidemic of typhoid
    (D) An epidemic of paralytic polio among infants
    (E) An epidemic of paralytic polio among adolescents and adults

Inference

Since the question asks for an inference about a lack of modern sanitation, begin by examining what the passage says about the presence of modern sanitation. Lines 9–11 explain the role of modern sanitation in delaying the onset of polio. Lines 14–16 state *the hygiene that helped prevent typhoid epidemics indirectly fostered a paralytic polio epidemic.* It is reasonable to infer from this statement that a lack of modern sanitation could lead to a typhoid epidemic.

A   Lyme disease is caused by the bacteria carried by deer ticks, not by a lack of sanitation.
B   The dengue virus is transmitted by a mosquito, not by a lack of sanitation.
C   **Correct.** Lines 14–15 show that typhoid epidemics were prevented by modern sanitation; therefore, typhoid might break out in the absence of modern sanitation.
D   Lines 12–14 show that infants did not typically suffer paralysis with polio.
E   When modern sanitation is not present, immunity to polio is acquired in infancy.

The correct answer is C.

7. According to the passage, the outbreak of dengue hemorrhagic fever in the 1950's occurred for which of the following reasons?

    (A) The mosquito *Aedes aegypti* was newly introduced into Asia.
    (B) The mosquito *Aedes aegypti* became more numerous.
    (C) The mosquito *Aedes albopictus* became infected with the dengue virus.
    (D) Individuals who would normally acquire immunity to the dengue virus as infants were not infected until later in life.
    (E) More people began to visit and inhabit areas in which mosquitoes live and breed.

    Supporting ideas

    The question asks for information explicitly stated in the passage, although in slightly different language. Look at lines 24–28, where the 1950's outbreak of dengue fever is discussed. The outbreak became an epidemic in Asia *because of ecological changes that caused Aedes aegypti, the mosquito that transmits the dengue virus, to proliferate.*

    A The sentence does not say that the mosquito was newly introduced into Asia.
    B **Correct.** Ecological conditions in Asia at that time allowed the mosquito *Aedes aegypti* to proliferate, that is, to grow numerous.
    C *Aedes albopictus* is another mosquito (lines 28–32) more recently connected with a potential epidemic; the passage does not suggest this mosquito was connected to the 1950's Asian epidemic.
    D Immunity to polio is acquired in infancy (lines 12–13), but no mention is made of a similar immunity to the dengue virus.
    E Population shifts may explain the prevalence of Lyme disease in parts of the United States (lines 16–22), but they are not cited as cause of the Asian epidemic.

    The correct answer is B.

8. It can be inferred from the passage that Lyme disease has become prevalent in parts of the United States because of which of the following?

    (A) The inadvertent introduction of Lyme disease bacteria to the United States
    (B) The inability of modern sanitation methods to eradicate Lyme disease bacteria
    (C) A genetic mutation in Lyme disease bacteria that makes them more virulent
    (D) The spread of Lyme disease bacteria from infected humans to non-infected humans
    (E) An increase in the number of humans who encounter deer ticks

    Inference

    To make an inference about Lyme disease, examine the discussion of Lyme disease in lines 16–24. The disease is caused by bacteria carried by deer ticks. It has become prevalent in parts of the United States as the deer population has grown. This population growth has occurred at the same time that the suburbs have expanded and outdoor activities in the deer's habitat have increased. What can be inferred about the growing prevalence of Lyme disease? It is logical to infer that more people are encountering the deer ticks that carry the disease.

    A No inadvertent introduction of the bacteria is mentioned in the passage.
    B Modern sanitation plays a role in typhoid and polio epidemics, but it is not linked to Lyme disease.
    C No genetic mutation of bacteria is discussed in the context of Lyme disease.
    D Transmission by deer ticks is discussed, but not human-to-human transmission.
    E **Correct.** As the deer population grows and as humans encroach on the deer habitat, more people encounter deer ticks and become infected with the disease.

    The correct answer is E.

9. Which of the following can most reasonably be concluded about the mosquito *Aedes albopictus* on the basis of information given in the passage?

   (A) It is native to the United States.
   (B) It can proliferate only in Asia.
   (C) It transmits the dengue virus.
   (D) It caused an epidemic of dengue hemorrhagic fever in the 1950's.
   (E) It replaced *Aedes aegypti* in Asia when ecological changes altered *Aedes aegypti's* habitat.

Inference

An inference is drawn from stated information rather than explicitly stated. Begin by finding the information given about this mosquito. The mosquito *Aedes albopictus* is mentioned in the final sentence of the passage, which says that this mosquito was inadvertently introduced into the United States and has spread widely. Because of this, the author states that *the stage is now set in the United States for a dengue epidemic.* It is reasonable to infer that this mosquito can transmit the dengue virus.

A It has been inadvertently introduced into the United States.

B The mosquito that proliferated in Asia during the 1950's was *Aedes aegypti*.

C **Correct.** The mosquito *Aedes albopictus* transmits the dengue virus.

D The mosquito *Aedes aegypti* caused the epidemic in the 1950's, not *Aedes albopictus*.

E No information in the passage supports this statement.

The correct answer is C.

10. Which of the following best describes the organization of the passage?

   (A) A paradox is stated, discussed, and left unresolved.
   (B) Two opposing explanations are presented, argued, and reconciled.
   (C) A theory is proposed and is then followed by descriptions of three experiments that support the theory.
   (D) A generalization is stated and is then followed by three instances that support the generalization.
   (E) An argument is described and is then followed by three counterexamples that refute the argument.

Logical structure

Analyze the structure of the passage in order to answer a question about how the passage is organized. The passage begins by explaining that some epidemics are not caused by genetic mutations in bacteria and viruses, but rather by social and ecological changes in an environment. Three specific examples, i.e., polio, Lyme disease, and dengue fever, are then used to support this general statement.

A The passage opens by showing that epidemics may be caused by different means; this is not a paradox.

B Only one explanation, having three supporting examples, is given.

C The three examples of epidemics are not experiments conducted to support a theory; they are documented cases of disease.

D **Correct.** A generalization is stated: *scientists have discovered the importance of social and ecological factors to epidemics* (lines 5–6). Three examples—polio, Lyme disease, and dengue fever—support the generalization.

E The examples in the passage support the author's generalization or argument; no counterexamples refuting the argument are included.

The correct answer is D.

11. Which of the following, if true, would most strengthen the author's assertion about the cause of the Lyme disease outbreak in the United States?

(A) The deer population was smaller in the late nineteenth century than in the mid twentieth century.

(B) Interest in outdoor recreation began to grow in the late nineteenth century.

(C) In recent years the suburbs have stopped growing.

(D) Outdoor recreation enthusiasts routinely take measures to protect themselves against Lyme disease.

(E) Scientists have not yet developed a vaccine that can prevent Lyme disease.

Logical structure

Examine the author's argument about the cause of Lyme disease. The author blames the recent prevalence of Lyme disease on the rise in the deer population and the growth of the suburbs, with people spending more time outside in the deer's habitat. The disease had appeared *only sporadically* during the late nineteenth century.

A **Correct.** If the deer population was smaller when the disease occurred *only sporadically*, then the author's claim that the mid-century rise in deer population is one of the causes of Lyme disease is strengthened.

B Increased interest in outdoor recreation does not mean that people engaged in outdoor activities in the deer's habitat; the assertion is not strengthened.

C The lack of growth of the suburbs weakens, rather than strengthens, the author's assertion.

D Protective measures against the disease are not relevant to an assertion about what causes the disease.

E The lack of a vaccine is irrelevant to an assertion about what causes the disease.

The correct answer is A.

Questions 12–15 refer to the passage on page 26.

12. Which of the following most accurately states the purpose of the passage?

(A) To compare two different approaches to the study of homeostasis

(B) To summarize the findings of several studies regarding organisms' maintenance of internal variables in extreme environments

(C) To argue for a particular hypothesis regarding various organisms' conservation of water in desert environments

(D) To cite examples of how homeostasis is achieved by various organisms

(E) To defend a new theory regarding the maintenance of adequate fluid balance

Main idea

To answer this question, look at the passage as a whole since the purpose is reflected in the entire passage. The first paragraph defines homeostasis and names three animals that must maintain internal fluid balance in difficult circumstances. The topic of the second paragraph is how desert rats maintain fluid balance. The third paragraph discusses how camels maintain fluid balance, while the final paragraph describes maintenance of water balance in marine vertebrates. Thus, the overall purpose is to give three examples of how homeostasis is achieved.

A Examples of homeostasis are given, but different approaches to studying it are not discussed.

B The passage describes examples but it does not summarize studies.

C While the passage does discuss two desert animals, it does not present any argument for a particular hypothesis.

D **Correct.** The passage discusses the examples of desert rats, camels, and marine invertebrates to show how these organisms are able to achieve homeostasis.

E The passage describes how three organisms maintain water balance, but it presents no theory about it.

The correct answer is D.

13. According to the passage, the camel maintains internal fluid balance in which of the following ways?

    I.   By behavioral avoidance of exposure to conditions that lead to fluid loss
    II. By an ability to tolerate high body temperatures
    III. By reliance on stored internal fluid supplies

    (A) I only
    (B) II only
    (C) I and II only
    (D) II and III only
    (E) I, II, and III

    Inference

    To answer this question about factual information stated in the passage, read the third paragraph carefully and compare its content to that of each statement. Line 26 says the camels cannot store water, so Statement III is obviously false. Since camels only pant and sweat when they reach temperatures that *would kill a human*, they must have an ability to tolerate high body temperatures. Therefore, Statement II is true. Finally, there is no evidence that camels avoid exposure to conditions that lead to fluid loss. Lines 30–32 show that camels suffer high levels of fluid loss. Therefore Statement I is false. The correct answer must include only Statement II, while excluding Statements I and III.

    A   Statement I is false.
    B   **Correct.** Statement II is the only true statement; lines 34–36 show that camels can tolerate high body temperatures.
    C   Statement II is true, but Statement I is false.
    D   Statement II is true, but Statement III is false.
    E   Statement II is true, but Statements I and III are false.

    The correct answer is B.

14. It can be inferred from the passage that some mechanisms that regulate internal body temperature, like sweating and panting, can lead to which of the following?

    (A) A rise in the external body temperature
    (B) A drop in the body's internal fluid level
    (C) A decrease in the osmotic pressure of the blood
    (D) A decrease in the amount of renal water loss
    (E) A decrease in the urine's salt content

    Inference

    An inference is drawn from stated information. To answer this question, look at the information about sweating and panting in lines 17–19 and 30–32. The passage states that desert rats are *avoiding loss of fluid through panting or sweating, which are regulatory mechanisms for maintaining internal body temperature by evaporative cooling.* These mechanisms reduce internal body temperatures. Additionally, camels conserve internal water (line 36) when they avoid sweating and panting. Therefore, they must lose internal water when they do sweat and pant. Sweating and panting lead to a loss of internal water.

    A   The passage does not discuss *external body temperature*; these mechanisms lower internal body temperature, and there is no reason to infer external body temperatures might rise.
    B   **Correct.** Sweating and panting lead to *loss of fluid,* and avoiding them helps camels *conserve internal water.*
    C   The passage states that desert rats are *able to maintain the osmotic pressure of their blood, as well as their total body-water content* (lines 14–16) and does not connect changes in osmotic pressure to temperature-regulating mechanisms such as sweating and panting.
    D   While the passage does discuss renal water loss, it does not relate this to temperature-regulating mechanisms like sweating and panting.
    E   The passage does not relate body temperature regulators like sweating and panting to changes in the urine's salt content.

    The correct answer is B.

15. It can be inferred from the passage that the author characterizes the camel's kidney as "entirely unexceptional" (line 27) primarily to emphasize that it

   (A) functions much as the kidney of a rat functions
   (B) does not aid the camel in coping with the exceptional water loss resulting from the extreme conditions of its environment
   (C) does not enable the camel to excrete as much salt as do the kidneys of marine vertebrates
   (D) is similar in structure to the kidneys of most mammals living in water-deprived environments
   (E) requires the help of other organs in eliminating excess salt

Inference

To answer this question, look at the phrase *entirely unexceptional* in the context of the passage. Desert rats and camels share the problem of conserving water in an environment where water is lacking, *temperature is high, and humidity is low* (lines 12–13). Desert rats have as part of their coping mechanisms exceptional kidneys that produce urine with a high salt content. The author compares camels' kidneys to those of desert rats and shows that the camels have ordinary kidneys that do not help the camels conserve water.

A   Since a contrast is drawn between the kidneys of camels and those of desert rats, the two must function differently.
B   **Correct.** The camel's kidney does nothing special to help the camel cope with its difficult environment.
C   No comparison between the kidneys of camels and the kidneys of marine vertebrates is made.
D   There is no information given about the kidney structure of most mammals in desert environments so this conclusion is not justified.
E   Marine vertebrates have other organs that help eliminate extra salt; camels do not.

The correct answer is B.

Questions 16–21 refer to the passage on page 28.

16. The primary purpose of the passage is to

   (A) enumerate reasons why both traditional scholarly methods and newer scholarly methods have limitations
   (B) identify a shortcoming in a scholarly approach and describe an alternative approach
   (C) provide empirical data to support a long-held scholarly assumption
   (D) compare two scholarly publications on the basis of their authors' backgrounds
   (E) attempt to provide a partial answer to a long-standing scholarly dilemma

Main idea

To find the primary purpose, look at what the author is doing in the entire passage. In the first paragraph, the author examines two approaches to political history, both of which suffer from the same flaw, the exclusion of women. In the second paragraph, the author reviews an alternative, more inclusive way to understand political history.

A   The first paragraph identifies only one reason that the two approaches are flawed; an alternative approach is discussed in the second paragraph.
B   **Correct.** The author points to the flaw in earlier approaches to history and shows an alternative way of thinking about political history.
C   No data are offered to support an assumption.
D   Only one historian is mentioned by name; her background is not mentioned.
E   No long-standing dilemma is discussed.

The correct answer is B.

17. The passage suggests which of the following concerning the techniques used by the new political historians described in the first paragraph of the passage?

    (A) They involved the extensive use of the biographies of political party leaders and political theoreticians.
    (B) They were conceived by political historians who were reacting against the political climates of the 1960's and 1970's.
    (C) They were of more use in analyzing the positions of United States political parties in the nineteenth century than in analyzing the positions of those in the twentieth century.
    (D) They were of more use in analyzing the political behavior of nineteenth-century voters than in analyzing the political activities of those who could not vote during that period.
    (E) They were devised as a means of tracing the influence of nineteenth-century political trends on twentieth-century political trends.

Inference

The question's use of the verb *suggests* is an indication that an inference must be made. Examine the first paragraph, where the *new school of political history* is discussed. These historians used techniques such as *quantitative analyses of election returns* that the author describes as *useless in analyzing the political activities of women, who were denied the vote until 1920* (lines 10–12). It can, however, be assumed that the same techniques did prove useful in understanding the *mass political behavior* of voters.

A The first sentence explains that these historians *sought to go beyond the traditional focus… on leaders and government institutions.*
B The passage does not indicate that the historians were reacting against their own historical moment.
C The historians examined *the political practices of ordinary citizens* (line 5), not the positions of political parties.

D **Correct.** Lines 7–11 explicitly state that the historians' techniques were *useless* in analyzing the political activities of those not allowed to vote; the same lines imply that the techniques were useful in analyzing the political behavior of voters.
E No information in the passage supports this explanation.

The correct answer is D.

18. It can be inferred that the author of the passage quotes Baker directly in the second paragraph primarily in order to

    (A) clarify a position before providing an alternative to that position
    (B) differentiate between a novel definition and traditional definitions
    (C) provide an example of a point agreed on by different generations of scholars
    (D) provide an example of the prose style of an important historian
    (E) amplify a definition given in the first paragraph

Logical structure

To analyze why the author uses a direct quotation, look at the logical structure of the passage in relation to the quotation. The historians discussed in the first paragraph define political activity as voting. Paula Baker, however, has a new definition of political activity, one that includes the activities of those who were not allowed to vote. It is reasonable to infer that the author quotes Baker to draw attention to this new definition, which provides an innovative, alternative way of thinking about political history.

A Paula Baker's is the alternative position offered; no alternative to hers is discussed.
B **Correct.** Baker is quoted to emphasize that her definition is new and that it differs significantly from the traditional definition used by other historians.
C The contrasting views expressed in the first and second paragraphs show that different generations of scholars have not agreed.
D The author does not comment on Baker's prose style.

E   Baker's definition contrasts with, rather than amplifies, the one offered in the first paragraph.

The correct answer is B.

19. According to the passage, Paula Baker and the new political historians of the 1960's and 1970's shared which of the following?

(A) A commitment to interest group politics
(B) A disregard for political theory and ideology
(C) An interest in the ways in which nineteenth-century politics prefigured contemporary politics
(D) A reliance on such quantitative techniques as the analysis of election returns
(E) An emphasis on the political involvement of ordinary citizens

Supporting ideas

Since the question uses the phrase *according to the passage,* the answer is explicitly stated in the passage. Look for a point on which the new political historians and Baker agree. The first sentence of the passage says that these new historians were interested in the political activities of *ordinary citizens* (line 5). Paula Baker is similarly interested in the political activities of *ordinary citizens* (line 16), especially of female citizens, who were not allowed to vote.

A   The personal political commitments of Baker and the political historians are not discussed.
B   The passage does not show that they disregarded political theory and ideology.
C   The passage only discusses Baker's interest in the way women's political activities in the nineteenth century prefigured twentieth-century trends (lines 22–29).
D   The passage explains that new historians relied on such techniques, but that Baker did not.
E   **Correct.** Both the new historians and Baker are said to have studied the political activities of *ordinary citizens.*

The correct answer is E.

20. Which of the following best describes the structure of the first paragraph of the passage?

(A) Two scholarly approaches are compared, and a shortcoming common to both is identified.
(B) Two rival schools of thought are contrasted, and a third is alluded to.
(C) An outmoded scholarly approach is described, and a corrective approach is called for.
(D) An argument is outlined, and counterarguments are mentioned.
(E) A historical era is described in terms of its political trends.

Logical structure

To answer this question, analyze the structure of the first paragraph. It compares *the old approach* of studying political history through emphasis on leaders and government institutions with *the new school of political history,* which turned instead to the political activities of ordinary citizens. Both approaches suffered from the same drawback: the failure to include women in their analyses.

A   **Correct.** Two approaches to history are discussed, and a flaw shared by both, the exclusion of women, is identified.
B   The first paragraph does not allude to a third school of thought.
C   A corrective approach is not discussed in the first paragraph.
D   The first paragraph presents neither an argument nor counterarguments.
E   The political trends of an historical era are not detailed in the first paragraph.

The correct answer is A.

21. The information in the passage suggests that a pre-1960's political historian would have been most likely to undertake which of the following studies?

    (A) An analysis of voting trends among women voters of the 1920's
    (B) A study of male voters' gradual ideological shift from party politics to issue-oriented politics
    (C) A biography of an influential nineteenth-century minister of foreign affairs
    (D) An analysis of narratives written by previously unrecognized women activists
    (E) A study of voting trends among naturalized immigrant laborers in a nineteenth-century logging camp

Inference

In using *suggests,* this question asks the reader to apply information stated in the passage to make an inference about the methods of historians before the 1960's. These methods are discussed in the first paragraph. Lines 1–4 say that the *old approach* to political history (before the advent of the new school of historians in the 1960's and 1970's) focused on leaders and government institutions. It is reasonable to infer that the pre-1960's historian was likely to focus on a leader or government institution.

A   Traditional historians did not focus on ordinary citizens, but on their leaders.
B   Baker is interested in this group shift, but traditional historians were not.
C   **Correct.** Traditional historians emphasized the work of leaders and government institutions; a biography of a foreign affairs minister fits this focus perfectly.
D   Such an analysis would be of interest to Baker, but not to traditional historians focusing on leaders and government.
E   The new historians would be interested in such a study, but not traditional historians, who did not look at the activities of ordinary citizens.

The correct answer is C.

Questions 22–28 refer to the passage on page 30.

22. The passage is primarily concerned with evaluating

    (A) the importance of Florence Nightingale's innovations in the field of nursing
    (B) contrasting approaches to the writing of historical biography
    (C) contradictory accounts of Florence Nightingale's historical significance
    (D) the quality of health care in nineteenth century England
    (E) the effect of the Crimean War on developments in the field of health care

Main idea

Consider the passage as a whole to answer this question. The author begins by announcing that two recent works about Florence Nightingale offer *different assessments* of her career and then summarizes those accounts. One book *seeks to debunk* her reputation and historical significance, while the other promotes her significance to *not only her own age but also subsequent generations.* In the final paragraph, the author takes a position synthesizing the two views.

A   Nightingale's involvement in nursing is discussed, but not her nursing innovations.
B   The passage concerns two books about an historical figure, not the writing of historical biography.
C   **Correct.** The passage focuses on two books with *different assessments* of Nightingale's significance.
D   The passage refers to some specific health care problems during and after the Crimean War, but it does not evaluate the general quality of health care over the course of the nineteenth century.
E   No such effects are discussed in the passage.

The correct answer is C.

23. According to the passage, the editors of Nightingale's letters credit her with contributing to which of the following?

   (A) Improvement of the survival rate for soldiers in British Army hospitals during the Crimean War
   (B) The development of a nurses' training curriculum that was far in advance of its day
   (C) The increase in the number of women doctors practicing in British Army hospitals
   (D) Establishment of the first facility for training nurses at a major British university
   (E) The creation of an organization for monitoring the peacetime living conditions of British soldiers

Supporting ideas

This question asks the reader to find specific information that is explicitly stated. In the second paragraph, lines 21–34 list the achievements the editors of her letters attribute to Nightingale. Among them is her work to improve sanitary conditions. When she learned how bad *the peacetime living conditions* of British soldiers were, she persuaded the government *to establish a Royal Commission on the Health of the Army.*

A   The passage discusses Nightingale's work after the war, but the survival rate during the war is not mentioned.
B   Nightingale founded a nurses' training hospital (line 30), but its curriculum is not examined.
C   No information is given about women doctors.
D   The passage does not discuss whether the nurses' training hospital that Nightingale founded was the first of its kind or whether it was at a major British university.
E   **Correct.** Nightingale persuaded the government to create a commission overseeing British soldiers' living conditions.

The correct answer is E.

24. The passage suggests which of the following about Nightingale's relationship with the British public of her day?

   (A) She was highly respected, her projects receiving popular and governmental support.
   (B) She encountered resistance both from the army establishment and the general public.
   (C) She was supported by the working classes and opposed by the wealthier classes.
   (D) She was supported by the military establishment but had to fight the governmental bureaucracy.
   (E) After initially being received with enthusiasm, she was quickly forgotten.

Inference

An inference is drawn from stated information. This question asks the reader to gather the hints appearing throughout the passage about Nightingale's relationship with her public. Nightingale was idealized and had a *heroic reputation* (line 5); she occupied a *place in the national pantheon* (line 15). Moreover her projects were successful: she persuaded the government to establish a health commission and the public to fund a nurses' training hospital. The logical inference from the information given is that Nightingale was respected by the British public.

A   **Correct.** Her *heroic reputation* implies that she was widely respected. Her success with both the government and the public allowed her projects to be realized.
B   The passage shows no evidence of resistance either from the army or from the public; indeed, the public contributed to her causes.
C   The passage does not divide her supporters from her detractors along class lines.
D   The passage does not mention either military support or government resistance.
E   She was not quickly forgotten, since the author refers to her as *the famous British nurse* who has earned *an eminent place among the ranks of social pioneers.*

The correct answer is A.

25. The passage suggests which of the following about sanitary conditions in Britain after the Crimean War?

    (A) While not ideal, they were superior to those in other parts of the world.
    (B) Compared with conditions before the war, they had deteriorated.
    (C) They were more advanced in rural areas than in the urban centers.
    (D) They were worse in military camps than in the neighboring civilian populations.
    (E) They were uniformly crude and unsatisfactory throughout England.

Inference

The question's use of the word *suggests* means that the answer depends on making an inference. The editors of Nightingale's letters illustrate *her ongoing efforts to reform sanitary conditions after the war* by giving an example of her activity. She found that the death rate of British soldiers was considerably higher than that of the civilians living near the soldiers' barracks, and she attributed the higher death rate to the *horrible* living conditions in the barracks (lines 23–26). Thus, it is reasonable to infer that the sanitary conditions were worse in military camps, or barracks, than they were in civilian populations near the camps.

A No comparison is made to other parts of the world.
B No comparison is made to conditions before the war.
C No comparison is made between rural and urban areas.
D **Correct.** When compared with the civilian death rate in neighboring areas, the far higher death rate among soldiers could be attributed to unsanitary living conditions; therefore the conditions must have been worse in the camps.
E No evidence supports a generalization about England as whole.

The correct answer is D.

26. With which of the following statements regarding the differing interpretations of Nightingale's importance would the author most likely agree?

    (A) Summers misunderstood both the importance of Nightingale's achievements during the Crimean War and her subsequent influence on British policy.
    (B) The editors of Nightingale's letters made some valid points about her practical achievements, but they still exaggerated her influence on subsequent generations.
    (C) Although Summers' account of Nightingale's role in the Crimean War may be accurate, she ignored evidence of Nightingale's subsequent achievement that suggests that her reputation as an eminent social reformer is well deserved.
    (D) The editors of Nightingale's letters mistakenly propagated the outdated idealization of Nightingale that only impedes attempts to arrive at a balanced assessment of her true role.
    (E) The evidence of Nightingale's letters supports Summers' conclusions both about Nightingale's activities and about her influence.

Application

Examine the final paragraph; the author's opinion of both accounts of Nightingale's work appears there. Summers' work claims that Nightingale's importance during the Crimean War was *exaggerated*, and the author concedes in lines 43–45 that Nightingale *may not have achieved all her goals during the Crimean War.* However, the author believes that Nightingale's *breadth of vision* and her accomplishment of *ambitious projects* earn her *an eminent place among the ranks of social pioneers.*

A The author at least partly concedes Summers' point about Nightingale's achievements during the Crimean War, but does not discuss Summers' treatment of Nightingale after the war.

B The author believes the letters should establish *continued respect for Nightingale's brilliance and creativity.*

C **Correct.** The author acknowledges the point Summers makes about Nightingale's contribution during the war but finds evidence in the letters and in Nightingale's accomplishments after the war to support a highly favorable view of her work. It is reasonable to infer that the author would agree that Summers ignored this important evidence.

D The author believes that the letters illustrate Nightingale's *brilliance and creativity* and that Nightingale herself has earned *an eminent place* among social pioneers. These positions are not consistent with agreeing that the editors idealized Nightingale and prevented a just assessment of her work.

E The evidence of the letters supports just the reverse, *brilliance and creativity.*

The correct answer is C.

27. Which of the following is an assumption underlying the author's assessment of Nightingale's creativity?

(A) Educational philosophy in Nightingale's day did not normally emphasize developing children's ability to observe.

(B) Nightingale was the first to notice the poor living conditions in British military barracks in peacetime.

(C) No educator before Nightingale had thought to enlist the help of village schoolmasters in introducing new teaching techniques.

(D) Until Nightingale began her work, there was no concept of organized help for the needy in nineteenth-century Britain.

(E) The British Army's medical services had no cost accounting system until Nightingale devised one in the 1860's.

Evaluation

Look at the last paragraph for a discussion of Nightingale's creativity. The author begins the last paragraph by asserting that Nightingale's letters demonstrate her *brilliance and creativity.* In the first of two examples that illustrate these qualities, Nightingale urges a schoolmaster to encourage children to use their powers of observation. Since the author uses this as an example of brilliance and creativity, it is apparent the author assumed that educators did not ordinarily encourage children's powers of observation.

A **Correct.** The author's citation of Nightingale's encouraging an educator to cultivate children's powers of observation implies the author's assumption that nineteenth-century educational philosophy did not pay attention to children's capacity to observe.

B While the author mentions the editors' discussion of Nightingale's efforts to remedy the poor conditions, the author does not suggest that she was the first to notice them.

C Although the author cites evidence from the letters that Nightingale counseled one schoolmaster, there is no suggestion that she was the first to have enlisted the help of schoolmasters.

D The author recognizes the modernism of Nightingale's approach to organized help for the needy, but there is no evidence that the author assumes she originated the concept.

E The author states only that Nightingale devised a system that remained in use for many years; there is no assumption regarding the lack of a system previously.

The correct answer is A.

28. In the last paragraph, the author is primarily concerned with

    (A) summarizing the arguments about Nightingale presented in the first two paragraphs
    (B) refuting the view of Nightingale's career presented in the preceding paragraph
    (C) analyzing the weaknesses of the evidence presented elsewhere in the passage
    (D) citing evidence to support a view of Nightingale's career
    (E) correcting a factual error occurring in one of the works under review

Main idea

The author begins the last paragraph in the first person, *I believe*, in order to take a position on Nightingale's historical significance. With one concession to Summers' work, the author uses the letters as evidence of Nightingale's extraordinary abilities. The author believes that Nightingale's work has earned her a respected place in history.

A   Beginning with *I believe* shows that the author intends to do more than simply summarize.
B   The author largely supports the view of Nightingale presented in the second paragraph.
C   The last paragraph does analyze weak evidence, but its purpose is to state a position.
D   **Correct.** The author cites evidence in Nightingale's letters and actions that support a highly favorable view of her career.
E   No such correction appears in the final paragraph.

The correct answer is D.

Questions 29–34 refer to the passage on page 32.

29. Which of the following best describes the organization of the passage?

    (A) The historical backgrounds of two currently used research methods are chronicled.
    (B) The validity of the data collected by using two different research methods is compared.
    (C) The usefulness of a research method is questioned and then a new method is proposed.
    (D) The use of a research method is described and the limitations of the results obtained are discussed.
    (E) A research method is evaluated and the changes necessary for its adaptation to other subject areas are discussed.

Logical structure

To answer a question about organization, determine the function of each paragraph in order to see the overall structure of the whole passage. The first paragraph introduces a research method, recording life stories. The second and third paragraphs discuss the problems of this method. According to the final paragraph, the method remains useful despite its limitations.

A   Only one research method is discussed in the passage.
B   The validity of data is questioned, but only one research method is discussed.
C   While the usefulness of the method is questioned, no new one is proposed.
D   **Correct.** The method of recording life stories is described, its limitations acknowledged, and its usefulness recognized.
E   A research method is evaluated, but no changes are proposed.

The correct answer is D.

3.6 Reading Comprehension **Answer Explanations**

30. Which of the following is most similar to the actions of nineteenth-century ethnologists in their editing of the life stories of Native Americans?

    (A) A witness in a jury trial invokes the Fifth Amendment in order to avoid relating personally incriminating evidence.
    (B) A stockbroker refuses to divulge the source of her information on the possible future increase in a stock's value.
    (C) A sports announcer describes the action in a team sport with which he is unfamiliar.
    (D) A chef purposely excludes the special ingredient from the recipe of his prizewinning dessert.
    (E) A politician fails to mention in a campaign speech the similarities in the positions held by her opponent for political office and by herself.

Application

To answer the question, determine what the author says about the ethnologists and apply the information to the examples given in the answer choices. Ethnologists believed that recording personal stories *could increase their understanding of cultures they had been observing from without* (lines 10–12). But they were criticized for not spending enough time in these cultures (lines 25–26) and thus not understanding the cultures well enough. Their position is most like that of the sports announcer, who is also an observer, but who is not familiar with the game (or, in the case of the ethnologists, the culture) being observed.

A The passage does not suggest that the ethnographers deliberately withheld evidence for personal reasons.
B The ethnologists were faulted for other reasons, not for withholding evidence.
C **Correct.** As do the ethnologists, the sports announcer observes and reports, but in neither case is the observer adequately familiar with the subject being observed.
D The ethnologists did not purposely exclude an item from their studies.
E The passage does not point to any similarities between the ethnologists and the people they studied.

The correct answer is C.

31. According to the passage, collecting life stories can be a useful methodology because

    (A) life stories provide deeper insights into a culture than the hypothesizing of academics who are not members of that culture
    (B) life stories can be collected easily and they are not subject to invalid interpretations
    (C) ethnologists have a limited number of research methods from which to choose
    (D) life stories make it easy to distinguish between the important and unimportant features of a culture
    (E) the collection of life stories does not require a culturally knowledgeable investigator

Supporting ideas

The phrase *according to the passage* indicates that the answer is stated in the passage. The final paragraph describes collecting life stories as *a useful tool* because the stories *are likely to throw more light on the working of the mind and emotions* of the people the ethnologists study than *any amount of speculation from an ethnologist... from another culture.*

A **Correct.** Because they come from within a culture, the life stories reveal more about it than can any of the theories developed by those outside the culture.
B Neither the ease nor the difficulty of gathering the stories is mentioned, but their vulnerability to misinterpretation is discussed in lines 19–28.
C The passage does not discuss how many research tools are available.
D The passage states that ethnologists regarded as *unimportant* some of the events that the subjects of the stories found *significant* (33–37).
E According to the passage, ethnologists were criticized for not being culturally knowledgeable enough (lines 25–26).

The correct answer is A.

32. Information in the passage suggests that which of the following may be a possible way to eliminate bias in the editing of life stories?

    (A) Basing all inferences made about the culture on an ethnological theory
    (B) Eliminating all of the emotion laden information reported by the informant
    (C) Translating the informant's words into the researcher's language
    (D) Reducing the number of questions and carefully specifying the content of the questions that the investigator can ask the informant
    (E) Reporting all of the information that the informant provides regardless of the investigator's personal opinion about its intrinsic value

Inference

The question's use of the word *suggests* means that the answer depends on making an inference. Lines 31–33 provide the reference for this question about biased editing: *Editors often decided what elements were significant to the field research on a given tribe.* The editors introduced bias with their choices about what was important. Therefore, it is reasonable to infer that, to eliminate bias, those choices must be eliminated. Reporting all the information, not just what the investigator or editor thinks is important, is a possible way to avoid bias.

A   The passage does not imply that bias results from veering away from a theory.
B   Investigators are criticized for allowing emotion to tinge their reports (lines 27–28), but informants are not criticized for having emotional material.
C   Lines 33–35 reveal that translations are not always possible.
D   The passage does not discuss the number and content of questions, so it cannot be inferred that restricting them would eliminate bias.
E   **Correct.** Reporting all the information, rather than choosing to report only what appears to the observer to be important, is a possible way to eliminate bias in editing life stories.

The correct answer is E.

33. The primary purpose of the passage as a whole is to

    (A) question an explanation
    (B) correct a misconception
    (C) critique a methodology
    (D) discredit an idea
    (E) clarify an ambiguity

Main idea

This question explicitly asks the reader to consider the passage as a whole in order to determine the author's intent. Start by asking: what is the subject of the passage? Collecting life stories is called a *method* (line 20) and a *useful tool* (line 43). The first paragraph introduces this research method, the middle paragraphs offer an extended critique of it, and the final paragraph reaffirms its usefulness.

A   Collecting life stories is not an explanation; it is a method to gain understanding of a culture.
B   The autobiographies may be misinterpreted, but they are not a misconception.
C   **Correct.** The passage is about a methodology; both its weaknesses and strengths are examined.
D   Collecting the stories is not an idea but a method; though its limitations are revealed, the method is not discredited.
E   The final paragraph implies that ambiguity is inherent in life stories; that ambiguity is not clarified.

The correct answer is C.

34. It can be inferred from the passage that a characteristic of the ethnological research on Native Americans conducted during the nineteenth century was the use of which of the following?

    (A) Investigators familiar with the culture under study
    (B) A language other than the informant's for recording life stories
    (C) Life stories as the ethnologist's primary source of information
    (D) Complete transcriptions of informants' descriptions of tribal beliefs
    (E) Stringent guidelines for the preservation of cultural data

Inference

An inference is drawn from stated information. To answer this question, find what the passage says about the ethnological research on Native American culture in the nineteenth century. The third paragraph tells us that *much was inevitably lost* (line 31) when investigators wrote the oral stories down. *Native Americans recognized that the essence of their lives could not be communicated in English* (lines 33–35). From these two statements, it is reasonable to infer that the stories were written down in a language different from that of the storyteller.

A The investigators were criticized for not being suitably familiar with the culture (lines 25–26).
B **Correct.** Native Americans believed that English could not express their culture; at least some investigators, therefore, must have written the stories down in English.
C Ethnologists wanted the stories to *supplement* their field work (lines 5–9), not to replace it as their primary means of investigation.
D Lines 32–34 reveal that the life stories were edited, not complete.
E The passage provides no information about such guidelines.

The correct answer is B.

Questions 35–40 refer to the passage on page 34.

35. The primary function of the passage as a whole is to

    (A) account for the popularity of a practice
    (B) evaluate the utility of a practice
    (C) demonstrate how to institute a practice
    (D) weigh the ethics of using a strategy
    (E) explain the reasons for pursuing a strategy

Main idea

This question explicitly requires looking at the passage *as a whole* in order to determine the author's purpose. The first paragraph explains the practice of offering guarantees and lists circumstances in which an unconditional guarantee may be an appropriate marketing tool. The second paragraph begins with *However*, implying that a contradiction is about to follow. The serious drawbacks to guarantees are examined, and the passage closes with a warning.

A The passage does not discuss the popularity of guarantees.
B **Correct.** The passage examines and judges the advantages and disadvantages of a business practice.
C The passage does not show how to put guarantees into place.
D The passage does not discuss ethics.
E The first paragraph does explain the reasons for offering guarantees, but that is only a portion of the passage, not the passage *as a whole*.

The correct answer is B.

36. All of the following are mentioned in the passage as circumstances in which professional service firms can benefit from offering an unconditional guarantee EXCEPT:

    (A) The firm is having difficulty retaining its clients of long standing.
    (B) The firm is having difficulty getting business through client recommendations.
    (C) The firm charges substantial fees for its services.
    (D) The adverse effects of poor performance by the firm are significant for the client.
    (E) The client is reluctant to incur risk.

Supporting ideas

The phrase *mentioned in the passage* indicates that the necessary information is explicitly stated. To answer this question, use the process of elimination to find the one example that is NOT mentioned in the passage. The question refers to lines 8–13, where the circumstances in which an unconditional guarantee might be beneficial to a firm are listed. Check each of the responses to the question against the list; the one that does not appear in the list is the correct answer.

A **Correct.** The sentence begins by noting that unconditional guarantees are particularly important with new clients; clients of long standing are not discussed.
B Lines 11–13 include the difficulty of getting business through referrals and word-of-mouth.
C Line 10 cites high fees as such a circumstance.
D Lines 10–11 include the severe repercussions of bad service.
E Lines 9–10 cite the cautiousness of the client.

The correct answer is A.

37. Which of the following is cited in the passage as a goal of some professional service firms in offering unconditional guarantees of satisfaction?

    (A) A limit on the firm's liability
    (B) Successful competition against other firms
    (C) Ability to justify fee increases
    (D) Attainment of an outstanding reputation in a field
    (E) Improvement in the quality of the firm's service

Supporting ideas

When the question says to find an answer *cited* in the passage, the answer will be explicitly stated information. The passage opens with an explanation of why some firms want to offer unconditional guarantees: *Seeking a competitive advantage* explains their rationale. Firms offer the guarantees to compete more effectively against firms that do not offer guarantees.

A The passage does not mention liability limits.
B **Correct.** Some firms offer unconditional guarantees as a way to compete successfully against firms that do not offer them.
C Fee increases are not discussed.
D The second paragraph suggests the reverse: offering a guarantee may hurt a firm's reputation.
E Improving the quality of service is not mentioned as a reason to offer guarantees.

The correct answer is B.

38. The passage's description of the issue raised by unconditional guarantees for health care or legal services most clearly implies that which of the following is true?

    (A) The legal and medical professions have standards of practice that would be violated by attempts to fulfill such unconditional guarantees.
    (B) The result of a lawsuit or medical procedure cannot necessarily be determined in advance by the professionals handling a client's case.
    (C) The dignity of the legal and medical professions is undermined by any attempts at marketing of professional services, including unconditional guarantees.
    (D) Clients whose lawsuits or medical procedures have unsatisfactory outcomes cannot be adequately compensated by financial settlements alone.
    (E) Predicting the monetary cost of legal or health care services is more difficult than predicting the monetary cost of other types of professional services.

Inference

The question's use of the word *implies* means that the answer depends on making an inference. This question refers to one sentence in the passage (lines 21–24), so it is essential to review what that sentence says in order to understand what it implies. An unconditional guarantee of satisfaction may have a particular disadvantage in the case of health care and legal services because clients may be misled into believing that lawsuits or medical procedures have guaranteed outcomes when they do not. Since an inference may be drawn only from explicitly stated information, the correct response must be about the problem of guarantees and outcomes.

A   Although this statement may be true, it cannot be derived from the cited reference.
B   **Correct.** Legal and medical professionals cannot guarantee the outcomes of their work.
C   This statement cannot be drawn from the description of the issue.
D   Compensation is not discussed in the reference.
E   Predicting costs is not discussed in the reference.

The correct answer is B.

39.   Which of the following hypothetical situations best exemplifies the potential problem noted in the second sentence of the second paragraph (lines 15–19)?

(A)   A physician's unconditional guarantee of satisfaction encourages patients to sue for malpractice if they are unhappy with the treatment they receive.
(B)   A lawyer's unconditional guarantee of satisfaction makes clients suspect that the lawyer needs to find new clients quickly to increase the firm's income.
(C)   A business consultant's unconditional guarantee of satisfaction is undermined when the consultant fails to provide all of the services that are promised.
(D)   An architect's unconditional guarantee of satisfaction makes clients wonder how often the architect's buildings fail to please clients.
(E)   An accountant's unconditional guarantee of satisfaction leads clients to believe that tax returns prepared by the accountant are certain to be accurate.

Application

This question involves taking the problem identified in lines 15–19 and applying it to the hypothetical situation that best fits it. Offering an unconditional guarantee may not work as a marketing strategy because potential clients may *doubt the … firm's ability to deliver the promised level of service.* This strategy may actually introduce doubts or reservations on the part of potential clients and in fact discourage them from ever hiring the firm or the individual providing the service.

A   In this case, the problem occurs after, not before, the service is rendered.
B   This situation exemplifies another problem of unconditional guarantees, the suggestion that *a firm is begging for business* (line 21).
C   The problem occurs after, not before, the service is rendered.
D   **Correct.** The architect's apparent need to offer an unconditional guarantee makes potential clients question the outcome of the architect's work by suggesting the likelihood of their dissatisfaction with the architectural services.
E   This situation contradicts the problem.

The correct answer is D.

40. The passage most clearly implies which of the following about the professional service firms mentioned in lines 24–25?

    (A) They are unlikely to have offered unconditional guarantees of satisfaction in the past.
    (B) They are usually profitable enough to be able to compensate clients according to the terms of an unconditional guarantee.
    (C) They usually practice in fields in which the outcomes are predictable.
    (D) Their fees are usually more affordable than those charged by other professional service firms.
    (E) Their clients are usually already satisfied with the quality of service that is delivered.

Inference

The question asks for the implications of this statement in lines 24–27: *professional service firms with outstanding reputations and performance to match have little to gain from offering unconditional guarantees.* Why is it logical to infer that these firms have little to gain from this strategy? If their performance and reputation are both *outstanding*, it is likely that their clients are already satisfied with the quality of the work they provide and that offering such guarantees would provide no competitive advantage.

A The statement in the passage concerns the present; nothing is implied about what may have been true in the past.
B The statement includes no information about profitability, so no inference may be drawn.
C No information is provided about specific fields or likely outcomes.
D Fees are not discussed in this statement.
E **Correct.** No guarantee is needed when clients are already satisfied with the quality of work provided.

The correct answer is E.

Questions 41–46 refer to the passage on page 36.

41. The primary purpose of the passage is to

    (A) contrast possible outcomes of a type of business investment
    (B) suggest more careful evaluation of a type of business investment
    (C) illustrate various ways in which a type of business investment could fail to enhance revenues
    (D) trace the general problems of a company to a certain type of business investment
    (E) criticize the way in which managers tend to analyze the costs and benefits of business investments

Main idea

Look at the passage as a whole to find the primary purpose. This passage uses an example, described in the second paragraph, to illustrate the principle of business practice explained in the first paragraph. The author begins by saying that efforts to improve service do not always result in a *competitive advantage* for a company. Thus, an investment in service must be carefully evaluated to determine if it will reduce costs or increase revenues (lines 4–8).

A Only one outcome, failure to gain a competitive advantage, is examined.
B **Correct.** Investments in service must be carefully evaluated for the returns they will bring.
C Only one way, an unnecessary investment in improved service, is discussed.
D The example of the bank is used only to illustrate a general business principle; the bank itself is not the focus of the passage.
E The passage criticizes the absence of such an analysis, not the way it is conducted.

The correct answer is B.

42. According to the passage, investments in service are comparable to investments in production and distribution in terms of the

    (A) tangibility of the benefits that they tend to confer
    (B) increased revenues that they ultimately produce
    (C) basis on which they need to be weighed
    (D) insufficient analysis that managers devote to them
    (E) degree of competitive advantage that they are likely to provide

Supporting ideas

The phrase *according to the passage* indicates that the question covers material that is explicitly stated in the passage. The answer to this question demands a careful reading of the second sentence (lines 4–8). Investments in service are like investments in production and distribution because they *must be balanced against other types of investments on the basis of direct, tangible benefits*. Thus, these investments should be weighed on the same basis.

A   The author is not equating the tangible benefits the different kinds of investments reap, but rather the basis on which decisions to make investments are made.
B   Revenues generated from investing in service are not said to be comparable to revenues generated from investing in production and distribution.
C   **Correct.** An evaluation of whether or not to make these investments must be made on the same basis.
D   How managers analyze investments in production and distribution is not discussed.
E   The competitive advantage of superior service is acknowledged, but not the degree of it; it is not mentioned at all in the context of production and distribution.

The correct answer is C.

43. The passage suggests which of the following about service provided by the regional bank prior to its investment in enhancing that service?

    (A) It enabled the bank to retain customers at an acceptable rate.
    (B) It threatened to weaken the bank's competitive position with respect to other regional banks.
    (C) It had already been improved after having caused damage to the bank's reputation in the past.
    (D) It was slightly superior to that of the bank's regional competitors.
    (E) It needed to be improved to attain parity with the service provided by competing banks.

Inference

Because the question uses the word *suggests*, finding the answer depends on making an inference about service at the bank. The paragraph that discusses the bank begins with the transitional expression, *this truth*, which refers to the previous sentence (lines 8–15). The *truth* is that investing in improved service is a waste *if a company is already effectively on a par with its competitors because it provides service that avoids a damaging reputation and keeps customers from leaving at an unacceptable rate*. Because of the way the author has linked this generalization to the description of the bank after investment, it is reasonable to infer that the hypothetical company's situation describes the bank prior to its investment in improved service.

A   **Correct.** The bank's service would have been good enough to avoid a damaging reputation and to retain customers at an acceptable rate.
B   The passage does not suggest that the bank's service was either poor or deficient to that of its competitors.
C   The passage implies that the bank's service avoided *a damaging reputation*.
D   The bank would have been *on a par with its competitors*, not superior to them.
E   The bank would have been *on a par with its competitors*, not inferior to them.

The correct answer is A.

44. The passage suggests that bank managers failed to consider whether or not the service improvement mentioned in line 19

    (A) was too complicated to be easily described to prospective customers
    (B) made a measurable change in the experiences of customers in the bank's offices
    (C) could be sustained if the number of customers increased significantly
    (D) was an innovation that competing banks could have imitated
    (E) was adequate to bring the bank's general level of service to a level that was comparable with that of its competitors

Inference

The question's use of the word *suggests* means that the answer depends on making an inference. To answer this question, look at the entire sentence that contains the reference (lines 20–23). Managers failed to think ahead. Would the service improvement attract new customers because other banks would find it difficult to copy? Or would the service improvement be easily imitated by competitors? The managers should have investigated this area before investing in improved service.

A   The passage states the improvement *could easily be described to customers* (lines 28–29).
B   No evidence in the passage shows that the managers failed to think about their customers' experience in the bank.
C   The passage does not imply that managers failed to consider an increase in clients.
D   **Correct.** The managers did not wonder if other banks would copy their service improvement.
E   Lines 8–12 imply that the bank enjoyed a comparable level of service before investing in service improvement.

The correct answer is D.

45. The discussion of the regional bank (lines 16–27) serves which of the following functions within the passage as a whole?

    (A) It describes an exceptional case in which investment in service actually failed to produce a competitive advantage.
    (B) It illustrates the pitfalls of choosing to invest in service at a time when investment is needed more urgently in another area.
    (C) It demonstrates the kind of analysis that managers apply when they choose one kind of service investment over another.
    (D) It supports the argument that investments in certain aspects of service are more advantageous than investments in other aspects of service.
    (E) It provides an example of the point about investment in service made in the first paragraph.

Logical structure

This question requires thinking about what the second paragraph contributes to the whole passage. The first paragraph makes a generalization about investing in improvements in service; in certain conditions, such improvements do not result in the *competitive advantage* a company hopes for. The second paragraph offers the bank as an example of this generalization.

A   The first sentence of the passage explains that improving service does not necessarily bring a *competitive advantage*, so the bank is not exceptional.
B   The bank illustrates the pitfall of not evaluating a service improvement on the basis of tangible benefits; other areas of the bank are not mentioned.
C   The passage does not discuss how managers analyze and choose different service investments.
D   Investments in different aspects of service are not evaluated in the passage.
E   **Correct.** The bank is an example of the position stated in the first paragraph that investing in improved service can be a waste if the investment is not evaluated carefully.

The correct answer is E.

46. The author uses the word "only" in line 27 most likely in order to

(A) highlight the oddity of the service improvement
(B) emphasize the relatively low value of the investment in service improvement
(C) distinguish the primary attribute of the service improvement from secondary attributes
(D) single out a certain merit of the service improvement from other merits
(E) point out the limited duration of the actual service improvement

Logical structure

The question asks you to consider the logic of the author's word choice. The previous two sentences discuss why the service improvement was a wasted investment. In contrast, the final sentence turns to the sole advantage of the service improvement, which is trivial by comparison. The author uses *only* to modify *merit* in order to emphasize the minimal nature of this advantage.

A The passage does not indicate that the service improvement is somehow strange or peculiar.
B Correct. *Only* emphasizes the low value attached to the single benefit.
C No attributes of the service improvement are mentioned.
D *Only* signifies that there was one sole merit of the service improvement.
E The duration of the benefit is not discussed in the passage.

The correct answer is B.

Questions 47–51 refer to the passage on page 38.

47. According to the passage, before the final results of the study were known, which of the following seemed likely?

(A) That workers with the highest productivity would also be the most accurate
(B) That workers who initially achieved high productivity ratings would continue to do so consistently
(C) That the highest performance ratings would be achieved by workers with the highest productivity
(D) That the most productive workers would be those whose supervisors claimed to value productivity
(E) That supervisors who claimed to value productivity would place equal value on customer satisfaction

Supporting ideas

Since this question uses the phrase *according to the passage*, the answer is stated in the passage. Only lines 18–20 refer to the expected outcome of the study: *there should have been a strong correlation between a monitored worker's productivity and the overall rating the worker received.*

A The passage does not state a prediction linking productivity with accuracy.
B No prediction is stated that workers rated highly productive would remain so.
C Correct. It was expected that the most productive workers would be the most highly rated.
D The passage does not state such a prediction.
E The passage makes no such prediction.

The correct answer is C.

48. It can be inferred that the author of the passage discusses "unmonitored workers" (line 12) primarily in order to

   (A) compare the ratings of these workers with the ratings of monitored workers
   (B) provide an example of a case in which monitoring might be effective
   (C) provide evidence of an inappropriate use of CPMCS
   (D) emphasize the effect that CPMCS may have on workers' perceptions of their jobs
   (E) illustrate the effect that CPMCS may have on workers' ratings

Inference

An inference is drawn from stated information. Go to the specific line reference in the question to find the reason that the author included the detail about unmonitored workers. Unmonitored workers are compared with monitored workers on a single point: what they believe to be the most important element of their job (and thus of their ratings). Unmonitored workers believe it is customer service, but monitored workers point to productivity. The logical inference from the information given is that the author is using this contrast to show that CPMCS affect how workers think about their jobs.

A   Unmonitored workers' ratings are not discussed in the passage.
B   The author does not link unmonitored workers with a potentially effective use of monitoring.
C   The author does not connect unmonitored workers and inappropriate uses of CPMCS.
D   Correct. The contrast in the workers' responses demonstrates that CPMCS may influence how workers think about their jobs.
E   The passage does not connect unmonitored workers with the effect of CPMCS on workers' ratings.

The correct answer is D.

49. Which of the following, if true, would most clearly have supported the conclusion referred to in lines 23–25?

   (A) Ratings of productivity correlated highly with ratings of both accuracy and attendance.
   (B) Electronic monitoring greatly increased productivity.
   (C) Most supervisors based overall ratings of performance on measures of productivity alone.
   (D) Overall ratings of performance correlated more highly with measures of productivity than the researchers expected.
   (E) Overall ratings of performance correlated more highly with measures of accuracy than with measures of productivity.

Logical structure

To answer this question look at the actual conclusion of the study: in rating workers' performances, supervisors *gave considerable weight to… attendance, accuracy, and indications of customer satisfaction.* What additional piece of information would support this conclusion? If one of these three criteria mattered as much as or more than productivity in assessing workers' performances, then the conclusion would be strengthened. Thus, the supervisors' overall performance ratings should correlate with measures of attendance, accuracy, or customer service to at least the same extent that they correlate with measures of productivity.

A   The conclusion is about the value supervisors place on criteria other than productivity, so a finding about productivity is irrelevant to the conclusion.
B   Increased productivity in not relevant to the conclusion, which concerns other criteria in performance assessment.
C   This statement contradicts the conclusion that supervisors value other criteria.
D   This statement contradicts the conclusion stated in lines 23–25.
E   Correct. When measures of accuracy, one of the three criteria supervisors consider other than productivity, correlate with overall performance ratings more highly than measures of productivity do, the conclusion is strengthened.

The correct answer is E.

50. According to the passage, a "hygiene factor" (line 27) is an aspect of a worker's performance that

    (A) has no effect on the rating of a worker's performance
    (B) is so basic to performance that it is assumed to be adequate for all workers
    (C) is given less importance than it deserves in rating a worker's performance
    (D) is not likely to affect a worker's rating unless it is judged to be inadequate
    (E) is important primarily because of the effect it has on a worker's rating

Supporting ideas

According to the passage means that the answer is explicitly stated in the passage. Why does *"hygiene factor"* appear in quotation marks? The author is calling attention to the expression, which is defined in lines 26–28. A *"hygiene factor"* is a criterion in assessing job performance that hurts the overall rating if it is too low, but that does not improve the rating beyond a certain point.

A If too low, a *"hygiene factor"* affects the rating negatively (lines 27–28).
B Because the *"hygiene factor"* can affect the rating, it is not assumed to be uniformly adequate.
C The passage does not provide enough information to make this determination.
D **Correct.** When low, it may affect workers' overall ratings negatively, but when high, it does not affect the ratings beyond a certain point.
E The passage does not assert that its primary importance is its effect on ratings.

The correct answer is D.

51. The primary purpose of the passage is to

    (A) explain the need for the introduction of an innovative strategy
    (B) discuss a study of the use of a particular method
    (C) recommend a course of action
    (D) resolve a difference of opinion
    (E) suggest an alternative approach

Main idea

To answer this question, look at the entire passage. What is its main point? It begins by explaining the use of CPMCS in some companies, and then it shows that a study of employees being monitored by CPMCS revealed unexpected results. The rest of the passage discusses the study.

A The passage reports rather than argues; it does not explain the need for a strategy.
B **Correct.** The passage presents a method of recording workers' activities, CPMCS, and then reports the findings of a study of this method.
C The passage describes a study of a method; it does not recommend actions.
D The passage provides study results, not conflicting opinions.
E No alternative to CPMCS is discussed in the passage.

The correct answer is B.

Questions 52–55 refer to the passage on page 40.

52. The primary purpose of the passage is to

(A) refute the idea that the zonation exhibited in mangrove forests is caused by adaptation to salinity

(B) describe the pattern of zonation typically found in Florida mangrove forests

(C) argue that Davis' succession paradigm cannot be successfully applied to Florida mangrove forests

(D) discuss hypotheses that attempt to explain the zonation of coastal mangrove forests

(E) establish that plants that do well in saline forest environments require salt to achieve maximum metabolic efficiency

Main idea

Look at the passage as a whole in order to find the author's primary concern. In the first paragraph the author discusses zonation and species distribution in mangrove forests. The second paragraph presents Davis' theory that zonation is caused by plant succession. The third paragraph discusses a challenge to Davis' theory. The final paragraph presents research on salinity tolerance and zonation in mangrove forests. The passage as a whole is concerned with different explanations of zonation in mangrove forests.

A The fourth paragraph discusses the relation of salinity and zonation, but the author does not refute this idea. Since this idea is only discussed in one paragraph, it cannot be the primary concern of the whole passage.

B Zonation is described in the first paragraph, but the author's primary interest is in the possible causes of zonation.

C The third paragraph shows that Davis' paradigm applies to some mangrove forests, but not to those on stable coastlines.

D **Correct.** The author's primary concern, as expressed throughout the passages, is looking at different explanations of the causes of zonation in mangrove forests.

E Salinity is discussed in the final paragraph but the passage states that salt is not required. The brief discussion of this point shows that it is not the primary concern of the passage.

The correct answer is D.

53. According to the passage, the earliest research on mangrove forests produced which of the following?

(A) Data that implied random patterns of mangrove species distribution

(B) Descriptions of species distributions suggesting zonation

(C) Descriptions of the development of mangrove forests over time

(D) Reclassification of species formerly thought to be identical

(E) Data that confirmed the "land-building" role of mangroves

Supporting ideas

As indicated by the phrase *according to the passage*, this question is based on factual information stated in the passage. Lines 5–8 describe the *earliest research on mangrove forests*. This research *produced descriptions of species distribution from shore to land*. This shore-to-land pattern is described as *zonal* in the first sentence.

A The passage suggests that the distribution was not random.

B **Correct.** The description of the species distribution goes from shore to land, fitting the definition of *zonal* in the first sentence.

C The passage does not indicate that the research looked at mangrove forest development over time.

D There is no evidence that the research involved reclassification.

E The research produced only descriptions; the land-building theory came later.

The correct answer is B.

54. It can be inferred from the passage that Davis' paradigm does NOT apply to which of the following?

    (A) The shoreline of Florida mangrove forests first studied by Davis
    (B) A shoreline in an area with weak currents
    (C) A shoreline in an area with weak tidal energy
    (D) A shoreline extended by "land-building" species of mangroves
    (E) A shoreline in which few sediments can accumulate

Application

To answer this question, apply Davis' paradigm to the situations in the answer choices. One situation will NOT fit the paradigm. According to Davis, the shoreline is extended seaward by *the land-building role of mangroves*. The third paragraph describes the circumstances favorable to the land-building process: weak currents, weak tidal energies, and the accumulation of sediments. In the absence of these conditions, land-building would not occur.

A Since this is the area Davis studied, it obviously fits the paradigm.
B Weak currents favor the land-building paradigm.
C Weak tidal energies favor the land-building paradigm.
D If land building has occurred, then the paradigm describing that land building applies.
E **Correct.** If few sediments can accumulate, land building is NOT able to occur.

The correct answer is E.

55. Information in the passage indicates that the author would most probably regard which of the following statements as INCORRECT?

    (A) Coastal mangrove forests are usually zonal.
    (B) Hurricanes interrupt the process of accretion and succession that extends existing shorelines.
    (C) Species of plants that thrive in a saline habitat require salt to flourish.
    (D) Plants with the highest metabolic efficiency in a given habitat tend to exclude other plants from that habitat.
    (E) Shorelines in areas with weak currents and tides are more likely to be extended through the process of accumulation of sediment than are shorelines with strong currents and tides.

Inference

Since authors try to provide correct information in their work, they would regard as incorrect any information that contradicts their work. To answer this question, check each statement against the information in the passage to find the one that is NOT in agreement with the passage.

A Lines 1–2 state that *neotropical coastal mangroves forests are usually "zonal."*
B Lines 17–19 state that hurricanes interrupt accretion and succession.
C **Correct.** This statement contradicts the statement in line 39 about mangroves not requiring salt.
D This general statement agrees with the more specific reference in lines 43–46 to the metabolic efficiency of mangroves in areas with high salinity; there is no reason to think the author would find it incorrect.
E The statement agrees with the information in the third paragraph that *in areas where weak currents and weak tidal energies allow the accumulation of sediments, mangroves will follow land formation and accelerate the rate of soil accretion.*

The correct answer is C.

Questions 56–63 refer to the passage on page 41.

56. The primary focus of the passage is on which of the following?

(A) Comparing two scientific theories and contrasting the predictions that each would make concerning a natural phenomenon

(B) Describing a new theoretical model and noting that it explains the nature of observations made of a particular natural phenomenon

(C) Evaluating the results of a particular scientific experiment and suggesting further areas for research

(D) Explaining how two different natural phenomena are related and demonstrating a way to measure them

(E) Analyzing recent data derived from observations of an actual phenomenon and constructing a model to explain the data

Main idea

To answer a question about the primary focus of a passage, look at the passage as a whole. The first paragraph describes the new theoretical model. The second paragraph discusses the data relevant to actual observation, and the third paragraph shows that actual observations were consistent with the theoretical model.

A Although the computer model revealed an unexpected finding, it confirmed the astronomers' hypothesis that meteor streams broaden with time. The passage does not contrast the predictions of competing theories.

B **Correct.** The computer model explains the structure of meteor streams; actual observations of meteor streams confirm the model's findings.

C No suggestions for further research are made.

D Only one natural phenomenon is studied.

E The model was created first and predicted what the observed data confirmed. The model was not constructed to explain the data.

The correct answer is B.

57. According to the passage, which of the following is an accurate statement concerning meteor streams?

(A) Meteor streams and comets start out with similar orbits, but only those of meteor streams are perturbed by planetary gravitation.

(B) Meteor streams grow as dust particles are attracted by the gravitational fields of comets.

(C) Meteor streams are composed of dust particles derived from comets.

(D) Comets may be composed of several kinds of materials, while meteor streams consist only of large dust particles.

(E) Once formed, meteor streams hasten the further disintegration of comets.

Supporting ideas

The phrase *according to the passage* indicates that the answer is explicitly stated in the passage; however, it may be stated in slightly different language. The passage begins with a definition of a meteor stream, which is *composed of dust particles that have been ejected from a parent comet at a variety of velocities.*

A Meteor streams and comets initially share the same orbit (line 3), and planetary gravitation fields affect the orbits of meteor streams (lines 7–10). However, no information is provided about the effect of planetary gravitation on comets' orbits, so the statement that *only* the orbits of meteor streams are affected is unjustified.

B Lines 7–10 explain that meteor streams grow, or broaden, because of the influence of planetary gravitational fields, not the gravitational fields of comets.

C **Correct.** The first sentence defines meteor streams as being composed of dust particles that come from comets.

D The passage does not describe the composition of comets.

E The passage does not explain the disintegration of comets.

The correct answer is C.

58. The author states that the research described in the first paragraph was undertaken in order to

    (A) determine the age of an actual meteor stream
    (B) identify the various structural features of meteor streams
    (C) explore the nature of a particularly interesting meteor stream
    (D) test the hypothesis that meteor streams become broader as they age
    (E) show that a computer model could help in explaining actual astronomical data

Supporting ideas

The question tells the reader where to look and what to look for: an explicit statement in the first paragraph about why the computer model was constructed. Lines 7–13 provide the reference needed to answer this question. Astronomers *hypothesized that a meteor stream should broaden with time... A recent computer-modeling experiment tested this hypothesis.* Thus, the research was conducted in order to test the hypothesis that meteor streams broaden with age.

A The last paragraph shows that the approximate age of the Geminid meteor stream was determined as a result of the research, but it was not the reason the research was undertaken in the first place.
B The computer model came up with an unexpected finding about the structure of meteor streams; however, the research was undertaken not to identify the structure of the meteor streams, but to determine if they broaden over time.
C The purpose of the research was to test a general hypothesis about all meteor streams, not to explore one meteor stream in particular.
D **Correct.** The purpose of the research is explicitly stated in the first paragraph: to test the hypothesis that meteor streams broaden as they age.
E Although the computer model did explain actual data, the purpose of the research was not to show the computer's usefulness, but rather to test the astronomers' hypothesis.

The correct answer is D.

59. It can be inferred from the passage that which of the following would most probably be observed during the Earth's passage through a meteor stream if the conventional theories mentioned in lines 18–19 were correct?

    (A) Meteor activity would gradually increase to a single, intense peak, and then gradually decline.
    (B) Meteor activity would be steady throughout the period of the meteor shower.
    (C) Meteor activity would rise to a peak at the beginning and at the end of the meteor shower.
    (D) Random bursts of very high meteor activity would be interspersed with periods of very little activity.
    (E) In years in which the Earth passed through only the outer areas of a meteor stream, meteor activity would be absent.

Inference

An inference is drawn from stated information. Begin by looking at the information about conventional theories in lines 18–21. Conventional theories held that *the distribution of particles would be increasingly dense toward the center of a meteor stream.* If the conventional theories were true, it could be inferred that there would be one intense period of activity as the Earth passed through the dense center of the meteor stream. The computer model showed instead that meteor stream resembled *a thick-walled, hollow pipe.* Lines 29–32 explain that, according to the computer model's prediction, Earth would experience two periods of meteor activity as it passed through the meteor stream, one as it entered the "pipe" and one as it exited. Observation of the Geminid meteor shower shows *just such a bifurcation.*

A **Correct.** Since the conventional theories predicted an *increasingly dense* center, Earth would experience a gradual increase of meteor activity, an intense peak at dense center, then a gradual decrease.
B For meteor activity to be steady, the distribution of dust particles would have to be more or less the same across the stream, not *increasingly dense toward the center.*

C   This bifurcated meteor activity was predicted by the computer model, not by conventional theories.

D   Conventional theories propose a dense center, which is not a structure that would result in such erratic meteor activity.

E   A meteor shower always occurs when Earth passes through a meteor stream (lines 24–25).

The correct answer is A.

60. According to the passage, why do the dust particles in a meteor stream eventually surround a comet's original orbit?

(A)   They are ejected by the comet at differing velocities.

(B)   Their orbits are uncontrolled by planetary gravitational fields.

(C)   They become part of the meteor stream at different times.

(D)   Their velocity slows over time.

(E)   Their ejection velocity is slower than that of the comet.

Supporting ideas

This question asks for information explicitly stated in the passage. The first paragraph describes the composition and behavior of meteor streams. The dust particles that make up the meteor stream are ejected from the comet *at a variety of velocities*. Eventually, *a shroud of dust surrounds the entire cometary orbit* because of the *differing velocities* of these dust particles.

A   **Correct.** Lines 1–7 show that, *due to their differing velocities*, the dust particles eventually surround the comet's orbit.

B   Lines 7–10 explain that the dust particles' orbits are dislocated by, and thus under the control of, planetary gravitational fields.

C   The passage does not indicate that the dust particles join the meteor stream at different times.

D   The passage gives no evidence that the velocity of the dust particles slows.

E   The passage does not say that the ejection velocity is slower than the comet's velocity.

The correct answer is A.

61. The passage suggests that which of the following is a prediction concerning meteor streams that can be derived from both the conventional theories mentioned in lines 18–19 and the new computer derived theory?

(A)   Dust particles in a meteor stream will usually be distributed evenly throughout any cross section of the stream.

(B)   The orbits of most meteor streams should cross the orbit of the Earth at some point and give rise to a meteor shower.

(C)   Over time the distribution of dust in a meteor stream will usually become denser at the outside edges of the stream than at the center.

(D)   Meteor showers caused by older meteor streams should be, on average, longer in duration than those caused by very young meteor streams.

(E)   The individual dust particles in older meteor streams should be, on average, smaller than those that compose younger meteor streams.

Inference

The question's use of the word *suggests* means that the answer depends on making an inference. Lines 7–8 state the hypothesis that *a meteor stream should broaden with time*; this hypothesis is consistent with both conventional and computer-derived theories regarding the nature of the center of the meteor stream. Thus, the broader the meteor stream is, the older it is. Lines 24–25 state that meteor showers occur whenever Earth passes through a meteor stream. It can be inferred that if the meteor stream is older and broader, Earth will experience longer periods of meteor showers as it passes through this broad stream than it would if the meteor stream were younger and therefore less broad.

A   Conventional theories predict a dense center, and the computer model predicts a pipe-like structure; neither theory is consistent with an even distribution of dust particles.

B   Neither theory makes predictions about the orbits of most meteor streams.

C   Conventional theories predict a dense center, not a dense exterior.

D   **Correct.** Both theories contend that meteor streams broaden over time. An older, broader meteor stream means that Earth will experience longer meteor showers from start to finish than it would if it were to pass through a younger, narrower meteor stream.

E   The passage does not discuss the size of individual dust particles.

The correct answer is D.

62.   It can be inferred from the last paragraph of the passage that which of the following must be true of the Earth as it orbits the Sun?

(A)   Most meteor streams it encounters are more than 2,000 years old.

(B)   When passing through a meteor stream, it usually passes near to the stream's center.

(C)   It crosses the Geminid meteor stream once every year.

(D)   It usually takes over a day to cross the actual Geminid meteor stream.

(E)   It accounts for most of the gravitational perturbation affecting the Geminid meteor stream.

Inference

An inference is drawn from stated information. To answer this question, reread the last paragraph and compare it with the inferences given in the answer choices. Earth experiences meteor showers every time it passes through a meteor stream. The last paragraph identifies the Geminid meteor showers as occurring *yearly* (line 37). Therefore, it is logical to infer that the Earth must pass through the Geminid meteor stream yearly.

A   The passage provides no evidence to support this generalization about the age of meteor streams.

B   Lines 32–34 state: *There is no reason why the Earth should always pass through the stream's exact center.*

C   **Correct.** Since the Geminid meteor showers occur yearly, the Earth must pass through the Geminid meteor stream yearly.

D   Lines 38–41 show that the Earth passed through the Geminid meteor stream in an average of 19 hours.

E   Lines 7–10 explain that dust particles' orbits are perturbed by planetary gravitation, but there is no reason to infer that Earth's gravitation affects the meteor stream more than other planets' gravitation.

The correct answer is C.

63.   Which of the following is an assumption underlying the last sentence of the passage?

(A)   In each of the years between 1970 and 1979, the Earth took exactly 19 hours to cross the Geminid meteor stream.

(B)   The comet associated with the Geminid meteor stream has totally disintegrated.

(C)   The Geminid meteor stream should continue to exist for at least 5,000 years.

(D)   The Geminid meteor stream has not broadened as rapidly as the conventional theories would have predicted.

(E)   The computer-model Geminid meteor stream provides an accurate representation of the development of the actual Geminid stream.

Logical structure

The last sentence establishes the approximate date of the Geminid meteor stream. How is this date determined? The computer model shows that the Earth would cross the meteor stream in a little more than 24 hours if the stream were 5,000 years old (lines 27–29). One decade's data show that the Earth crossed the meteor stream in an average of 19 hours (lines 38–41). The conclusion that the stream is about 3,000 years old assumes that the computer model is accurate.

A   The data provide an average time, not an exact time for each year.

B   The passage does not mention the comet associated with the meteor stream.

C   The passage does not predict the longevity of the meteor stream.

D   The computer model confirmed the hypothesis about broadening over time proposed by conventional theories; to do this, it projected a 5,000 year period, but that does not mean that astronomers expected the actual stream to be older or broader than it was.

E   **Correct.** The assumption is that the computer model accurately represents the development of the actual Geminid meteor stream.

The correct answer is E.

Questions 64–69 refer to the passage on page 44.

64.   The primary purpose of the passage is to

   (A)   discuss a plan for investigation of a phenomenon that is not yet fully understood

   (B)   present two explanations of a phenomenon and reconcile the differences between them

   (C)   summarize two theories and suggest a third theory that overcomes the problems encountered in the first two

   (D)   describe an alternative hypothesis and provide evidence and arguments that support it

   (E)   challenge the validity of a theory by exposing the inconsistencies and contradictions in it

Main idea

Examining the structure of the whole passage helps to identify the passage's primary purpose or main idea. The first paragraph introduces a recent hypothesis about how caffeine affects behavior. The second paragraph looks at an earlier, widely accepted hypothesis and then presents the objections to it made by the scientists proposing the more recent hypothesis. The third and fourth paragraphs provide evidence to support that newer hypothesis. Since most of the passage is devoted to the recent hypothesis, clearly the primary purpose must be to present that hypothesis to readers.

A   The passage discusses a current investigation, not one planned for the future.

B   The passage examines two explanations, but the earlier theory is discussed only to expose its weakness. Most of the passage is devoted to the more recent theory.

C   Only two theories are presented in the passage.

D   Correct. The recent hypothesis provides an alternative to an earlier one and is supported by evidence and arguments.

E   Lines 28–33 do pose such a challenge to the earlier theory; however, the challenge is a small part of the whole passage. Similarly, in the final paragraph, an exception to the more recent theory is introduced, only to be dismissed as an unimportant concern.

The correct answer is D.

65.   According to Snyder et al, caffeine differs from adenosine in that caffeine

   (A)   stimulates behavior in mice and in humans, whereas adenosine stimulates behavior in humans only

   (B)   has mixed effects in the brain, whereas adenosine has only a stimulatory effect

   (C)   increases cyclic AMP concentrations in target neurons, whereas adenosine decreases such concentrations

   (D)   permits release of neurotransmitters when it is bound to adenosine receptors, whereas adenosine inhibits such release

   (E)   inhibits both neuron firing and the production of phosphodiesterase when there is a sufficient concentration in the brain, whereas adenosine inhibits only neuron firing

Supporting ideas

To answer this question, look for the section that discusses adenosine and caffeine. The first paragraph leads the reader through how adenosine (lines 7–11) and caffeine (lines 4–6) work in the brain, according to Snyder et al. Adenosine *depresses neuron firing* by *inhibiting the release of neurotransmitters*; it is able to achieve this by binding to *specific receptors on neuronal membranes*. Caffeine interrupts this process by binding to the receptors, which prevents adenosine from attaching to them, and the neurons then *fire more readily than they otherwise would*.

A   The passage includes no evidence that adenosine stimulates behavior.

B   While the final paragraph reveals that caffeine displays mixed effects, the passage does not state that adenosine has a stimulatory effect.

C   Increasing cyclic AMP concentrations is part of the earlier theory, not that of Snyder et al.

D   Correct. Lines 7–19 explain that caffeine binds to the receptors, releasing neurotransmitters, whereas adenosine hinders that release.

E   Inhibiting the production of phosphodiesterase is discussed in the earlier theory, not in the work of Snyder et al.

The correct answer is D.

66. In response to experimental results concerning IBMX, Snyder et al contended that it is not uncommon for psychoactive drugs to have

    (A) mixed effects in the brain
    (B) inhibitory effects on enzymes in the brain
    (C) close structural relationships with caffeine
    (D) depressive effects on mouse locomotion
    (E) the ability to dislodge caffeine from receptors in the brain

Supporting ideas

To answer this question, look at the last paragraph, which discusses the effects of IBMX. This compound binds to the adenosine receptors, but instead of acting as a stimulant as other caffeine derivatives do, it was found to depress locomotion in mice. Snyder et al explain that IBMX *has mixed effects in the brain, a not unusual occurrence with psychoactive drugs* (lines 58–60).

A **Correct.** The results of one experiment can be explained by *mixed effects in the brain,* which Snyder et al say may be expected with psychoactive drugs.
B This response refers back to the earlier theory, not to Snyder et al's work.
C Caffeine is only included within the broad category of psychoactive drugs.
D This effect is attributed to one compound, IBMX, not to all psychoactive drugs.
E This ability is not discussed in the passage.

The correct answer is A.

67. According to Snyder et al, all of the following compounds can bind to specific receptors in the brain EXCEPT

    (A) IBMX
    (B) caffeine
    (C) adenosine
    (D) theophylline
    (E) phosphodiesterase

Supporting ideas

This question asks the reader to rule out all the possibilities discussed in the text, leaving the single exception. The first paragraph explains that both adenosine and caffeine bind to receptors in the brain. The fourth paragraph attests to the ability of theophylline to bind to the receptors. The last paragraph describes IBMX as a compound that binds to adenosine receptors. Thus the exception has to be the enzyme phosphodiesterase.

A Lines 54–55 show that IBMX binds to receptors.
B Lines 17–19 show that caffeine binds to receptors.
C Lines 13–14 show that adenosine binds to receptors.
D Lines 48–50 show that theophylline binds to receptors.
E **Correct.** The passage includes no evidence that phosphodiesterase binds to receptors.

The correct answer is E.

68. Snyder et al suggest that caffeine's ability to bind to A_1 and A_2 receptors can be at least partially attributed to which of the following?

    (A) The chemical relationship between caffeine and phosphodiesterase
    (B) The structural relationship between caffeine and adenosine
    (C) The structural similarity between caffeine and neurotransmitters
    (D) The ability of caffeine to stimulate behavior
    (E) The natural occurrence of caffeine and adenosine in the brain

Inference

This question asks the reader to find information that is suggested but not directly stated in the passage. The A_1 and A_2 receptors are mentioned in line 16, so look at the surrounding material. Snyder et al propose that caffeine, *which is structurally similar to adenosine*, binds to both types of receptors, just as adenosine does. Caffeine's ability to bind to these receptors may be due to this structural similarity to adenosine.

A   Phosphodiesterase is discussed in an entirely different context in lines 22–25.
B   **Correct.** Lines 17–19 suggest that caffeine's structural similarity to adenosine may be responsible for its ability to bind to A_1 and A_2 receptors.
C   Caffeine acts on neurotransmitters; it is not structurally similar to them.
D   Caffeine's ability to stimulate behavior results from, rather than causes, this process.
E   The passage does not discuss the natural occurrence of these compounds.

The correct answer is B.

69. The author quotes Snyder et al in lines 43–48 most probably in order to

    (A) reveal some of the assumptions underlying their theory
    (B) summarize a major finding of their experiments
    (C) point out that their experiments were limited to mice
    (D) indicate that their experiments resulted only in general correlations
    (E) refute the objections made by supporters of the older theory

Logical structure

To find the reason that the author quotes Snyder et al, examine the third paragraph, where the quotation appears. The paragraph starts with evidence supporting the new hypothesis on the basis of experiments with mice. The quotation then begins *in general*, a phrase that implies a summary of the results of the work with mice. The quoted material explains that the more the compounds were able to bind to the receptors, the greater the stimulatory effect. This major finding supports the hypothesis.

A   The quotation explains results of an experiment, not assumptions about theory.
B   **Correct.** The quotation summarizes the experiment with mice and reports a major finding in support of the hypothesis.
C   The quotation generalizes on the basis of the experiment; it does not limit the finding to mice.
D   Specific correlations were made between the ability to bind to receptors and to stimulate locomotion.
E   The passage includes no such objections; therefore no refutations are needed.

The correct answer is B.

Questions 70–77 refer to the passage on page 46.

70. According to the passage, job segregation by sex in the United States was

(A) greatly diminished by labor mobilization during the Second World War
(B) perpetuated by those textile-mill owners who argued in favor of women's employment in wage labor
(C) one means by which women achieved greater job security
(D) reluctantly challenged by employers except when the economic advantages were obvious
(E) a constant source of labor unrest in the young textile industry

Supporting ideas

The question uses the phrase *according to the passage*, indicating that the answer is based on information stated in the passage. The second paragraph explains that *a prevailing definition of femininity* often dictates what jobs are given to women. For example, textile-mill owners used *hoary stereotypes associated with… homemaking activities* in order to justify their employment of women, claiming that *women were by nature skillful at detailed tasks and patient in carrying out repetitive chores.*

A   Lines 43–45 show just the reverse to be true: *job segregation by sex characterized even the most important war industries.*
B   **Correct.** Textile-mill owners exploited stereotypes about women and the work suited to them in order to justify employing them as wage laborers.
C   Many *"female"* jobs were *less secure* (lines 34–35).
D   No information in the passage leads to this conclusion; in fact, employers showed little interest in challenging job segregation *even when higher profits beckoned* (lines 40–41).
E   Labor unrest among textile-mill workers is not discussed.

The correct answer is B.

71. According to the passage, historians of women's labor focused on factory work as a more promising area of research than service-sector work because factory work

(A) involved the payment of higher wages
(B) required skill in detailed tasks
(C) was assumed to be less characterized by sex segregation
(D) was more readily accepted by women than by men
(E) fitted the economic dynamic of industrialism better

Supporting ideas

The phrase *according to the passage* indicates that the answer is stated in the passage. Look at the first paragraph, which discusses historians of women's labor. These historians disregarded service work in favor of factory work not only because factory work differed from traditional *"women's work,"* but also because the forces of industrialism were *presumed to be gender-blind* (lines 5–9).

A   The passage does not indicate that historians studied factory workers because of higher wages.
B   The passage gives no evidence that historians chose this research area for this reason.
C   **Correct.** The passage indicates that the historians chose this research area because they assumed that sex segregation was less prevalent in factory work than in service-sector work.
D   Women's ready acceptance of factory work is not mentioned in the passage as the reason why historians turned their attention to factory work rather than service-sector work.
E   Factory work may have fitted the dynamic of industrialism better, but this is not the reason the passage gives for the historians' choice.

The correct answer is C.

72. It can be inferred from the passage that early historians of women's labor in the United States paid little attention to women's employment in the service sector of the economy because

    (A) the extreme variety of these occupations made it very difficult to assemble meaningful statistics about them
    (B) fewer women found employment in the service sector than in factory work
    (C) the wages paid to workers in the service sector were much lower than those paid in the industrial sector
    (D) women's employment in the service sector tended to be much more short-term than in factory work
    (E) employment in the service sector seemed to have much in common with the unpaid work associated with homemaking

Inference

Since this question asks for an inference, the answer is not directly stated in the passage; it must instead be derived from the information given. To answer this question, look at what the first paragraph says about the historians' focus on factory work. The historians *disregarded* service work and *focused instead* on factory work in part because *it seemed so different from traditional, unpaid "women's work" in the home* (lines 5–7). Since the two kinds of work are explicitly contrasted, it is reasonable to infer that what is not true of factory work is true of service work; service work is similar to *traditional, unpaid "women's work" in the home.*

A No mention of statistics is made in the passage.
B The numbers of women in each kind of work are not compared.
C Wages earned in the two kinds of work are not compared.
D Duration of employment in the two kinds of work is not compared.
E **Correct.** Historians disregarded service work because it was similar to *"women's work"* at home.

The correct answer is E.

73. The passage supports which of the following statements about the early mill owners mentioned in the second paragraph?

    (A) They hoped that by creating relatively unattractive "female" jobs they would discourage women from losing interest in marriage and family life.
    (B) They sought to increase the size of the available labor force as a means to keep men's wages low.
    (C) They argued that women were inherently suited to do well in particular kinds of factory work.
    (D) They thought that factory work bettered the condition of women by emancipating them from dependence on income earned by men.
    (E) They felt guilty about disturbing the traditional division of labor in the family.

Supporting ideas

Look at the second paragraph to see what it says about the assumptions and actions of the mill owners. To answer this question, look for a perspective or action that the paragraph explicitly supports. The mill owners accepted and perpetuated the stereotypes of women, including their greater attention to detail and patience with repetitive tasks, and thus argued that women were inherently (*by nature*) suited to the work in a textile mill.

A The mill owners assumed that women's *"real" aspirations were for marriage and family life,* which they used as an excuse to pay women less.
B The passage does not say that mill owners tried to keep men's wages low.
C **Correct.** The mill owners contended that certain factory work was suitable to a woman's alleged patient, detail-oriented nature.
D The passage does not credit mill owners with trying to emancipate women.
E There is no indication in the passage that the mill owners felt any guilt.

The correct answer is C.

74. It can be inferred from the passage that the "unfinished revolution" the author mentions in line 14 refers to the

(A) entry of women into the industrial labor market
(B) recognition that work done by women as homemakers should be compensated at rates comparable to those prevailing in the service sector of the economy
(C) development of a new definition of femininity unrelated to the economic forces of industrialism
(D) introduction of equal pay for equal work in all professions
(E) emancipation of women wage earners from gender-determined job allocation

Inference

An inference requires going beyond the material explicitly stated in the passage to the author's ideas that underlie that material. To understand this reference, it is first necessary to analyze its context. The first paragraph explains that historians focused on factory work on the assumption that it was *gender-blind* and *emancipatory in effect*. However, the paragraph concludes, *emancipation has been less profound than expected, for not even industrial wage labor has escaped continued sex segregation in the workplace*. The phrase *this unfinished revolution* appears in the next sentence, and it refers back to *continued sex segregation in the workplace*. Here the passage implies that the author believes the revolution is unfinished because jobs are still allocated to women on the basis of their sex.

A The first paragraph has established that women are in the industrial workforce.
B Compensation for work at home is not discussed in the passage.
C The only definition of femininity referred to in the passage is said to determine the kinds of jobs available to women.
D Equal pay for equal work is not addressed in the passage.
E **Correct.** The *unfinished revolution* refers to an emancipation that is incomplete because job segregation on the basis of sex continues.

The correct answer is E.

75. The passage supports which of the following statements about hiring policies in the United States?

(A) After a crisis many formerly "male" jobs are reclassified as "female" jobs.
(B) Industrial employers generally prefer to hire women with previous experience as homemakers.
(C) Post-Second World War hiring policies caused women to lose many of their wartime gains in employment opportunity.
(D) Even war industries during the Second World War were reluctant to hire women for factory work.
(E) The service sector of the economy has proved more nearly gender-blind in its hiring policies than has the manufacturing sector.

Supporting ideas

Look at each answer choice to see if it is explicitly supported by information in the passage. The last sentence of the passage states that, once World War II was over, men returned to take the *"male"* jobs that women had been temporarily allowed to master. Thus, the gains women had been allowed to make during the war (despite continued job segregation) were lost to them after men returned to work.

A The last paragraph shows that after World War II, *"male"* jobs that had been held by women during the war were returned to men.
B No information in the passage supports this claim.
C **Correct.** After World War II, women lost many employment opportunities that had been available to them during the war.
D The passage says that job segregation persisted in the war, but it does not indicate that war industries were reluctant to hire women.
E No comparison is made in the passage to support this conclusion.

The correct answer is C.

76. Which of the following words best expresses the opinion of the author of the passage concerning the notion that women are more skillful than men in carrying out detailed tasks?

    (A) "patient" (line 23)
    (B) "repetitive" (line 23)
    (C) "hoary" (line 25)
    (D) "homemaking" (line 26)
    (E) "purview" (line 27)

    Tone

    This question asks about the author's attitude. Word choice may reveal attitude, as it does here when the author describes the *hoary stereotypes* about women that mill owners perpetuated. *Hoary* means old—literally white with age—and so the stereotypes are being dismissed by the author as old-fashioned, even obsolete.

    A The mill owners stereotyped women as *patient*; this does not express the author's opinion.
    B Mill owners claimed that women were suited to *repetitive* work; this does not express the author's opinion.
    C **Correct.** *Hoary* carries with it a judgment. In the author's eyes, the mill owners' stereotypes are impossibly antiquated.
    D *Homemaking* describes activities but does not reveal the author's opinion.
    E *Purview* simply means a range or a scope; it does not reveal an opinion.

    The correct answer is C.

77. Which of the following best describes the relationship of the final paragraph to the passage as a whole?

    (A) The central idea is reinforced by the citation of evidence drawn from twentieth-century history.
    (B) The central idea is restated in such a way as to form a transition to a new topic for discussion.
    (C) The central idea is restated and juxtaposed with evidence that might appear to contradict it.
    (D) A partial exception to the generalizations of the central idea is dismissed as unimportant.
    (E) Recent history is cited to suggest that the central idea's validity is gradually diminishing.

    Logical structure

    Consider the final paragraph in the context of the whole passage to evaluate its relationship to the whole. The first two paragraphs examine job segregation in an unspecified but earlier time. The final paragraph brings the reader into the twentieth century, when, as the example drawn from World War II shows, job segregation persisted. Thus, the final paragraph updates and reinforces the author's thesis about the persistence of job segregation.

    A **Correct.** The central idea that sex segregation continues in the workplace is reinforced with an example from World War II.
    B The central idea is the persistence of job segregation, which is the only topic in the paragraph.
    C The last paragraph supports the passage; no apparently contradictory evidence is introduced.
    D The last paragraph supports the central idea with a more modern example; no exceptions are either entertained or dismissed.
    E More recent history is cited to support the central idea, not to show that it is diminishing.

    The correct answer is A.

Questions 78–83 refer to the passage on page 48.

78. The author of the passage alludes to the well-established nature of the concept of individual rights in the Anglo-Saxon legal and political tradition in order to

    (A) illustrate the influence of individualist feminist thought on more general intellectual trends in English history
    (B) argue that feminism was already a part of the larger Anglo-Saxon intellectual tradition, even though this has often gone unnoticed by critics of women's emancipation
    (C) explain the decline in individualist thinking among feminists in non-English speaking countries

(D)　help account for an increasing shift toward individualist feminism among feminists in English-speaking countries

(E)　account for the philosophical differences between individualist and relational feminists in English-speaking countries

Logical structure

This question asks for the reason that the author has chosen to include the information about the Anglo-Saxon tradition in lines 23–26. The concept of individual rights was *well established* in this tradition, and that is the reason that *individualist feminism came to predominate in English-speaking countries.* Thus, this detail explains why feminists in English-speaking countries turned to individualist, rather than relational, feminism.

A　This statement reverses the order: the more general intellectual trends in English history influenced individualist feminism.

B　Feminism is not said to be a part of the Anglo-Saxon tradition.

C　While relational feminism predominates among European and non-Western feminists, no evidence shows a decline in individualist feminism among these groups.

D　Correct. The author uses the information about individual rights and the Anglo-Saxon tradition to explain why individualist feminism predominated in English-speaking countries.

E　The Anglo-Saxon tradition is not said to account for all the philosophical differences between the two feminisms in English-speaking countries, but only for the fact that individualist feminism became predominant.

The correct answer is D.

79.　The passage suggests that the author of the passage believes which of the following?

(A)　The predominance of individualist feminism in English-speaking countries is a historical phenomenon, the causes of which have not yet been investigated.

(B)　The individualist and relational feminist views are irreconcilable, given their theoretical differences concerning the foundations of society.

(C)　A consensus concerning the direction of future feminist politics will probably soon emerge, given the awareness among feminists of the need for cooperation among women.

(D)　Political adversaries of feminism often misuse arguments predicated on differences between the sexes to argue that the existing social system should be maintained.

(E)　Relational feminism provides the best theoretical framework for contemporary feminist politics, but individualist feminism could contribute much toward refining and strengthening modern feminist thought.

Supporting ideas

To answer this question, look for an idea that the author explicitly supports in the passage. The first sentence of the last paragraph states that the relational feminists' argument—that women's biological role gives them a special (and undervalued) place in society—may be used by opponents of feminism to reinforce the existing dominance of men.

A　In lines 23–26, the author identifies one cause for the situation.

B　In lines 46–50, the author implies that a reconciliation might be possible, making this an overstatement.

C　The author does not suggest that consensus is likely to happen soon; cooperation is not discussed.

D　Correct. This statement is consistent with the view that the author expressed in the third paragraph.

E　The last paragraph discusses the problems of both feminisms, but the author does not say one is better than the other.

The correct answer is D.

80. It can be inferred from the passage that the individualist feminist tradition denies the validity of which of the following causal statements?

(A) A division of labor in a social group can result in increased efficiency with regard to the performance of group tasks.

(B) A division of labor in a social group causes inequities in the distribution of opportunities and benefits among group members.

(C) A division of labor on the basis of gender in a social group is necessitated by the existence of sex-linked biological differences between male and female members of the group.

(D) Culturally determined distinctions based on gender in a social group foster the existence of differing attitudes and opinions among group members.

(E) Educational programs aimed at reducing inequalities based on gender among members of a social group can result in a sense of greater well-being for all members of the group.

Inference

To make an inference about the individualist feminist tradition, begin by rereading the first paragraph, which sets forth the differing arguments of the two feminisms. Relational feminism holds that the biological differences of the sexes must result in a division of labor based on those differences (lines 5–10). *By contrast*, individualist feminism downplays the importance of gender roles and attaches little importance to the biological function of childbearing (lines 10–15). Thus, it can be inferred that individualist feminists would disagree with the statement that biological differences should determine a gender-based division of labor in society.

A The passage neither discusses increased efficiency nor implies that individualist feminists would reject it.

B The passage does not indicate that individualist feminists would disagree with this statement.

C **Correct.** This statement reflects the position of the relational feminists, which the individualist feminists oppose, stressing instead individual rights and personal autonomy.

D The passage offers no evidence that individualist feminists would disagree with this statement.

E Nothing in the passage indicates that individualist feminists would disagree with this statement.

The correct answer is C.

81. According to the passage, relational feminists and individualist feminists agree that

(A) individual human rights take precedence over most other social claims

(B) the gender-based division of labor in society should be eliminated

(C) laws guaranteeing equal treatment for all citizens regardless of gender should be passed

(D) a greater degree of social awareness concerning the importance of motherhood would be beneficial to society

(E) the same educational and economic opportunities should be available to both sexes

Supporting ideas

This question asks for information that is explicitly stated in the passage in slightly different language. While the passage is largely devoted to the differences between the two feminisms, lines 28–32 indicate a point of convergence. Individualist feminists believe in *equal rights for all*. Relational feminists believe that *equal educational and economic opportunities* should be available to women.

A Only individualist feminists believe that individual rights are most important (lines 10–15).

B Relational feminists do believe in a gender-based division of labor (lines 5–10).

C Lines 30–37 show that relational feminists do not believe in gender-blind equal rights laws.

D Only relational feminists believe in the importance of women's *special contributions to society* (line 33).

E **Correct.** Practitioners of both feminisms believe that equal educational and economic opportunities should be available to both sexes.

The correct answer is E.

82. According to the author, which of the following was true of feminist thought in Western societies before 1890?

(A) Individualist feminist arguments were not found in the thought or writing of non-English-speaking feminists.

(B) Individualist feminism was a strain in feminist thought, but another strain, relational feminism, predominated.

(C) Relational and individualist approaches were equally prevalent in feminist thought and writing.

(D) The predominant view among feminists held that the welfare of women was ultimately less important than the welfare of children.

(E) The predominant view among feminists held that the sexes should receive equal treatment under the law.

Supporting ideas

To answer this question, look at what the author states in lines 16–20, where the years before and after 1890 are discussed. The second paragraph begins by explaining that the two feminisms *coexisted* up until the late nineteenth century, although relational feminism *had been the dominant strain in feminist thought.*

A If relational feminism was *the dominant strain* of the two views that *coexisted*, the individualist arguments must have existed as well.

B **Correct.** Lines 19–20 explicitly state that relational feminism *had been the dominant strain in feminist thought* before 1890.

C The passage shows that the two feminisms were not equally prevalent; relational feminism predominated.

D No evidence in the passage supports this statement.

E The passage does not show that most feminists before 1890 took this position.

The correct answer is B.

83. The author implies that which of the following was true of most feminist thinkers in England and the United States after 1920?

(A) They were less concerned with politics than with intellectual issues.

(B) They began to reach a broader audience and their programs began to be adopted by mainstream political parties.

(C) They called repeatedly for international cooperation among women's groups to achieve their goals.

(D) They moderated their initial criticism of the economic systems that characterized their societies.

(E) They did not attempt to unite the two different feminist approaches in their thought.

Inference

Answering this question involves making an inference. Before 1890, the two feminisms *coexisted.* After 1920, *the goals of the two approaches began to seem increasingly irreconcilable* (lines 27–28). Lines 28–37 provide details on the differing and even opposing priorities of the relational and individualist feminists in England and the United States. It is reasonable to infer that both feminisms pursued their own goals and did not try to reconcile the two different approaches in their work. The final paragraph reveals that the two feminisms continue to remain separate, although the author offers a possibility for their harmonization.

A Individualist feminists advocated a *system with equal rights,* and relational feminists sought *protective legislation,* so it is clear both groups were politically active; the author does not imply they were more interested in intellectual issues.

B The passage offers no evidence to show broader or growing support for their ideas.

C International cooperation is not discussed in the passage.

D No information in the passage supports this statement.

E **Correct.** As the goals of the two feminisms grew *increasingly irreconcilable,* feminists in England and the United States did not try to harmonize the two strains in their thinking.

The correct answer is E.

Questions 84–90 refer to the passage on page 50.

84. According to the passage, all of the following were benefits of privatizing state-owned industries in the United Kingdom EXCEPT:

    (A) Privatized industries paid taxes to the government.
    (B) The government gained revenue from selling state-owned industries.
    (C) The government repaid some of its national debt.
    (D) Profits from industries that were still state-owned increased.
    (E) Total borrowings and losses of state-owned industries decreased.

    Supporting ideas

    This question begins with the phrase *according to the passage*, indicating that it can be answered using facts stated in the passage. The first paragraph lists the benefits of privatization. Use the process of elimination and check the five possible answer choices against the benefits described in lines 8–12. The point that is NOT discussed in the passage is the correct answer.

    A   Lines 11–12 discuss tax revenues.
    B   Lines 10–11 discuss revenue from the sales.
    C   Lines 14–16 discuss debt repayment.
    D   **Correct.** Profits from state-owned industries are not discussed.
    E   Lines 9–10 discuss decreased borrowings and losses.

    The correct answer is D.

85. According to the passage, which of the following resulted in increased productivity in companies that have been privatized?

    (A) A large number of employees chose to purchase shares in their companies.
    (B) Free shares were widely distributed to individual shareholders.
    (C) The government ceased to regulate major industries.
    (D) Unions conducted wage negotiations for employees.
    (E) Employee-owners agreed to have their wages lowered.

    Supporting ideas

    This question is based on information explicitly stated in the passage. The second paragraph describes the increased productivity, and the third paragraph begins by stating one reason for it: *employees of privatized industries were given the opportunity to buy shares in their own companies* (lines 29–31). The paragraph also cites the high percentage of employees buying shares in three privatized companies, supporting the idea that many employees bought shares.

    A   **Correct.** Productivity increased after employees became shareholders in their companies.
    B   The theoretical advantages and disadvantages of free shares are discussed (lines 43–52), but the passage does not say that any were given away.
    C   The passage does not examine governmental regulation.
    D   The passage does not analyze the relation between wages and productivity.
    E   Lines 39–42 cite one example of employee-owner willingness to accept lower wages, but this is not said to have resulted in increased productivity.

    The correct answer is A.

86. It can be inferred from the passage that the author considers labor disruptions to be

   (A) an inevitable problem in a weak national economy
   (B) a positive sign of employee concern about a company
   (C) a predictor of employee reactions to a company's offer to sell shares to them
   (D) a phenomenon found more often in state-owned industries than in private companies
   (E) a deterrence to high performance levels in an industry

Inference

This question states that an inference is required; this inference is based on material presented in the second paragraph. To demonstrate that privatization has *raised the level of performance in every area,* the author gives three examples (lines 20–27). One example is the disappearance of labor disruptions, once common. If the absence of labor disruptions raises the level of performance, then the author must believe that the presence of labor disruptions impedes a high level of performance.

A   The author does not link labor disruptions with a weak national economy.
B   The author does not interpret labor disruptions in a positive light.
C   The author does not identify labor disruptions as a predictor of employees' responses to opportunities to buy a company's shares.
D   Labor disruptions in state-owned and private industries are not compared.
E   **Correct.** The author implies that labor disruptions interfere with high levels of performance in industry.

The correct answer is E.

87. The passage supports which of the following statements about employees buying shares in their own companies?

   (A) At three different companies, approximately nine out of ten of the workers were eligible to buy shares in their companies.
   (B) Approximately 90 percent of the eligible workers at three different companies chose to buy shares in their companies.
   (C) The opportunity to buy shares was discouraged by at least some labor unions.
   (D) Companies that demonstrated the highest productivity were the first to allow their employees the opportunity to buy shares.
   (E) Eligibility to buy shares was contingent on employees' agreeing to increased work loads.

Supporting ideas

Check each statement by comparing it to the information presented in the passage. Only one statement is supported. The third paragraph presents the percentages of the eligible employees who purchased shares in their companies: 89 percent at one company, 90 percent at a second, and 92 percent at a third (lines 32–35). Thus, it is true that roughly 90 percent of the eligible work force at three different companies bought shares in their companies once they were given the opportunity to do so.

A   The passage cites the percentages of the eligible employees who bought shares, not the percentages of the total work force who were eligible.
B   **Correct.** The passage shows that roughly 90 percent of the eligible employees at three different companies bought shares in their companies.
C   The passage does not show the attitude of labor unions toward employee share buying.
D   The passage offers no evidence that companies with high productivity were the first to offer shares to their employees.
E   The passage does not show eligibility to be dependent on increased workload.

The correct answer is B.

88. Which of the following statements is most consistent with the principle described in lines 36–38?

(A) A democratic government that decides it is inappropriate to own a particular industry has in no way abdicated its responsibilities as guardian of the public interest.

(B) The ideal way for a government to protect employee interests is to force companies to maintain their share of a competitive market without government subsidies.

(C) The failure to harness the power of self-interest is an important reason that state-owned industries perform poorly.

(D) Governments that want to implement privatization programs must try to eliminate all resistance to the free-market system.

(E) The individual shareholder will reap only a minute share of the gains from whatever sacrifices he or she makes to achieve these gains.

Application

First identify the principle involved, and then find the statement that is most compatible with that principle. Lines 36–38 argue that having *a personal stake* in a business makes employees *work to make it prosper.* When there is no personal stake, or self-interest, involved, employees do not have the same incentive to work hard to make their industry *prosper.* Thus, the poor performance of state-owned industries can be ascribed in part to the lack of motivation employees suffer when they have no personal stake in the business.

A The principle involves a personal, rather than governmental, relationship.

B Self-interest may inspire people to do more; government coercion is not consistent with this principle.

C **Correct.** State-owned industries perform poorly in part because employees do not have the powerful motivation of self-interest.

D The principle has to do with the motivation of individuals, not governments.

E Lines 36–38 describe the principle of self-interest, not self-sacrifice.

The correct answer is C.

89. Which of the following can be inferred from the passage about the privatization process in the United Kingdom?

(A) It depends to a potentially dangerous degree on individual ownership of shares.

(B) It conforms in its most general outlines to Thomas Paine's prescription for business ownership.

(C) It was originally conceived to include some giving away of free shares.

(D) It has been successful, even though privatization has failed in other countries.

(E) It is taking place more slowly than some economists suggest is necessary.

Inference

Answering this question requires looking at each possible inference to see if it is supported somewhere in the passage. Support for the inference about the pace of privatization is provided by the suggestion of some economists that giving away free shares *would provide a needed acceleration of the privatization process* (lines 44–45). If privatization needs to be accelerated, then it must be going too slowly, at least according to these economists.

A The passage does not allude to any danger in individual ownership of shares.

B Paine is quoted only in reference to receiving free shares as opposed to buying shares; also, the process of privatization had occurred before employees bought shares in the newly privatized companies.

C No evidence supports the distribution of free shares as part of the plan to privatize.

D The failure of privatization in other countries is not mentioned.

E **Correct.** The economists' suggestion comes from what they see as the need to speed up a process that is currently taking too long.

The correct answer is E.

90. The quotation in lines 46–47 is most probably used to

(A) counter a position that the author of the passage believes is incorrect
(B) state a solution to a problem described in the previous sentence
(C) show how opponents of the viewpoint of the author of the passage have supported their arguments
(D) point out a paradox contained in a controversial viewpoint
(E) present a historical maxim to challenge the principle introduced in the third paragraph

Logical structure

Looking at the quotation's context leads to an understanding of why the quotation was used. Paine's quotation offers a concise and time-honored counterargument to the view voiced in the preceding sentence. The economists suggest giving away free shares, but the author notes that these economists are forgetting that, according to Paine, people do not value what they get too cheaply. The author uses the quotation to show the basic error in the economists' thinking.

A **Correct.** The author uses Paine's quotation as an apt counter to the economists' suggestion.
B The quotation attacks the solution posed in the previous sentence.
C The author agrees with Paine, as is evident in the final lines of the passage.
D The author implies that a viewpoint is ill advised, but does not say it is controversial.
E Paine's maxim does not challenge the principle of self-interest.

The correct answer is A.

Questions 91–97 refer to the passage on page 52.

91. In the passage, the author is primarily concerned with doing which of the following?

(A) Comparing two different approaches to a problem
(B) Describing a problem and proposing a solution
(C) Defending an established method
(D) Presenting data and drawing conclusions from the data
(E) Comparing two different analyses of a current situation

Main idea

To answer this question, analyze what the author is doing in each paragraph of the passage. The first paragraph presents a problem: the failure of shareholders and managers to enhance a company's long-term productivity. The second paragraph proposes a possible solution to that problem.

A Only one approach to a problem is explored.
B **Correct.** The first paragraph describes a problem, and the second paragraph proposes a solution.
C The author criticizes the established method, or current practice, as described in the first paragraph.
D The author presents not data, but a problem.
E Only one analysis of the current situation is presented.

The correct answer is B.

92. It can be inferred from the passage that which of the following is true of majority shareholders in a corporation?

  (A) They make the corporation's operational management decisions.
  (B) They are not allowed to own more than 50 percent of the corporation's stock.
  (C) They cannot make quick profits by selling off large amounts of their stock in the corporation.
  (D) They are more interested in profits than in productivity.
  (E) They cannot sell any of their stock in the corporation without giving the public advance notice.

Inference

An inference is drawn from stated information. To answer this question, look at what the passage says about *individual capitalists who owned enough stock to dominate the board of directors and dictate company policy*. The logical inference from this information is that these *individual capitalists* were majority stockholders; they are the only majority shareholders discussed in the passage. Lines 6–8 indicate that these capitalists *could not sell out for a quick profit and instead had to concentrate on …long-term productivity*.

A While majority shareholders might *dictate company policy* (line 4), there is no suggestion that they would make operational decisions.
B The passage does discuss current limitations on minority shareholders, but there is no discussion of limitations on majority shareholders.
C **Correct.** Lines 2–6 show that *individual capitalists*, and thus majority shareholders, cannot make quick profits because *putting such large amounts of stock on the market would only depress its value*.
D In lines 6–8, the author argues exactly the opposite of this point.
E Majority shareholders may sell as much stock as they want; the only constraint they face is the economic one of quickly depressing the share price.

The correct answer is C.

93. According to the passage, the purpose of the requirement suggested in lines 33–36 would be which of the following?

  (A) To encourage institutional stockholders to sell stock that they believe will decrease in value
  (B) To discourage institutional stockholders from intervening in the operation of a company whose stock they own
  (C) To discourage short-term profit taking by institutional stockholders
  (D) To encourage a company's employees to take an active role in the ownership of stock in the company
  (E) To encourage investors to diversify their stock holdings

Supporting ideas

This question asks for information explicitly stated in the passage regarding the purpose of the author's proposed requirement for advance notice of major institutional shareholders' intent to sell stock. The author explains that *old-style* capitalists did not put large amounts of stock on the market because it would only depress its value; *they could not sell out for a quick profit and instead had to concentrate on improving the long-term productivity of their companies* (lines 6–8). The requirement that major institutional shareholders notify the public before a significant sale of stock fulfills the same purpose. They would not be able to make a quick profit by *trading shares at a propitious moment* and would instead have to work toward increasing the long-term productivity of the companies in which they invest (lines 42–46).

A In this case, *the value of the stock would plummet* (lines 38–39), so it is not the author's reason for the requirement.
B The author believes institutions should *take a more active role in the operations of the companies in which they invest* (lines 31–33); the requirement should foster this participation.
C **Correct.** Throughout the passage, the author argues for investing in the long-term productivity of a company rather than making only short-term profits.

D   The passage does not discuss employee ownership of a company.

E   The passage does not discuss diversification of stock holdings.

The correct answer is C.

94. The author suggests that which of the following is a true statement about people who typify the "old-style capitalist" referred to in line 25?

(A)   They now rely on outdated management techniques.

(B)   They seldom engaged in short-term trading of the stock they owned.

(C)   They did not influence the investment policies of the corporations in which they invested.

(D)   They now play a very small role in the stock market as a result of antitrust legislation.

(E)   They were primarily concerned with maximizing the short-term profitability of the corporations in which they owned stock.

Inference

The question's use of the word *suggests* means that the answer depends on making an inference. *Old-style capitalist* refers back to lines 1–8 where there is a fuller description of the former investment environment, from which it is reasonable to infer what may be said to typify these investors. Such capitalists *owned enough stock to dominate the board of directors and dictate company policy.* Since putting a lot of their stock on the market would only depress its value, these capitalists *could not sell out for a quick profit and instead had to concentrate on improving the long-term productivity of their companies.*

A   The passage gives no indication that management techniques are outdated.

B   **Correct.** The passage explicitly states that they did not *sell out for a quick profit.*

C   The passage says just the reverse: they dictated company policy.

D   The capitalists were individual investors, and the passage does not indicate what role individual investors now play in the stock market.

E   Lines 6–8 show the reverse to be true.

The correct answer is B.

95. It can be inferred that the author makes which of the following assumptions about the businesses once controlled by individual capitalists?

(A)   These businesses were less profitable than are businesses today.

(B)   Improving long-term productivity led to increased profits.

(C)   Each business had only a few stockholders.

(D)   There was no short-term trading in the stock of these businesses.

(E)   Institutions owned no stock in these companies.

Logical Structure

To answer a question about an assumption, look at the logical structure of the author's argument. The author argues that current shareholders and managers should follow the practice of *old-style* capitalists in seeking *to enhance long-term productivity (and hence long-term profitability)* of the companies in which they invest. Since the productivity and profitability are explicitly linked in current times, the author must assume that the companies controlled by the old-style capitalists were profitable.

A   The author does not compare the profitability of past and present companies.

B   **Correct.** The author assumes that long-term productivity yields long-term profitability, in the past as well in the present.

C   Although a single investor could play a powerful role (lines 1–4), the author makes no mention of how many total shareholders there might be in any one business.

D   Investors who owned a major share of stock were not likely to sell it for quick profit (lines 4–7). The author does not suggest that other shareholders avoided short-term trading.

E   Lines 9–11 show that institutions currently hold stock, but nothing indicates that institutions did not hold stock in the past.

The correct answer is B.

96. The author suggests that the role of large institutions as stockholders differs from that of the "old-style capitalist" in part because large institutions

    (A) invest in the stock of so many companies that they cannot focus attention on the affairs of any single corporation
    (B) are prohibited by law from owning a majority of a corporation's stock
    (C) are influenced by brokers who advise against long-term ownership of stocks
    (D) are able to put large amounts of stock on the market without depressing the stock's value
    (E) are attracted to the stocks of corporations that demonstrate long-term gains in productivity

Supporting ideas

This question involves looking at the contrast the author draws between individual capitalists, who once *owned enough stock to dominate the board of directors,* and institutions, which are *prohibited by antitrust laws from owning a majority of a company's stock.*

A The passage does not indicate the number of companies institutions invest in.
B Correct. Unlike the *old-style capitalist,* an institution is prohibited by law from owning a majority of a company's stock.
C The passage never mentions brokers.
D Lines 38–39 explain that *the value of the stock would plummet.*
E No reasons are given for the institutions' choices of corporations.

The correct answer is B.

97. The primary function of the second paragraph of the passage is to

    (A) identify problems
    (B) warn of consequences
    (C) explain effects
    (D) evaluate solutions
    (E) recommend actions

Logical structure

In order to determine the purpose of the second paragraph, look at the whole passage and follow the structure of the author's argument. The author identifies a problem in the first paragraph, warning of the consequences if the problem is allowed to continue. The author then turns to a possible solution, making specific recommendations in lines 28–35. The language the author uses is a call to action: *legal limits… should be removed*; *institutions* should be *encouraged*; *any institution… should be forced.*

A The author has identified the problem in the previous paragraph.
B The author has warned of the consequences in the previous paragraph.
C The majority of the paragraph is devoted to proposing specific actions rather than to explaining effects.
D The author describes a solution, but does not evaluate either that solution or other solutions.
E Correct. In lines 28–35, the author recommends specific actions to solve the problem identified in the first paragraph.

The correct answer is E.

Questions 98–105 refer to the passage on page 54.

98. The author's main point is that

    (A) modern multinationals originated in the sixteenth and seventeenth centuries with the establishment of chartered trading companies
    (B) the success of early chartered trading companies, like that of modern multinationals, depended primarily on their ability to carry out complex operations

(C)   early chartered trading companies should be more seriously considered by scholars studying the origins of modern multinationals

(D)   scholars are quite mistaken concerning the origins of modern multinationals

(E)   the management structures of early chartered trading companies are fundamentally the same as those of modern multinationals

Main idea

To understand the main point of the whole passage, review what the author does in each paragraph. The first paragraph presents the general view that the conditions in which early trading companies operated were too primitive to make a comparison to modern multinational corporations interesting. The second paragraph corrects this impression by citing their complex activities, and the third paragraph, after reminding the reader of important differences between them, closes by saying that early trading companies *merit further study as analogues of more modern structures* (lines 53-54). The author's main point is to show that an interesting comparison between early trading companies and modern multinational companies exists and deserves further study.

A   Early trading companies share similarities with modern multinational companies but are not credited with having originated them.

B   Early trading companies are compared to modern companies on the basis of their complex activities, but their success is not discussed.

C   Correct. An interesting comparison between early trading companies and modern multinational companies may be drawn and should be further studied.

D   The author does not say that the general view is mistaken, only that a comparison of early and modern companies deserves *further study*.

E   Early trading companies had *hierarchical management structures* (line 28), but the author does not say they were the same as those in modern companies.

The correct answer is C.

99.   According to the passage, early chartered trading companies are usually described as

(A)   irrelevant to a discussion of the origins of the modern multinational corporation

(B)   interesting but ultimately too unusual to be good subjects for economic study

(C)   analogues of nineteenth-century British trading firms

(D)   rudimentary and very early forms of the modern multinational corporation

(E)   important national institutions because they existed to further the political aims of the governments of their home countries

Supporting ideas

The question uses the phrase *according to the passage,* indicating that the answer is explicitly stated in the passage. In the first paragraph, early trading companies are called *irrelevant* to a discussion about the origins of modern multinational corporations (lines 12–19).

A   Correct. The early trading companies are usually dismissed as *irrelevant* to a discussion of the origins of modern multinational corporations.

B   The passage does not characterize the early trading companies as *unusual*.

C   The passage compares the early trading companies to modern companies, not nineteenth-century ones.

D   The author argues that, in contrast to the discussions that *usually* dismiss their relevance, early trading companies do offer an interesting comparison to the modern multinationals.

E   Early trading companies *acted abroad to promote national interests* (lines 43–44), but no claim is made that they existed for solely political ends.

The correct answer is A.

100. It can be inferred from the passage that the author would characterize the activities engaged in by early chartered trading companies as being

   (A) complex enough in scope to require a substantial amount of planning and coordination on the part of management
   (B) too simple to be considered similar to those of a modern multinational corporation
   (C) as intricate as those carried out by the largest multinational corporations today
   (D) often unprofitable due to slow communications and unreliable means of transportation
   (E) hampered by the political demands imposed on them by the governments of their home countries

Inference

To discover what the author believes about the activities of early trading companies, look at the beginning of the second paragraph. The previous paragraph had ended with the prevailing dismissal of these companies as unimportant. The author begins the second paragraph with a transitional expression, *in reality, however*, to emphasize a contrasting point of view. The first sentence lists an impressive array of complex activities, and then the author notes that *the large volume of transactions associated with these activities seems to have necessitated hierarchical management structures* (lines 26–28). The author believes the complex activities of the early companies required a multi-leveled management structure to oversee them.

   A Correct. The activities of early trading companies were so complex that they required *hierarchical management structures* to oversee them (line 28).
   B This is the prevailing view rather than the author's view.
   C The author demonstrates their complexity, but does not claim they are as intricate as those of modern multinational corporations.
   D The *large volume of transactions* suggests they were profitable, but the author's focus is on the complexity of the activities rather than on their outcomes.

   E The author shows they *depended heavily* on the governments of their counties (lines 37–38), but does not imply they were *hampered* by politics.

The correct answer is A.

101. The author lists the various activities of early chartered trading companies in order to

   (A) analyze the various ways in which these activities contributed to changes in management structure in such companies
   (B) demonstrate that the volume of business transactions of such companies exceeded that of earlier firms
   (C) refute the view that the volume of business undertaken by such companies was relatively low
   (D) emphasize the international scope of these companies' operations
   (E) support the argument that such firms coordinated such activities by using available means of communication and transport

Logical structure

To find the purpose of the list in lines 20–26, look at the context that surrounds it. The previous paragraph closes with the point of view, not shared by the author, that the volume of transactions of these early companies is assumed to be *low*. The author immediately contradicts this evaluation and counters it by listing the activities the trading companies actually engaged in, noting the *large volume of transactions associated with these activities*. Thus, the author includes this list in order to attack the common assumption that the volume of business transactions was low.

A   Management structures were necessary to oversee the activities, but the passage does not mention specific ways in which the activities contributed to changes.

B   No comparison to earlier firms is made.

C   **Correct.** The list contradicts the statement in the previous paragraph that the volume of transactions was low.

D   The international scope of the activities is not in question (lines 13–15) and does not need to be defended.

E   The list is included to argue against a common assumption, not to argue for a position that this passage does not call into question.

The correct answer is C.

102.   With which of the following generalizations regarding management structures would the author of the passage most probably agree?

(A)   Hierarchical management structures are the most efficient management structures possible in a modern context.

(B)   Firms that routinely have a high volume of business transactions find it necessary to adopt hierarchical management structures.

(C)   Hierarchical management structures cannot be successfully implemented without modern communications and transportation.

(D)   Modern multinational firms with a relatively small volume of business transactions usually do not have hierarchically organized management structures.

(E)   Companies that adopt hierarchical management structures usually do so in order to facilitate expansion into foreign trade.

Application

Consider what the author says about *hierarchical management structures* in the second paragraph in order to find a statement (independent of the passage) with which the author would agree. After listing activities of the early trading companies, the author says in lines 26–28: *The large volume of transactions associated with these activities seems to have necessitated hierarchical management structures.* Thus, it is likely that the author would agree that, in general, firms with large volumes of transactions must have *hierarchical management structures.*

A   Since the passage does not discuss hierarchical management as the most efficient possible in a modern context, there is no evidence that the author would agree.

B   **Correct.** The author would agree that firms with large volumes of transactions need hierarchical management structures.

C   This statement is explicitly contradicted in lines 26–28.

D   The passage links hierarchical management with a high volume of business but provides no evidence about a low volume of business.

E   The high volume of transactions, rather than foreign trade, necessitates hierarchical management.

The correct answer is B.

103. The passage suggests that modern multinationals differ from early chartered trading companies in that

(A) the top managers of modern multinationals own stock in their own companies rather than simply receiving a salary

(B) modern multinationals depend on a system of capitalist international trade rather than on less modern trading systems

(C) modern multinationals have operations in a number of different foreign countries rather than merely in one or two

(D) the operations of modern multinationals are highly profitable despite the more stringent environmental and safety regulations of modern governments

(E) the overseas operations of modern multinationals are not governed by the national interests of their home countries

Inference

Since the question asks about differences, focus on the third paragraph, where differences are described. The first sentence is a general statement, indicating that the early trading companies *did differ strikingly from modern multinationals in many respects*. Because the author sets up this first general statement as a contrast between the early and modern companies, the examples that follow it imply that whatever is true of the early trading companies is not true of modern multinationals. Thus, when the author says the early companies *depended heavily* on their national governments, the implication is that modern companies do not.

A Lines 45–47 contradict this statement: *Senior managers' holdings in modern multinationals are usually insignificant.*

B Lines 48–49 show that the early trading companies established *a system of capitalist international trade.*

C The passage does not say that early trading companies conducted business with only one or two foreign countries.

D The passage does not imply that early trading companies failed to make profits, nor does it discuss modern regulations.

E **Correct.** The passage implies that modern multinational companies, unlike early trading companies, need not *depend heavily* on their national governments or *promote national interests* abroad.

The correct answer is E.

104. The author mentions the artisan and peasant production systems of early chartered trading companies as an example of

(A) an area of operations of these companies that was unhampered by rudimentary systems of communications and transport

(B) a similarity that allows fruitful comparison of these companies with modern multinationals

(C) a positive achievement of these companies in the face of various difficulties

(D) a system that could not have emerged in the absence of management hierarchies

(E) a characteristic that distinguishes these companies from modern multinationals

Logical structure

To answer this question, examine how the author uses this reference. It occurs in lines 47–50 as the last of three examples that show the differences between early trading companies and modern multinational companies. The trading companies *operated in a preindustrial world*, dependent on *a premodern system of artisan and peasant production*. With this example, the author is showing one of the differences between early and modern companies.

A The author does not show that artisan and peasant production systems were unhampered by primitive communication and transport.

B This reference points to a dissimilarity, not a similarity.

C The passage does not show artisan and peasant production as a positive achievement.

D The author does not link artisan and peasant production with management hierarchies.

E **Correct.** The author uses the example of artisan and peasant production systems to illustrate one of the differences between early and modern companies.

The correct answer is E.

105. The passage suggests that one of the reasons that early chartered trading companies deserve comparison with early modern multinationals is

   (A) the degree to which they both depended on new technology
   (B) the similar nature of their management structures
   (C) similarities in their top managements' degree of ownership in the company
   (D) their common dependence on political stability abroad in order to carry on foreign operations
   (E) their common tendency to revolutionize systems of production

Inference

Since the questions uses the word *suggests,* the answer depends on making an inference. In order to make an inference about one of the similarities between early and modern companies, draw together information from different parts of the passage. The author begins by noting that the modern multinational corporation is usually said to have begun when the owner-managers of nineteenth-century firms *were replaced by teams of salaried managers organized into hierarchies* (lines 4–6). The author thus associates a hierarchical management structure with modern multinational corporations. In the second paragraph, the author shows that the many transactions of early trading companies required *hierarchical management structures* to oversee them. Both early and modern companies share similar management structures.

   A The passage does not describe their dependence on new technology.
   B **Correct.** Their similar management structures lead the author to conclude that the early trading companies may aptly be compared with modern multinationals.
   C Lines 41–44 point to a difference rather than a similarity in the top managers' degree of ownership.
   D The passage does not discuss their need for political stability abroad.
   E A common tendency to revolutionize production systems is not mentioned.

The correct answer is B.

4.0 Critical Reasoning

4.0 Critical Reasoning

Critical reasoning questions appear in the Verbal section of the GMAT® exam. The Verbal section uses multiple-choice questions to measure your ability to read and comprehend written material, to reason and evaluate arguments, and to correct written material to conform to standard written English. Because the Verbal section includes content from a variety of topics, you may be generally familiar with some of the material; however, neither the passages nor the questions assume knowledge of the topics discussed. Critical reasoning questions are intermingled with reading comprehension and sentence correction questions throughout the Verbal section of the exam.

You will have 75 minutes to complete the Verbal section, or about 1¾ minutes to answer each question. Although critical reasoning questions are based on written passages, these passages are shorter than reading-comprehension passages. They tend to be less than 100 words in length and generally are followed by one or two questions. For these questions, you will see a split computer screen. The written passage will remain visible as each question associated with that passage appears in turn on the screen. You will see only one question at a time.

Critical reasoning questions are designed to test the reasoning skills involved in (1) making arguments, (2) evaluating arguments, and (3) formulating or evaluating a plan of action. The materials on which questions are based are drawn from a variety of sources. The GMAT® test does not suppose any familiarity with the subject matter of those materials.

In these questions, you are to analyze the situation on which each question is based, and then select the answer choice that most appropriately answers the question. Begin by reading the passages carefully, then read the five answer choices. If the correct answer is not immediately obvious to you, see whether you can eliminate some of the wrong answers. Reading the passage a second time may be helpful in illuminating subtleties that were not immediately evident.

Answering critical reasoning questions requires no specialized knowledge of any particular field; you don't have to have knowledge of the terminology and conventions of formal logic. The sample critical reasoning questions in this chapter illustrate the variety of topics the exam may cover, the kinds of questions it may ask, and the level of analysis it requires.

The following pages describe what critical reasoning questions are designed to measure and present the directions that will precede questions of this type. Sample questions and explanations of the correct answers follow.

4.1 What Is Measured

Critical reasoning questions are designed to provide one measure of your ability to reason effectively in the following areas:

- **Argument Construction**

  Questions in this category may ask you to recognize such things as the basic structure of an argument, properly drawn conclusions, underlying assumptions, well-supported explanatory hypotheses, or parallels between structurally similar arguments.

- **Argument Evaluation**

  These questions may ask you to analyze a given argument and to recognize such things as factors that would strengthen or weaken the given argument; reasoning errors committed in making that argument; or aspects of the method by which the argument proceeds.

- **Formulating and evaluating a plan of action**

  This type of question may ask you to recognize such things as the relative appropriateness, effectiveness, or efficiency of different plans of action; factors that would strengthen or weaken the prospects of success for a proposed plan of action; or assumptions underlying a proposed plan of action.

4.2 Test-Taking Strategies for Critical Reasoning Questions

1. **Read very carefully the set of statements on which a question is based.**

   Pay close attention to—

   - what is put forward as factual information;

   - what is not said but necessarily follows from what is said;

   - what is claimed to follow from facts that have been put forward; and

   - how well substantiated are any claims that a particular conclusion follows from the facts that have been put forward.

   In reading the arguments, it is important to pay attention to the logical reasoning used; the actual truth of statements portrayed as fact is not important.

2. **Identify the conclusion.**

   The conclusion does not necessarily come at the end of the text; it may come somewhere in the middle, or even at the beginning. Be alert to clues in the text that an argument follows logically from another statement or statements in the text.

3. **Determine exactly what each question asks.**

   You might find it helpful to read the question first, before reading the material on which it is based; don't assume that you know what you will be asked about an argument. An argument may have obvious flaws, and one question may ask you to detect them. But another question may direct you to select the one answer choice that does NOT describe a flaw in the argument.

4. **Read all the answer choices carefully.**

   Do not assume that a given answer is the best without first reading all the choices.

4.3 The Directions

These are the directions you will see for critical reasoning questions when you take the GMAT® test. If you read them carefully and understand them clearly before going to sit for the exam, you will not need to spend too much time reviewing them when you are at the test center and the exam is under way.

For this question, select the best of the answer choices given.

4.4 Critical Reasoning Sample Questions

For these questions, select the best of the answer choices given.

1. Which of the following best completes the passage below?

    In a survey of job applicants, two-fifths admitted to being at least a little dishonest. However, the survey may underestimate the proportion of job applicants who are dishonest, because_____.

    (A) some dishonest people taking the survey might have claimed on the survey to be honest
    (B) some generally honest people taking the survey might have claimed on the survey to be dishonest
    (C) some people who claimed on the survey to be at least a little dishonest may be very dishonest
    (D) some people who claimed on the survey to be dishonest may have been answering honestly
    (E) some people who are not job applicants are probably at least a little dishonest

2. Increases in the level of high-density lipoprotein (HDL) in the human bloodstream lower bloodstream cholesterol levels by increasing the body's capacity to rid itself of excess cholesterol. Levels of HDL in the bloodstream of some individuals are significantly increased by a program of regular exercise and weight reduction.

    Which of the following can be correctly inferred from the statements above?

    (A) Individuals who are underweight do not run any risk of developing high levels of cholesterol in the bloodstream.
    (B) Individuals who do not exercise regularly have a high risk of developing high levels of cholesterol in the bloodstream late in life.
    (C) Exercise and weight reduction are the most effective methods of lowering bloodstream cholesterol levels in humans.
    (D) A program of regular exercise and weight reduction lowers cholesterol levels in the bloodstream of some individuals.
    (E) Only regular exercise is necessary to decrease cholesterol levels in the bloodstream of individuals of average weight.

3. A cost-effective solution to the problem of airport congestion is to provide high-speed ground transportation between major cities lying 200 to 500 miles apart. The successful implementation of this plan would cost far less than expanding existing airports and would also reduce the number of airplanes clogging both airports and airways.

    Which of the following, if true, could proponents of the plan above most appropriately cite as a piece of evidence for the soundness of their plan?

    (A) An effective high-speed ground-transportation system would require major repairs to many highways and mass-transit improvements.
    (B) One-half of all departing flights in the nation's busiest airport head for a destination in a major city 225 miles away.
    (C) The majority of travelers departing from rural airports are flying to destinations in cities over 600 miles away.
    (D) Many new airports are being built in areas that are presently served by high-speed ground-transportation systems.
    (E) A large proportion of air travelers are vacationers who are taking long-distance flights.

4.	The price the government pays for standard weapons purchased from military contractors is determined by a pricing method called "historical costing." Historical costing allows contractors to protect their profits by adding a percentage increase, based on the current rate of inflation, to the previous year's contractual price.

Which of the following statements, if true, is the best basis for a criticism of historical costing as an economically sound pricing method for military contracts?

(A)	The government might continue to pay for past inefficient use of funds.
(B)	The rate of inflation has varied considerably over the past twenty years.
(C)	The contractual price will be greatly affected by the cost of materials used for the products.
(D)	Many taxpayers question the amount of money the government spends on military contracts.
(E)	The pricing method based on historical costing might not encourage the development of innovative weapons.

5.	Which of the following best completes the passage below? Established companies concentrate on defending what they already have. Consequently, they tend not to be innovative themselves and tend to underestimate the effects of the innovations of others. The clearest example of this defensive strategy is the fact that_____.

(A)	ballpoint pens and soft-tip markers have eliminated the traditional market for fountain pens, clearing the way for the marketing of fountain pens as luxury or prestige items
(B)	a highly successful automobile was introduced by the same company that had earlier introduced a model that had been a dismal failure
(C)	a once-successful manufacturer of slide rules reacted to the introduction of electronic calculators by trying to make better slide rules
(D)	one of the first models of modern accounting machines, designed for use in the banking industry, was purchased by a public library as well as by banks
(E)	the inventor of a commonly used anesthetic did not intend the product to be used by dentists, who currently account for almost the entire market for that drug

6.	Since the mayor's publicity campaign for Greenville's bus service began six months ago, morning automobile traffic into the midtown area of the city has decreased seven percent. During the same period, there has been an equivalent rise in the number of persons riding buses into the midtown area. Obviously, the mayor's publicity campaign has convinced many people to leave their cars at home and ride the bus to work.

Which of the following, if true, casts the most serious doubt on the conclusion drawn above?

(A)	Fares for all bus routes in Greenville have risen an average of five percent during the past six months.
(B)	The mayor of Greenville rides the bus to City Hall in the city's midtown area.
(C)	Road reconstruction has greatly reduced the number of lanes available to commuters in major streets leading to the midtown area during the past six months.
(D)	The number of buses entering the midtown area of Greenville during the morning hours is exactly the same now as it was one year ago.
(E)	Surveys show that longtime bus riders are no more satisfied with the Greenville bus service than they were before the mayor's publicity campaign began.

7. A researcher discovered that people who have low levels of immune-system activity tend to score much lower on tests of mental health than do people with normal or high immune-system activity. The researcher concluded from this experiment that the immune system protects against mental illness as well as against physical disease.

The researcher's conclusion depends on which of the following assumptions?

(A) High immune-system activity protects against mental illness better than normal immune-system activity does.

(B) Mental illness is similar to physical disease in its effects on body systems.

(C) People with high immune-system activity cannot develop mental illness.

(D) Mental illness does not cause people's immune-system activity to decrease.

(E) Psychological treatment of mental illness is not as effective as is medical treatment.

8. It is true that it is against international law to sell plutonium to countries that do not yet have nuclear weapons. But if United States companies do not do so, companies in other countries will.

Which of the following is most like the argument above in its logical structure?

(A) It is true that it is against the police department's policy to negotiate with kidnappers. But if the police want to prevent loss of life, they must negotiate in some cases.

(B) It is true that it is illegal to refuse to register for military service. But there is a long tradition in the United States of conscientious objection to serving in the armed forces.

(C) It is true that it is illegal for a government official to participate in a transaction in which there is an apparent conflict of interest. But if the facts are examined carefully, it will clearly be seen that there was no actual conflict of interest in the defendant's case.

(D) It is true that it is against the law to burglarize people's homes. But someone else certainly would have burglarized that house if the defendant had not done so first.

(E) It is true that company policy forbids supervisors to fire employees without two written warnings. But there have been many supervisors who have disobeyed this policy.

9. Extinction is a process that can depend on a variety of ecological, geographical, and physiological variables. These variables affect different species of organisms in different ways, and should, therefore, yield a random pattern of extinctions. However, the fossil record shows that extinction occurs in a surprisingly definite pattern, with many species vanishing at the same time.

Which of the following, if true, forms the best basis for at least a partial explanation of the patterned extinctions revealed by the fossil record?

(A) Major episodes of extinction can result from widespread environmental disturbances that affect numerous different species.

(B) Certain extinction episodes selectively affect organisms with particular sets of characteristics unique to their species.

(C) Some species become extinct because of accumulated gradual changes in their local environments.

(D) In geologically recent times, for which there is no fossil record, human intervention has changed the pattern of extinctions.

(E) Species that are widely dispersed are the least likely to become extinct.

10. Which of the following best completes the passage below?

At a recent conference on environmental threats to the North Sea, most participating countries favored uniform controls on the quality of effluents, whether or not specific environmental damage could be attributed to a particular source of effluent. What must, of course, be shown, in order to avoid excessively restrictive controls, is that_____.

(A) any uniform controls that are adopted are likely to be implemented without delay

(B) any substance to be made subject to controls can actually cause environmental damage

(C) the countries favoring uniform controls are those generating the largest quantities of effluents

(D) all of any given pollutant that is to be controlled actually reaches the North Sea at present

(E) environmental damage already inflicted on the North Sea is reversible

11. Shelby Industries manufactures and sells the same gauges as Jones Industries. Employee wages account for forty percent of the cost of manufacturing gauges at both Shelby Industries and Jones Industries. Shelby Industries is seeking a competitive advantage over Jones Industries. Therefore, to promote this end, Shelby Industries should lower employee wages.

Which of the following, if true, would most weaken the argument above?

(A) Because they make a small number of precision instruments, gauge manufacturers cannot receive volume discounts on raw materials.

(B) Lowering wages would reduce the quality of employee work, and this reduced quality would lead to lowered sales.

(C) Jones Industries has taken away twenty percent of Shelby Industries' business over the last year.

(D) Shelby Industries pays its employees, on average, ten percent more than does Jones Industries.

(E) Many people who work for manufacturing plants live in areas in which the manufacturing plant they work for is the only industry.

12. Large national budget deficits do not cause large trade deficits. If they did, countries with the largest budget deficits would also have the largest trade deficits. In fact, when deficit figures are adjusted so that different countries are reliably comparable to each other, there is no such correlation.

If the statements above are all true, which of the following can properly be inferred on the basis of them?

(A) Countries with large national budget deficits tend to restrict foreign trade.

(B) Reliable comparisons of the deficit figures of one country with those of another are impossible.

(C) Reducing a country's national budget deficit will not necessarily result in a lowering of any trade deficit that country may have.

(D) When countries are ordered from largest to smallest in terms of population, the smallest countries generally have the smallest budget and trade deficits.

(E) Countries with the largest trade deficits never have similarly large national budget deficits.

13. A famous singer recently won a lawsuit against an advertising firm for using another singer in a commercial to evoke the famous singer's well-known rendition of a certain song. As a result of the lawsuit, advertising firms will stop using imitators in commercials. Therefore, advertising costs will rise, since famous singers' services cost more than those of their imitators.

The conclusion above is based on which of the following assumptions?

(A) Most people are unable to distinguish a famous singer's rendition of a song from a good imitator's rendition of the same song.

(B) Commercials using famous singers are usually more effective than commercials using imitators of famous singers.

(C) The original versions of some well-known songs are unavailable for use in commercials.

(D) Advertising firms will continue to use imitators to mimic the physical mannerisms of famous singers.

(E) The advertising industry will use well-known renditions of songs in commercials.

14. The sustained massive use of pesticides in farming has two effects that are especially pernicious. First, it often kills off the pests' natural enemies in the area. Second, it often unintentionally gives rise to insecticide-resistant pests, since those insects that survive a particular insecticide will be the ones most resistant to it, and they are the ones left to breed.

From the passage above, it can be properly inferred that the effectiveness of the sustained massive use of pesticides can be extended by doing which of the following, assuming that each is a realistic possibility?

(A) Using only chemically stable insecticides
(B) Periodically switching the type of insecticide used
(C) Gradually increasing the quantities of pesticides used
(D) Leaving a few fields fallow every year
(E) Breeding higher-yielding varieties of crop plants

15. Treatment for hypertension forestalls certain medical expenses by preventing strokes and heart disease. Yet any money so saved amounts to only one-fourth of the expenditures required to treat the hypertensive population. Therefore, there is no economic justification for preventive treatment for hypertension.

Which of the following, if true, is most damaging to the conclusion above?

(A) The many fatal strokes and heart attacks resulting from untreated hypertension cause insignificant medical expenditures but large economic losses of other sorts.
(B) The cost, per patient, of preventive treatment for hypertension would remain constant even if such treatment were instituted on a large scale.
(C) In matters of health care, economic considerations should ideally not be dominant.
(D) Effective prevention presupposes early diagnosis, and programs to ensure early diagnosis are costly.

(E) The net savings in medical resources achieved by some preventive health measures are smaller than the net losses attributable to certain other measures of this kind.

16. In an attempt to promote the widespread use of paper rather than plastic, and thus reduce non-biodegradable waste, the council of a small town plans to ban the sale of disposable plastic goods for which substitutes made of paper exist. The council argues that since most paper is entirely biodegradable, paper goods are environmentally preferable.

Which of the following, if true, indicates that the plan to ban the sale of disposable plastic goods is ill suited to the town council's environmental goals?

(A) Although biodegradable plastic goods are now available, members of the town council believe biodegradable paper goods to be safer for the environment.
(B) The paper factory at which most of the townspeople are employed plans to increase production of biodegradable paper goods.
(C) After other towns enacted similar bans on the sale of plastic goods, the environmental benefits were not discernible for several years.
(D) Since most townspeople prefer plastic goods to paper goods in many instances, they are likely to purchase them in neighboring towns where plastic goods are available for sale.
(E) Products other than those derived from wood pulp are often used in the manufacture of paper goods that are entirely biodegradable.

17. Since the deregulation of airlines, delays at the nation's increasingly busy airports have increased by 25 percent. To combat this problem, more of the takeoff and landing slots at the busiest airports must be allocated to commercial airlines.

Which of the following, if true, casts the most doubt on the effectiveness of the solution proposed above?

(A) The major causes of delays at the nation's busiest airports are bad weather and overtaxed air traffic control equipment.

(B) Since airline deregulation began, the number of airplanes in operation has increased by 25 percent.

(C) Over 60 percent of the takeoff and landing slots at the nation's busiest airports are reserved for commercial airlines.

(D) After a small Midwestern airport doubled its allocation of takeoff and landing slots, the number of delays that were reported decreased by 50 percent.

(E) Since deregulation the average length of delay at the nation's busiest airports has doubled.

18. Unlike the wholesale price of raw wool, the wholesale price of raw cotton has fallen considerably in the last year. Thus, although the retail price of cotton clothing at retail clothing stores has not yet fallen, it will inevitably fall.

Which of the following, if true, most seriously weakens the argument above?

(A) The cost of processing raw cotton for cloth has increased during the last year.

(B) The wholesale price of raw wool is typically higher than that of the same volume of raw cotton.

(C) The operating costs of the average retail clothing store have remained constant during the last year.

(D) Changes in retail prices always lag behind changes in wholesale prices.

(E) The cost of harvesting raw cotton has increased in the last year.

19. Reviewer: The book Art's Decline argues that European painters today lack skills that were common among European painters of preceding centuries. In this the book must be right, since its analysis of 100 paintings, 50 old and 50 contemporary, demonstrates convincingly that none of the contemporary paintings are executed as skillfully as the older paintings.

Which of the following points to the most serious logical flaw in the reviewer's argument?

(A) The paintings chosen by the book's author for analysis could be those that most support the book's thesis.

(B) There could be criteria other than the technical skill of the artist by which to evaluate a painting.

(C) The title of the book could cause readers to accept the book's thesis even before they read the analysis of the paintings that supports it.

(D) The particular methods currently used by European painters could require less artistic skill than do methods used by painters in other parts of the world.

(E) A reader who was not familiar with the language of art criticism might not be convinced by the book's analysis of the 100 paintings.

20. A computer equipped with signature-recognition software, which restricts access to a computer to those people whose signatures are on file, identifies a person's signature by analyzing not only the form of the signature but also such characteristics as pen pressure and signing speed. Even the most adept forgers cannot duplicate all of the characteristics the program analyzes.

Which of the following can be logically concluded from the passage above?

(A) The time it takes to record and analyze a signature makes the software impractical for everyday use.

(B) Computers equipped with the software will soon be installed in most banks.

(C) Nobody can gain access to a computer equipped with the software solely by virtue of skill at forging signatures.

(D) Signature-recognition software has taken many years to develop and perfect.

(E) In many cases even authorized users are denied legitimate access to computers equipped with the software.

21. Start-up companies financed by venture capitalists have a much lower failure rate than companies financed by other means Source of financing, therefore, must be a more important causative factor in the success of a start-up company than are such factors as the personal characteristics of the entrepreneur, the quality of strategic planning, or the management structure of the company.

Which of the following, if true, most seriously weakens the argument above?

(A) Venture capitalists tend to be more responsive than other sources of financing to changes in a start-up company's financial needs.

(B) The strategic planning of a start-up company is a less important factor in the long-term success of the company than are the personal characteristics of the entrepreneur.

(C) More than half of all new companies fail within five years.

(D) The management structures of start-up companies are generally less formal than the management structures of ongoing businesses.

(E) Venture capitalists base their decisions to fund start-up companies on such factors as the characteristics of the entrepreneur and quality of strategic planning of the company.

Questions 22–23 are based on the following:

Half of the subjects in an experiment—the experimental group—consumed large quantities of a popular artificial sweetener. Afterward, this group showed lower cognitive abilities than did the other half of the subjects—the control group—who did not consume the sweetener. The detrimental effects were attributed to an amino acid that is one of the sweetener's principal constituents.

22. Which of the following, if true, would best support the conclusion that some ingredient of the sweetener was responsible for the experimental results?

(A) Most consumers of the sweetener do not consume as much of it as the experimental group members did.

(B) The amino acid referred to in the conclusion is a component of all proteins, some of which must be consumed for adequate nutrition.

(C) The quantity of the sweetener consumed by individuals in the experimental group is considered safe by federal food regulators.

(D) The two groups of subjects were evenly matched with regard to cognitive abilities prior to the experiment.

(E) A second experiment in which subjects consumed large quantities of the sweetener lacked a control group of subjects who were not given the sweetener.

23. Which of the following, if true, would best help explain how the sweetener might produce the observed effect?

(A) The government's analysis of the artificial sweetener determined that it was sold in relatively pure form.

(B) A high level of the amino acid in the blood inhibits the synthesis of a substance required for normal brain functioning.

(C) Because the sweetener is used primarily as a food additive, adverse reactions to it are rarely noticed by consumers.

(D) The amino acid that is a constituent of the sweetener is also sold separately as a dietary supplement.

(E) Subjects in the experiment did not know whether they were consuming the sweetener or a second, harmless substance.

24. In the arid land along the Colorado River, use of the river's water supply is strictly controlled: farms along the river each have a limited allocation that they are allowed to use for irrigation. But the trees that grow in narrow strips along the river's banks also use its water. Clearly, therefore, if farmers were to remove those trees, more water would be available for crop irrigation.

    Which of the following, if true, most seriously weakens the argument?

    (A) The trees along the river's banks shelter it from the sun and wind, thereby greatly reducing the amount of water lost through evaporation.
    (B) Owners of farms along the river will probably not undertake the expense of cutting down trees along the banks unless they are granted a greater allocation of water in return.
    (C) Many of the tree species currently found along the river's banks are specifically adapted to growing in places where tree roots remain constantly wet.
    (D) The strip of land where trees grow along the river's banks would not be suitable for growing crops if the trees were removed.
    (E) The distribution of water allocations for irrigation is intended to prevent farms farther upstream from using water needed by farms farther downstream.

25. Near Chicago a newly built hydroponic spinach "factory," a completely controlled environment for growing spinach, produces on 1 acre of floor space what it takes 100 acres of fields to produce. Expenses, especially for electricity, are high, however, and the spinach produced costs about four times as much as washed California field spinach, the spinach commonly sold throughout the United States.

    Which of the following, if true, best supports a projection that the spinach-growing facility near Chicago will be profitable?

    (A) Once the operators of the facility are experienced, they will be able to cut operating expenses by about 25 percent.
    (B) There is virtually no scope for any further reduction in the cost per pound for California field spinach.
    (C) Unlike washed field spinach, the hydroponically grown spinach is untainted by any pesticides or herbicides and thus will sell at exceptionally high prices to such customers as health food restaurants.
    (D) Since spinach is a crop that ships relatively well, the market for the hydroponically grown spinach is no more limited to the Chicago area than the market for California field spinach is to California.
    (E) A second hydroponic facility is being built in Canada, taking advantage of inexpensive electricity and high vegetable prices.

26. Automobile Dealer's Advertisement:

    The Highway Traffic Safety Institute reports that the PZ 1000 has the fewest injuries per accident of any car in its class. This shows that the PZ 1000 is one of the safest cars available today.

    Which of the following, if true, most seriously weakens the argument in the advertisement?

    (A) The Highway Traffic Safety Institute report listed many cars in other classes that had more injuries per accident than did the PZ 1000.
    (B) In recent years many more PZ 1000's have been sold than have any other kind of car in its class.
    (C) Cars in the class to which the PZ 1000 belongs are more likely to be involved in accidents than are other types of cars.
    (D) The difference between the number of injuries per accident for the PZ 1000 and that for other cars in its class is quite pronounced.
    (E) The Highway Traffic Safety Institute issues reports only once a year.

27. Editorial: The mayor plans to deactivate the city's fire alarm boxes, because most calls received from them are false alarms. The mayor claims that the alarm boxes are no longer necessary, since most people now have access to either public or private telephones. But the city's commercial district, where there is the greatest risk of fire, has few residents and few public telephones, so some alarm boxes are still necessary.

Which of the following, if true, most seriously weakens the editorial's argument?

(A) Maintaining the fire alarm boxes costs the city more than five million dollars annually.
(B) Commercial buildings have automatic fire alarm systems that are linked directly to the fire department.
(C) The fire department gets less information from an alarm box than it does from a telephone call.
(D) The city's fire department is located much closer to the residential areas than to the commercial district.
(E) On average, almost 25 percent of the public telephones in the city are out of order.

28. State spokesperson: Many businesspeople who have not been to our state believe that we have an inadequate road system. Those people are mistaken, as is obvious from the fact that in each of the past six years, our state has spent more money per mile on road improvements than any other state.

Which of the following, if true, most seriously undermines the reasoning in the spokesperson's argument?

(A) In the spokesperson's state, spending on road improvements has been increasing more slowly over the past six years than it has in several other states.
(B) Adequacy of a state's road system is generally less important to a businessperson considering doing business there than is the availability of qualified employees.
(C) Over the past six years, numerous businesses have left the spokesperson's state, but about as many businesses have moved into the state.

(D) In general, the number of miles of road in a state's road system depends on both the area and the population of the state.
(E) Only states with seriously inadequate road systems need to spend large amounts of money on road improvements.

29. A program instituted in a particular state allows parents to prepay their children's future college tuition at current rates. The program then pays the tuition annually for the child at any of the state's public colleges in which the child enrolls. Parents should participate in the program as a means of decreasing the cost for their children's college education.

Which of the following, if true, is the most appropriate reason for parents not to participate in the program?

(A) The parents are unsure about which public college in the state the child will attend.
(B) The amount of money accumulated by putting the prepayment funds in an interest-bearing account today will be greater than the total cost of tuition for any of the public colleges when the child enrolls.
(C) The annual cost of tuition at the state's public colleges is expected to increase at a faster rate than the annual increase in the cost of living.
(D) Some of the state's public colleges are contemplating large increases in tuition next year.
(E) The prepayment plan would not cover the cost of room and board at any of the state's public colleges.

30. Company Alpha buys free-travel coupons from people who are awarded the coupons by Bravo Airlines for flying frequently on Bravo airplanes. The coupons are sold to people who pay less for the coupons than they would pay by purchasing tickets from Bravo. This marketing of coupons results in lost revenue for Bravo.

To discourage the buying and selling of free-travel coupons, it would be best for Bravo Airlines to restrict the

(A) number of coupons that a person can be awarded in a particular year

(B) use of the coupons to those who were awarded the coupons and members of their immediate families

(C) days that the coupons can be used to Monday through Friday

(D) amount of time that the coupons can be used after they are issued

(E) number of routes on which travelers can use the coupons

31. Toughened hiring standards have not been the primary cause of the present staffing shortage in public schools. The shortage of teachers is primarily caused by the fact that in recent years teachers have not experienced any improvements in working conditions and their salaries have not kept pace with salaries in other professions.

Which of the following, if true, would most support the claims above?

(A) Many teachers already in the profession would not have been hired under the new hiring standards.

(B) Today more teachers are entering the profession with a higher educational level than in the past.

(C) Some teachers have cited higher standards for hiring as a reason for the current staffing shortage.

(D) Many teachers have cited low pay and lack of professional freedom as reasons for their leaving the profession.

(E) Many prospective teachers have cited the new hiring standards as a reason for not entering the profession.

32. A proposed ordinance requires the installation in new homes of sprinklers automatically triggered by the presence of a fire. However, a home builder argued that because more than 90 percent of residential fires are extinguished by a household member, residential sprinklers would only marginally decrease property damage caused by residential fires.

Which of the following, if true, would most seriously weaken the home builder's argument?

(A) Most individuals have no formal training in how to extinguish fires.

(B) Since new homes are only a tiny percentage of available housing in the city, the new ordinance would be extremely narrow in scope.

(C) The installation of smoke detectors in new residences costs significantly less than the installation of sprinklers.

(D) In the city where the ordinance was proposed, the average time required by the fire department to respond to a fire was less than the national average.

(E) The largest proportion of property damage that results from residential fires is caused by fires that start when no household member is present.

33. A recent spate of launching and operating mishaps with television satellites led to a corresponding surge in claims against companies underwriting satellite insurance. As a result, insurance premiums shot up, making satellites more expensive to launch and operate. This, in turn, had added to the pressure to squeeze more performance out of currently operating satellites.

Which of the following, if true, taken together with the information above, best supports the conclusion that the cost of television satellites will continue to increase?

(A) Since the risk to insurers of satellites is spread over relatively few units, insurance premiums are necessarily very high.

(B) When satellites reach orbit and then fail, the causes of failure are generally impossible to pinpoint with confidence.

(C) The greater the performance demands placed on satellites, the more frequently those satellites break down.

(D) Most satellites are produced in such small numbers that no economies of scale can be realized.

(E) Since many satellites are built by unwieldy international consortia, inefficiencies are inevitable.

Questions 34–35 refer to the following:

If the airspace around centrally located airports were restricted to commercial airliners and only those private planes equipped with radar, most of the private-plane traffic would be forced to use outlying airfields. Such a reduction in the amount of private-plane traffic would reduce the risk of midair collision around the centrally located airports.

34. The conclusion drawn in the first sentence depends on which of the following assumptions?

   (A) Outlying airfields would be as convenient as centrally located airports for most pilots of private planes.
   (B) Most outlying airfields are not equipped to handle commercial-airline traffic.
   (C) Most private planes that use centrally located airports are not equipped with radar.
   (D) Commercial airliners are at greater risk of becoming involved in midair collisions than are private planes.
   (E) A reduction in the risk of midair collision would eventually lead to increases in commercial airline traffic.

35. Which of the following, if true, would most strengthen the conclusion drawn in the second sentence?

   (A) Commercial airliners are already required by law to be equipped with extremely sophisticated radar systems.
   (B) Centrally located airports are experiencing overcrowded airspace primarily because of sharp increases in commercial-airline traffic.
   (C) Many pilots of private planes would rather buy radar equipment than be excluded from centrally located airports.
   (D) The number of midair collisions that occur near centrally located airports has decreased in recent years.
   (E) Private planes not equipped with radar systems cause a disproportionately large number of midair collisions around centrally located airports.

36. Two decades after the Emerald River Dam was built, none of the eight fish species native to the Emerald River was still reproducing adequately in the river below the dam. Since the dam reduced the annual range of water temperature in the river below the dam from 50 degrees to 6 degrees, scientists have hypothesized that sharply rising water temperatures must be involved in signaling the native species to begin the reproductive cycle.

   Which of the following statements, if true, would most strengthen the scientists' hypothesis?

   (A) The native fish species were still able to reproduce only in side streams of the river below the dam where the annual temperature range remains approximately 50 degrees.
   (B) Before the dam was built, the Emerald River annually overflowed its banks, creating backwaters that were critical breeding areas for the native species of fish.
   (C) The lowest recorded temperature of the Emerald River before the dam was built was 34 degrees, whereas the lowest recorded temperature of the river after the dam was built has been 43 degrees.
   (D) Nonnative species of fish, introduced into the Emerald River after the dam was built, have begun competing with the declining native fish species for food and space.
   (E) Five of the fish species native to the Emerald River are not native to any other river in North America.

37. Certain messenger molecules fight damage to the lungs from noxious air by telling the muscle cells encircling the lungs' airways to contract. This partially seals off the lungs. An asthma attack occurs when the messenger molecules are activated unnecessarily, in response to harmless things like pollen or household dust.

   Which of the following, if true, points to the most serious flaw of a plan to develop a medication that would prevent asthma attacks by blocking receipt of any messages sent by the messenger molecules referred to above?

(A)   Researchers do not yet know how the body produces the messenger molecules that trigger asthma attacks.
(B)   Researchers do not yet know what makes one person's messenger molecules more easily activated than another's.
(C)   Such a medication would not become available for several years, because of long lead times in both development and manufacture.
(D)   Such a medication would be unable to distinguish between messages triggered by pollen and household dust and messages triggered by noxious air.
(E)   Such a medication would be a preventative only and would be unable to alleviate an asthma attack once it had started.

38.   Which of the following best completes the passage below?

The more worried investors are about losing their money, the more they will demand a high potential return on their investment; great risks must be offset by the chance of great rewards. This principle is the fundamental one in determining interest rates, and it is illustrated by the fact that_____.

(A)   successful investors are distinguished by an ability to make very risky investments without worrying about their money
(B)   lenders receive higher interest rates on unsecured loans than on loans backed by collateral
(C)   in times of high inflation, the interest paid to depositors by banks can actually be below the rate of inflation
(D)   at any one time, a commercial bank will have a single rate of interest that it will expect all of its individual borrowers to pay
(E)   the potential return on investment in a new company is typically lower than the potential return on investment in a well-established company

39.   A certain mayor has proposed a fee of five dollars per day on private vehicles entering the city, claiming that the fee will alleviate the city's traffic congestion. The mayor reasons that, since the fee will exceed the cost of round-trip bus fare from many nearby points, many people will switch from using their cars to using the bus.

Which of the following statements, if true, provides the best evidence that the mayor's reasoning is flawed?

(A)   Projected increases in the price of gasoline will increase the cost of taking a private vehicle into the city.
(B)   The cost of parking fees already makes it considerably more expensive for most people to take a private vehicle into the city than to take a bus.
(C)   Most of the people currently riding the bus do not own private vehicles.
(D)   Many commuters opposing the mayor's plan have indicated that they would rather endure traffic congestion than pay a five-dollar-per-day fee.
(E)   During the average workday, private vehicles owned and operated by people living within the city account for 20 percent of the city's traffic congestion.

40. Dental researchers recently discovered that toothbrushes can become contaminated with bacteria that cause pneumonia and strep throat. They found that contamination usually occurs after toothbrushes have been used for four weeks. For that reason, people should replace their toothbrushes at least once a month.

Which of the following, if true, would most weaken the conclusion above?

(A) The dental researchers could not discover why toothbrush contamination usually occurred only after toothbrushes had been used for four weeks.

(B) The dental researchers failed to investigate contamination of toothbrushes by viruses, yeasts, and other pathogenic microorganisms.

(C) The dental researchers found that among people who used toothbrushes contaminated with bacteria that cause pneumonia and strep throat, the incidence of these diseases was no higher than among people who used uncontaminated toothbrushes.

(D) The dental researchers found that people who rinsed their toothbrushes thoroughly in hot water after each use were as likely to have contaminated toothbrushes as were people who only rinsed their toothbrushes hurriedly in cold water after each use.

(E) The dental researchers found that, after six weeks of use, greater length of use of a toothbrush did not correlate with a higher number of bacteria being present.

41. Leaders of a miners' union on strike against Coalco are contemplating additional measures to pressure the company to accept the union's contract proposal. The union leaders are considering as their principal new tactic a consumer boycott against Gasco gas stations, which are owned by Energy Incorporated, the same corporation that owns Coalco.

The answer to which of the following questions is LEAST directly relevant to the union leaders' consideration of whether attempting a boycott of Gasco will lead to acceptance of their contract proposal?

(A) Would revenue losses by Gasco seriously affect Energy Incorporated?

(B) Can current Gasco customers easily obtain gasoline elsewhere?

(C) Have other miners' unions won contracts similar to the one proposed by this union?

(D) Have other unions that have employed a similar tactic achieved their goals with it?

(E) Do other corporations that own coal companies also own gas stations?

Questions 42–43 are based on the following:

Transnational cooperation among corporations is experiencing a modest renaissance among United States firms, even though projects undertaken by two or more corporations under a collaborative agreement are less profitable than projects undertaken by a single corporation. The advantage of transnational cooperation is that such joint international projects may allow United States firms to win foreign contracts that they would not otherwise be able to win.

42. Which of the following statements by a United States corporate officer best fits the situation of United States firms as described in the passage above?

(A) "We would rather make only a share of the profit and also risk only a share of a possible loss than run the full risk of a loss."

(B) "We would rather make a share of a relatively modest profit than end up making none of a potentially much bigger profit."

(C) "We would rather cooperate and build good will than poison the business climate by all-out competition."

(D) "We would rather have foreign corporations join us in American projects than join them in projects in their home countries."

(E) "We would rather win a contract with a truly competitive bid of our own than get involved in less profitable collaborative agreements."

43. Which of the following is information provided by the passage above?

    (A) Transnational cooperation involves projects too big for a single corporation to handle.
    (B) Transnational cooperation results in a pooling of resources leading to high-quality performance.
    (C) Transnational cooperation has in the past been both more common and less common than it is now among United States firms.
    (D) Joint projects between United States and foreign corporations are not profitable enough to be worth undertaking.
    (E) Joint projects between United States and foreign corporations benefit only those who commission the projects.

44. Laws requiring the use of headlights during daylight hours can prevent automobile collisions. However, since daylight visibility is worse in countries farther from the equator, any such laws would obviously be more effective in preventing collisions in those countries. In fact, the only countries that actually have such laws are farther from the equator than is the continental United States.

    Which of the following conclusions could be most properly drawn from the information given above?

    (A) Drivers in the continental United States who used their headlights during the day would be just as likely to become involved in a collision as would drivers who did not use their headlights.
    (B) In many countries that are farther from the equator than is the continental United States poor daylight visibility is the single most important factor in automobile collisions.
    (C) The proportion of automobile collisions that occur in the daytime is greater in the continental United States than in the countries that have daytime headlight laws.
    (D) Fewer automobile collisions probably occur each year in countries that have daytime headlight laws than occur within the continental United States.
    (E) Daytime headlight laws would probably do less to prevent automobile collisions in the continental United States than they do in the countries that have the laws.

Questions 45–46 are based on the following

Bank depositors in the United States are all financially protected against bank failure because the government insures all individuals' bank deposits. An economist argues that this insurance is partly responsible for the high rate of bank failures, since it removes from depositors any financial incentive to find out whether the bank that holds their money is secure against failure. If depositors were more selective, then banks would need to be secure in order to compete for dositors' money.

45. The economist's argument makes which of the following assumptions?

    (A) Bank failures are caused when big borrowers default on loan repayments.
    (B) A significant proportion of depositors maintain accounts at several different banks.
    (C) The more a depositor has to deposit, the more careful he or she tends to be in selecting a bank.
    (D) The difference in the interest rates paid to depositors by different banks is not a significant factor in bank failures.
    (E) Potential depositors are able to determine which banks are secure against failure.

46. Which of the following, if true, most seriously weakens the economist's argument?

    (A) Before the government started to insure depositors against bank failure, there was a lower rate of bank failure than there is now.
    (B) When the government did not insure deposits, frequent bank failures occurred as a result of depositors' fears of losing money in bank failures.
    (C) Surveys show that a significant proportion of depositors are aware that their deposits are insured by the government.
    (D) There is an upper limit on the amount of an individual's deposit that the government will insure, but very few individuals' deposits exceed this limit.
    (E) The security of a bank against failure depends on the percentage of its assets that are loaned out and also on how much risk its loans involve.

47. A study of marital relationships in which one partner's sleeping and waking cycles differ from those of the other partner reveals that such couples share fewer activities with each other and have more violent arguments than do couples in a relationship in which both partners follow the same sleeping and waking patterns. Thus, mismatched sleeping and waking cycles can seriously jeopardize a marriage.

Which of the following, if true, most seriously weakens the argument above?

(A) Married couples in which both spouses follow the same sleeping and waking patterns also occasionally have arguments that can jeopardize the couple's marriage.

(B) The sleeping and waking cycles of individuals tend to vary from season to season.

(C) The individuals who have sleeping and waking cycles that differ significantly from those of their spouses tend to argue little with colleagues at work.

(D) People in unhappy marriages have been found to express hostility by adopting different sleeping and waking cycles from those of their spouses.

(E) According to a recent study, most people's sleeping and waking cycles can be controlled and modified easily.

48. In the past most airline companies minimized aircraft weight to minimize fuel costs. The safest airline seats were heavy, and airlines equipped their planes with few of these seats. This year the seat that has sold best to airlines has been the safest one—a clear indication that airlines are assigning a higher priority to safe seating than to minimizing fuel costs.

Which of the following, if true, most seriously weakens the argument above?

(A) Last year's best-selling airline seat was not the safest airline seat on the market.

(B) No airline company has announced that it would be making safe seating a higher priority this year.

(C) The price of fuel was higher this year than it had been in most of the years when the safest airline seats sold poorly.

(D) Because of increases in the cost of materials, all airline seats were more expensive to manufacture this year than in any previous year.

(E) Because of technological innovations, the safest airline seat on the market this year weighed less than most other airline seats on the market.

49. Division Manager: I want to replace the Microton computers in my division with Vitech computers.

General Manager: Why?

Division Manager: It costs 28 percent less to train new staff on the Vitech.

General Manager: But that is not a good enough reason. We can simply hire only people who already know how to use the Microton computer.

Which of the following, if true, most seriously undermines the general manager's objection to the replacement of Microton computers with Vitechs?

(A) Currently all employees in the company are required to attend workshops on how to use Microton computers in new applications.

(B) Once employees learn how to use a computer, they tend to change employers more readily than before.

(C) Experienced users of Microton computers command much higher salaries than do prospective employees who have no experience in the use of computers.

(D) The average productivity of employees in the general manager's company is below the average productivity of the employees of its competitors.

(E) The high costs of replacement parts make Vitech computers more expensive to maintain than Microton computers.

50. Crops can be traded on the futures market before they are harvested. If a poor corn harvest is predicted, prices of corn futures rise; if a bountiful corn harvest is predicted, prices of corn futures fall. This morning meteorologists are predicting much-needed rain for the corn-growing region starting tomorrow. Therefore, since adequate moisture is essential for the current crop's survival, prices of corn futures will fall sharply today.

    Which of the following, if true, most weakens the argument above?

    (A)   Corn that does not receive adequate moisture during its critical pollination stage will not produce a bountiful harvest.
    (B)   Futures prices for corn have been fluctuating more dramatically this season than last season.
    (C)   The rain that meteorologists predicted for tomorrow is expected to extend well beyond the corn-growing region.
    (D)   Agriculture experts announced today that a disease that has devastated some of the corn crop will spread widely before the end of the growing season.
    (E)   Most people who trade in corn futures rarely take physical possession of the corn they trade.

51. The interview is an essential part of a successful hiring program because, with it, job applicants who have personalities that are unsuited to the requirements of the job will be eliminated from consideration.

    The argument above logically depends on which of the following assumptions?

    (A)   A hiring program will be successful if it includes interviews.
    (B)   The interview is a more important part of a successful hiring program than is the development of a job description.
    (C)   Interviewers can accurately identify applicants whose personalities are unsuited to the requirements of the job.

    (D)   The only purpose of an interview is to evaluate whether job applicants' personalities are suited to the requirements of the job.
    (E)   The fit of job applicants' personalities to the requirements of the job was once the most important factor in making hiring decisions.

52. Useful protein drugs, such as insulin, must still be administered by the cumbersome procedure of injection under the skin. If proteins are taken orally, they are digested and cannot reach their target cells. Certain nonprotein drugs, however, contain chemical bonds that are not broken down by the digestive system. They can, thus, be taken orally.

    The statements above most strongly support a claim that a research procedure that successfully accomplishes which of the following would be beneficial to users of protein drugs?

    (A)   Coating insulin with compounds that are broken down by target cells, but whose chemical bonds are resistant to digestion
    (B)   Converting into protein compounds, by procedures that work in the laboratory, the nonprotein drugs that resist digestion
    (C)   Removing permanently from the digestive system any substances that digest proteins
    (D)   Determining, in a systematic way, what enzymes and bacteria are present in the normal digestive system and whether they tend to be broken down within the body
    (E)   Determining the amount of time each nonprotein drug takes to reach its target cells

53. There is a great deal of geographical variation in the frequency of many surgical procedures—up to tenfold variation per hundred thousand people among different areas in the numbers of hysterectomies, prostatectomies, and tonsillectomies.

To support a conclusion that much of the variation is due to unnecessary surgical procedures, it would be most important to establish which of the following?

(A) A local board of review at each hospital examines the records of every operation to determine whether the surgical procedure was necessary.

(B) The variation is unrelated to factors (other than the surgical procedures themselves) that influence the incidence of diseases for which surgery might be considered.

(C) There are several categories of surgical procedure (other than hysterectomies, prostatectomies, and tonsillectomies) that are often performed unnecessarily.

(D) For certain surgical procedures, it is difficult to determine after the operation whether the procedures were necessary or whether alternative treatment would have succeeded.

(E) With respect to how often they are performed unnecessarily, hysterectomies, prostatectomies, and tonsillectomies are representative of surgical procedures in general.

54. A museum has been offered an undocumented statue, supposedly Greek and from the sixth century B.C. Possibly the statue is genuine but undocumented because it was recently unearthed or because it has been privately owned. However, an ancient surface usually has uneven weathering, whereas the surface of this statue has the uniform quality characteristically produced by a chemical bath used by forgers to imitate a weathered surface. Therefore, the statue is probably a forgery.

Which of the following, if true, most seriously weakens the argument?

(A) Museums can accept a recently unearthed statue only with valid export documentation from its country of origin.

(B) The subject's pose and other aspects of the subject's treatment exhibit all the most common features of Greek statues of the sixth century B.C.

(C) The chemical bath that forgers use was at one time used by dealers and collectors to remove the splotchy surface appearance of genuinely ancient sculptures.

(D) Museum officials believe that forgers have no technique that can convincingly simulate the patchy weathering characteristic of the surfaces of ancient sculptures.

(E) An allegedly Roman sculpture with a uniform surface similar to that of the statue being offered to the museum was recently shown to be a forgery.

55. Studies have shown that elderly people who practice a religion are much more likely to die immediately after an important religious holiday period than immediately before one. Researchers have concluded that the will to live can prolong life, at least for short periods of time.

Which of the following, if true, would most strengthen the researchers' conclusion?

(A) Elderly people who practice a religion are less likely to die immediately before or during an important religious holiday than at any other time of the year.

(B) Elderly people who practice a religion appear to experience less anxiety at the prospect of dying than do other people.

(C) Some elderly people who do practice a religion live much longer than most elderly people who do not.

(D) Most elderly people who participate in religious holidays have different reasons for participating than young people do.

(E) Many religions have important holidays in the spring and fall, seasons with the lowest death rates for elderly people.

56. Gortland has long been narrowly self-sufficient in both grain and meat. However, as per capita income in Gortland has risen toward the world average, per capita consumption of meat has also risen toward the world average, and it takes several pounds of grain to produce one pound of meat. Therefore, since per capita income continues to rise, whereas domestic grain production will not increase, Gortland will soon have to import either grain or meat or both.

Which of the following is an assumption on which the argument depends?

(A) The total acreage devoted to grain production in Gortland will not decrease substantially.

(B) The population of Gortland has remained relatively constant during the country's years of growing prosperity.

(C) The per capita consumption of meat in Gortland is roughly the same across all income levels.

(D) In Gortland, neither meat nor grain is subject to government price controls.

(E) People in Gortland who increase their consumption of meat will not radically decrease their consumption of grain.

57. Meteorite explosions in the Earth's atmosphere as large as the one that destroyed forests in Siberia, with approximately the force of a 12-megaton nuclear blast, occur about once a century.

The response of highly automated systems controlled by complex computer programs to unexpected circumstances is unpredictable.

Which of the following conclusions can most properly be drawn, if the statements above are true, about a highly automated nuclear-missile defense system controlled by a complex computer program?

(A) Within a century after its construction, the system would react inappropriately and might accidentally start a nuclear war.

(B) The system would be destroyed if an explosion of a large meteorite occurred in the Earth's atmosphere.

(C) It would be impossible for the system to distinguish the explosion of a large meteorite from the explosion of a nuclear weapon.

(D) Whether the system would respond inappropriately to the explosion of a large meteorite would depend on the location of the blast.

(E) It is not certain what the system's response to the explosion of a large meteorite would be, if its designers did not plan for such a contingency.

Questions 58–59 are based on the following:

If there is an oil-supply disruption resulting in higher international oil prices, domestic oil prices in open-market countries such as the United States will rise as well, whether such countries import all or none of their oil.

58. If the statement above concerning oil-supply disruptions is true, which of the following policies in an open-market nation is most likely to reduce the long-term economic impact on that nation of sharp and unexpected increases in international oil prices?

(A) Maintaining the quantity of oil imported at constant yearly levels

(B) Increasing the number of oil tankers in its fleet

(C) Suspending diplomatic relations with major oil-producing nations

(D) Decreasing oil consumption through conservation

(E) Decreasing domestic production of oil

59. Which of the following conclusions is best supported by the statement above?

    (A) Domestic producers of oil in open-market countries are excluded from the international oil market when there is a disruption in the international oil supply.

    (B) International oil-supply disruptions have little, if any, effect on the price of domestic oil as long as an open-market country has domestic supplies capable of meeting domestic demand.

    (C) The oil market in an open-market country is actually part of the international oil market, even if most of that country's domestic oil is usually sold to consumers within its borders.

    (D) Open-market countries that export little or none of their oil can maintain stable domestic oil prices even when international oil prices rise sharply.

    (E) If international oil prices rise, domestic distributors of oil in open-market countries will begin to import more oil than they export.

60. Most archaeologists have held that people first reached the Americas less than 20,000 years ago by crossing a land bridge into North America. But recent discoveries of human shelters in South America dating from 32,000 years ago have led researchers to speculate that people arrived in South America first, after voyaging across the Pacific, and then spread northward.

    Which of the following, if it were discovered, would be pertinent evidence against the speculation above?

    (A) A rock shelter near Pittsburgh, Pennsylvania, contains evidence of use by human beings 19,000 years ago.

    (B) Some North American sites of human habitation predate any sites found in South America.

    (C) The climate is warmer at the 32,000-year-old South American site than at the oldest known North American site.

    (D) The site in South America that was occupied 32,000 years ago was continuously occupied until 6,000 years ago.

    (E) The last Ice Age, between 11,500 and 20,000 years ago, considerably lowered worldwide sea levels.

61. The tobacco industry is still profitable and projections are that it will remain so. In the United States this year, the total amount of tobacco sold by tobacco farmers has increased, even though the number of adults who smoke has decreased.

    Each of the following, if true, could explain the simultaneous increase in tobacco sales and decrease in the number of adults who smoke EXCEPT:

    (A) During this year, the number of women who have begun to smoke is greater than the number of men who have quit smoking.

    (B) The number of teenage children who have begun to smoke this year is greater than the number of adults who have quit smoking during the same period.

    (C) During this year, the number of nonsmokers who have begun to use chewing tobacco or snuff is greater than the number of people who have quit smoking.

    (D) The people who have continued to smoke consume more tobacco per person than they did in the past.

    (E) More of the cigarettes made in the United States this year were exported to other countries than was the case last year.

62. A milepost on the towpath read "21" on the side facing the hiker as she approached it and "23" on its back. She reasoned that the next milepost forward on the path would indicate that she was halfway between one end of the path and the other. However, the milepost one mile further on read "20" facing her and "24" behind.

    Which of the following, if true, would explain the discrepancy described above?

(A) The numbers on the next milepost had been reversed.

(B) The numbers on the mileposts indicate kilometers, not miles.

(C) The facing numbers indicate miles to the end of the path, not miles from the beginning.

(D) A milepost was missing between the two the hiker encountered.

(E) The mileposts had originally been put in place for the use of mountain bikers, not for hikers.

63. Traditionally, decision making by managers that is reasoned step-by-step has been considered preferable to intuitive decision making. However, a recent study found that top managers used intuition significantly more than did most middle- or lower-level managers. This confirms the alternative view that intuition is actually more effective than careful, methodical reasoning.

The conclusion above is based on which of the following assumptions?

(A) Methodical, step-by-step reasoning is inappropriate for making many real-life management decisions.

(B) Top managers have the ability to use either intuitive reasoning or methodical, step-by-step reasoning in making decisions.

(C) The decisions made by middle- and lower-level managers can be made as easily by using methodical reasoning as by using intuitive reasoning.

(D) Top managers use intuitive reasoning in making the majority of their decisions.

(E) Top managers are more effective at decision making than middle- or lower-level managers.

64. High levels of fertilizer and pesticides, needed when farmers try to produce high yields of the same crop year after year, pollute water supplies. Experts therefore urge farmers to diversify their crops and to rotate their plantings yearly.

To receive governmental price-support benefits for a crop, farmers must have produced that same crop for the past several years.

The statements above, if true, best support which of the following conclusions?

(A) The rules for governmental support of farm prices work against efforts to reduce water pollution.

(B) The only solution to the problem of water pollution from fertilizers and pesticides is to take farmland out of production.

(C) Farmers can continue to make a profit by rotating diverse crops, thus reducing costs for chemicals, but not by planting the same crop each year.

(D) New farming techniques will be developed to make it possible for farmers to reduce the application of fertilizers and pesticides.

(E) Governmental price supports for farm products are set at levels that are not high enough to allow farmers to get out of debt.

Questions 65–66 are based on the following:

Hardin argued that grazing land held in common (that is, open to any user) would always be used less carefully than private grazing land. Each rancher would be tempted to overuse common land because the benefits would accrue to the individual, while the costs of reduced land quality that result from overuse would be spread among all users. But a study comparing 217 million acres of common grazing land with 433 million acres of private grazing land showed that the common land was in better condition.

65. The answer to which of the following questions would be most useful in evaluating the significance, in relation to Hardin's claim, of the study described above?

(A) Did any of the ranchers whose land was studied use both common and private land?

(B) Did the ranchers whose land was studied tend to prefer using common land over using private land for grazing?

(C) Was the private land that was studied of comparable quality to the common land before either was used for grazing?

(D) Were the users of the common land that was studied at least as prosperous as the users of the private land?

(E) Were there any owners of herds who used only common land, and no private land, for grazing?

66. Which of the following, if true and known by the ranchers, would best help explain the results of the study?

(A) With private grazing land, both the costs and the benefits of overuse fall to the individual user.

(B) The cost in reduced land quality that is attributable to any individual user is less easily measured with common land than it is with private land.

(C) An individual who overuses common grazing land might be able to achieve higher returns than other users can, with the result that he or she would obtain a competitive advantage.

(D) If one user of common land overuses it even slightly, the other users are likely to do so even more, with the consequence that the costs to each user outweigh the benefits.

(E) There are more acres of grazing land held privately than there are held in common.

67. A compelling optical illusion called the illusion of velocity and size makes objects appear to be moving more slowly the larger the objects are. Therefore, a motorist's estimate of the time available for crossing a highway with a small car approaching is bound to be lower than it would be with a large truck approaching.

The conclusion above would be more properly drawn if it were made clear that the_____.

(A) truck's speed is assumed to be lower than the car's

(B) truck's speed is assumed to be the same as the car's

(C) truck's speed is assumed to be higher than the car's

(D) motorist's estimate of time available is assumed to be more accurate with cars approaching than with trucks approaching

(E) motorist's estimate of time available is assumed to be more accurate with trucks approaching than with cars approaching

68. Advocates of a large-scale space-defense research project conclude that it will represent a net benefit to civilian business. They say that since government-sponsored research will have civilian applications, civilian businesses will reap the rewards of government-developed technology.

Each of the following, if true, raises a consideration arguing against the conclusion above, EXCEPT:

(A) The development of cost-efficient manufacturing techniques is of the highest priority for civilian business and would be neglected if resources go to military projects, which do not emphasize cost efficiency.

(B) Scientific and engineering talent needed by civilian business will be absorbed by the large-scale project.

(C) Many civilian businesses will receive subcontracts to provide materials and products needed by the research project.

(D) If government research money is devoted to the space project, it will not be available for specifically targeted needs of civilian business, where it could be more efficiently used.

(E) The increase in taxes or government debt needed to finance the project will severely reduce the vitality of the civilian economy.

69. Manufacturers sometimes discount the price of a product to retailers for a promotion period when the product is advertised to consumers. Such promotions often result in a dramatic increase in amount of product sold by the manufacturers to retailers. Nevertheless, the manufacturers could often make more profit by not holding the promotions.

Which of the following, if true, most strongly supports the claim above about the manufacturers' profit?

(A) The amount of discount generally offered by manufacturers to retailers is carefully calculated to represent the minimum needed to draw consumers' attention to the product.

(B) For many consumer products the period of advertising discounted prices to consumers is about a week, not sufficiently long for consumers to become used to the sale price.

(C) For products that are not newly introduced, the purpose of such promotions is to keep the products in the minds of consumers and to attract consumers who are currently using competing products.

(D) During such a promotion retailers tend to accumulate in their warehouses inventory bought at discount; they then sell much of it later at their regular price.

(E) If a manufacturer fails to offer such promotions but its competitor offers them, that competitor will tend to attract consumers away from the manufacturer's product.

70. When people evade income taxes by not declaring taxable income, a vicious cycle results. Tax evasion forces lawmakers to raise income tax rates, which causes the tax burden on non-evading taxpayers to become heavier. This, in turn, encourages even more taxpayers to evade income taxes by hiding taxable income.

The vicious cycle described above could not result unless which of the following were true?

(A) An increase in tax rates tends to function as an incentive for taxpayers to try to increase their pretax incomes.

(B) Some methods for detecting tax evaders, and thus recovering some tax revenue lost through evasion, bring in more than they cost, but their success rate varies from year to year.

(C) When lawmakers establish income tax rates in order to generate a certain level of revenue, they do not allow adequately for revenue that will be lost through evasion.

(D) No one who routinely hides some taxable income can be induced by a lowering of tax rates to stop hiding such income unless fines for evaders are raised at the same time.

(E) Taxpayers do not differ from each other with respect to the rate of taxation that will cause them to evade taxes.

71. Because postage rates are rising, *Home Decorator* magazine plans to maximize its profits by reducing by one-half the number of issues it publishes each year. The quality of articles, the number of articles published per year, and the subscription price will not change. Market research shows that neither subscribers nor advertisers will be lost if the magazine's plan is instituted.

Which of the following, if true, provides the strongest evidence that the magazine's profits are likely to decline if the plan is instituted?

(A) With the new postage rates, a typical issue under the proposed plan would cost about one-third more to mail than a typical current issue would.

(B) The majority of the magazine's subscribers are less concerned about a possible reduction in the quantity of the magazine's articles than about a possible loss of the current high quality of its articles.

(C) Many of the magazine's long-time subscribers would continue their subscriptions even if the subscription price were increased.

(D) Most of the advertisers that purchase advertising space in the magazine will continue to spend the same amount on advertising per issue as they have in the past.

(E) Production costs for the magazine are expected to remain stable.

72. A discount retailer of basic household necessities employs thousands of people and pays most of them at the minimum wage rate. Yet following a federally mandated increase of the minimum wage rate that increased the retailer's operating costs considerably, the retailer's profits increased markedly.

Which of the following, if true, most helps to resolve the apparent paradox?

(A) Over half of the retailer's operating costs consist of payroll expenditures; yet only a small percentage of those expenditures go to pay management salaries.

(B) The retailer's customer base is made up primarily of people who earn, or who depend on the earnings of others who earn, the minimum wage.

(C) The retailer's operating costs, other than wages, increased substantially after the increase in the minimum wage rate went into effect.

(D) When the increase in the minimum wage rate went into effect, the retailer also raised the wage rate for employees who had been earning just above minimum wage.

(E) The majority of the retailer's employees work as cashiers, and most cashiers are paid the minimum wage.

73. The cotton farms of Country Q became so productive that the market could not absorb all that they produced. Consequently, cotton prices fell. The government tried to boost cotton prices by offering farmers who took 25 percent of their cotton acreage out of production direct support payments up to a specified maximum per farm.

The government's program, if successful, will not be a net burden on the budget. Which of the following, if true, is the best basis for an explanation of how this could be so?

(A) Depressed cotton prices meant operating losses for cotton farms, and the government lost revenue from taxes on farm profits.

(B) Cotton production in several countries other than Q declined slightly the year that the support-payment program went into effect in Q.

(C) The first year that the support-payment program was in effect, cotton acreage in Q was 5 percent below its level in the base year for the program.

(D) The specified maximum per farm meant that for very large cotton farms the support payments were less per acre for those acres that were withdrawn from production than they were for smaller farms.

(E)   Farmers who wished to qualify for support payments could not use the cotton acreage that was withdrawn from production to grow any other crop.

74.   United States hospitals have traditionally relied primarily on revenues from paying patients to offset losses from unreimbursed care. Almost all paying patients now rely on governmental or private health insurance to pay hospital bills. Recently, insurers have been strictly limiting what they pay hospitals for the care of insured patients to amounts at or below actual costs.

Which of the following conclusions is best supported by the information above?

(A)   Although the advance of technology has made expensive medical procedures available to the wealthy, such procedures are out of the reach of low-income patients.

(B)   If hospitals do not find ways of raising additional income for unreimbursed care, they must either deny some of that care or suffer losses if they give it.

(C)   Some patients have incomes too high for eligibility for governmental health insurance but are unable to afford private insurance for hospital care.

(D)   If the hospitals reduce their costs in providing care, insurance companies will maintain the current level of reimbursement, thereby providing more funds for unreimbursed care.

(E)   Even though philanthropic donations have traditionally provided some support for the hospitals, such donations are at present declining.

75.   Generally scientists enter their field with the goal of doing important new research and accept as their colleagues those with similar motivation. Therefore, when any scientist wins renown as an expounder of science to general audiences, most other scientists conclude that this popularizer should no longer be regarded as a true colleague.

The explanation offered above for the low esteem in which scientific popularizers are held by research scientists assumes that

(A)   serious scientific research is not a solitary activity, but relies on active cooperation among a group of colleagues

(B)   research scientists tend not to regard as colleagues those scientists whose renown they envy

(C)   a scientist can become a famous popularizer without having completed any important research

(D)   research scientists believe that those who are well known as popularizers of science are not motivated to do important new research

(E)   no important new research can be accessible to or accurately assessed by those who are not themselves scientists

76.   Country Y uses its scarce foreign-exchange reserves to buy scrap iron for recycling into steel. Although the steel thus produced earns more foreign exchange than it costs, that policy is foolish. Country Y's own territory has vast deposits of iron ore, which can be mined with minimal expenditure of foreign exchange.

Which of the following, if true, provides the strongest support for Country Y's policy of buying scrap iron abroad?

(A)   The price of scrap iron on international markets rose significantly in 1987.

(B)   Country Y's foreign-exchange reserves dropped significantly in 1987.

(C)   There is virtually no difference in quality between steel produced from scrap iron and that produced from iron ore.

(D)   Scrap iron is now used in the production of roughly half the steel used in the world today, and experts predict that scrap iron will be used even more extensively in the future.

(E)   Furnaces that process scrap iron can be built and operated in Country Y with substantially less foreign exchange than can furnaces that process iron ore.

77. Parasitic wasps lay their eggs directly into the eggs of various host insects in exactly the right numbers for any suitable size of host egg. If they laid too many eggs in a host egg, the developing wasp larvae would compete with each other to the death for nutrients and space. If too few eggs were laid, portions of the host egg would decay, killing the wasp larvae.

    Which of the following conclusions can properly be drawn from the information above?

    (A) The size of the smallest host egg that a wasp could theoretically parasitize can be determined from the wasp's egg-laying behavior.
    (B) Host insects lack any effective defenses against the form of predation practiced by parasitic wasps.
    (C) Parasitic wasps learn from experience how many eggs to lay into the eggs of different host species.
    (D) Failure to lay enough eggs would lead to the death of the developing wasp larvae more quickly than would laying too many eggs.
    (E) Parasitic wasps use visual clues to calculate the size of a host egg.

78. Consumer health advocate: Your candy company adds caffeine to your chocolate candy bars so that each one delivers a specified amount of caffeine. Since caffeine is highly addictive, this indicates that you intend to keep your customers addicted.

    Candy manufacturer: Our manufacturing process results in there being less caffeine in each chocolate candy bar than in the unprocessed cacao beans from which the chocolate is made.

    The candy manufacturer's response is flawed as a refutation of the consumer health advocate's argument because it_____.

    (A) fails to address the issue of whether the level of caffeine in the candy bars sold by the manufacturer is enough to keep people addicted
    (B) assumes without warrant that all unprocessed cacao beans contain a uniform amount of caffeine

    (C) does not specify exactly how caffeine is lost in the manufacturing process
    (D) treats the consumer health advocate's argument as though it were about each candy bar rather than about the manufacturer's candy in general
    (E) merely contradicts the consumer health advocate's conclusion without giving any reason to believe that the advocate's reasoning is unsound

79. To evaluate a plan to save money on office-space expenditures by having its employees work at home, XYZ Company asked volunteers from its staff to try the arrangement for six months. During this period, the productivity of these employees was as high as or higher than before.

    Which of the following, if true, would argue most strongly against deciding, on the basis of the trial results, to implement the company's plan?

    (A) The employees who agreed to participate in the test of the plan were among the company's most self-motivated and independent workers.
    (B) The savings that would accrue from reduced office-space expenditures alone would be sufficient to justify the arrangement for the company, apart from any productivity increases.
    (C) Other companies that have achieved successful results from work-at-home plans have work forces that are substantially larger than that of XYZ.
    (D) The volunteers who worked at home were able to communicate with other employees as necessary for performing the work.
    (E) Minor changes in the way office work is organized at XYZ would yield increases in employee productivity similar to those achieved in the trial.

80. Vitacorp, a manufacturer, wishes to make its information booth at an industry convention more productive in terms of boosting sales. The booth offers information introducing the company's new products and services. To achieve the desired result, Vitacorp's marketing department will attempt to attract more people to the booth. The marketing director's first measure was to instruct each salesperson to call his or her five best customers and personally invite them to visit the booth.

Which of the following, if true, most strongly supports the prediction that the marketing director's first measure will contribute to meeting the goal of boosting sales?

(A) Vitacorp's salespeople routinely inform each important customer about new products and services as soon as the decision to launch them has been made.

(B) Many of Vitacorp's competitors have made plans for making their own information booths more productive in increasing sales.

(C) An information booth that is well attended tends to attract visitors who would not otherwise have attended the booth.

(D) Most of Vitacorp's best customers also have business dealings with Vitacorp's competitors.

(E) Vitacorp has fewer new products and services available this year than it had in previous years.

81. An eyeglass manufacturer tried to boost sales for the summer quarter by offering its distributors a special discount if their orders for that quarter exceeded those for last year's summer quarter by at least 20 percent. Many distributors qualified for this discount. Even with much merchandise discounted, sales increased enough to produce a healthy gain in net profits. The manufacturer plans to repeat this success by offering the same sort of discount for the fall quarter.

Which of the following, if true, most clearly points to a flaw in the manufacturer's plan to repeat the successful performance of the summer quarter?

(A) In general, a distributor's orders for the summer quarter are no higher than those for the spring quarter.

(B) Along with offering special discounts to qualifying distributors, the manufacturer increased newspaper and radio advertising in those distributors' sales areas.

(C) The distributors most likely to qualify for the manufacturer's special discount are those whose orders were unusually low a year earlier.

(D) The distributors who qualified for the manufacturer's special discount were free to decide how much of that discount to pass on to their own customers.

(E) The distributors' ordering more goods in the summer quarter left them overstocked for the fall quarter.

82. Consumer advocate: It is generally true, at least in this state, that lawyers who advertise a specific service charge less for that service than lawyers who do not advertise. It is also true that **each time restrictions on the advertising of legal services have been eliminated, the number of lawyers advertising their services has increased and legal costs to consumers have declined in consequence.** However, eliminating the state requirement that legal advertisements must specify fees for specific services would almost certainly increase rather than further reduce consumers' legal costs. Lawyers would **no longer have an incentive to lower their fees when they begin advertising and if no longer required to specify fee arrangements, many lawyers who now advertise would increase their fees.**

In the consumer advocate's argument, the two portions in boldface play which of the following roles?

(A) The first is a generalization that the consumer advocate accepts as true; the second is presented as a consequence that follows from the truth of that generalization.

(B) The first is a pattern of cause and effect that the consumer advocate argues will be repeated in the case at issue; the second acknowledges a circumstance in which that pattern would not hold.

(C) The first is a pattern of cause and effect that the consumer advocate predicts will not hold in the case at issue; the second offers a consideration in support of that prediction.

(D) The first is evidence that the consumer advocate offers in support of a certain prediction; the second is that prediction.

(E) The first acknowledges a consideration that weighs against the main position that the consumer advocate defends; the second is that position.

4.5 Critical Reasoning Answer Key

1.	A	32.	E	63.	E
2.	D	33.	C	64.	A
3.	B	34.	C	65.	C
4.	A	35.	E	66.	D
5.	C	36.	A	67.	B
6.	C	37.	D	68.	C
7.	D	38.	B	69.	D
8.	D	39.	B	70.	C
9.	A	40.	C	71.	D
10.	B	41.	E	72.	B
11.	B	42.	B	73.	A
12.	C	43.	C	74.	B
13.	E	44.	E	75.	D
14.	B	45.	E	76.	E
15.	A	46.	B	77.	A
16.	D	47.	D	78.	A
17.	A	48.	E	79.	A
18.	A	49.	C	80.	C
19.	A	50.	D	81.	E
20.	C	51.	C	82.	C
21.	E	52.	A		
22.	D	53.	B		
23.	B	54.	C		
24.	A	55.	A		
25.	C	56.	E		
26.	C	57.	E		
27.	B	58.	D		
28.	E	59.	C		
29.	B	60.	B		
30.	B	61.	A		
31.	D	62.	C		

4.6 Critical Reasoning Answer Explanations

The following discussion is intended to familiarize you with the most efficient and effective approaches to critical reasoning questions. The particular questions in this chapter are generally representative of the kinds of critical reasoning questions you will encounter on the GMAT®. Remember that it is the problem solving strategy that is important, not the specific details of a particular question.

1. Which of the following best completes the passage below?

    In a survey of job applicants, two-fifths admitted to being at least a little dishonest. However, the survey may underestimate the proportion of job applicants who are dishonest, because_____.

    (A) some dishonest people taking the survey might have claimed on the survey to be honest

    (B) some generally honest people taking the survey might have claimed on the survey to be dishonest

    (C) some people who claimed on the survey to be at least a little dishonest may be very dishonest

    (D) some people who claimed on the survey to be dishonest may have been answering honestly

    (E) some people who are not job applicants are probably at least a little dishonest

    Argument Evaluation

    Situation   Survey asking about dishonesty may underestimate dishonesty.

    Reasoning   *How could the survey present an underestimate?* Accurate survey results depend on honest answers. If some dishonest people say they are honest, then the real number of dishonest people is actually higher than the survey states. The survey therefore may underestimate how many people are dishonest.

    A   **Correct.** This statement properly identifies the error in the survey method.
    B   This leads to an overestimate, not an underestimate.
    C   The degree of dishonesty is irrelevant.
    D   This leads to a correct estimate, not an underestimate.
    E   People who are not job applicants are irrelevant.

    The correct answer is A.

2. Increases in the level of high-density lipoprotein (HDL) in the human bloodstream lower bloodstream cholesterol levels by increasing the body's capacity to rid itself of excess cholesterol. Levels of HDL in the bloodstream of some individuals are significantly increased by a program of regular exercise and weight reduction.

Which of the following can be correctly inferred from the statements above?

(A) Individuals who are underweight do not run any risk of developing high levels of cholesterol in the bloodstream.

(B) Individuals who do not exercise regularly have a high risk of developing high levels of cholesterol in the bloodstream late in life.

(C) Exercise and weight reduction are the most effective methods of lowering bloodstream cholesterol levels in humans.

(D) A program of regular exercise and weight reduction lowers cholesterol levels in the bloodstream of some individuals.

(E) Only regular exercise is necessary to decrease cholesterol levels in the bloodstream of individuals of average weight.

Argument Construction

Situation   Higher HDL levels in the bloodstream reduce cholesterol. Regular exercise and weight reduction promote higher HDL levels in some people.

Reasoning   *What inference is supported by this information?* The first statement is a general one, applying to all people. The second one applies only to some people. The resulting inference can be made only about some people, not everyone. Because some people achieve higher HDL levels through a program of regular exercise and weight reduction, these individuals will have lower cholesterol levels.

A   The passage draws no comparison between being underweight and having lower cholesterol levels.

B   The passage does not discuss lack of regular exercise as a risk factor for the development of high bloodstream cholesterol late in life.

C   Other possible methods of lowering cholesterol levels are not discussed, and so a program of exercise and weight reduction cannot be inferred to be the best method. Moreover, a general inference applying to all humans cannot be made of the basis of some individuals.

D   **Correct.** This statement properly identifies the inference that, since a program of exercise and weight reduction raises HDL for *some* people, that program should lower cholesterol for *some* people.

E   The passage explicitly states that the two elements of regular exercise and weight reduction together contribute to *some* individuals' ability to increase their HDL levels. It cannot be inferred that all individuals of average weight can lower their cholesterol with regular exercise alone.

The correct answer is D.

3. A cost-effective solution to the problem of airport congestion is to provide high-speed ground transportation between major cities lying 200 to 500 miles apart. The successful implementation of this plan would cost far less than expanding existing airports and would also reduce the number of airplanes clogging both airports and airways.

Which of the following, if true, could proponents of the plan above most appropriately cite as a piece of evidence for the soundness of their plan?

(A) An effective high-speed ground-transportation system would require major repairs to many highways and mass-transit improvements.

(B) One-half of all departing flights in the nation's busiest airport head for a destination in a major city 225 miles away.

(C) The majority of travelers departing from rural airports are flying to destinations in cities over 600 miles away.

(D) Many new airports are being built in areas that are presently served by high-speed ground-transportation systems.

(E) A large proportion of air travelers are vacationers who are taking long-distance flights.

Evaluation of a Plan

Situation   Providing high-speed ground transportation between cities 200 to 500 miles apart is a more cost-effective and efficient way to reduce airport congestion than expanding existing airports.

Reasoning   *What evidence supports the plan?* The transportation plan will work only if people are likely to use the high-speed ground transportation. If half the flights leaving the busiest airport fly to destinations within range (200–500 miles) of ground transportation, then many people might choose it over air travel. Fewer flights would be needed and airport congestion would decrease.

A   Expensive repairs are an argument against, not for, ground transportation.

B   **Correct.** This statement properly identifies evidence that supports the plan.

C   Rural travelers are not included in this proposal, which addresses travel between major cities.

D   New airports covering the same routes are a threat to the plan.

E   The information that the airports are congested because of long-distance travelers, rather than those heading to destinations within 500 miles, argues against the proposal.

The correct answer is B.

4. The price the government pays for standard weapons purchased from military contractors is determined by a pricing method called "historical costing." Historical costing allows contractors to protect their profits by adding a percentage increase, based on the current rate of inflation, to the previous year's contractual price.

Which of the following statements, if true, is the best basis for a criticism of historical costing as an economically sound pricing method for military contracts?

(A) The government might continue to pay for past inefficient use of funds.

(B) The rate of inflation has varied considerably over the past twenty years.

(C) The contractual price will be greatly affected by the cost of materials used for the products.

(D) Many taxpayers question the amount of money the government spends on military contracts.

(E) The pricing method based on historical costing might not encourage the development of innovative weapons.

Argument Evaluation

Situation   Military contractors add a percentage increase, based on the rate of inflation, to prices specified in previous contracts for standard weapons.

Reasoning   *What could be wrong in simply adding a percentage increase each year?* If the original contract price accommodated the contractors' inefficiencies, the government's overpayments for these inefficiencies are simply perpetuated, and money continues to be wasted. Additionally, historical costing assumes costs only go up, never down.

A   **Correct.** This statement properly identifies a serious problem with historical costing.

B   Pointing out the variable rate of inflation shows a strength, rather than a weakness, of historical costing.

C   Identifying the importance of the cost of materials, which also varies with inflation, is a strength of the method.

D   Taxpayers' concerns are outside the scope of this question.

E   The contract is for standard weapons only; innovative weapons are not discussed.

The correct answer is A.

5. Which of the following best completes the passage below? Established companies concentrate on defending what they already have. Consequently, they tend not to be innovative themselves and tend to underestimate the effects of the innovations of others. The clearest example of this defensive strategy is the fact that_____.

    (A) ballpoint pens and soft-tip markers have eliminated the traditional market for fountain pens, clearing the way for the marketing of fountain pens as luxury or prestige items

    (B) a highly successful automobile was introduced by the same company that had earlier introduced a model that had been a dismal failure

    (C) a once-successful manufacturer of slide rules reacted to the introduction of electronic calculators by trying to make better slide rules

    (D) one of the first models of modern accounting machines, designed for use in the banking industry, was purchased by a public library as well as by banks

    (E) the inventor of a commonly used anesthetic did not intend the product to be used by dentists, who currently account for almost the entire market for that drug

Argument Construction

Situation   Established companies focus on defending their existing products, rather than seeking opportunities for innovation. They also underestimate the importance of other companies' innovations.

Reasoning   *Which example clearly shows the use of a defensive strategy?* A company is using a defensive strategy when it limits its business focus strictly to the improvement of an existing product instead of recognizing and responding to a significant innovation. The producer of slide rules who reacts to the introduction of electronic calculators by trying to make better slide rules is a perfect example of the failure of a company to respond appropriately to innovation.

A   Fountain pens have not been rendered obsolete by innovations in writing instruments; fountain-pen producers responded to the innovations by redefining the market for their product.

B   The automobile company did not respond defensively and simply reproduce the same failed model; it produced a new, successful model.

C   Correct. This statement properly identifies an example of defensive strategy.

D   A product's ability to appeal to an unintended audience is not an example of a defensive strategy.

E   The anesthetic finds a different market than its inventor anticipated; this is not a defensive strategy.

The correct answer is C.

6. Since the mayor's publicity campaign for Greenville's bus service began six months ago, morning automobile traffic into the midtown area of the city has decreased seven percent. During the same period, there has been an equivalent rise in the number of persons riding buses into the midtown area. Obviously, the mayor's publicity campaign has convinced many people to leave their cars at home and ride the bus to work.

Which of the following, if true, casts the most serious doubt on the conclusion drawn above?

(A) Fares for all bus routes in Greenville have risen an average of five percent during the past six months.

(B) The mayor of Greenville rides the bus to City Hall in the city's midtown area.

(C) Road reconstruction has greatly reduced the number of lanes available to commuters in major streets leading to the midtown area during the past six months.

(D) The number of buses entering the midtown area of Greenville during the morning hours is exactly the same now as it was one year ago.

(E) Surveys show that longtime bus riders are no more satisfied with the Greenville bus service than they were before the mayor's publicity campaign began.

Argument Evaluation

Situation   Traffic into midtown has decreased by seven percent, and bus ridership has increased by an equivalent amount. The mayor's publicity campaign is responsible for this change.

Reasoning   *What casts doubt on this conclusion?* Another reasonable cause for the decrease in automobile traffic and the increase in bus ridership would make this conclusion suspect. Road construction impeding access to midtown over the same period of time is a reasonable alternative explanation. The road construction projects would likely have caused fewer people to drive to midtown; many of these people have probably taken the bus.

A   An increase in fares might be a reasonable explanation for decreased, rather than this increased, ridership.

B   The mayor's decision to ride the bus sets a good example for citizens, and his example tends to strengthen the conclusion.

C   **Correct.** This statement properly identifies an explanation that weakens the conclusion.

D   An alternative explanation based on the running of more buses can be eliminated.

E   Passengers perceive bus service to be the same, so better service can be eliminated as a possible cause of the increased ridership.

The correct answer is C.

7. A researcher discovered that people who have low levels of immune-system activity tend to score much lower on tests of mental health than do people with normal or high immune-system activity. The researcher concluded from this experiment that the immune system protects against mental illness as well as against physical disease.

The researcher's conclusion depends on which of the following assumptions?

(A) High immune-system activity protects against mental illness better than normal immune-system activity does.

(B) Mental illness is similar to physical disease in its effects on body systems.

(C) People with high immune-system activity cannot develop mental illness.

(D) Mental illness does not cause people's immune-system activity to decrease.

(E) Psychological treatment of mental illness is not as effective as is medical treatment.

Argument Construction

Situation   Finding that people with low immune-system activity score lower on mental health tests than people with normal or high levels of immune activity, a researcher concludes that the immune system protects mental as well as physical health.

Reasoning   *What assumption does the researcher make?* The researcher asserts that immune-system activity can inhibit mental illness as it does physical illness. While it is possible that mental illness might itself depress immune-system activity, the researcher assumes that this is not the case. If mental illness caused a decline in immune-system activity, then lower levels of immune-system activity would be expected as a result, and the higher levels would merely indicate the absence of illness rather than any effect on illness.

A   The researcher does not distinguish between high and normal levels of immune-system activity, so this assumption is not needed.

B   The researcher is investigating only mental illness, not physical disease, so this assumption is not needed.

C   Immune-system activity could protect mental health without offering total prevention of mental illness; this assumption is not needed.

D   **Correct.** This statement properly identifies the researcher's underlying assumption that mental illness does not decrease immune system activity.

E   Since different treatments are not discussed, any assumption about them is unnecessary.

The correct answer is D.

8. It is true that it is against international law to sell plutonium to countries that do not yet have nuclear weapons. But if United States companies do not do so, companies in other countries will.

   Which of the following is most like the argument above in its logical structure?

   (A) It is true that it is against the police department's policy to negotiate with kidnappers. But if the police want to prevent loss of life, they must negotiate in some cases.

   (B) It is true that it is illegal to refuse to register for military service. But there is a long tradition in the United States of conscientious objection to serving in the armed forces.

   (C) It is true that it is illegal for a government official to participate in a transaction in which there is an apparent conflict of interest. But if the facts are examined carefully, it will clearly be seen that there was no actual conflict of interest in the defendant's case.

   (D) It is true that it is against the law to burglarize people's homes. But someone else certainly would have burglarized that house if the defendant had not done so first.

   (E) It is true that company policy forbids supervisors to fire employees without two written warnings. But there have been many supervisors who have disobeyed this policy.

Argument Construction

Situation   If American companies comply with international law and refuse to sell plutonium to countries without nuclear weapons, companies in other countries will go ahead and sell plutonium illegally.

Reasoning   *Which argument has the same logical structure as the argument about selling plutonium?* Consider how the argument proceeds. The plutonium argument first identifies a law. Then it makes an excuse for breaking that law by asserting that the law will inevitably be broken by others in the future. This implies that it is acceptable to break the law now because it will be broken sometime.

A   This argument states a reason for breaking the law, preventing loss of life, but it does not say that the law will inevitably be broken in the future.

B   This argument acknowledges the law has been broken in the past; it says nothing about the future.

C   This argument shows that the law does not apply to a particular case.

D   Correct. This statement properly identifies an argument that is parallel in logical structure to the plutonium argument because it too asserts the inevitability that the law will be broken at some time by someone and excuses the defendant as merely being the first to do so.

E   This argument demonstrates that a policy has been previously disobeyed; it does not state that it will be disobeyed in the future.

The correct answer is D.

9. Extinction is a process that can depend on a variety of ecological, geographical, and physiological variables. These variables affect different species of organisms in different ways, and should, therefore, yield a random pattern of extinctions. However, the fossil record shows that extinction occurs in a surprisingly definite pattern, with many species vanishing at the same time.

Which of the following, if true, forms the best basis for at least a partial explanation of the patterned extinctions revealed by the fossil record?

(A) Major episodes of extinction can result from widespread environmental disturbances that affect numerous different species.

(B) Certain extinction episodes selectively affect organisms with particular sets of characteristics unique to their species.

(C) Some species become extinct because of accumulated gradual changes in their local environments.

(D) In geologically recent times, for which there is no fossil record, human intervention has changed the pattern of extinctions.

(E) Species that are widely dispersed are the least likely to become extinct.

Argument Construction

Situation   The fossil record reveals that species become extinct in a surprisingly definite pattern, with multiple species vanishing simultaneously.

Reasoning   *Which point provides a basis for explaining the pattern?* The passage states that the process of extinction depends on so many variables—in the ecology and geography of the environment and in the physiology of the species—that the expected outcome would be a random pattern of extinctions. Yet a definite pattern is found instead. What could explain the disappearance of multiple species at the same time? What if the magnitude of one variable is so overwhelming that it prevails over the impact of the other variables? It is possible that significant widespread changes in the environment might affect multiple species simultaneously, causing their extinction.

A   **Correct.** This statement properly identifies a basis for explaining the pattern of many species becoming extinct simultaneously.

B   This explanation of selective extinction does not explain how many species become extinct at the same time.

C   This explanation addresses only *some* species, not *many* species.

D   The passage is based on what the fossil record suggests; more recent times, having no fossil record, are outside the consideration of the passage.

E   Indicating which species are least likely to become extinct does not explain a pattern of simultaneous extinction of many species.

The correct answer is A.

10. Which of the following best completes the passage below?

    At a recent conference on environmental threats to the North Sea, most participating countries favored uniform controls on the quality of effluents, whether or not specific environmental damage could be attributed to a particular source of effluent. What must, of course, be shown, in order to avoid excessively restrictive controls, is that_____.

    (A) any uniform controls that are adopted are likely to be implemented without delay
    (B) any substance to be made subject to controls can actually cause environmental damage
    (C) the countries favoring uniform controls are those generating the largest quantities of effluents
    (D) all of any given pollutant that is to be controlled actually reaches the North Sea at present
    (E) environmental damage already inflicted on the North Sea is reversible

Argument Construction

Situation   In the face of environmental threats to the North Sea, restrictions on effluents are considered.

Reasoning   *How can excessively restrictive controls be avoided?* To prevent pollutants from entering the North Sea, countries decide to control the quality of effluents. They need to control only those effluents that cause environmental damage. There is no need to restrict harmless effluents.

A   The immediacy of adopting controls does not prevent the controls from being overly restrictive.

B   **Correct.** This statement properly identifies the fact that controls on harmless effluents would be excessively restrictive and so should be avoided.

C   Avoiding unnecessary restrictions involves analyzing the quality of the effluents, not the composition of the countries favoring the restrictions.

D   It is not necessary to prove that all of a pollutant reaches the North Sea. It is necessary to prove only that some of it does.

E   The environmental damage that has already been caused is outside the scope of the restrictions. Finding that the damage is reversible will do nothing to prevent unnecessary restrictions.

The correct answer is B.

11. Shelby Industries manufactures and sells the same gauges as Jones Industries. Employee wages account for forty percent of the cost of manufacturing gauges at both Shelby Industries and Jones Industries. Shelby Industries is seeking a competitive advantage over Jones Industries. Therefore, to promote this end, Shelby Industries should lower employee wages.

Which of the following, if true, would most weaken the argument above?

(A) Because they make a small number of precision instruments, gauge manufacturers cannot receive volume discounts on raw materials.

(B) Lowering wages would reduce the quality of employee work, and this reduced quality would lead to lowered sales.

(C) Jones Industries has taken away twenty percent of Shelby Industries' business over the last year.

(D) Shelby Industries pays its employees, on average, ten percent more than does Jones Industries.

(E) Many people who work for manufacturing plants live in areas in which the manufacturing plant they work for is the only industry.

Evaluation of a Plan

Situation   Two industries manufacture the same product, and employee wages at both industries account for the same percentage of the manufacturing cost. One company seeks a competitive edge by lowering employee wages.

Reasoning   *What point weakens the argument in favor of lowering wages?* The company anticipates that the result of lowering wages will be a competitive edge, presumably gained through offering its products at lower prices as the result of having lower production costs. If evidence can be shown that lowering wages will not result in gaining a competitive advantage, the argument is weakened. If instead the result of lowered wages is lowered employee morale, and thus a lower quality of work and products, the declining quality could lead to a loss of sales. In this case, the action would not only fail to provide a competitive edge, it would put the company and its products at a disadvantage.

A   Because the company is unable to get lower costs on its raw materials, it is more likely seek other ways of lowering its costs, such as reducing wages. This statement tends to support the argument.

B   Correct. This statement properly identifies a factor that weakens the argument.

C   The loss of business would only encourage the Shelby company to seek a competitive edge, perhaps by cutting employee wages, so this statement does not weaken the conclusion.

D   Its relatively higher employee wages show only why the company might reduce wages; the conclusion about gaining a competitive advantage is not weakened.

E   Because of the location of the company, employees are likely to continue working even if wages are lowered; this statement strengthens, rather than weakens, the conclusion.

The correct answer is B.

12. Large national budget deficits do not cause large trade deficits. If they did, countries with the largest budget deficits would also have the largest trade deficits. In fact, when deficit figures are adjusted so that different countries are reliably comparable to each other, there is no such correlation.

If the statements above are all true, which of the following can properly be inferred on the basis of them?

(A) Countries with large national budget deficits tend to restrict foreign trade.

(B) Reliable comparisons of the deficit figures of one country with those of another are impossible.

(C) Reducing a country's national budget deficit will not necessarily result in a lowering of any trade deficit that country may have.

(D) When countries are ordered from largest to smallest in terms of population, the smallest countries generally have the smallest budget and trade deficits.

(E) Countries with the largest trade deficits never have similarly large national budget deficits.

Argument Construction

Situation   No correlation is found between large national budget deficits and large trade deficits.

Reasoning   *What inference can be drawn from this information?* The inference must be based on the stated information. Since the passage states that national budget deficits are not tied to trade deficits, it is logical to anticipate an inference about the independent nature of the relationship between the two kinds of deficits. One possible inference is that reducing one deficit has no impact on the reduction of the other.

A   An inference about restricting foreign trade cannot be drawn because no information about such restrictions is given.

B   The passage states that reliable comparisons have been developed.

C   **Correct.** This statement properly identifies an inference that can be drawn from the given information.

D   There is no information in the passage about population size, so no inference about it can be drawn.

E   The two kinds of deficits are independent of each other; it cannot be inferred that such independence prohibits both deficits from being large.

The correct answer is C.

13. A famous singer recently won a lawsuit against an advertising firm for using another singer in a commercial to evoke the famous singer's well-known rendition of a certain song. As a result of the lawsuit, advertising firms will stop using imitators in commercials. Therefore, advertising costs will rise, since famous singers' services cost more than those of their imitators.

The conclusion above is based on which of the following assumptions?

(A) Most people are unable to distinguish a famous singer's rendition of a song from a good imitator's rendition of the same song.

(B) Commercials using famous singers are usually more effective than commercials using imitators of famous singers.

(C) The original versions of some well-known songs are unavailable for use in commercials.

(D) Advertising firms will continue to use imitators to mimic the physical mannerisms of famous singers.

(E) The advertising industry will use well-known renditions of songs in commercials.

Argument Construction

Situation   A famous singer successfully sues an advertising company for using an imitator of that singer in a commercial. Advertising costs will now rise because the fees of famous singers are higher than the fees of their imitators.

Reasoning   *What assumption must be true to support the argument that costs will rise?* Consider what specifically is assumed to be driving the rise in advertising costs. It is not the fact of an increased production cost for a certain element of the commercials; it is the choice of those who make decisions about what elements to include in their commercials. The assumption is that, despite the outcome of the suit, the companies will still want to use well-known versions of songs in their commercials and thus will have to hire the famous singers of those songs and pay their higher fees.

A   Whether or not the audience can tell the difference between the singers is beside the point; the audience's listening aptitude does not cause advertising costs to rise.

B   The effectiveness of the commercials is not in question; the cause of the rising costs is the issue.

C   The lack of availability of some songs is not relevant to the rise in advertising costs. The same songs would not have been available even when production costs were lower.

D   The passage explicitly states that, after the lawsuit, *advertising firms will stop using imitators in commercials.* This statement contradicts the passage and cannot possibly be assumed.

E   **Correct.** This statement properly identifies an assumption that underlies the conclusion that costs will rise.

The correct answer is E.

14. The sustained massive use of pesticides in farming has two effects that are especially pernicious. First, it often kills off the pests' natural enemies in the area. Second, it often unintentionally gives rise to insecticide resistant pests, since those insects that survive a particular insecticide will be the ones most resistant to it, and they are the ones left to breed.

    From the passage above, it can be properly inferred that the effectiveness of the sustained massive use of pesticides can be extended by doing which of the following, assuming that each is a realistic possibility?

    (A) Using only chemically stable insecticides

    (B) Periodically switching the type of insecticide used

    (C) Gradually increasing the quantities of pesticides used

    (D) Leaving a few fields fallow every year

    (E) Breeding higher-yielding varieties of crop plants

Evaluation of a Plan

Situation   Continued high-level pesticide use often kills off the targeted pests' natural enemies. In addition, the pests that survive the application of the pesticide may become resistant to it, and these pesticide-resistant pests will continue breeding.

Reasoning   *What can be done to prolong the effectiveness of pesticide use?* It can be inferred that the ongoing use of a particular pesticide will not continue to be effective against the future generations of pests with an inherent resistance to that pesticide. What would be effective against these future generations? If farmers periodically change the particular pesticide they use, then pests resistant to one kind of pesticide might be killed by another. This would continue, with pests being killed off in cycles as the pesticides are changed. It is also possible that this rotation might allow some of the pests' natural enemies to survive, at least until the next cycle.

A   Not enough information about chemically stable insecticides is given to make a sound inference.

B   **Correct.** This statement properly identifies an action that could extend the effectiveness of pesticide use.

C   Gradually increasing the amount of the pesticides being used will not help the situation since the pests are already resistant to it.

D   Continued use of pesticides is assumed as part of the argument. Since pesticides would be unnecessary for fallow fields, this suggestion is irrelevant.

E   Breeding higher-yielding varieties of crops does nothing to extend the effectiveness of the use of pesticides.

The correct answer is B.

15. Treatment for hypertension forestalls certain medical expenses by preventing strokes and heart disease. Yet any money so saved amounts to only one-fourth of the expenditures required to treat the hypertensive population. Therefore, there is no economic justification for preventive treatment for hypertension.

Which of the following, if true, is most damaging to the conclusion above?

(A) The many fatal strokes and heart attacks resulting from untreated hypertension cause insignificant medical expenditures but large economic losses of other sorts.

(B) The cost, per patient, of preventive treatment for hypertension would remain constant even if such treatment were instituted on a large scale.

(C) In matters of health care, economic considerations should ideally not be dominant.

(D) Effective prevention presupposes early diagnosis, and programs to ensure early diagnosis are costly.

(E) The net savings in medical resources achieved by some preventive health measures are smaller than the net losses attributable to certain other measures of this kind.

Argument Evaluation

Situation   The preventive treatment of hypertension cannot be economically justified because the costs of treating the entire hypertensive population are far greater than the costs of treating the strokes and heart disease that some hypertensive patients might suffer.

Reasoning   *Which evidence most damages the argument?* The argument compares only two costs: the preventive treatment of hypertension and the treatment of strokes and heart disease. The conclusion is based solely on that comparison. What if there are other significant costs? If other large economic losses occur when hypertension goes untreated, then treatment may be economically justified, and the argument is damaged.

A   **Correct.** This statement properly identifies evidence that damages the conclusion.

B   The passage asserts that preventive treatment costs would be too high; that the cost would be constant neither changes that opinion nor damages the conclusion.

C   The conclusion can only be damaged by an objection that is framed in the same terms, in this case, in economic terms. The opinion stated here is not relevant to the conclusion.

D   Since early diagnosis programs increase the costs of preventive care, this statement supports rather than damages the conclusion.

E   This statement provides no specific information about hypertension; other preventive health measures are irrelevant to the conclusion.

The correct answer is A.

16. In an attempt to promote the widespread use of paper rather than plastic, and thus reduce non-biodegradable waste, the council of a small town plans to ban the sale of disposable plastic goods for which substitutes made of paper exist. The council argues that since most paper is entirely biodegradable, paper goods are environmentally preferable.

Which of the following, if true, indicates that the plan to ban the sale of disposable plastic goods is ill suited to the town council's environmental goals?

(A) Although biodegradable plastic goods are now available, members of the town council believe biodegradable paper goods to be safer for the environment.

(B) The paper factory at which most of the townspeople are employed plans to increase production of biodegradable paper goods.

(C) After other towns enacted similar bans on the sale of plastic goods, the environmental benefits were not discernible for several years.

(D) Since most townspeople prefer plastic goods to paper goods in many instances, they are likely to purchase them in neighboring towns where plastic goods are available for sale.

(E) Products other than those derived from wood pulp are often used in the manufacture of paper goods that are entirely biodegradable.

Evaluation of a Plan

Situation   A town council considers banning the sale of disposable plastic goods for which there are paper substitutes because paper is biodegradable and therefore environmentally preferable.

Reasoning   *What problem might there be in the council's plan?* The plan is intended to reduce the amount of plastic used by the citizens of the town. The town council's plan is, however, only as effective as the support it has from the town's citizens. If the citizens prefer disposable plastic goods and if the goods are also readily available in neighboring towns, there is nothing to stop them from buying the plastic goods elsewhere if that is their preference.

A   The existence of biodegradable plastic does not make the town's plan to ban disposable plastic goods unsuitable to its environmental goal.

B   The town's plan is no less appropriate for its goal if the local paper factory makes biodegradable paper goods.

C   Environmental benefits need not be immediate. Even though benefits were not perceived *for several years* after similar bans, the benefits did occur.

D   **Correct.** This statement properly identifies the problem with the council's plan.

E   The specific materials that go into making nonbiodegradable paper are not in question. This statement is irrelevant to the plan.

The correct answer is D.

17. Since the deregulation of airlines, delays at the nation's increasingly busy airports have increased by 25 percent. To combat this problem, more of the takeoff and landing slots at the busiest airports must be allocated to commercial airlines.

Which of the following, if true, casts the most doubt on the effectiveness of the solution proposed above?

(A) The major causes of delays at the nation's busiest airports are bad weather and overtaxed air traffic control equipment.

(B) Since airline deregulation began, the number of airplanes in operation has increased by 25 percent.

(C) Over 60 percent of the takeoff and landing slots at the nation's busiest airports are reserved for commercial airlines.

(D) After a small Midwestern airport doubled its allocation of takeoff and landing slots, the number of delays that were reported decreased by 50 percent.

(E) Since deregulation the average length of delay at the nation's busiest airports has doubled.

Evaluation of a Plan

Situation   To reduce delays, more takeoff and landing slots at the busiest airports should go to commercial airlines.

Reasoning   *What point casts the most doubt on the proposed solution?* Evaluating the effectiveness of this solution means examining the relation between the problem, an increase in delays, and the solution, an increase in takeoff and landing slots. Could the delays be caused by other factors that the solution fails to address? If the major causes for delays are related to weather and air traffic control equipment, not to the number of slots for takeoff and landing, then the proposed solution of changing the allocations of the slots is bound to be less effective.

A   **Correct.** This statement properly identifies a weakness in the proposed solution.

B   The increasing number of planes shows why airports are busier. Since there is no information about whether these planes are private or commercial, this statement neither casts doubt on the solution nor supports it.

C   This statement suggests that there are slots available to be allocated to commercial airlines and thus offers some support for the proposed solution.

D   The example of one airport shows that the solution may work.

E   The increase in length of delay shows the scope of the problem; this fact does not cast doubt on the solution.

The correct answer is A.

18. Unlike the wholesale price of raw wool, the wholesale price of raw cotton has fallen considerably in the last year. Thus, although the retail price of cotton clothing at retail clothing stores has not yet fallen, it will inevitably fall.

Which of the following, if true, most seriously weakens the argument above?

(A) The cost of processing raw cotton for cloth has increased during the last year.

(B) The wholesale price of raw wool is typically higher than that of the same volume of raw cotton.

(C) The operating costs of the average retail clothing store have remained constant during the last year.

(D) Changes in retail prices always lag behind changes in wholesale prices.

(E) The cost of harvesting raw cotton has increased in the last year.

Argument Evaluation

Situation   Since the wholesale price of raw cotton has fallen significantly, the retail price of cotton clothing in stores will inevitably fall.

Reasoning   *What point weakens this argument?* Consider carefully the difference between the two products for which costs are being compared: cotton and cloth. This argument assumes that lower wholesale prices for a raw product must necessarily result in lower retail prices for a processed product. What other factors could have an impact on the final retail prices of cotton clothing? If any of the costs of transforming the raw product into a processed product increase, then the retail prices of cotton clothing will not necessarily fall.

A   **Correct.** This statement properly identifies a weakness in the argument.

B   The relative prices of raw wool and raw cotton are irrelevant to price changes in raw cotton and processed cotton.

C   One step between wholesale and retail prices is the operating cost of the retail store. If that operating cost has been constant rather than rising, it is possible that the retail prices could follow the lower wholesale prices. Thus the argument is not weakened.

D   The argument notes that the wholesale price has fallen *in the last year* and that though the retail price *has not yet fallen, it will inevitably fall*. The argument has already taken the lag into account and is not weakened by this statement.

E   Harvesting costs are part of the assumed increased price of raw cotton and do not affect current retail prices.

The correct answer is A.

19.   Reviewer: The book _Art's Decline_ argues that European painters today lack skills that were common among European painters of preceding centuries. In this the book must be right, since its analysis of 100 paintings, 50 old and 50 contemporary, demonstrates convincingly that none of the contemporary paintings are executed as skillfully as the older paintings.

Which of the following points to the most serious logical flaw in the reviewer's argument?

(A)   The paintings chosen by the book's author for analysis could be those that most support the book's thesis.

(B)   There could be criteria other than the technical skill of the artist by which to evaluate a painting.

(C)   The title of the book could cause readers to accept the book's thesis even before they read the analysis of the paintings that supports it.

(D)   The particular methods currently used by European painters could require less artistic skill than do methods used by painters in other parts of the world.

(E)   A reader who was not familiar with the language of art criticism might not be convinced by the book's analysis of the 100 paintings.

Argument Evaluation

Situation   Comparing 50 contemporary paintings with 50 earlier paintings, a book argues that contemporary European painters lack the skills of earlier European painters. The reviewer endorses the book's thesis by noting that the contemporary paintings are not as skillfully done as the older paintings.

Reasoning   _What is the flaw in the reasoning?_ The argument is based on two samples of 50 paintings each, but there is no evidence that the samples are representative. It is quite possible that the book presents and discusses only those paintings that support its argument and ignores those paintings that do not support the argument. The reviewer accepts the selected samples of artwork without questioning how truly representative they are.

A   **Correct.** This statement properly identifies a logical flaw in the reviewer's argument.

B   This statement critiques the narrow focus of the book, not the reasoning of its argument, which is endorsed by the reviewer.

C   This statement shows that the reasoning of readers may be flawed if they accept the thesis on the basis of the book's title; it does not point to a flaw in the author's or the reviewer's reasoning.

D   The book compares two groups of European painters. Comparisons to painters in other parts of the world are irrelevant.

E   This statement focuses on the reader's possible confusion, not on an error of reasoning on the part of the reviewer or author.

The correct answer is A.

4.6 Critical Reasoning **Answer Explanations**

20. A computer equipped with signature-recognition software, which restricts access to a computer to those people whose signatures are on file, identifies a person's signature by analyzing not only the form of the signature but also such characteristics as pen pressure and signing speed. Even the most adept forgers cannot duplicate all of the characteristics the program analyzes.

Which of the following can be logically concluded from the passage above?

(A) The time it takes to record and analyze a signature makes the software impractical for everyday use.

(B) Computers equipped with the software will soon be installed in most banks.

(C) Nobody can gain access to a computer equipped with the software solely by virtue of skill at forging signatures.

(D) Signature-recognition software has taken many years to develop and perfect.

(E) In many cases even authorized users are denied legitimate access to computers equipped with the software.

Argument Construction

Situation   Forgers cannot duplicate all the characteristics that signature-recognition software analyzes, including the form of a signature, pen pressure, and signing speed. Computers equipped with this software restrict access to those whose signatures are on file.

Reasoning   *What conclusion can be reached about computers equipped with this software?* The passage states that the software detects more characteristics in a signature than the most accomplished forger can possibly reproduce. Thus, skill at forging signatures is not enough to allow someone to gain access to a computer equipped with the software.

A   No information about the speed of the analysis is given, so no such conclusion can be drawn.

B   Since the passage never mentions banks, no conclusion can be drawn about banks' use of the software.

C   **Correct.** This statement properly identifies a conclusion that can be drawn from the passage.

D   The time required to develop the software is irrelevant to the argument.

E   Since errors are not discussed, any conclusion about errors is unwarranted.

The correct answer is C.

21. Start-up companies financed by venture capitalists have a much lower failure rate than companies financed by other means. Source of financing, therefore, must be a more important causative factor in the success of a start-up company than are such factors as the personal characteristics of the entrepreneur, the quality of strategic planning, or the management structure of the company.

    Which of the following, if true, most seriously weakens the argument above?

    (A) Venture capitalists tend to be more responsive than other sources of financing to changes in a start-up company's financial needs.

    (B) The strategic planning of a start-up company is a less important factor in the long-term success of the company than are the personal characteristics of the entrepreneur.

    (C) More than half of all new companies fail within five years.

    (D) The management structures of start-up companies are generally less formal than the management structures of ongoing businesses.

    (E) Venture capitalists base their decisions to fund start-up companies on such factors as the characteristics of the entrepreneur and quality of strategic planning of the company.

Argument Evaluation

Situation   When venture capitalists fund start-up companies, the failure rate is much lower than when the companies are funded by other means. The success of start-up companies, then, may be attributed more to their source of funding than to any other factor.

Reasoning   *What point weakens the argument?* The argument concludes that the source of funding is the single most important factor in determining the success of a start-up company. But what if the source of that funding, venture capitalists, considers other factors before making its investment? Venture capitalists may evaluate the characteristics of the entrepreneur as well as the company's strategic plan and management structure before deciding to fund the start-up company. If this is the case, then the most important element in determining the success of the company cannot be said to be the source of the funding.

A   The responsiveness of venture capitalists is a point in favor of the argument, not against it.

B   This statement about the relative importance of strategic planning and the personality of the entrepreneur does not weaken the argument because it does not address the issue of financial backing.

C   The argument concerns only successful start-up companies, so high failure rates are irrelevant.

D   A comparison between start-up companies and existing businesses is not relevant to an argument about the funding of start-ups.

E   **Correct.** This statement properly identifies evidence that weakens the argument.

The correct answer is E.

Questions 22–23 are based on the following:

Half of the subjects in an experiment—the experimental group—consumed large quantities of a popular artificial sweetener. Afterward, this group showed lower cognitive abilities than did the other half of the subjects—the control group—who did not consume the sweetener. The detrimental effects were attributed to an amino acid that is one of the sweetener's principal constituents.

22. Which of the following, if true, would best support the conclusion that some ingredient of the sweetener was responsible for the experimental results?

(A) Most consumers of the sweetener do not consume as much of it as the experimental group members did.

(B) The amino acid referred to in the conclusion is a component of all proteins, some of which must be consumed for adequate nutrition.

(C) The quantity of the sweetener consumed by individuals in the experimental group is considered safe by federal food regulators.

(D) The two groups of subjects were evenly matched with regard to cognitive abilities prior to the experiment.

(E) A second experiment in which subjects consumed large quantities of the sweetener lacked a control group of subjects who were not given the sweetener.

Argument Evaluation

Situation   The experimental group in a study consumed large quantities of an artificial sweetener and afterward showed lower cognitive abilities; the control group consumed no artificial sweetener and revealed no cognitive decline. An amino acid in the sweetener is said to have caused the decline.

Reasoning   *Which point best supports the conclusion?* After the experiment, the two groups showed a difference in cognitive ability. According to the passage, it could therefore be concluded that this difference was the result of the experiment. What unstated information would support the conclusion? Matching the subjects' cognitive ability beforehand eliminates the possibility that one group may have had lower cognitive abilities to begin with. The similarity of the two groups prior to the experiment supports the conclusion that an ingredient in the sweetener is responsible for the difference afterward.

A   The smaller quantity consumed by most people is not relevant to the findings of the experiment.

B   It is logical to assume that all members of both groups were consuming some of this amino acid in their maintenance of "adequate nutrition" for themselves. If the amounts consumed were small, the conclusion is unaffected. If the amounts consumed were large, the conclusion that this amino acid causes cognitive decline is weakened, not strengthened.

C   Safety determinations by food regulators are irrelevant to the outcome of the experiment.

D   Correct. This statement properly identifies evidence that supports the conclusion.

E   A second experiment without a control group does not strengthen or weaken the first experiment's findings.

The correct answer is D.

23. Which of the following, if true, would best help explain how the sweetener might produce the observed effect?

(A) The government's analysis of the artificial sweetener determined that it was sold in relatively pure form.

(B) A high level of the amino acid in the blood inhibits the synthesis of a substance required for normal brain functioning.

(C) Because the sweetener is used primarily as a food additive, adverse reactions to it are rarely noticed by consumers.

(D) The amino acid that is a constituent of the sweetener is also sold separately as a dietary supplement.

(E) Subjects in the experiment did not know whether they were consuming the sweetener or a second, harmless substance.

Argument Construction

Situation   The experimental group in a study consumed large quantities of an artificial sweetener and afterward showed lower cognitive abilities; the control group consumed no artificial sweetener and revealed no cognitive decline. An amino acid in the sweetener is said to have caused the decline. (The same as the item above.)

Reasoning   *How can the effect of the sweetener on cognitive ability best be explained?* This question asks the reader to consider only the amino acid in the sweetener and the lower cognitive abilities found in the experimental group. What could link them? The fact that the amino acid inhibits a process necessary for ordinary brain function would explain the decline in cognitive ability found in the experimental group.

A   The pure form of the sweetener does not explain the experiment's results.

B   **Correct.** This statement properly explains how the amino acid might cause the lower cognitive abilities.

C   Consumers' failure to notice adverse effects from the sweetener does not explain the sweetener's effect on the experimental group.

D   The availability of the amino acid as a dietary supplement does not explain how consuming the amino acid in the sweetener produces lower cognitive abilities.

E   The use of a standard experimental procedure does not explain how the sweetener affects cognitive ability.

The correct answer is B.

24. In the arid land along the Colorado River, use of the river's water supply is strictly controlled: farms along the river each have a limited allocation that they are allowed to use for irrigation. But the trees that grow in narrow strips along the river's banks also use its water. Clearly, therefore, if farmers were to remove those trees, more water would be available for crop irrigation.

Which of the following, if true, most seriously weakens the argument?

(A) The trees along the river's banks shelter it from the sun and wind, thereby greatly reducing the amount of water lost through evaporation.

(B) Owners of farms along the river will probably not undertake the expense of cutting down trees along the banks unless they are granted a greater allocation of water in return.

(C) Many of the tree species currently found along the river's banks are specifically adapted to growing in places where tree roots remain constantly wet.

(D) The strip of land where trees grow along the river's banks would not be suitable for growing crops if the trees were removed.

(E) The distribution of water allocations for irrigation is intended to prevent farms farther upstream from using water needed by farms farther downstream.

Argument Evaluation

Situation   Water is scarce and precious in the land along the Colorado River, and the amount allocated for irrigating farmland is strictly controlled. Farmers would have more water available for crop irrigation if the riverside trees, which also use the water, were removed.

Reasoning   *What point weakens the argument?* The reason given for removing the trees is to make more water available for crops. What if the trees actually conserve water rather than simply consume it? If the trees protect the river from sun and wind, their presence can greatly reduce the amount of river water lost to evaporation. Thus, the farmers would lose water, not gain it, by cutting down the trees.

A   **Correct.** This statement properly identifies a weakness in the argument.

B   The argument is about the greater availability of water once the trees are removed; it is not about what the farmers might or might not do. This statement does not weaken the argument.

C   This statement may lead the reader to believe that particular species along the river may use more water than other trees, which could support the argument. The species themselves, however, are not the focus of the argument; removal of the trees, no matter what species they are, is the focus.

D   The argument concerns the greater availability of water, not the greater availability of arable land.

E   The reason for the water allocation does not have any bearing on whether removing the trees will provide more water for irrigation.

The correct answer is A.

25. Near Chicago a newly built hydroponic spinach "factory," a completely controlled environment for growing spinach, produces on 1 acre of floor space what it takes 100 acres of fields to produce. Expenses, especially for electricity, are high, however, and the spinach produced costs about four times as much as washed California field spinach, the spinach commonly sold throughout the United States.

Which of the following, if true, best supports a projection that the spinach-growing facility near Chicago will be profitable?

(A) Once the operators of the facility are experienced, they will be able to cut operating expenses by about 25 percent.

(B) There is virtually no scope for any further reduction in the cost per pound for California field spinach.

(C) Unlike washed field spinach, the hydroponically grown spinach is untainted by any pesticides or herbicides and thus will sell at exceptionally high prices to such customers as health food restaurants.

(D) Since spinach is a crop that ships relatively well, the market for the hydroponically grown spinach is no more limited to the Chicago area than the market for California field spinach is to California.

(E) A second hydroponic facility is being built in Canada, taking advantage of inexpensive electricity and high vegetable prices.

Argument Evaluation

Situation   Spinach grown hydroponically in a controlled environment at a facility near Chicago is four times as expensive as the popular washed field spinach grown in California.

Reasoning   *What point best supports the projection of profitability for the hydroponic spinach?* The hydroponic spinach cannot compete with the California spinach in price. What might be another way for the hydroponic spinach to compete successfully against the field-washed spinach? That is, what feature of the hydroponic spinach is the California spinach unable to match? If the California spinach is tainted with pesticides or herbicides, health-conscious consumers could be willing to pay much higher prices for hydroponic spinach that is grown in pristine conditions without herbicides or pesticides.

A   The 25 percent reduction in operating costs cannot compensate for the much larger price difference, so this statement does not support the projection.

B   Knowing that the price of California spinach can go no lower does not help to explain how the hydroponic spinach can possibly compensate for the huge price difference between the two products.

C   **Correct.** This statement properly identifies a value that allows the high-priced hydroponic spinach to compete successfully with the less expensive California spinach.

D   The ease of shipping is an advantage shared equally by the two types of spinach.

E   The existence of a facility in Canada does nothing to assure the profitability of the Chicago facility.

The correct answer is C.

26. Automobile Dealer's Advertisement:

The Highway Traffic Safety Institute reports that the PZ 1000 has the fewest injuries per accident of any car in its class. This shows that the PZ 1000 is one of the safest cars available today.

Which of the following, if true, most seriously weakens the argument in the advertisement?

(A) The Highway Traffic Safety Institute report listed many cars in other classes that had more injuries per accident than did the PZ 1000.

(B) In recent years many more PZ 1000's have been sold than have any other kind of car in its class.

(C) Cars in the class to which the PZ 1000 belongs are more likely to be involved in accidents than are other types of cars.

(D) The difference between the number of injuries per accident for the PZ 1000 and that for other cars in its class is quite pronounced.

(E) The Highway Traffic Safety Institute issues reports only once a year.

Argument Evaluation

Situation   An advertisement claims that the PZ 1000 is one of the safest cars available; it bases this claim on the Highway Traffic Safety Institute's report that this model had the fewest injuries per accident of any car in its class.

Reasoning   *What point weakens the advertisement's claim?* Examine closely the difference between the report and the advertising position. While the Highway Traffic Safety Institute compares the PZ 1000 to other cars *in its class*, the advertisement compares the PZ 1000 to *all cars available today*. What if the class of cars to which the PZ 1000 belongs is a more dangerous class of cars? In that case, while the PZ 1000 may be the safest car of a dangerous class, it cannot be said to be one of the safest cars available.

A   The higher incidence of injuries per accident in other classes of cars supports rather than weakens the advertisement's argument.

B   Because the argument is about the safety of the car, not its popularity, this statement is not relevant.

C   **Correct.** This statement properly identifies a weakness in the advertisement's argument.

D   Since it is already known that the PZ 1000 has the lowest rate of injury per accident in its class, this statement does not provide any new information to support or weaken the argument.

E   The frequency of the reports is irrelevant to the advertisement's claim.

The correct answer is C.

27. <u>Editorial</u>: The mayor plans to deactivate the city's fire alarm boxes, because most calls received from them are false alarms. The mayor claims that the alarm boxes are no longer necessary, since most people now have access to either public or private telephones. But the city's commercial district, where there is the greatest risk of fire, has few residents and few public telephones, so some alarm boxes are still necessary.

Which of the following, if true, most seriously weakens the editorial's argument?

(A) Maintaining the fire alarm boxes costs the city more than five million dollars annually.

(B) Commercial buildings have automatic fire alarm systems that are linked directly to the fire department.

(C) The fire department gets less information from an alarm box than it does from a telephone call.

(D) The city's fire department is located much closer to the residential areas than to the commercial district.

(E) On average, almost 25 percent of the public telephones in the city are out of order.

Argument Evaluation

Situation   The mayor considers fire alarm boxes unnecessary since most people have access to public or private phones. An editorial argues that some boxes should be kept in the commercial district since the district has few residents and few public phones.

Reasoning   *What point weakens the editorial's argument?* The editorial argues that the commercial district has few residents (to discover any fires) and few public phones (to report them), but recognizes that the lack of potential witnesses to fires raises the question of whether the limited number of commercial-district residents could report fires more effectively with access to alarm boxes rather than to public phones. What if alternative systems to notify the fire department are already in place in the commercial district? If the commercial buildings are already using automatic fire alarm systems that are directly linked to the fire department and provide automated notifications, then the alarm boxes are indeed unnecessary.

A   The editorial's argument is about fires in the commercial district; it is not about the maintenance costs of the alarm boxes. This point fails to undermine the editorial.

B   **Correct.** This statement properly identifies a weakness in the editorial's argument.

C   The argument is not about varying amounts of information; it is about notifying the fire department of the existence of a fire in the first place.

D   The greater distance that the fire department must travel to the commercial district addresses the importance of response time; this point does not weaken the argument.

E   Alarm boxes would be more necessary, not less, if public telephones were frequently out of order, so this statement supports the editorial.

The correct answer is B.

28. State spokesperson: Many businesspeople who have not been to our state believe that we have an inadequate road system. Those people are mistaken, as is obvious from the fact that in each of the past six years, our state has spent more money per mile on road improvements than any other state.

    Which of the following, if true, most seriously undermines the reasoning in the spokesperson's argument?

    (A) In the spokesperson's state, spending on road improvements has been increasing more slowly over the past six years than it has in several other states.

    (B) Adequacy of a state's road system is generally less important to a businessperson considering doing business there than is the availability of qualified employees.

    (C) Over the past six years, numerous businesses have left the spokesperson's state, but about as many businesses have moved into the state.

    (D) In general, the number of miles of road in a state's road system depends on both the area and the population of the state.

    (E) Only states with seriously inadequate road systems need to spend large amounts of money on road improvements.

Argument Evaluation

Situation   A state spokesperson responds to the criticism that the road system is inadequate by observing that the state has spent more money per mile on road improvements than any other state has spent.

Reasoning   *What point undermines the spokesperson's reasoning?* When might heavy spending on road improvements <u>not</u> result in an adequate road system? If the state has needed to spend more money on road improvements than any other state, it suggests that its roads have needed more improving than those in any other state. The high level of state spending on road improvements provides evidence only that the road system was in dire need of improvement and not that it has yet achieved adequacy.

A   A slower rate of increases in spending does not contradict the spokesperson's statement that the state has spent more than others, and it offers no information on the adequacy of the road system.

B   The argument is about the adequacy of the road system, not about finding employees, so this point does not undermine the argument.

C   Since the road system is not mentioned as a reason that businesses left the state or came to it, this point is irrelevant to the argument.

D   The background information about area and population does not affect the argument about the adequacy of the road system.

E   **Correct.** This statement properly identifies a point that undermines the spokesperson's reasoning.

The correct answer is E.

29. A program instituted in a particular state allows parents to prepay their children's future college tuition at current rates. The program then pays the tuition annually for the child at any of the state's public colleges in which the child enrolls. Parents should participate in the program as a means of decreasing the cost for their children's college education.

Which of the following, if true, is the most appropriate reason for parents not to participate in the program?

(A) The parents are unsure about which public college in the state the child will attend.

(B) The amount of money accumulated by putting the prepayment funds in an interest-bearing account today will be greater than the total cost of tuition for any of the public colleges when the child enrolls.

(C) The annual cost of tuition at the state's public colleges is expected to increase at a faster rate than the annual increase in the cost of living.

(D) Some of the state's public colleges are contemplating large increases in tuition next year.

(E) The prepayment plan would not cover the cost of room and board at any of the state's public colleges.

Evaluation of a Plan

Situation   The state plan lets parents prepay tuition at state colleges to reduce future costs.

Reasoning   *What could be an appropriate reason to avoid the plan?* The plan is intended to assure parents that they will be able to cover the cost of their children's tuition while minimizing how much they have to spend. If an alternative approach lets them spend less and still assures that the cost of the tuition is covered, they should choose the alternative approach rather than the state plan.

A   Freedom to choose any state college is a strength of the state plan.

B   Correct. This statement properly identifies an alternative to the state plan.

C   Protection from tuition increases is a strength of the state plan.

D   Protection from tuition increases is a strength of the state plan.

E   Nontuition costs are irrelevant to the state plan.

The correct answer is B.

30. Company Alpha buys free-travel coupons from people who are awarded the coupons by Bravo Airlines for flying frequently on Bravo airplanes. The coupons are sold to people who pay less for the coupons than they would pay by purchasing tickets from Bravo. This marketing of coupons results in lost revenue for Bravo.

    To discourage the buying and selling of free-travel coupons, it would be best for Bravo Airlines to restrict the

    (A) number of coupons that a person can be awarded in a particular year

    (B) use of the coupons to those who were awarded the coupons and members of their immediate families

    (C) days that the coupons can be used to Monday through Friday

    (D) amount of time that the coupons can be used after they are issued

    (E) number of routes on which travelers can use the coupons

Evaluation of a Plan

Situation   A company that buys and sells travel coupons reduces the revenue of an airline. The airline wants to discourage the trade in coupons.

Reasoning   *How can the airline discourage its customers from selling their coupons?* Limiting the use of the coupons to those who earned them and their immediate families rewards passengers for flying the airline and encourages them to continue to do so while at the same time making the sale of the coupons useless.

A   Limiting the number of coupons awarded a year does nothing to discourage their resale.

B   **Correct.** This statement properly identifies a limitation that makes the sale of coupons useless while maintaining the coupons' value as a reward.

C   Limiting the time of use to weekdays does not discourage resale and makes the coupons less valuable to the airline's customers.

D   Imposing a date by which the coupons must be used does not discourage resale and diminishes the coupons' value as a reward.

E   Restricting the routes available does not discourage resale but does reduce the coupons' value as a reward.

The correct answer is B.

31. Toughened hiring standards have not been the primary cause of the present staffing shortage in public schools. The shortage of teachers is primarily caused by the fact that in recent years teachers have not experienced any improvements in working conditions and their salaries have not kept pace with salaries in other professions.

Which of the following, if true, would most support the claims above?

(A) Many teachers already in the profession would not have been hired under the new hiring standards.

(B) Today more teachers are entering the profession with a higher educational level than in the past.

(C) Some teachers have cited higher standards for hiring as a reason for the current staffing shortage.

(D) Many teachers have cited low pay and lack of professional freedom as reasons for their leaving the profession.

(E) Many prospective teachers have cited the new hiring standards as a reason for not entering the profession.

Argument Evaluation

Situation   The teacher shortage can be explained by poor working conditions and poor salaries rather than by stricter hiring practices.

Reasoning   *Which statement supports this point of view?* This argument about the cause of the teacher shortage dismisses one possibility, obstacles created by higher standards in hiring, and endorses another, the failure to improve working conditions and salaries. Only a response that gives information about working conditions and salaries can support the conclusion.

A   The argument is about the cause of the present teacher shortage. The quality of the current members of the profession is not at issue.

B   More teachers with relatively higher education levels may be entering the field, but this statement is irrelevant to the cause of the present teacher shortage.

C   This opinion supports the explanation that the argument rejects.

D   **Correct.** This statement properly identifies evidence that pay and working conditions have caused teachers to leave the profession and thus supports the claim that these factors are causes of the teacher shortage.

E   This statement strengthens the opposing point of view.

The correct answer is D.

32. A proposed ordinance requires the installation in new homes of sprinklers automatically triggered by the presence of a fire. However, a home builder argued that because more than 90 percent of residential fires are extinguished by a household member, residential sprinklers would only marginally decrease property damage caused by residential fires.

    Which of the following, if true, would most seriously weaken the home builder's argument?

    (A)   Most individuals have no formal training in how to extinguish fires.

    (B)   Since new homes are only a tiny percentage of available housing in the city, the new ordinance would be extremely narrow in scope.

    (C)   The installation of smoke detectors in new residences costs significantly less than the installation of sprinklers.

    (D)   In the city where the ordinance was proposed, the average time required by the fire department to respond to a fire was less than the national average.

    (E)   The largest proportion of property damage that results from residential fires is caused by fires that start when no household member is present.

Argument Evaluation

Situation   A home builder claims that requiring automatic sprinklers in new homes will not significantly decrease property damage from residential fires because more than 90 percent of home fires are put out by a household member.

Reasoning   *Which point weakens the argument?* The home builder unites one element, 90 percent of all home fires, with another, total property damage from all residential fires. But the greatest damage may occur in that small window of less than 10 percent of all home fires, when no household member is home to put out the fire. This is precisely the situation that the automatic sprinklers would remedy.

A   If more than 90 percent of residential fires are successfully extinguished by the individuals who live there, then no formal training appears to be necessary.

B   The small percentage of new homes supports the builder's position; it does not weaken the argument.

C   The argument is not about the kind of smoke detection or the costs of the installations.

D   The argument is not about a comparison between fire departments and sprinkler systems.

E   **Correct.** This statement properly identifies a weakness in the home builder's argument by showing that the most damage occurs when no household member is present to put out the fire.

The correct answer is E.

33. A recent spate of launching and operating mishaps with television satellites led to a corresponding surge in claims against companies underwriting satellite insurance. As a result, insurance premiums shot up, making satellites more expensive to launch and operate. This, in turn, had added to the pressure to squeeze more performance out of currently operating satellites.

Which of the following, if true, taken together with the information above, best supports the conclusion that the cost of television satellites will continue to increase?

(A) Since the risk to insurers of satellites is spread over relatively few units, insurance premiums are necessarily very high.

(B) When satellites reach orbit and then fail, the causes of failure are generally impossible to pinpoint with confidence.

(C) The greater the performance demands placed on satellites, the more frequently those satellites break down.

(D) Most satellites are produced in such small numbers that no economies of scale can be realized.

(E) Since many satellites are built by unwieldy international consortia, inefficiencies are inevitable.

Argument Evaluation

Situation A rise in the number of claims after a series of accidents has forced insurance companies to raise prices for coverage of television satellites. Consequently, new satellites are more expensive, and existing satellites must perform more. The cost of television satellites will continue to increase.

Reasoning *Why will the cost continue to increase?* The passage says that the existing satellites are being asked to work harder than previously. If that increase in workload brings with it an increased number of breakdowns, growing satellite repair and replacement costs will add to the already increased cost of insurance premiums.

A The high rate of premiums is a given; nothing in this statement reflects why the costs would increase further.

B The difficulty of diagnosing the causes of satellite failure shows one reason the costs are high; it does not show why they are increasing.

C **Correct.** This statement properly identifies a factor that explains why costs will continue to increase.

D The small number of satellites shows one reason they are expensive; it does not explain why costs would continue to increase.

E The inefficiencies may partially account for initial high costs; nothing in this statement explains an increase in costs.

The correct answer is C.

Questions 34–35 refer to the following:

If the airspace around centrally located airports were restricted to commercial airliners and only those private planes equipped with radar, most of the private-plane traffic would be forced to use outlying airfields. Such a reduction in the amount of private-plane traffic would reduce the risk of midair collision around the centrally located airports.

34. The conclusion drawn in the first sentence depends on which of the following assumptions?

   (A) Outlying airfields would be as convenient as centrally located airports for most pilots of private planes.

   (B) Most outlying airfields are not equipped to handle commercial-airline traffic.

   (C) Most private planes that use centrally located airports are not equipped with radar.

   (D) Commercial airliners are at greater risk of becoming involved in midair collisions than are private planes.

   (E) A reduction in the risk of midair collision would eventually lead to increases in commercial airline traffic.

Argument Construction

Situation   Only commercial airliners and private planes with radar would be allowed to use the airspace around centrally located airports; most private-plane traffic would use outlying airfields instead. The result would be fewer midair collisions around centrally located airports.

Reasoning   *What assumption underlies the conclusion that most private planes would be forced to use outlying airfields?* The passage states that private planes with radar may continue to use the centrally located airports. If, as a result of the restriction, most private planes could no longer use these airports, it must be assumed that most private planes do not have radar. This assumption concerns only the number of private planes being rerouted; no other issue is involved.

A   Convenience is not at issue.

B   The capacity of outlying airfields is outside the scope of the question.

C   **Correct.** This statement properly identifies the assumption that most of these private planes lack radar and would no longer be allowed to land at the centrally located airports.

D   The assumption is about the number of private planes only; commercial airlines are outside the scope of the question.

E   The future of commercial airline traffic is beyond the scope of the question.

The correct answer is C.

35. Which of the following, if true, would most strengthen the conclusion drawn in the second sentence?

    (A) Commercial airliners are already required by law to be equipped with extremely sophisticated radar systems.

    (B) Centrally located airports are experiencing overcrowded airspace primarily because of sharp increases in commercial-airline traffic.

    (C) Many pilots of private planes would rather buy radar equipment than be excluded from centrally located airports.

    (D) The number of midair collisions that occur near centrally located airports has decreased in recent years.

    (E) Private planes not equipped with radar systems cause a disproportionately large number of midair collisions around centrally located airports.

Argument Evaluation

Situation   Only commercial airliners and private planes with radar would be allowed to use the airspace around centrally located airports; most private-plane traffic would use outlying airfields instead. The result would be fewer midair collisions around centrally located airports. (The same as the item above.)

Reasoning   *What point strengthens the conclusion that midair collisions would be reduced?* Restricting private-plane traffic to planes having radar would reduce collisions. Why is this true? It must be that private planes without radar are responsible for a disproportionately large number of the midair collisions near centrally located airports; fewer of these planes should mean fewer collisions.

A   The conclusion is about private planes, not about commercial airliners.

B   Increases in commercial-airline traffic are irrelevant to the question of private-plane traffic.

C   The desirability of radar equipment is not being questioned. The link between the lack of radar and midair collisions is the issue.

D   A recent reduction of the number of collisions does not explain their cause.

E   **Correct.** This statement properly identifies a factor that strengthens the conclusion.

The correct answer is E.

36. Two decades after the Emerald River Dam was built, none of the eight fish species native to the Emerald River was still reproducing adequately in the river below the dam. Since the dam reduced the annual range of water temperature in the river below the dam from 50 degrees to 6 degrees, scientists have hypothesized that sharply rising water temperatures must be involved in signaling the native species to begin the reproductive cycle.

Which of the following statements, if true, would most strengthen the scientists' hypothesis?

(A) The native fish species were still able to reproduce only in side streams of the river below the dam where the annual temperature range remains approximately 50 degrees.

(B) Before the dam was built, the Emerald River annually overflowed its banks, creating backwaters that were critical breeding areas for the native species of fish.

(C) The lowest recorded temperature of the Emerald River before the dam was built was 34 degrees, whereas the lowest recorded temperature of the river after the dam was built has been 43 degrees.

(D) Nonnative species of fish, introduced into the Emerald River after the dam was built, have begun competing with the declining native fish species for food and space.

(E) Five of the fish species native to the Emerald River are not native to any other river in North America.

Argument Evaluation

Situation   The construction of a dam has significantly reduced the range of water temperatures in the river below the dam. Scientists have implicated this change in the failure of native fish species to reproduce adequately.

Reasoning   *What evidence would strengthen the hypothesis?* To test the hypothesis, scientists need to study the same fish in the same river, but with only one variable, the temperature range of the water, changed. If the same species of fish successfully reproduce in water that retains the same temperature range that the river had before the dam was built, then the scientists have likely found the cause of the problem.

A   **Correct.** This statement properly identifies evidence that strengthens the scientists' hypothesis.

B   The overflow's creation of breeding areas offers an alternative hypothesis; it rivals rather than strengthens the hypothesis about temperature range.

C   These specific temperatures provide data, but they do not point to a cause.

D   The hypothesis is concerned only with a comparison of native fish species before and after the dam was built; the introduction of nonnative fish species after the dam's construction is irrelevant.

E   The rareness of certain species points to the severity of the problem, not to its cause.

The correct answer is A.

37. Certain messenger molecules fight damage to the lungs from noxious air by telling the muscle cells encircling the lungs' airways to contract. This partially seals off the lungs. An asthma attack occurs when the messenger molecules are activated unnecessarily, in response to harmless things like pollen or household dust.

Which of the following, if true, points to the most serious flaw of a plan to develop a medication that would prevent asthma attacks by blocking receipt of any messages sent by the messenger molecules referred to above?

(A) Researchers do not yet know how the body produces the messenger molecules that trigger asthma attacks.

(B) Researchers do not yet know what makes one person's messenger molecules more easily activated than another's.

(C) Such a medication would not become available for several years, because of long lead times in both development and manufacture.

(D) Such a medication would be unable to distinguish between messages triggered by pollen and household dust and messages triggered by noxious air.

(E) Such a medication would be a preventative only and would be unable to alleviate an asthma attack once it had started.

Evaluation of a Plan

Situation The lungs are partially sealed off when certain molecules signal the muscle cells of the airway to contract. While this process prevents damage to the lungs from noxious air, harmless substances can trigger the process in asthma patients. A medication to block this process is considered.

Reasoning *Why is the plan to develop the medication flawed?* Consider the action that the medication is intended to perform. How might that action be problematic? The process initiated by the messenger molecules has the useful and necessary purpose of protecting the lungs against harmful agents in the air. A medication to block the process completely would not distinguish between when the process is unnecessary, in the presence of harmless substances, and when that process is entirely necessary, in the presence of noxious air. Thus the medication would leave asthma patients unprotected from potential damage to their lungs.

A Understanding how the body produces the messenger molecules is not relevant to understanding how the action of the medication might be flawed.

B The greater sensitivity of some people's messenger molecules is not the issue.

C Pointing out long lead times does not explain a flaw in the medication.

D Correct. This statement properly identifies the fact that the medication is flawed because it could do harm by preventing a necessary process.

E The proposed medication makes no claim to alleviate asthma attacks once they have begun.

The correct answer is D.

38. Which of the following best completes the passage below?

The more worried investors are about losing their money, the more they will demand a high potential return on their investment; great risks must be offset by the chance of great rewards. This principle is the fundamental one in determining interest rates, and it is illustrated by the fact that_____.

(A) successful investors are distinguished by an ability to make very risky investments without worrying about their money

(B) lenders receive higher interest rates on unsecured loans than on loans backed by collateral

(C) in times of high inflation, the interest paid to depositors by banks can actually be below the rate of inflation

(D) at any one time, a commercial bank will have a single rate of interest that it will expect all of its individual borrowers to pay

(E) the potential return on investment in a new company is typically lower than the potential return on investment in a well-established company

Argument Construction

Situation   The principle of determining interest rates is related to the risk involved in making the investment of a loan. Potentially greater rewards will lead lenders (investors) to accept greater risks.

Reasoning   *Which example illustrates the principle that greater risks should produce greater rewards?* The example must be about the relationship of risk to benefit. Lenders take a greater risk when loans are not backed by collateral because there is a chance they could lose their money entirely. Consequently, the lenders (by definition, they are investors) should receive the reward of higher interest rates.

A   The freedom from anxiety enjoyed by some investors is not relevant. While risky investments are mentioned, this statement does not mention their return.

B   **Correct.** This statement properly identifies the example that shows that riskier loans, those not backed by collateral, receive the benefit of higher interest rates.

C   This discussion of interest rates in times of inflation does not mention potential risk or potential benefit.

D   A single rate of interest for all investments, no matter the level of risk, contradicts the principle and so cannot possibly be an example of it.

E   New companies are generally riskier than established ones. A lower rate of return for such riskier new companies contradicts the principle.

The correct answer is B.

39.   A certain mayor has proposed a fee of five dollars per day on private vehicles entering the city, claiming that the fee will alleviate the city's traffic congestion. The mayor reasons that, since the fee will exceed the cost of round-trip bus fare from many nearby points, many people will switch from using their cars to using the bus.

Which of the following statements, if true, provides the best evidence that the mayor's reasoning is flawed?

(A)   Projected increases in the price of gasoline will increase the cost of taking a private vehicle into the city.

(B)   The cost of parking fees already makes it considerably more expensive for most people to take a private vehicle into the city than to take a bus.

(C)   Most of the people currently riding the bus do not own private vehicles.

(D)   Many commuters opposing the mayor's plan have indicated that they would rather endure traffic congestion than pay a five-dollar-per-day fee.

(E)   During the average workday, private vehicles owned and operated by people living within the city account for 20 percent of the city's traffic congestion.

Evaluation of a Plan

Situation   In order to alleviate traffic congestion, the mayor proposes a five dollar daily fee on private vehicles entering the city. Because the fee is more than the round-trip bus fare, the mayor believes many drivers will switch to buses.

Reasoning   *What flaw exists in the mayor's reasoning?* The mayor apparently believes that saving money is the decisive issue for drivers. If, however, drivers are already paying more in parking fees than they would in fares as bus commuters, then saving money is not the reason they are choosing to drive their cars rather than take the bus. These drivers will not change their behavior simply to save money.

A   The increased cost of fuel does not point to a weakness of the mayor's plan; it could possibly be a reason that citizens would endorse it.

B   **Correct.** This statement properly identifies a flaw in the mayor's reasoning.

C   Current bus riders are not relevant to the mayor's plan, which anticipates only the newly added bus riders coming from among the current drivers.

D   Many drivers may continue to commute in their private vehicles, but others might switch to buses. The mayor's plan does not anticipate a switch by all drivers.

E   The 20 percent figure shows that most congestion is caused by vehicles entering from outside the city; this does not point out a weakness in the mayor's plan.

The correct answer is B.

40. Dental researchers recently discovered that toothbrushes can become contaminated with bacteria that cause pneumonia and strep throat. They found that contamination usually occurs after toothbrushes have been used for four weeks. For that reason, people should replace their toothbrushes at least once a month.

Which of the following, if true, would most weaken the conclusion above?

(A) The dental researchers could not discover why toothbrush contamination usually occurred only after toothbrushes had been used for four weeks.

(B) The dental researchers failed to investigate contamination of toothbrushes by viruses, yeasts, and other pathogenic microorganisms.

(C) The dental researchers found that among people who used toothbrushes contaminated with bacteria that cause pneumonia and strep throat, the incidence of these diseases was no higher than among people who used uncontaminated toothbrushes.

(D) The dental researchers found that people who rinsed their toothbrushes thoroughly in hot water after each use were as likely to have contaminated toothbrushes as were people who only rinsed their toothbrushes hurriedly in cold water after each use.

(E) The dental researchers found that, after six weeks of use, greater length of use of a toothbrush did not correlate with a higher number of bacteria being present.

Argument Evaluation

Situation   Researchers have found that, after four weeks of use, toothbrushes may become contaminated with disease bacteria. Therefore, toothbrushes should be replaced once a month.

Reasoning   *What information weakens the conclusion?* The passage concludes that contaminated toothbrushes should be replaced monthly. Clearly, the assumption that underlies this conclusion is that such replacement is necessary because the bacterial contamination is potentially harmful to the user of the toothbrush; the user could become ill as a result of contact with these disease bacteria. Do people actually become ill because of their use of contaminated toothbrushes? Comparing disease rates for people using uncontaminated toothbrushes and for people using contaminated toothbrushes shows no difference between the groups, and the assumption about the potential harm is proven wrong. The conclusion is thus weakened when contaminated toothbrushes are not shown to be more likely to cause illness.

A   The recommendation to change every four weeks is not weakened simply because researchers cannot explain why it takes that long for contamination to occur.

B   The failure to investigate other possible contaminants of toothbrushes does not weaken the recommendation.

C   **Correct.** This statement properly identifies the information that weakens the conclusion: using contaminated toothbrushes is no more likely to result in disease than using uncontaminated ones, and thus changing toothbrushes every month is unnecessary.

D   Since even careful maintenance of toothbrushes does not reduce contamination, the recommendation is strengthened.

E   If the contamination still remains at six weeks, even if it is not worse, the recommendation based on the bacteria existing at four weeks is not weakened.

The correct answer is C.

41. Leaders of a miners' union on strike against Coalco are contemplating additional measures to pressure the company to accept the union's contract proposal. The union leaders are considering as their principal new tactic a consumer boycott against Gasco gas stations, which are owned by Energy Incorporated, the same corporation that owns Coalco.

The answer to which of the following questions is LEAST directly relevant to the union leaders' consideration of whether attempting a boycott of Gasco will lead to acceptance of their contract proposal?

(A) Would revenue losses by Gasco seriously affect Energy Incorporated?

(B) Can current Gasco customers easily obtain gasoline elsewhere?

(C) Have other miners' unions won contracts similar to the one proposed by this union?

(D) Have other unions that have employed a similar tactic achieved their goals with it?

(E) Do other corporations that own coal companies also own gas stations?

Evaluation of a Plan

Situation   In an effort to pressure Coalco to accept their contract proposal, union leaders consider organizing a consumer boycott of gas stations owned by Coalco's parent company.

Reasoning   *Which question is LEAST relevant to the boycott decision?* Union leaders have a number of questions to consider in deciding what to do. This problem requires finding the one question that is NOT relevant to deciding if a boycott would be an effective tactic. Examine each in turn. Whether other corporations that own coal companies also own gas stations is NOT directly relevant to whether a boycott of Gasco gas stations will coerce Coalco to accept a proposal.

A   Knowing how seriously the parent corporation would be hurt by revenue losses from the boycott is relevant.

B   If consumers cannot easily get gas elsewhere, the boycott is likely to fail, so this question is relevant.

C   If other miners' unions have won similar contracts, then the union's proposal is reasonable. This question is relevant.

D   If other unions have succeeded (or failed) with a similar plan, that information is relevant to the likely success (or failure) of this plan.

E   **Correct.** This question is the only one that does not clearly bear upon the plan; an answer to it is the one least directly relevant to the boycott decision.

The correct answer is E.

Questions 42–43 are based on the following:

Transnational cooperation among corporations is experiencing a modest renaissance among United States firms, even though projects undertaken by two or more corporations under a collaborative agreement are less profitable than projects undertaken by a single corporation. The advantage of transnational cooperation is that such joint international projects may allow United States firms to win foreign contracts that they would not otherwise be able to win.

42. Which of the following statements by a United States corporate officer best fits the situation of United States firms as described in the passage above?

   (A) "We would rather make only a share of the profit and also risk only a share of a possible loss than run the full risk of a loss."

   (B) "We would rather make a share of a relatively modest profit than end up making none of a potentially much bigger profit."

   (C) "We would rather cooperate and build good will than poison the business climate by all-out competition."

   (D) "We would rather have foreign corporations join us in American projects than join them in projects in their home countries."

   (E) "We would rather win a contract with a truly competitive bid of our own than get involved in less profitable collaborative agreements."

Argument Construction

Situation   When U.S. corporations share projects with other corporations, those projects yield less profit, but there is a decided benefit nonetheless. By participating in joint transnational projects, U.S. corporations can win (and participate in the profits of) foreign contracts they otherwise could not.

Reasoning   *Which statement describes this situation from the viewpoint of a U.S. corporate officer?* By cooperating with other corporations, a firm is more likely to win a contract than it would be if it just sought the contract on its own. There are more profits to be made if the contract is not shared, but the business opportunity itself is less likely.

A   This statement emphasizes minimizing risk when profits are shared, but the passage does not discuss risk.

B   **Correct.** This statement properly identifies a viewpoint consistent with the passage: a corporate officer would prefer having the modest profit of a collaborative project to having no contract or profit at all.

C   This statement contrasts cooperation with competition, but competition is not discussed in the passage.

D   This statement contrasts two modes of transnational cooperation and indicates a preference for one over another. No mention is made in the passage of foreign corporations joining American projects, and no preference is stated.

E   This statement completely contradicts the passage in dismissing the value of collaborative agreements.

The correct answer is B.

43. Which of the following is information provided by the passage above?

(A) Transnational cooperation involves projects too big for a single corporation to handle.

(B) Transnational cooperation results in a pooling of resources leading to high-quality performance.

(C) Transnational cooperation has in the past been both more common and less common than it is now among United States firms.

(D) Joint projects between United States and foreign corporations are not profitable enough to be worth undertaking.

(E) Joint projects between United States and foreign corporations benefit only those who commission the projects.

Argument Construction

Situation   When U.S. corporations share projects with other corporations, those projects yield less profit, but there is a decided benefit nonetheless. By participating in joint transnational projects, U.S. corporations can win (and participate in the profits of) foreign contracts they otherwise could not. (The same as the item above.)

Reasoning   *What information can be inferred from the passage?* Answering this question requires careful attention to the words used in the passage. The first sentence states that the United States is experiencing *a modest renaissance* of transnational cooperation. The word *renaissance*, meaning the revival of a former state of affairs or the resurgence after an intervening lull, indicates that transnational cooperation was once well established among American firms; it further implies that the practice once died out and now is making a comeback. The use of the word *modest* in describing this comeback suggests that transnational cooperation is not currently as widespread as it had been at one time.

A   The passage does not indicate that the shared projects are too big for one corporation.

B   The passage makes no claims about the quality of the performance.

C   **Correct.** This statement properly identifies information provided in the first sentence of the passage.

D   The passage indicates that the joint projects are indeed sufficiently profitable to be worth undertaking.

E   The passage does not suggest that benefits go only to those who commission projects.

The correct answer is C.

44. Laws requiring the use of headlights during daylight hours can prevent automobile collisions. However, since daylight visibility is worse in countries farther from the equator, any such laws would obviously be more effective in preventing collisions in those countries. In fact, the only countries that actually have such laws are farther from the equator than is the continental United States.

Which of the following conclusions could be most properly drawn from the information given above?

(A) Drivers in the continental United States who used their headlights during the day would be just as likely to become involved in a collision as would drivers who did not use their headlights.

(B) In many countries that are farther from the equator than is the continental United States poor daylight visibility is the single most important factor in automobile collisions.

(C) The proportion of automobile collisions that occur in the daytime is greater in the continental United States than in the countries that have daytime headlight laws.

(D) Fewer automobile collisions probably occur each year in countries that have daytime headlight laws than occur within the continental United States.

(E) Daytime headlight laws would probably do less to prevent automobile collisions in the continental United States than they do in the countries that have the laws.

Argument Construction

Situation   Laws requiring the use of headlights during the daytime are more effective at preventing car collisions in countries with lower daylight visibility, that is, in countries at greater distances from the equator. The only countries having these laws are those located farther from the equator than is the continental U.S.

Reasoning   *What conclusion can be drawn from this information?* Countries with daytime headlight laws are all farther from the equator than is the continental U.S. The location is significant because daytime visibility is worse in those countries than it is in the continental U.S. How effective at preventing collisions would such laws be in the continental United States with its greater proximity to the equator? It is reasonable to conclude that such laws would be less effective at preventing collisions there than they are in the countries farther from the equator.

A   This contradicts the given information that daytime headlight laws *can prevent automobile collisions.* Although daytime headlight use may be less effective in countries with more daylight, it cannot be concluded that U.S. drivers using daytime headlights would gain no benefit from them and would have collisions the same as those who do not.

B   The passage offers no evidence for the conclusion that poor visibility is the *greatest* cause for collisions in these countries.

C   Data are required to make judgments about the proportion of daytime collisions.

D   Without specific data, no conclusion can be drawn about the relative number of accidents that occur.

E   **Correct.** This statement properly identifies a conclusion to be drawn from the given information.

The correct answer is E.

Questions 45–46 are based on the following:

Bank depositors in the United States are all financially protected against bank failure because the government insures all individuals' bank deposits. An economist argues that this insurance is partly responsible for the high rate of bank failures, since it removes from depositors any financial incentive to find out whether the bank that holds their money is secure against failure. If depositors were more selective, then banks would need to be secure in order to compete for depositors' money.

45. The economist's argument makes which of the following assumptions?

(A) Bank failures are caused when big borrowers default on loan repayments.

(B) A significant proportion of depositors maintain accounts at several different banks.

(C) The more a depositor has to deposit, the more careful he or she tends to be in selecting a bank.

(D) The difference in the interest rates paid to depositors by different banks is not a significant factor in bank failures.

(E) Potential depositors are able to determine which banks are secure against failure.

Argument Construction

Situation   An economist contends that the high rate of bank failures can partly be blamed on federal insurance of bank deposits. The insurance removes any financial incentive for depositors to seek those banks that are the most secure against failure. In the absence of more selective depositors, the banks need not be secure to compete for deposits.

Reasoning   *What assumption underlies the economist's argument?* The economist argues that banks would have to be more secure in a competitive environment with more discriminating depositors. The economist encourages potential depositors to be *more selective* in choosing a bank and therefore must believe that they know what makes a bank secure against failure. Only with this knowledge could depositors choose the best bank.

A   This statement explains how a bank failure may occur, but it is not a necessary assumption for the economist's argument about how depositors choose a bank.

B   The argument never discusses multiple accounts, so this statement cannot be assumed.

C   The economist argues that depositors are not careful in selecting banks; this statement contradicts that position, at least for some depositors, so it cannot possibly be assumed.

D   In arguing about choosing banks, the economist mentions nothing about the relation of interest rates to bank failures, so this statement is not assumed.

E   **Correct.** This statement properly identifies the economist's underlying assumption that potential depositors are able to determine which banks are more secure.

The correct answer is E.

46. Which of the following, if true, most seriously weakens the economist's argument?

    (A) Before the government started to insure depositors against bank failure, there was a lower rate of bank failure than there is now.

    (B) When the government did not insure deposits, frequent bank failures occurred as a result of depositors' fears of losing money in bank failures.

    (C) Surveys show that a significant proportion of depositors are aware that their deposits are insured by the government.

    (D) There is an upper limit on the amount of an individual's deposit that the government will insure, but very few individuals' deposits exceed this limit.

    (E) The security of a bank against failure depends on the percentage of its assets that are loaned out and also on how much risk its loans involve.

Argument Evaluation

Situation   An economist contends that the high rate of bank failures can partly be blamed on federal insurance of bank deposits. The insurance removes any financial incentive for depositors to seek those banks that are the most secure against failure. In the absence of more selective depositors, the banks need not be secure to compete for deposits. (The same as the item above.)

Reasoning   *What point most weakens the economist's argument?* The economist identifies federal insurance of deposits as a partial cause of the high rate of bank failures, citing depositors' complacency regarding the safety of their savings and their resultant lack of concern about the banks' being secure. What circumstance might have led to frequent bank failures before the federal insurance program started? If banks often failed because depositors acted on their fears that their savings were in jeopardy, then the economist's conclusion blaming the program is weakened.

A   If there was a lower rate of bank failure before federal insurance, then the economist's argument is supported, not weakened.

B   **Correct.** This statement properly identifies a factor that weakens the economist's argument.

C   The knowledge that their deposits are insured no matter which bank they choose may lead depositors to be less selective in their choice of bank; this statement supports rather than weakens the argument.

D   Since most depositors are covered by federal insurance, they can continue to be less selective in choosing a bank, and thus the argument is not weakened.

E   Nothing in this statement about assets and risks is linked to federal insurance of deposits, so this statement is irrelevant to the argument.

The correct answer is B.

47. A study of marital relationships in which one partner's sleeping and waking cycles differ from those of the other partner reveals that such couples share fewer activities with each other and have more violent arguments than do couples in a relationship in which both partners follow the same sleeping and waking patterns. Thus, mismatched sleeping and waking cycles can seriously jeopardize a marriage.

Which of the following, if true, most seriously weakens the argument above?

(A) Married couples in which both spouses follow the same sleeping and waking patterns also occasionally have arguments that can jeopardize the couple's marriage.

(B) The sleeping and waking cycles of individuals tend to vary from season to season.

(C) The individuals who have sleeping and waking cycles that differ significantly from those of their spouses tend to argue little with colleagues at work.

(D) People in unhappy marriages have been found to express hostility by adopting different sleeping and waking cycles from those of their spouses.

(E) According to a recent study, most people's sleeping and waking cycles can be controlled and modified easily.

Argument Evaluation

Situation   A study of married couples reveals that spouses with different sleeping and waking cycles tend to have fewer activities in common and more intense arguments than spouses with similar sleeping and waking cycles. Thus, different sleep-wake cycles may severely endanger a marriage.

Reasoning   *Which evidence weakens the conclusion?* This problem asks the reader to consider patterns of cause and effect. The conclusion assumes that different sleep-wake cycles are in place, causing the marital problems. What if the marital problems are in place, resulting in different sleep-wake cycles? The conclusion is weakened by evidence showing that unhappily married spouses express hostility by deliberately adopting cycles different from those of their spouses.

A   The argument does not say that mismatched cycles are the *only* cause of the arguments jeopardizing a marriage or that only couples with such a mismatch have such arguments.

B   This statement does not show how seasonal variability affects mismatched cycles in marriage, and so it is irrelevant.

C   The conclusion is about the effect of mismatched cycles on a marriage, and so the relationship with colleagues is irrelevant.

D   Correct. This statement properly identifies a weakness in the argument by changing the argument's perspective: instead of blaming the patterns for the hostility, it blames the hostility for the patterns. This alternative explanation of the study's findings weakens the argument.

E   While suggesting that sleep-wake behaviors can be modified, this statement still does not provide evidence that weakens the conclusion.

The correct answer is D.

48. In the past most airline companies minimized aircraft weight to minimize fuel costs. The safest airline seats were heavy, and airlines equipped their planes with few of these seats. This year the seat that has sold best to airlines has been the safest one—a clear indication that airlines are assigning a higher priority to safe seating than to minimizing fuel costs.

    Which of the following, if true, most seriously weakens the argument above?

    (A) Last year's best-selling airline seat was not the safest airline seat on the market.

    (B) No airline company has announced that it would be making safe seating a higher priority this year.

    (C) The price of fuel was higher this year than it had been in most of the years when the safest airline seats sold poorly.

    (D) Because of increases in the cost of materials, all airline seats were more expensive to manufacture this year than in any previous year.

    (E) Because of technological innovations, the safest airline seat on the market this year weighed less than most other airline seats on the market.

Argument Evaluation

Situation   The safest airline seats were heavy, but since additional weight meant higher fuel costs, airlines had bought few of these seats. Because the best-selling seats this year are the safest ones, the airlines have clearly reset their priorities, choosing safe seating over minimizing fuel costs.

Reasoning   *What information weakens this argument?* The argument moves from reporting that the best-selling seats are now the safest ones to concluding that the airlines must have changed their priorities. Any information about the new seats that suggests the airlines have not had to change their priorities to change their customary seat-buying practices would weaken this argument. If the safest seat this year was also among the lightest, the airlines may simply be pursuing their previous priority of minimizing fuel costs by reducing weight.

A   Noting that a change has occurred between *last year*, when the best-selling seat was not the safest, and *this year*, when it is, does not weaken the argument.

B   A change in priorities can occur without any public announcement, so this statement does not weaken the argument.

C   Stating that fuel costs are higher this year than in the past does not connect those higher costs with the airlines' priorities, so the argument is not weakened.

D   Revealing the increased production costs of all seats, regardless of their degree of safety, does not weaken the conclusion about the airlines' priorities.

E   **Correct.** This statement properly identifies information that weakens the argument.

The correct answer is E.

49. Division Manager: I want to replace the Microton computers in my division with Vitech computers.

    General Manager: Why?

    Division Manager: It costs 28 percent less to train new staff on the Vitech.

    General Manager: But that is not a good enough reason. We can simply hire only people who already know how to use the Microton computer.

    Which of the following, if true, most seriously undermines the general manager's objection to the replacement of Microton computers with Vitechs?

    (A) Currently all employees in the company are required to attend workshops on how to use Microton computers in new applications.

    (B) Once employees learn how to use a computer, they tend to change employers more readily than before.

    (C) Experienced users of Microton computers command much higher salaries than do prospective employees who have no experience in the use of computers.

    (D) The average productivity of employees in the general manager's company is below the average productivity of the employees of its competitors.

    (E) The high costs of replacement parts make Vitech computers more expensive to maintain than Microton computers.

Argument Evaluation

Situation   A division manager wants to replace Microton computers with Vitech computers in order to reduce training costs for new staff. The general manager objects to this reasoning, arguing that the company can hire only those people who already know how to use the Microton computers.

Reasoning   *What point weakens the general manager's argument?* The division manager's preference for Vitech equipment is based on reduced personnel-training costs. The general manager rejects this cost-reduction rationale and counters by suggesting a way to avoid these costs altogether. Both managers thus accept costs as the basis for making the decision between the two brands. Any evidence that overall costs would be higher when using the Microton computers weakens the general manager's argument. If the costs associated with employing experienced Microton users are greater, then hiring exclusively from this pool and paying their *much higher* salaries may result in higher overall costs for the company than the costs for training new staff on the Vitechs.

A   This information about Microton training does not compare the costs related to the two types of computers, and so it is irrelevant to the general manager's argument.

B   This point suggest that hiring experienced workers will be easy and so strengthens the general manager's argument.

C   **Correct.** This statement properly identifies evidence that undermines the general manager's argument.

D   Productivity at the company and at its competitors is not at issue.

E   The higher ongoing costs for Vitech replacement parts would strengthen the general manager's cost-based argument.

The correct answer is C.

50. Crops can be traded on the futures market before they are harvested. If a poor corn harvest is predicted, prices of corn futures rise; if a bountiful corn harvest is predicted, prices of corn futures fall. This morning meteorologists are predicting much-needed rain for the corn-growing region starting tomorrow. Therefore, since adequate moisture is essential for the current crop's survival, prices of corn futures will fall sharply today.

Which of the following, if true, most weakens the argument above?

(A) Corn that does not receive adequate moisture during its critical pollination stage will not produce a bountiful harvest.

(B) Futures prices for corn have been fluctuating more dramatically this season than last season.

(C) The rain that meteorologists predicted for tomorrow is expected to extend well beyond the corn-growing region.

(D) Agriculture experts announced today that a disease that has devastated some of the corn crop will spread widely before the end of the growing season.

(E) Most people who trade in corn futures rarely take physical possession of the corn they trade.

Argument Evaluation

Situation   Crop futures rise when a harvest is expected to be small and drop when a harvest is expected to be large. Today's weather forecast for the corn-growing area predicts much-needed rain, so corn futures will fall today.

Reasoning   *What information weakens the argument that corn futures will fall?* The prediction that corn futures will drop sharply today is made solely on the basis of the rain, forecasted for tomorrow, which promises an abundant crop. What about further announcements regarding the other factors that could affect the crop? If it is made known that a devastating disease will severely affect the corn crop before the end of the growing season, then the prospect of a smaller harvest will make futures rise rather than fall.

A   This statement tells at what exact point in the growing cycle rain is critical to a good harvest, but it gives no information about this year's harvest.

B   This comparison of past price fluctuations does not affect what will happen to today's corn futures on account of the predicted rain. The argument is not weakened.

C   The only rain that matters is the rain that affects the corn-growing region, not areas beyond it; this statement is irrelevant to the prediction.

D   Correct. This statement properly identifies information that weakens the argument.

E   Physical possession of the corn is irrelevant to the price of corn futures.

The correct answer is D.

51. The interview is an essential part of a successful hiring program because, with it, job applicants who have personalities that are unsuited to the requirements of the job will be eliminated from consideration.

The argument above logically depends on which of the following assumptions?

(A) A hiring program will be successful if it includes interviews.

(B) The interview is a more important part of a successful hiring program than is the development of a job description.

(C) Interviewers can accurately identify applicants whose personalities are unsuited to the requirements of the job.

(D) The only purpose of an interview is to evaluate whether job applicants' personalities are suited to the requirements of the job.

(E) The fit of job applicants' personalities to the requirements of the job was once the most important factor in making hiring decisions.

Argument Construction

Situation   The interview is a necessary part of hiring because candidates with unsuitable personalities are eliminated from consideration.

Reasoning   *What is being assumed in this argument?* The argument puts forth one reason that the interview is important: it eliminates candidates with unsuitable personalities. The argument is logical only if it is assumed that interviewing does indeed eliminate such candidates. The argument assumes that interviewers can successfully screen candidates and rule out those whose personalities do not fit the needs of the job.

A   The argument does not go so far as to say that interviews guarantee a successful hiring program.

B   The argument does not prioritize the parts of a hiring program.

C   **Correct.** This statement properly identifies the assumption underlying the argument.

D   The argument gives one reason that the interview is important, but it does not say it is the *only* reason.

E   The argument does not indicate that past practice affects how hiring decisions are currently being made.

The correct answer is C.

52. Useful protein drugs, such as insulin, must still be administered by the cumbersome procedure of injection under the skin. If proteins are taken orally, they are digested and cannot reach their target cells. Certain nonprotein drugs, however, contain chemical bonds that are not broken down by the digestive system. They can, thus, be taken orally.

The statements above most strongly support a claim that a research procedure that successfully accomplishes which of the following would be beneficial to users of protein drugs?

(A) Coating insulin with compounds that are broken down by target cells, but whose chemical bonds are resistant to digestion

(B) Converting into protein compounds, by procedures that work in the laboratory, the nonprotein drugs that resist digestion

(C) Removing permanently from the digestive system any substances that digest proteins

(D) Determining, in a systematic way, what enzymes and bacteria are present in the normal digestive system and whether they tend to be broken down within the body

(E) Determining the amount of time each nonprotein drug takes to reach its target cells

Argument Construction

Situation   Since protein drugs taken orally are digested and do not reach their target cells, they must be injected under the skin. Some nonprotein drugs have chemical bonds resistant to digestion and may be taken orally.

Reasoning   *What procedure might be beneficial for users of protein drugs?* Clearly it would be beneficial for users if protein drugs could be administered orally rather than by injection. Digestion has been the obstacle to the oral use of such drugs. Some nonprotein drugs have chemical bonds that resist digestion. If protein drugs such as insulin could use similar chemical bonds to resist digestion, thus allowing the protein to reach its target cells, then the protein drugs could be taken orally, a clear benefit to the users of those drugs.

A   **Correct.** This statement properly identifies a procedure that would be beneficial for users of protein drugs: coating a protein drug (such as insulin) so that it is resistant to digestion but able to reach its target cells would allow users to take it orally rather than by injection.

B   No benefit for users of protein drugs is gained by converting nonprotein drugs into protein compounds because then they too would need to be injected rather than taken orally.

C   The digestive system needs the substances that digest protein in order to function normally, so this procedure would do more harm than good.

D   Determining whether normally present enzymes and bacteria are broken down in the body does not offer any specific benefits for users of protein drugs.

E   The time required by nonprotein drugs to reach target cells is irrelevant to the question of benefits to users of protein drugs.

The correct answer is A.

53. There is a great deal of geographical variation in the frequency of many surgical procedures—up to tenfold variation per hundred thousand people among different areas in the numbers of hysterectomies, prostatectomies, and tonsillectomies.

   To support a conclusion that much of the variation is due to unnecessary surgical procedures, it would be most important to establish which of the following?

   (A) A local board of review at each hospital examines the records of every operation to determine whether the surgical procedure was necessary.

   (B) The variation is unrelated to factors (other than the surgical procedures themselves) that influence the incidence of diseases for which surgery might be considered.

   (C) There are several categories of surgical procedure (other than hysterectomies, prostatectomies, and tonsillectomies) that are often performed unnecessarily.

   (D) For certain surgical procedures, it is difficult to determine after the operation whether the procedures were necessary or whether alternative treatment would have succeeded.

   (E) With respect to how often they are performed unnecessarily, hysterectomies, prostatectomies, and tonsillectomies are representative of surgical procedures in general.

Argument Construction

Situation   The frequency of certain surgical procedures, e.g., hysterectomies, prostatectomies, and tonsillectomies, varies dramatically by geographical region. It may be possible to conclude that the disparity is to a large extent the result of the performance of unnecessary surgeries.

Reasoning   *What additional information must be true for this conclusion to hold?* Is it possible that different factors in different regions might reasonably account for the variation? Diseases or medical conditions for which these surgical procedures are appropriate might be more common in one geographical area than another. If the possibility of such geographical variations in the incidence of pertinent medical conditions is ruled out, it is fair to conclude that the variation can be attributed to unnecessary surgical procedures.

A   This statement undermines such a conclusion since it cites a process in place for preventing or reducing unnecessary procedures.

B   **Correct.** This statement properly identifies additional information that eliminates the possibility that the geographical variation is due to legitimate factors.

C   The argument is concerned only with hysterectomies, prostatectomies, and tonsillectomies; other surgical procedures are irrelevant.

D   The difficulty in determining whether or not surgery is necessary makes any conclusion ambiguous, so this statement will not lead to the intended conclusion.

E   The argument involves only the three kinds of surgery cited in the passage, so this statement is irrelevant to the conclusion.

The correct answer is B.

54. A museum has been offered an undocumented statue, supposedly Greek and from the sixth century B.C. Possibly the statue is genuine but undocumented because it was recently unearthed or because it has been privately owned. However, an ancient surface usually has uneven weathering, whereas the surface of this statue has the uniform quality characteristically produced by a chemical bath used by forgers to imitate a weathered surface. Therefore, the statue is probably a forgery.

Which of the following, if true, most seriously weakens the argument?

(A) Museums can accept a recently unearthed statue only with valid export documentation from its country of origin.

(B) The subject's pose and other aspects of the subject's treatment exhibit all the most common features of Greek statues of the sixth century B.C.

(C) The chemical bath that forgers use was at one time used by dealers and collectors to remove the splotchy surface appearance of genuinely ancient sculptures.

(D) Museum officials believe that forgers have no technique that can convincingly simulate the patchy weathering characteristic of the surfaces of ancient sculptures.

(E) An allegedly Roman sculpture with a uniform surface similar to that of the statue being offered to the museum was recently shown to be a forgery.

Argument Evaluation

Situation   The authenticity of an undocumented statue, supposed to be Greek from the sixth century B.C., is questioned. Its surface shows a uniform quality typically achieved from a chemical bath, a technique used by forgers. Thus the statue is probably a forgery.

Reasoning   *What point weakens the argument that the statue is a forgery?* The argument that the statue is a forgery rests on one point: the statue's uniform surface suggests it may have been treated in a chemical bath used by forgers to simulate weathering. If the statue acquired its surface in some legitimate way, then the conclusion that it is not a true antiquity is weakened. If art dealers or collectors once used for esthetic reasons the same chemical baths now used by forgers for a different purpose, that fact would throw into doubt the conclusion about the statue's lack of authenticity.

A   Since the argument is about what might make the statue a forgery, not about museums' acquisition protocols, this statement fails to weaken the argument.

B   Since successful forgers of antiquities might well be expected to produce a counterfeit work that typifies its supposed historical period, this statement does not affect the argument.

C   **Correct.** This statement properly identifies a possible historical source of the statue's uniform surface and thus undermines the one-point argument that the statue is a forgery.

D   This statement is not relevant to this case since the statue in question does not have patchy weathering, but rather a uniform surface.

E   A similar example suggests that this statue, too, could be proven a forgery, so the conclusion is not weakened.

The correct answer is C.

55. Studies have shown that elderly people who practice a religion are much more likely to die immediately after an important religious holiday period than immediately before one. Researchers have concluded that the will to live can prolong life, at least for short periods of time.

Which of the following, if true, would most strengthen the researchers' conclusion?

(A) Elderly people who practice a religion are less likely to die immediately before or during an important religious holiday than at any other time of the year.

(B) Elderly people who practice a religion appear to experience less anxiety at the prospect of dying than do other people.

(C) Some elderly people who do practice a religion live much longer than most elderly people who do not.

(D) Most elderly people who participate in religious holidays have different reasons for participating than young people do.

(E) Many religions have important holidays in the spring and fall, seasons with the lowest death rates for elderly people.

Argument Evaluation

Situation Using studies that show elderly people who practice a religion tend to die immediately after, rather than immediately before, a major religious holiday, researchers conclude that the will to live can prolong life, at least for a short period of time.

Reasoning *What point strengthens the conclusion?* The broader the scope of the research, the stronger the conclusion. The researchers based their conclusion on a comparison of deaths immediately before and after major religious holidays. What would happen if the comparison of death rates were expanded to the entire year? If it is learned that the elderly who practice a religion are less likely to die before or during a major religious holiday than at any other time of year, the conclusion that they can prolong their lives temporarily through a specific holiday event is considerably strengthened.

A **Correct.** This statement properly identifies a point that strengthens the researchers' conclusion.

B The conclusion is about whether the will to live can prolong life, not about attitudes toward death, so this point is irrelevant.

C The conclusion is not about who lives longest in general, but about how the will to live through a specific event can prolong life.

D A recognized difference in motivation between elderly and younger people does not provide a direct reason to conclude that the elderly can will themselves to live through a holiday.

E The conclusion is about the ability to prolong life on a short-term basis through a specific holiday, so more general seasonal information does not affect the conclusion.

The correct answer is A.

56. Gortland has long been narrowly self-sufficient in both grain and meat. However, as per capita income in Gortland has risen toward the world average, per capita consumption of meat has also risen toward the world average, and it takes several pounds of grain to produce one pound of meat. Therefore, since per capita income continues to rise, whereas domestic grain production will not increase, Gortland will soon have to import either grain or meat or both.

Which of the following is an assumption on which the argument depends?

(A) The total acreage devoted to grain production in Gortland will not decrease substantially.

(B) The population of Gortland has remained relatively constant during the country's years of growing prosperity.

(C) The per capita consumption of meat in Gortland is roughly the same across all income levels.

(D) In Gortland, neither meat nor grain is subject to government price controls.

(E) People in Gortland who increase their consumption of meat will not radically decrease their consumption of grain.

Argument Construction

Situation   A country previously self-sufficient in grain and meat will soon have to import one or the other or both. Consumption of meat has risen as per capita income has risen, and it takes several pounds of grain to produce one pound of meat.

Reasoning   *What conditions must be true for the conclusion to be true?* Meat consumption is rising. What about grain consumption? A sharp reduction in the amount of grain consumed could compensate for increased meat consumption, making the conclusion false. If people did radically decrease their grain consumption, it might not be necessary to import grain or meat or both. Since the argument concludes the imports are necessary, it assumes grain consumption will not plunge.

A   The argument makes no assumptions about the acreage devoted to grain; it assumes only that the demand for grain will rise.

B   The argument is based on rising per capita income, not population levels.

C   The argument involves only meat consumption in general, not its distribution by income level.

D   Since the argument does not refer to price controls, it cannot depend on an assumption about them.

E   **Correct.** This statement properly identifies the assumption that there will be no great decrease in grain consumption.

The correct answer is E.

57. Meteorite explosions in the Earth's atmosphere as large as the one that destroyed forests in Siberia, with approximately the force of a 12-megaton nuclear blast, occur about once a century.

The response of highly automated systems controlled by complex computer programs to unexpected circumstances is unpredictable.

Which of the following conclusions can most properly be drawn, if the statements above are true, about a highly automated nuclear-missile defense system controlled by a complex computer program?

(A) Within a century after its construction, the system would react inappropriately and might accidentally start a nuclear war.

(B) The system would be destroyed if an explosion of a large meteorite occurred in the Earth's atmosphere.

(C) It would be impossible for the system to distinguish the explosion of a large meteorite from the explosion of a nuclear weapon.

(D) Whether the system would respond inappropriately to the explosion of a large meteorite would depend on the location of the blast.

(E) It is not certain what the system's response to the explosion of a large meteorite would be, if its designers did not plan for such a contingency.

Argument Construction

Situation   A meteorite explosion equivalent to a nuclear blast occurs approximately once a century. Automated systems, controlled by computer programs, respond to unexpected occurrences unpredictably.

Reasoning   *What conclusion can be drawn about a highly automated defense system?* The response of the system is *unpredictable*, which means that no certain conclusion is possible because the system may react either appropriately or inappropriately. Any conclusion must allow for this uncertainty.

A   The system cannot be assumed to react inappropriately, nor can it be concluded that the result of any inappropriate reaction would be nuclear war. Furthermore, a meteorite explosion may not occur within a century.

B   The premises offer no evidence that the system would be destroyed.

C   A system may or may not have the capability to distinguish between a nuclear blast and a meteorite explosion.

D   No information is given in the two premises about the location of the explosion and its effect on the system, so no conclusion can be drawn about proximity.

E   **Correct.** This statement properly identifies the conclusion that, since the system responds *unpredictably*, its response to a meteorite would be uncertain.

The correct answer is E.

Questions 58–59 are based on the following:

If there is an oil-supply disruption resulting in higher international oil prices, domestic oil prices in open-market countries such as the United States will rise as well, whether such countries import all or none of their oil.

58. If the statement above concerning oil-supply disruptions is true, which of the following policies in an open-market nation is most likely to reduce the long-term economic impact on that nation of sharp and unexpected increases in international oil prices?

   (A) Maintaining the quantity of oil imported at constant yearly levels

   (B) Increasing the number of oil tankers in its fleet

   (C) Suspending diplomatic relations with major oil-producing nations

   (D) Decreasing oil consumption through conservation

   (E) Decreasing domestic production of oil

Evaluation of a Plan

Situation   International oil prices rise when a disruption in the oil supply occurs; in this event, open-market countries experience a rise in domestic oil prices, even if they do not import any oil.

Reasoning   *What policy will reduce the economic impact of oil price increases?* All open-market countries experience a rise in oil prices, even when they do not import oil. Thus importing oil is not the issue. A nation can soften the impact of price hikes by using less oil because decreasing oil consumption would decrease the need to purchase oil at increased prices; conservation is a way to lower consumption.

   A   Not all countries import oil; for those that do, maintaining the level of oil imports when prices fluctuate would affect the economy.

   B   The number of oil tankers is irrelevant to the effect on the economy.

   C   The diplomatic relationship among countries is irrelevant to the effect on the economy.

   D   **Correct.** This statement properly identifies a factor that will reduce the economic impact of increases in oil prices.

   E   Decreasing domestic oil production would only make the situation worse.

The correct answer is D.

59. Which of the following conclusions is best supported by the statement above?

(A) Domestic producers of oil in open-market countries are excluded from the international oil market when there is a disruption in the international oil supply.

(B) International oil-supply disruptions have little, if any, effect on the price of domestic oil as long as an open-market country has domestic supplies capable of meeting domestic demand.

(C) The oil market in an open-market country is actually part of the international oil market, even if most of that country's domestic oil is usually sold to consumers within its borders.

(D) Open-market countries that export little or none of their oil can maintain stable domestic oil prices even when international oil prices rise sharply.

(E) If international oil prices rise, domestic distributors of oil in open-market countries will begin to import more oil than they export.

Argument Construction

Situation   International oil prices rise when a disruption in the oil supply occurs; in this event, open-market countries experience a rise in domestic oil prices, even if they do not import any oil. (The same as the item above.)

Reasoning   *What conclusion can be drawn from this information?* The passage says that domestic oil prices rise when international oil prices rise. Thus any open-market country, even one that produces most of the oil it uses, is a participant in the international market rather than functioning independently of that market.

A   The passage gives no information about domestic producers of oil, so no conclusion about them can be drawn.

B   This is a direct contradiction of the information in the passage.

C   **Correct.** This statement properly identifies the conclusion that can be drawn from the evidence.

D   This contradicts the passage by saying that domestic prices remain stable when international prices rise.

E   No information is given about distributors of oil, so no conclusion may be drawn.

The correct answer is C.

60. Most archaeologists have held that people first reached the Americas less than 20,000 years ago by crossing a land bridge into North America. But recent discoveries of human shelters in South America dating from 32,000 years ago have led researchers to speculate that people arrived in South America first, after voyaging across the Pacific, and then spread northward.

Which of the following, if it were discovered, would be pertinent evidence against the speculation above?

(A) A rock shelter near Pittsburgh, Pennsylvania, contains evidence of use by human beings 19,000 years ago.

(B) Some North American sites of human habitation predate any sites found in South America.

(C) The climate is warmer at the 32,000-year-old South American site than at the oldest known North American site.

(D) The site in South America that was occupied 32,000 years ago was continuously occupied until 6,000 years ago.

(E) The last Ice Age, between 11,500 and 20,000 years ago, considerably lowered worldwide sea levels.

Argument Evaluation

Situation   People are assumed to have crossed to the Americas less than 20,000 years ago by a land bridge to North America. However, human shelters dating much earlier have been found in South America, suggesting that people arrived first in South America and then spread northward.

Reasoning   *Which evidence weakens the idea that people arrived first in South America?* The evidence in favor of the idea is the existence of human shelters dating from 32,000 years ago. If there were evidence of human shelters existing in North America at an even earlier date, then the speculation about South America would be invalid because people must have arrived first in North America.

A   The rock shelter does not predate the South American shelters, so this does not weaken the argument.

B   **Correct.** This statement properly identifies evidence that weakens the argument.

C   The climate difference is irrelevant to the question of dates.

D   The continuous occupation of the site for a period of time does not give any information that counters the speculation.

E   The lower sea levels are irrelevant; moreover, the dates given are after, not before, the date of the South American shelters.

The correct answer is B.

61. The tobacco industry is still profitable and projections are that it will remain so. In the United States this year, the total amount of tobacco sold by tobacco farmers has increased, even though the number of adults who smoke has decreased.

    Each of the following, if true, could explain the simultaneous increase in tobacco sales and decrease in the number of adults who smoke EXCEPT:

    (A) During this year, the number of women who have begun to smoke is greater than the number of men who have quit smoking.

    (B) The number of teenage children who have begun to smoke this year is greater than the number of adults who have quit smoking during the same period.

    (C) During this year, the number of nonsmokers who have begun to use chewing tobacco or snuff is greater than the number of people who have quit smoking.

    (D) The people who have continued to smoke consume more tobacco per person than they did in the past.

    (E) More of the cigarettes made in the United States this year were exported to other countries than was the case last year.

Argument Construction

Situation   The number of adult Americans who smoke has decreased, but the amount of tobacco sold has increased.

Reasoning   *Which point does NOT help explain the paradoxical decrease in smokers and increase in tobacco sales?* Many possible explanations exist: an increase in teenage smokers, tobacco's use in products that are not smoked, increased consumption by the remaining smokers, an increase in tobacco exports, and so on. To answer this question, use the process of elimination to find the choice that does NOT provide an explanation.

A   **Correct.** This statement properly identifies a contradiction to the facts given in the passage and so cannot possibly be used to explain those facts. If the number of women who begin to smoke is greater than the number of men who quit, then the number of adult American smokers has increased.

B   A rise in teenage smokers would offset the decline in adult smokers and so could explain the paradox.

C   Rising tobacco sales despite a decrease in smokers could be explained by an increase in the use of snuff and chewing tobacco by nonsmokers.

D   Even though there are now fewer smokers, if these remaining smokers smoked substantially more, then the rise in tobacco sales could be explained.

E   Rising exports could explain rising tobacco sales at a time when fewer adult Americans smoke.

The correct answer is A.

62. A milepost on the towpath read "21" on the side facing the hiker as she approached it and "23" on its back. She reasoned that the next milepost forward on the path would indicate that she was halfway between one end of the path and the other. However, the milepost one mile further on read "20" facing her and "24" behind.

Which of the following, if true, would explain the discrepancy described above?

(A) The numbers on the next milepost had been reversed.

(B) The numbers on the mileposts indicate kilometers, not miles.

(C) The facing numbers indicate miles to the end of the path, not miles from the beginning.

(D) A milepost was missing between the two the hiker encountered.

(E) The mileposts had originally been put in place for the use of mountain bikers, not for hikers.

Argument Construction

Situation   A hiker sees a milepost marked *21* on one side and *23* on the other, She expects the next milepost to read *22* on both sides. However, the actual sign says *20* and *24*.

Reasoning   *What explains the discrepancy?* The hiker assumes that the number facing her is the distance she has traveled from the path's beginning and the other number is the distance to the path's end, that is, that she has come *23* miles and has *21* miles left to go at the first milepost. In fact, the numbers are actually the reverse of her reasoning. At the second milepost she has come *24* miles and has *20* left to go. The first number is the distance to the end, and the second number is the distance she has already traveled.

A   Reversing the numbers would not make any difference; according to the hiker's reasoning, both numbers would be *22*.

B   The units are irrelevant since the discrepancy between the expectation and the actual would still exist.

C   **Correct.** This statement properly resolves the logical discrepancy by showing the hiker's interpretation of the logic used in numbering was faulty.

D   A missing milepost would not explain the discrepancy. If the missing milepost did say *22* on each side, there would still be a discrepancy with the *20/24* milepost.

E   The numbers are measures of distance, not time, so the mode of transportation is irrelevant.

The correct answer is C.

63. Traditionally, decision making by managers that is reasoned step-by-step has been considered preferable to intuitive decision making. However, a recent study found that top managers used intuition significantly more than did most middle- or lower-level managers. This confirms the alternative view that intuition is actually more effective than careful, methodical reasoning.

The conclusion above is based on which of the following assumptions?

(A) Methodical, step-by-step reasoning is inappropriate for making many real-life management decisions.

(B) Top managers have the ability to use either intuitive reasoning or methodical, step-by-step reasoning in making decisions.

(C) The decisions made by middle- and lower-level managers can be made as easily by using methodical reasoning as by using intuitive reasoning.

(D) Top managers use intuitive reasoning in making the majority of their decisions.

(E) Top managers are more effective at decision making than middle- or lower-level managers.

Argument Construction

Situation   Intuition, used significantly more by top managers than by middle- or low-level managers, is found to be more effective than step-by-step reasoning in making decisions.

Reasoning   *What assumption does the argument make?* The study shows that top managers use intuition more in decision making than the other managers do. The conclusion is then drawn that intuition is more effective. What would make this true? Between the study's finding and the conclusion lies the assumption that top managers are better decision makers. If this were not the case, there would be no basis for the conclusion.

A   While the argument is consistent with this idea, the inappropriateness of step-by-step reasoning is not assumed.

B   Managers' ability to switch modes is not the issue; the issue is the quality of the decisions made.

C   The effectiveness of decisions, not the ease with which they are made, is the subject of the conclusion and must be the subject of the assumption as well.

D   The proportion of time the top managers use intuition rather than methodical reasoning is not being questioned.

E   **Correct.** This statement properly identifies the underlying assumption that top managers make better decisions than middle- and lower-level managers do.

The correct answer is E.

64. High levels of fertilizer and pesticides, needed when farmers try to produce high yields of the same crop year after year, pollute water supplies. Experts therefore urge farmers to diversify their crops and to rotate their plantings yearly.

    To receive governmental price-support benefits for a crop, farmers must have produced that same crop for the past several years.

    The statements above, if true, best support which of the following conclusions?

    (A) The rules for governmental support of farm prices work against efforts to reduce water pollution.

    (B) The only solution to the problem of water pollution from fertilizers and pesticides is to take farmland out of production.

    (C) Farmers can continue to make a profit by rotating diverse crops, thus reducing costs for chemicals, but not by planting the same crop each year.

    (D) New farming techniques will be developed to make it possible for farmers to reduce the application of fertilizers and pesticides.

    (E) Governmental price supports for farm products are set at levels that are not high enough to allow farmers to get out of debt.

Argument Construction

Situation   Farmers are urged to rotate crops annually because the chemicals they must use when continuing to produce the same crops pollute water supplies. On the other hand, farmers may receive federal price-support benefits only if they continue to produce the same crop.

Reasoning   *What conclusion can be drawn from this information?* Farmers wish to receive the price-support benefits offered by the government, so they grow the same crop for several years. In order to continue getting good yields, they use the high levels of chemicals necessary when the same crop is grown from year to year. The result is water pollution. The government's rules for price-support benefits work against the efforts to reduce water pollution.

A   **Correct.** This statement properly identifies the conclusion supported by the evidence.

B   The experts cited in the passage believe that the rotation of crops is the solution, not the removal of farmland from production.

C   The passage does not discuss how the farmers make a profit; it discusses the problems associated with continued farming of one crop and the government's encouragement of one-crop farming with its price-support benefits.

D   The conclusion must be drawn from the two statements in the passage taken together. Nothing in those two statements leads to a conclusion about farming techniques in the future.

E   This conclusion is unwarranted because there is no information in the two statements about the levels of the price supports and of the farmers' debts.

The correct answer is A.

Questions 65–66 are based on the following:

Hardin argued that grazing land held in common (that is, open to any user) would always be used less carefully than private grazing land. Each rancher would be tempted to overuse common land because the benefits would accrue to the individual, while the costs of reduced land quality that results from overuse would be spread among all users. But a study comparing 217 million acres of common grazing land with 433 million acres of private grazing land showed that the common land was in better condition.

65. The answer to which of the following questions would be most useful in evaluating the significance, in relation to Hardin's claim, of the study described above?

(A) Did any of the ranchers whose land was studied use both common and private land?

(B) Did the ranchers whose land was studied tend to prefer using common land over using private land for grazing?

(C) Was the private land that was studied of comparable quality to the common land before either was used for grazing?

(D) Were the users of the common land that was studied at least as prosperous as the users of the private land?

(E) Were there any owners of herds who used only common land, and no private land, for grazing?

Argument Evaluation

Situation Hardin claims that common grazing land is used less carefully than private grazing land because each rancher tries to get the most benefit from the common land, thus overusing it. Contrary to this claim, a study comparing common grazing land with private grazing land found the common ground to be in better condition.

Reasoning *What other information might be useful in evaluating the study?* The study finds that common grazing land was in better condition than private grazing land, which contradicts Hardin's argument. Because the study concerns only the condition of the common and private lands, the relevant question must be about the lands themselves, not about the users of those lands. Since the comparison deals with the conditions of the two types of land only *after* the ranchers' use, it would be useful to know how the lands compared *before* that use.

A It does not matter whether ranchers used one or both types of lands; only the relative condition of the two kinds of lands matters.

B The ranchers' preferences are not being questioned.

C **Correct.** This statement properly identifies information that would be useful in evaluating the results of the study.

D The prosperity of the ranchers is irrelevant to the condition of the two types of grazing lands.

E It does not matter if some ranchers used only common lands because it is the relative condition of the lands that is important.

The correct answer is C.

66. Which of the following, if true and known by the ranchers, would best help explain the results of the study?

    (A) With private grazing land, both the costs and the benefits of overuse fall to the individual user.

    (B) The cost in reduced land quality that is attributable to any individual user is less easily measured with common land than it is with private land.

    (C) An individual who overuses common grazing land might be able to achieve higher returns than other users can, with the result that he or she would obtain a competitive advantage.

    (D) If one user of common land overuses it even slightly, the other users are likely to do so even more, with the consequence that the costs to each user outweigh the benefits.

    (E) There are more acres of grazing land held privately than there are held in common.

Argument Construction

Situation   Hardin claims that common grazing land is used less carefully than private grazing land because each rancher tries to get the most benefit from the common land, thus overusing it. Contrary to this claim, a study comparing common grazing land with private grazing land found the common ground to be in better condition. (The same as the item above.)

Reasoning   *What do the ranchers know that explains the better condition of the common grazing land?* The better condition of the common land may indeed reflect better land use, contrary to Hardin's claim that ranchers will exploit common land to its detriment. What knowledge would keep the ranchers from abusing the common land? Exploitation would be less likely if the ranchers fully realize that the potential costs of overuse could outweigh the benefits of having access to common land. If each rancher knows that overuse by one rancher sets an example for all ranchers, then it is in each rancher's self-interest to avoid the kind of overuse that could lead to more widespread exploitation.

A   This statement is about private grazing land only and thus irrelevant to an analysis of the use of common grazing land.

B   The lack of accountability would offer ranchers increased opportunities to exploit the common land; this statement does not explain why the common land is in better condition.

C   This statement offers a reason that ranchers would overuse the common land; it does not explain why the common land remains in better condition.

D   **Correct.** This statement properly identifies the ranchers' knowledge of the balance to be applied; such understanding would explain the results of the study.

E   The greater amount of private grazing land is not in question since the study is about quality, not quantity.

The correct answer is D.

67. A compelling optical illusion called the illusion of velocity and size makes objects appear to be moving more slowly the larger the objects are. Therefore, a motorist's estimate of the time available for crossing a highway with a small car approaching is bound to be lower than it would be with a large truck approaching.

The conclusion above would be more properly drawn if it were made clear that the_____.

(A) truck's speed is assumed to be lower than the car's

(B) truck's speed is assumed to be the same as the car's

(C) truck's speed is assumed to be higher than the car's

(D) motorist's estimate of time available is assumed to be more accurate with cars approaching than with trucks approaching

(E) motorist's estimate of time available is assumed to be more accurate with trucks approaching than with cars approaching

Argument Construction

Situation   An optical illusion makes objects appear to be moving more slowly the larger they are. It is explained that a driver's estimate of the time available to cross a highway is therefore lower when a small car is approaching than it would be if a large truck were approaching.

Reasoning   *What underlying assumption should be made more clear in the explanation of how the illusion works?* It is given that the motorist underestimates the approach time of a large truck compared to the approach time of a small car, that is, a driver estimates that the time it will take for the small car to approach is less than the time it will take for the large truck to approach because the operative illusion makes the larger truck seem to be moving more slowly than the small car. What unstated assumption clarifies the operation of this illusion? If the vehicles are moving at the same speed, the illusion makes it appear that the large truck is moving more slowly when in fact it is not. The illusion thus occurs when the objects are traveling at the same speed. The explanation, and the conclusion, would be clearer if this were specifically stated.

A   If the truck is moving more slowly than the car, then the driver's perception is based on the true condition, not on the illusion.

B   Correct. This statement properly identifies an assumption that contributes to understanding the explanation and conclusion: only when the vehicles are moving at the same speed does the illusion lead to the driver's perception; at the same speed the larger object appears to move more slowly than the smaller object.

C   If the truck is moving faster than the car, the illusion might make the two vehicles appear to be moving at the same speed.

D   It does not matter for which type of vehicle the driver's estimate of lead time is more accurate; this assumption is not helpful in explaining the conclusion that the illusion makes larger objects appear to be moving more slowly than small objects.

E   It does not matter for which type of vehicle the driver's estimate of lead time is more accurate; this assumption is not helpful in explaining the conclusion that the illusion makes larger objects appear to be moving more slowly than small objects.

The correct answer is B.

68. Advocates of a large-scale space-defense research project conclude that it will represent a net benefit to civilian business. They say that since government-sponsored research will have civilian applications, civilian businesses will reap the rewards of government-developed technology.

    Each of the following, if true, raises a consideration arguing against the conclusion above, EXCEPT:

    (A) The development of cost-efficient manufacturing techniques is of the highest priority for civilian business and would be neglected if resources go to military projects, which do not emphasize cost efficiency.

    (B) Scientific and engineering talent needed by civilian business will be absorbed by the large-scale project.

    (C) Many civilian businesses will receive subcontracts to provide materials and products needed by the research project.

    (D) If government research money is devoted to the space project, it will not be available for specifically targeted needs of civilian business, where it could be more efficiently used.

    (E) The increase in taxes or government debt needed to finance the project will severely reduce the vitality of the civilian economy.

Argument Evaluation

Situation   Civilian businesses will benefit from a large-scale, space-defense research project sponsored by the government.

Reasoning   *Which point supports the conclusion?* Identify the aspect of the research project that shows a clear benefit for civilian businesses. If civilian businesses are employed as subcontractors on this project, then they do plainly benefit from it; the conclusion is supported.

A   The neglect of cost efficiency, considered to be the *highest priority* by civilian businesses, is an important point in an argument against the project.

B   The loss of scientific and engineering talent would be a significant blow, not a benefit, to civilian businesses.

C   **Correct.** This statement properly identifies the consideration that strengthens the conclusion.

D   The loss of government funding for specifically targeted needs of civilian businesses cannot be perceived as a benefit, only a detriment.

E   Financing the project would hurt, not help, civilian businesses by reducing the vitality of the civilian economy.

The correct answer is C.

69. Manufacturers sometimes discount the price of a product to retailers for a promotion period when the product is advertised to consumers. Such promotions often result in a dramatic increase in amount of product sold by the manufacturers to retailers. Nevertheless, the manufacturers could often make more profit by not holding the promotions.

Which of the following, if true, most strongly supports the claim above about the manufacturers' profit?

(A) The amount of discount generally offered by manufacturers to retailers is carefully calculated to represent the minimum needed to draw consumers' attention to the product.

(B) For many consumer products the period of advertising discounted prices to consumers is about a week, not sufficiently long for consumers to become used to the sale price.

(C) For products that are not newly introduced, the purpose of such promotions is to keep the products in the minds of consumers and to attract consumers who are currently using competing products.

(D) During such a promotion retailers tend to accumulate in their warehouses inventory bought at discount; they then sell much of it later at their regular price.

(E) If a manufacturer fails to offer such promotions but its competitor offers them, that competitor will tend to attract consumers away from the manufacturer's product.

Argument Construction

Situation   During promotion periods, manufacturers discount prices and dramatically increase the amount of product sold to retailers. However, manufacturers might make more profit without the promotions.

Reasoning   *How could promotion periods cut profits?* It is stated that promotion periods result in increased product sales to retailers. How could such sales decrease the manufacturers' potential profits? If retailers buy more than they can sell during the promotion period, they will store the surplus in warehouses and sell it later at the regular price. Manufacturers lose their normal profits on these sales. This loss may be greater than any gains from increasing sales or winning new customers during the brief promotion period.

A   Calculating the minimum amount of discount should lead to greater profit for manufacturers, so this statement does not explain the potential loss of profit.

B   The brevity of the promotion period favors manufacturers because consumers do not become accustomed to the lower price.

C   Attracting customers' attention should contribute to higher, not lower, profit.

D   **Correct.** This statement properly identifies a factor that strengthens the argument.

E   Since the failure to offer promotions results in loss of customers to competitors, this statement shows that manufacturers gain by promotions.

The correct answer is D.

70. When people evade income taxes by not declaring taxable income, a vicious cycle results. Tax evasion forces lawmakers to raise income tax rates, which causes the tax burden on non-evading taxpayers to become heavier. This, in turn, encourages even more taxpayers to evade income taxes by hiding taxable income.

The vicious cycle described above could not result unless which of the following were true?

(A) An increase in tax rates tends to function as an incentive for taxpayers to try to increase their pretax incomes.

(B) Some methods for detecting tax evaders, and thus recovering some tax revenue lost through evasion, bring in more than they cost, but their success rate varies from year to year.

(C) When lawmakers establish income tax rates in order to generate a certain level of revenue, they do not allow adequately for revenue that will be lost through evasion.

(D) No one who routinely hides some taxable income can be induced by a lowering of tax rates to stop hiding such income unless fines for evaders are raised at the same time.

(E) Taxpayers do not differ from each other with respect to the rate of taxation that will cause them to evade taxes.

Argument Construction

Situation   When some people evade income taxes by hiding taxable income, income tax rates must be raised, placing a heavier tax burden on honest taxpayers. The higher rate, in turn, encourages more people to conceal taxable income.

Reasoning   *What must be true in order for this cycle to occur?* Consider the factors that are assumed to drive this cycle. It is said that tax evasion *forces* legislative increases in tax rates to cover the loss of tax revenues. Under what conditions would this underlying assumption hold true? When considering income tax rates in the first place, lawmakers must not take into account the amount of revenue that will inevitably be lost to evasion.

A   Any incentive to increase pretax incomes would counter the reported tendency to conceal income and thus break the cycle.

B   Success in detecting tax evaders, no matter how variable or cost effective, inhibits tax evasion and breaks the cycle.

C   **Correct.** This statement properly identifies the argument's underlying assumption that lawmakers fail to consider the revenue lost to evasion when they determine tax rates, forcing the increased tax rates that drive the cycle.

D   Higher fines deter evaders and thus break the cycle.

E   If taxpayers did not differ, the cycle could never get started. Either everyone would evade taxes or no one would. This statement must be false.

The correct answer is C.

71. Because postage rates are rising, *Home Decorator* magazine plans to maximize its profits by reducing by one-half the number of issues it publishes each year. The quality of articles, the number of articles published per year, and the subscription price will not change. Market research shows that neither subscribers nor advertisers will be lost if the magazine's plan is instituted.

Which of the following, if true, provides the strongest evidence that the magazine's profits are likely to decline if the plan is instituted?

(A) With the new postage rates, a typical issue under the proposed plan would cost about one-third more to mail than a typical current issue would.

(B) The majority of the magazine's subscribers are less concerned about a possible reduction in the quantity of the magazine's articles than about a possible loss of the current high quality of its articles.

(C) Many of the magazine's long-time subscribers would continue their subscriptions even if the subscription price were increased.

(D) Most of the advertisers that purchase advertising space in the magazine will continue to spend the same amount on advertising per issue as they have in the past.

(E) Production costs for the magazine are expected to remain stable.

Evaluation of a Plan

Situation In the face of rising postage costs, a magazine decides to cut in half the number of issues it publishes a year, though the quality and quantity of the articles as well as the subscription price will remain the same. Market research indicates that this plan will not cost the magazine any subscribers or advertisers.

Reasoning *How might the plan cause profits to decline?* The magazine plans to maximize profits by reducing costs. What could lead to lower profits despite lower costs? Loss of revenue could cause profits to go down. Revenue will be lost if advertisers spend the same amount on advertising per issue but there are only *half* as many issues in which to place advertising. When the advertising revenues are cut in half, a significant decline in profits is likely to result.

A If the number of issues is cut in half and the postage rate per issue goes up by a third, then mailing costs still go down. This statement does not suggest that the plan will cause a decline in profits.

B This statement is irrelevant to the magazine's profitability given the stated point that the quantity and quality of articles will not change.

C The passage says that the subscription price will not increase under the plan, so this statement provides no useful evidence.

D **Correct.** This statement properly identifies evidence of a flaw in the plan. While market research shows that *advertisers* will not be lost, this statement shows that a significant amount of *advertising* will be lost.

E Stable production costs would not lead to a decline in profits.

The correct answer is D.

72. A discount retailer of basic household necessities employs thousands of people and pays most of them at the minimum wage rate. Yet following a federally mandated increase of the minimum wage rate that increased the retailer's operating costs considerably, the retailer's profits increased markedly.

    Which of the following, if true, most helps to resolve the apparent paradox?

    (A) Over half of the retailer's operating costs consist of payroll expenditures; yet only a small percentage of those expenditures go to pay management salaries.

    (B) The retailer's customer base is made up primarily of people who earn, or who depend on the earnings of others who earn, the minimum wage.

    (C) The retailer's operating costs, other than wages, increased substantially after the increase in the minimum wage rate went into effect.

    (D) When the increase in the minimum wage rate went into effect, the retailer also raised the wage rate for employees who had been earning just above minimum wage.

    (E) The majority of the retailer's employees work as cashiers, and most cashiers are paid the minimum wage.

Argument Evaluation

Situation   A discount retailer of household necessities pays the minimum wage to most of its employees. When the minimum wages goes up, the retailer's operating costs rise. However, its profits also rise.

Reasoning   *What information helps resolve this paradox?* The retailer's profits paradoxically rise as its costs rise. What can be happening to account for this? Consider the nature of the cost increase: wages have gone up. If the retailer's customer base includes many people who earn minimum wage, their buying power has risen with the minimum wage and they can spend more. When customers spend more, the retailer's profits are likely to rise, and the seeming paradox is explained.

A   This statement emphasizes how substantially operating costs have risen. It does not suggest how rising costs could possibly lead to profits.

B   **Correct.** This statement properly explains the apparent paradox.

C   If the retailer's other costs also rose, then the paradox of the retailer's profits is even more mysterious.

D   Increasing other wages contributes to even higher operating costs; there is no information to explain how higher costs could lead to profits.

E   This detail about minimum-wage jobs does not explain how the retailer could be gaining profits when costs are rising.

The correct answer is B.

73. The cotton farms of Country Q became so productive that the market could not absorb all that they produced. Consequently, cotton prices fell. The government tried to boost cotton prices by offering farmers who took 25 percent of their cotton acreage out of production direct support payments up to a specified maximum per farm.

The government's program, if successful, will not be a net burden on the budget. Which of the following, if true, is the best basis for an explanation of how this could be so?

(A) Depressed cotton prices meant operating losses for cotton farms, and the government lost revenue from taxes on farm profits.

(B) Cotton production in several countries other than Q declined slightly the year that the support-payment program went into effect in Q.

(C) The first year that the support-payment program was in effect, cotton acreage in Q was 5 percent below its level in the base year for the program.

(D) The specified maximum per farm meant that for very large cotton farms the support payments were less per acre for those acres that were withdrawn from production than they were for smaller farms.

(E) Farmers who wished to qualify for support payments could not use the cotton acreage that was withdrawn from production to grow any other crop.

Evaluation of a Plan

Situation Overproduction of cotton led to falling prices. To boost prices, the government offered direct support payments to farmers who took 25 percent of their cotton acreage out of production. This plan is not expected to be a net burden on the budget.

Reasoning *What would explain why this plan is not a net burden?* The plan's success will mean that the government will be receiving in return as much as or more than it pays out in support payments. What government revenues would account for such an increase in receipts? If, when cotton prices fell, the cotton farmers had lower profits, they were paying lower taxes to the government. When cotton prices increase (because less land is in production and less cotton is offered in the market) and cotton farmers make greater profits, the government is able to tax those profits. In the program, the increased tax revenue compensates for the added expenditure.

A **Correct.** This statement properly identifies the information that explains how the plan functions.

B The decline in cotton production in other countries does not explain why the program will not be a burden on the budget.

C The difference in cotton acreage does not explain how the government can recover the costs of the direct-payment plan.

D The direct payments are presumably scaled to the size of the farm since the passage states that payments are made *up to* a specified maximum. Nothing in this statement explains how the government will be able to compensate for making the payments.

E How farmers use the land taken out of production is irrelevant, since the plan is concerned only with the cotton crop.

The correct answer is A.

74. United States hospitals have traditionally relied primarily on revenues from paying patients to offset losses from unreimbursed care. Almost all paying patients now rely on governmental or private health insurance to pay hospital bills. Recently, insurers have been strictly limiting what they pay hospitals for the care of insured patients to amounts at or below actual costs.

Which of the following conclusions is best supported by the information above?

(A) Although the advance of technology has made expensive medical procedures available to the wealthy, such procedures are out of the reach of low-income patients.

(B) If hospitals do not find ways of raising additional income for unreimbursed care, they must either deny some of that care or suffer losses if they give it.

(C) Some patients have incomes too high for eligibility for governmental health insurance but are unable to afford private insurance for hospital care.

(D) If the hospitals reduce their costs in providing care, insurance companies will maintain the current level of reimbursement, thereby providing more funds for unreimbursed care.

(E) Even though philanthropic donations have traditionally provided some support for the hospitals, such donations are at present declining.

Argument Construction

Situation   Hospitals have historically used the revenues from paying patients to compensate for the costs of unreimbursed care, and most paying patients now rely on insurance to pay the hospital bills. However, health insurers now strictly limit what is paid to the hospitals to amounts at or below the hospitals' actual costs.

Reasoning   *What conclusion can be drawn from the information in the passage?* The passage shows that the source that hospitals have turned to in the past to cover the costs of unreimbursed care—paying patients—has now disappeared. What will happen to unreimbursed care? Either the hospitals must figure out a new way to cover the costs, or they must deny care. The only other option is to suffer the losses incurred by unreimbursed care.

A   The passage does not examine specific medical procedures, so the conclusion that they are available only to some is not warranted.

B   **Correct.** This statement properly identifies a conclusion that can be drawn from the passage.

C   The passage does not discuss these patients, so no conclusion about them can be drawn.

D   The passage states that insurance companies will only reimburse *amounts at or below actual costs*, so it is unlikely that insurance companies will continue to reimburse at the same level if the hospitals reduce costs.

E   No information is provided about the role of philanthropic donations, so no conclusion about them may be drawn.

The correct answer is B.

75. Generally scientists enter their field with the goal of doing important new research and accept as their colleagues those with similar motivation. Therefore, when any scientist wins renown as an expounder of science to general audiences, most other scientists conclude that this popularizer should no longer be regarded as a true colleague.

The explanation offered above for the low esteem in which scientific popularizers are held by research scientists assumes that

(A) serious scientific research is not a solitary activity, but relies on active cooperation among a group of colleagues

(B) research scientists tend not to regard as colleagues those scientists whose renown they envy

(C) a scientist can become a famous popularizer without having completed any important research

(D) research scientists believe that those who are well known as popularizers of science are not motivated to do important new research

(E) no important new research can be accessible to or accurately assessed by those who are not themselves scientists

Argument Construction

Situation   Research scientists expect that they and their colleagues will do important new research. When a scientist becomes popular among a general audience for explaining principles of science, other scientists have less esteem for this popularizer, no longer regarding such a scientist as a serious colleague.

Reasoning   *What assumption do research scientists make about scientists who become popularizers?* The community of scientists shares a common goal: to do important new research. What would cause this community to disapprove of a popularizer? Any scientist who becomes a popularizer appears to have given up this shared goal in order to explain science to a general audience instead. This popularizer may be assumed to have lost the motivation to do important new research.

A   The issue is the scientists' goal, not the methods they use to achieve it.

B   This statement gives another reason that scientists may reject a popularizer, but because it is not the reason implied in the passage, it cannot be assumed.

C   The argument applies to all popularizers, including those who have done important research. This assumption is too limited.

D   Correct. This statement properly identifies the research scientists' underlying assumption.

E   The passage is not concerned with who understands science, but rather with who is doing important new research in science.

The correct answer is D.

76. Country Y uses its scarce foreign-exchange reserves to buy scrap iron for recycling into steel. Although the steel thus produced earns more foreign exchange than it costs, that policy is foolish. Country Y's own territory has vast deposits of iron ore, which can be mined with minimal expenditure of foreign exchange.

Which of the following, if true, provides the strongest support for Country Y's policy of buying scrap iron abroad?

(A)   The price of scrap iron on international markets rose significantly in 1987.

(B)   Country Y's foreign-exchange reserves dropped significantly in 1987.

(C)   There is virtually no difference in quality between steel produced from scrap iron and that produced from iron ore.

(D)   Scrap iron is now used in the production of roughly half the steel used in the world today, and experts predict that scrap iron will be used even more extensively in the future.

(E)   Furnaces that process scrap iron can be built and operated in Country Y with substantially less foreign exchange than can furnaces that process iron ore.

Evaluation of a Plan

Situation   A country could mine its vast deposits of iron ore with minimal expenditure of foreign exchange. Nevertheless, it uses its scarce foreign-exchange reserves to buy scrap iron for recycling into steel; this steel does earn more foreign exchange than it costs.

Reasoning   *Which statement supports the policy of buying scrap iron abroad?* The country is using scant foreign-exchange reserves to buy scrap iron when it could instead be mining its own iron ore with minimal expenditure of foreign exchange. What makes this approach seem foolish? It would be illogical if iron-processing costs are otherwise equal with regard to the expenditure of foreign exchange. What could justify this decision? If processing the scrap iron involves far less expenditure of foreign exchange than processing the raw iron ore, the policy is supported.

A   A significant increase in the international price of scrap iron would be a reason against the policy.

B   A significant drop in foreign-exchange reserves means that conserving the reserves is all the more important, but this statement provides no reason to support the current policy.

C   This statement merely shows that the quality of steel achieved by the two methods, and thus the likely selling price for the steel, is similar; it does not give a reason for supporting the current policy.

D   The increasing use of scrap iron for recycling into steel suggests that it is a good alternative to mining iron ore, but this statement is general and does not address the particular problems of a country that must use scarce foreign-exchange reserves to buy the scrap iron.

E   **Correct.** This statement properly identifies a factor that supports the policy.

The correct answer is E.

77. Parasitic wasps lay their eggs directly into the eggs of various host insects in exactly the right numbers for any suitable size of host egg. If they laid too many eggs in a host egg, the developing wasp larvae would compete with each other to the death for nutrients and space. If too few eggs were laid, portions of the host egg would decay, killing the wasp larvae.

Which of the following conclusions can properly be drawn from the information above?

(A) The size of the smallest host egg that a wasp could theoretically parasitize can be determined from the wasp's egg-laying behavior.

(B) Host insects lack any effective defenses against the form of predation practiced by parasitic wasps.

(C) Parasitic wasps learn from experience how many eggs to lay into the eggs of different host species.

(D) Failure to lay enough eggs would lead to the death of the developing wasp larvae more quickly than would laying too many eggs.

(E) Parasitic wasps use visual clues to calculate the size of a host egg.

Argument Construction

Situation   Parasitic wasps lay their eggs inside suitably sized host eggs. The wasps must be exact about the numbers of eggs they lay in the host eggs. If they lay too many, the wasp larvae have to compete for nutrients and space; if they lay too few, the host egg decays, killing the wasp larvae.

Reasoning   *What is the best-supported conclusion to be drawn from this information?* Approach this question by eliminating first the suggested conclusions that lack logical support, and then consider the content and logic of the remaining possibilities. A review of the alternatives seems to rule out four options, so consider and confirm the first. The first sentence of the passage explains that the wasps lay eggs *in exactly the right numbers* for the size of the host egg. The wasps' behavior could be examined by comparing different sizes of the host eggs in which wasps have laid different numbers of eggs. It would be possible then to determine the size of the smallest host egg that the wasp could lay its egg(s) in successfully.

A   **Correct.** This statement properly identifies the conclusion that an examination of the wasps' egg-laying behavior would reveal, at least in theory, the size of the smallest host egg a wasp could lay its egg(s) in.

B   The passage is about the parasitic wasps, not about the host insects, so a conclusion that is about the hosts is not supported.

C   The passage does not discuss how the wasps have the ability to lay the right number of eggs, so the conclusion that they learn by experience is not earned.

D   The passage does not present any information about the relative speed with which too many or too few developing larvae die, so this conclusion is not founded.

E   No information in the passage supports the wasps' use of visual clues, so this conclusion is not warranted.

The correct answer is A.

78. <u>Consumer health advocate</u>: Your candy company adds caffeine to your chocolate candy bars so that each one delivers a specified amount of caffeine. Since caffeine is highly addictive, this indicates that you intend to keep your customers addicted.

    <u>Candy manufacturer</u>: Our manufacturing process results in there being less caffeine in each chocolate candy bar than in the unprocessed cacao beans from which the chocolate is made.

    The candy manufacturer's response is flawed as a refutation of the consumer health advocate's argument because it_____.

    (A) fails to address the issue of whether the level of caffeine in the candy bars sold by the manufacturer is enough to keep people addicted

    (B) assumes without warrant that all unprocessed cacao beans contain a uniform amount of caffeine

    (C) does not specify exactly how caffeine is lost in the manufacturing process

    (D) treats the consumer health advocate's argument as though it were about each candy bar rather than about the manufacturer's candy in general

    (E) merely contradicts the consumer health advocate's conclusion without giving any reason to believe that the advocate's reasoning is unsound

Argument Evaluation

Situation   A candy manufacturer is accused of adding caffeine, an addictive substance, to its chocolate candy bars with the intent of keeping its customers addicted. The candy manufacturer responds to this accusation by saying that there is less caffeine in each chocolate candy bar than in the unprocessed cacao beans from which the chocolate is made.

Reasoning   *What is the flaw in the candy manufacturer's response?* First consider whether the response indeed refutes the advocate's charge. In actuality, instead of meeting the terms of the accusation, the candy maker veers away from the subject of adding caffeine to its chocolate bars or keeping customers addicted. The manufacturer substitutes an entirely different subject, the amount of caffeine in cacao beans, instead. The manufacturer's response is a diversion, not an answer.

A   **Correct.** This statement properly identifies the flaw in the response. The candy manufacturer does not answer the question about the amount of caffeine added to candy bars or the intent of making them addictive.

B   Even if the manufacturer did make this assumption, the information is not relevant to the accusation, which is not concerned with naturally occurring caffeine in cacao beans; the manufacturer would still be evading the question.

C   The addition of caffeine is the issue needing to be addressed in the answer, not the loss of caffeine through the manufacturing process.

D   The manufacturer does not treat the health advocate's argument this way; the argument is not addressed at all. Instead, the manufacturer compares the caffeine in chocolate bars and cacao beans.

E   The manufacturer does not contradict the accusation, but rather avoids it.

The correct answer is A.

79. To evaluate a plan to save money on office-space expenditures by having its employees work at home, XYZ Company asked volunteers from its staff to try the arrangement for six months. During this period, the productivity of these employees was as high as or higher than before.

Which of the following, if true, would argue most strongly against deciding, on the basis of the trial results, to implement the company's plan?

(A) The employees who agreed to participate in the test of the plan were among the company's most self-motivated and independent workers.

(B) The savings that would accrue from reduced office-space expenditures alone would be sufficient to justify the arrangement for the company, apart from any productivity increases.

(C) Other companies that have achieved successful results from work-at-home plans have work forces that are substantially larger than that of XYZ.

(D) The volunteers who worked at home were able to communicate with other employees as necessary for performing the work.

(E) Minor changes in the way office work is organized at XYZ would yield increases in employee productivity similar to those achieved in the trial.

Evaluation of a Plan

Situation To save money on office space expenditures, a company considers having employees work at home. A six-month trial with employees who have volunteered to test the plan shows their productivity to be as high as or higher than before.

Reasoning *Given these trial results, what is a good reason NOT to implement the plan?* Generalizing from a small sample to the group depends on having a sample that is representative. In this case, the employees who participated in the trial are not representative of all employees. The employees who volunteered for the trial, because of their self-motivation and independence, are the employees who would be most likely to work successfully at home. It would not be wise to base a generalization about all employees on this sample.

A **Correct.** This statement properly identifies a flaw in the trial results that are the basis for the plan.

B This statement supports the implementation of the plan. Moreover, it is not based on the trial results, so it does not answer the question.

C While the difference in the size of the work force may be significant to the success of the plan, such a determination cannot be derived from the trial results.

D Nothing indicates that the ease of communicating would change if the plan were implemented, so this statement does not provide a reason against the plan.

E The goal of the plan is to save money on office space, not to increase productivity, so an alternative plan to increase productivity is irrelevant.

The correct answer is A.

80. Vitacorp, a manufacturer, wishes to make its information booth at an industry convention more productive in terms of boosting sales. The booth offers information introducing the company's new products and services. To achieve the desired result, Vitacorp's marketing department will attempt to attract more people to the booth. The marketing director's first measure was to instruct each salesperson to call his or her five best customers and personally invite them to visit the booth.

Which of the following, if true, most strongly supports the prediction that the marketing director's first measure will contribute to meeting the goal of boosting sales?

(A) Vitacorp's salespeople routinely inform each important customer about new products and services as soon as the decision to launch them has been made.

(B) Many of Vitacorp's competitors have made plans for making their own information booths more productive in increasing sales.

(C) An information booth that is well attended tends to attract visitors who would not otherwise have attended the booth.

(D) Most of Vitacorp's best customers also have business dealings with Vitacorp's competitors.

(E) Vitacorp has fewer new products and services available this year than it had in previous years.

Evaluation of a Plan

Situation   A manufacturer wants increased sales from its information booth at an industry convention. To boost sales, the marketing department seeks to attract more people to the booth, and the marketing director tells the salespeople to invite their best customers to visit the booth.

Reasoning   *Which point best supports the marketing director's plan?* First ask what would be a valid reason for inviting faithful customers to visit the booth. Such invitations should assure that the booth will generally be busy with visitors. If people are more attracted to a well-attended booth than to an empty one, then more potential customers are likely to visit the busy booth, and more visitors should produce more sales. The marketing director is operating on the principle that success breeds success. Making sure that the booth is well attended by Vitacorp's current customers is likely to attract more potential customers and thus boost sales.

A   If the best customers already have all available new product and service information, they are unlikely to respond to the invitation to visit the booth; this point is a weakness in the plan.

B   Competitors' efforts toward the same goal may hurt Vitacorp's efforts, so this point does not support the plan.

C   **Correct.** This statement properly identifies a point supporting the marketing director's plan.

D   The plan simply aims to attract more visitors to Vitacorp's booth to encourage more sales and does not address the fact that Vitacorp shares its customers with its competitors.

E   Again, the plan merely seeks to attract an increased number of booth visitors, and thus potential buyers, to boost sales, no matter what new products and services may be offered this year.

The correct answer is C.

81. An eyeglass manufacturer tried to boost sales for the summer quarter by offering its distributors a special discount if their orders for that quarter exceeded those for last year's summer quarter by at least 20 percent. Many distributors qualified for this discount. Even with much merchandise discounted, sales increased enough to produce a healthy gain in net profits. The manufacturer plans to repeat this success by offering the same sort of discount for the fall quarter.

Which of the following, if true, most clearly points to a flaw in the manufacturer's plan to repeat the successful performance of the summer quarter?

(A) In general, a distributor's orders for the summer quarter are no higher than those for the spring quarter.

(B) Along with offering special discounts to qualifying distributors, the manufacturer increased newspaper and radio advertising in those distributors' sales areas.

(C) The distributors most likely to qualify for the manufacturer's special discount are those whose orders were unusually low a year earlier.

(D) The distributors who qualified for the manufacturer's special discount were free to decide how much of that discount to pass on to their own customers.

(E) The distributors' ordering more goods in the summer quarter left them overstocked for the fall quarter.

Evaluation of a Plan

Situation   A manufacturer successfully boosted sales and gained net profits for the summer quarter by giving distributors a discount if their orders exceeded the previous summer's orders by 20 percent. The manufacturer plans to repeat the success by offering the discount again in the fall quarter.

Reasoning   *What is the flaw in the manufacturer's plan?* The plan assumes that an action that succeeded once will work a second time. Why might the plan not work this time? If the distributors increased their orders during the summer simply because they were eager to take advantage of the discount, the result may be that they are now overstocked for the fall quarter. If so, they will not need to place orders for more goods, and the plan of continuing the discount will have less chance of success now.

A   This is irrelevant to the plan since the two quarters being compared are the two summer quarters one year apart, not spring and summer quarters.

B   Increased advertising should continue to contribute to the plan's success.

C   Even if the qualifying distributors only reached normal levels of sales, there is no reason to think that this success will not continue in the fall.

D   The distributors' freedom to decide how much of the discount to pass on to customers is equally true in both summer and fall quarters and should not affect the success of the plan.

E   **Correct.** This statement properly identifies a flaw in the plan.

The correct answer is E.

82. <u>Consumer advocate</u>: It is generally true, at least in this state, that lawyers who advertise a specific service charge less for that service than lawyers who do not advertise. It is also true that **each time restrictions on the advertising of legal services have been eliminated, the number of lawyers advertising their services has increased and legal costs to consumers have declined in consequence.** However, eliminating the state requirement that legal advertisements must specify fees for specific services would almost certainly increase rather than further reduce consumers' legal costs. Lawyers would no longer have an incentive to lower their fees when they begin advertising and **if no longer required to specify fee arrangements, many lawyers who now advertise would increase their fees.**

In the consumer advocate's argument, the two portions in boldface play which of the following roles?

(A) The first is a generalization that the consumer advocate accepts as true; the second is presented as a consequence that follows from the truth of that generalization.

(B) The first is a pattern of cause and effect that the consumer advocate argues will be repeated in the case at issue; the second acknowledges a circumstance in which that pattern would not hold.

(C) The first is a pattern of cause and effect that the consumer advocate predicts will not hold in the case at issue; the second offers a consideration in support of that prediction.

(D) The first is evidence that the consumer advocate offers in support of a certain prediction; the second is that prediction.

(E) The first acknowledges a consideration that weighs against the main position that the consumer advocate defends; the second is that position.

Argument Construction

Situation   Lawyers who advertise charge less. In the past, **when advertising restrictions have been removed, the number of lawyers advertising rose and legal costs to consumers fell.** However, eliminating the requirement to specify fees in advertisements would raise consumers' legal costs. **If lawyers are not required to specify their fees in ads, many lawyers who advertise will raise their fees, and consumer costs are likely to rise.**

Reasoning   *What part do the two sentences in **boldface** play in the argument?* This question asks the reader to look carefully at how the advocate's argument is constructed and in particular at how the two sentences in **boldface** are related. It is necessary to understand the consumer advocate's main point: if lawyers are not required to specify fees in advertisements, consumers' legal costs are likely to rise. The first **boldface** sentence shows the cause-and-effect relation of lawyers' ads and falling consumer costs, a relation the advocate predicts will not continue in the current case. The second **boldface** sentence explains why that relation will change.

A   The first sentence is presented as true, but the second sentence does not follow as a consequence; rather, it contradicts the first sentence.

B   The first sentence shows cause and effect, but the consumer advocate does not argue that it will be repeated. The advocate argues that it will not be repeated.

C   **Correct.** The first sentence shows general cause and effect in a situation that the advocate argues will not be true in this particular case. The second sentence explains why it will not be true.

D   The consumer advocate predicts legal costs will rise; the first sentence does not offer evidence in support of that prediction, but rather evidence that costs have always fallen.

E   The first sentence gives a general cause-and-effect relationship, not a special consideration; the second sentence shows how that relationship could change.

The correct answer is C.

5.0 Sentence Correction

5.0 Sentence Correction

Sentence correction questions appear in the Verbal section of the GMAT® exam. The Verbal section uses multiple-choice questions to measure your ability to read and comprehend written material, to reason and evaluate arguments, and to correct written material to conform to standard written English. Because the Verbal section includes passages from several different content areas, you may be generally familiar with some of the material; however, neither the passages nor the questions assume detailed knowledge of the topics discussed. Sentence correction questions are intermingled with critical reasoning and reading comprehension questions throughout the Verbal section of the exam. You will have 75 minutes to complete the Verbal section, or about 1¾ minutes to answer each question.

Sentence correction questions present a statement in which words are underlined. The questions ask you to select from the answer options the best expression of the idea or relationship described in the underlined section. The first answer choice always repeats the original phrasing, whereas the other four provide alternatives. In some cases, the original phrasing is the best choice. In other cases, the underlined section has obvious or subtle errors that require correction. These questions require you to be familiar with the stylistic conventions and grammatical rules of standard written English and to demonstrate your ability to improve incorrect or ineffective expressions.

You should begin these questions by reading the sentence carefully. Note whether there are any obvious grammatical errors as you read the underlined section. Then read the five answer choices carefully. If there was a subtle error you did not recognize the first time you read the sentence, it may become apparent after you have read the answer choices. If the error is still unclear, see whether you can eliminate some of the answers as being incorrect. Remember that in some cases, the original selection may be the best answer.

5.1 Basic English Grammar Rules

Sentence correction questions ask you to recognize and potentially correct at least one of the following grammar rules. However, these rules are not exhaustive. If you are interested in learning more about English grammar as a way to prepare for the GMAT® exam, there are several resources available on the Web.

Agreement

Standard English requires elements within a sentence to be consistent. There are two types of agreement: noun-verb and pronoun.

Noun-verb agreement: Singular subjects take singular verbs, whereas plural subjects take plural verbs.
Examples:
Correct: "I walk to the store." Incorrect: "I walks to the store."
Correct: "We go to school." Incorrect: "We goes to school."
Correct: "The number of residents has grown." Incorrect: "The number of residents have grown."
Correct: "The masses have spoken." Incorrect: "The masses has spoken."
Pronoun agreement: A pronoun must agree with the noun or pronoun it refers to in person, number, and gender.
Examples:
Correct: "When you dream, you are usually asleep."
Incorrect: "When one dreams, you are usually asleep."

Correct: "When the kids went to sleep, they slept like logs."
Incorrect: "When the kids went to sleep, he slept like a log."

Diction
Words should be chosen to correctly and effectively reflect the appropriate part of speech. There are several words that are commonly used incorrectly. When answering sentence correction questions, pay attention to the following conventions.

Among/between: Among is used to refer to relationships involving more than two objects. *Between* is used to refer to relationships involving only two objects.
Examples:
Correct: "We divided our winnings among the three of us." Incorrect: "We divided our winnings between the three of us."
Correct: "She and I divided the cake between us." Incorrect: "She and I divided the cake among us."

As/like: As can be a preposition meaning "in the capacity of," but more often is a conjunction of manner and is followed by a verb. *Like* is generally used as a preposition, and therefore is followed by a noun, an object pronoun, or a verb ending in "ing."
Examples:
Correct: "I work as a librarian." Incorrect: "I work like a librarian."
Correct: "Do as I say, not as I do." Incorrect: "Do like I say, not like I do."
Correct: "It felt like a dream." Incorrect: "It felt as a dream."
Correct: "People like you inspire me." Incorrect: "People as you inspire me."
Correct: "There's nothing like biking on a warm, autumn day." Incorrect: "There's nothing as biking on a warm fall day."

Mass and count words: Mass words are nouns quantified by an amount rather than by a number. *Count* nouns can be quantified by a number.
Examples:
Correct: "We bought a loaf of bread." Incorrect: "We bought one bread."
Correct: "He wished me much happiness." Incorrect: "He wished me many happinesses."
Correct: "We passed many buildings." Incorrect: "We passed much buildings."

Pronouns: Myself should not be used as a substitute for *I* or *me*.
Examples:
Correct: "Mom and I had to go to the store." Incorrect: "Mom and myself had to go to the store."
Correct: "He gave the present to Dad and me." Incorrect: "He gave the present to Dad and myself."

Grammatical Construction
Good grammar requires complete sentences. Be on the lookout for improperly formed constructions.

Fragments: Parts of a sentence that are disconnected from the main clause are called fragments.
Example:
Correct: "We saw the doctor and his nurse at the party." Incorrect: "We saw the doctor at the party. And his nurse."

Run-on sentences: A run-on sentence is two independent clauses that run together without proper punctuation.
Example:
Correct: "Jose Canseco is still a feared batter; most pitchers don't want to face him."
Incorrect: "Jose Canseco is still a feared batter most pitchers don't want to face him."

Constructions: Avoid wordy, redundant constructions.
Example:
Correct: "We could not come to the meeting because of a conflict." Incorrect: "The reason we could not come to the meeting is because of a conflict."

Idiom

It is important to avoid nonstandard expressions, though English idioms sometimes do not follow conventional grammatical rules. Be careful to use the correct idiom when using the constructions and parts of speech.

Prepositions: Specific prepositions have specific purposes.
Examples:
Correct: "She likes to jog in the morning." Incorrect: "She likes to jog on the morning."
Correct: "They ranged in age from 10 to 15." Incorrect: "They ranged in age from 10 up to 15."

Correlatives: Word combinations such as "not only . . . but also" should be followed by an element of the same grammatical type.
Example:
Correct: "I have called not only to thank her but also to tell her about the next meeting."
Incorrect: "I have called not only to thank her but also I told her about the next meeting."

Forms of comparison: Many forms follow precise constructions. *Fewer* refers to a specific number, whereas *less than* refers to a continuous quantity. *Between . . . and* is the correct form to designate a choice. *Farther* refers to distance, whereas *further* refers to degree.
Example:
Correct: "There were fewer children in my class this year." Incorrect: "There were less children in my class this year."
Correct: "There was less devastation than I was told." Incorrect: "There was fewer devastation than I was told."
Correct: "We had to choose between chocolate and vanilla." Incorrect: "We had to choose between chocolate or vanilla." (It is also correct to say, "We had to choose chocolate or vanilla.")
Correct: "I ran farther than John, but he took his weight training further than I did." Incorrect: "I ran further than John, but he took his weight training farther than I did."

Logical Predication

Watch out for phrases that detract from the logical argument.

Modification problems: Modifiers should be positioned so it is clear what word or words they are meant to modify. If modifiers are not positioned clearly, they can cause illogical references or comparisons, or distort the meaning of the statement.
Examples:
Correct: "I put the cake that I baked by the door." Incorrect: "I put the cake by the door that I baked."

Correct: "Reading my mind, she gave me the delicious cookie." Incorrect: "Reading my mind, the cookie she gave me was delicious."
Correct: "In the Middle Ages, the world was believed to be flat." Incorrect: "In the Middle Ages, the world was flat."

Parallelism
Constructing a sentence that is parallel in structure depends on making sure that the different elements in the sentence balance each other; this is a little bit like making sure that the two sides of a mathematical equation are balanced. To make sure that a sentence is grammatically correct, check to see that phrases, clauses, verbs, and other sentence elements parallel each other.
Examples:
Correct: "I took a bath, went to sleep, and woke up refreshed." Incorrect: "I took a bath, sleeping, and waking up refreshed."
Correct: "The only way to know is to take the plunge." Incorrect: "The only way to know is taking the plunge."

Rhetorical Construction
Good sentence structure avoids constructions that are awkward, wordy, redundant, imprecise, or unclear, even when they are free of grammatical errors.
Example:
Correct: "Before we left on vacation, we watered the plants, checked to see that the stove was off, and set the burglar alarm." Incorrect: "Before we left to go on our vacation, we watered, checked to be sure that the stove had been turned off, and set it."

Verb Form
In addition to watching for problems of agreement or parallelism, make sure that verbs are used in the correct tense. Be alert to whether a verb should reflect past, present, or future tense.
Example:
Correct: "I went to school yesterday." "I go to school every weekday." "I will go to school tomorrow."

Each tense also has a perfect form (used with the past participle—i.e., walked, ran), a progressive form (used with the present participle—i.e., walking, running), and a perfect progressive form (also used with the present participle—i.e., walking, running).

Present perfect: Used with *has* or *have*, the present perfect tense describes an action that occurred at an indefinite time in the past or that began in the past and continues into the present.
Examples:
Correct: "I have traveled all over the world." (at an indefinite time)
Correct: "He has gone to school since he was five years old." (continues into the present)

Past perfect: This verb form is used with *had* to show the order of two events that took place in the past.
Example:
Correct: "By the time I left for school, the cake had been baked."

Future perfect: Used with *will have*, this verb form describes an event in the future that will precede another event.
Example:
Present progressive: Used with *am, is,* or *are,* this verb form describes an ongoing action that is happening now.

Example:
Correct: "I am studying for exams." "The student is studying for exams." "We are studying for exams."

Past progressive: Used with *was* or *were,* this verb form describes something that was happening when another action occurred.
Example:
Correct: "The student was studying when the fire alarm rang." "They were studying when the fire broke out."

Future progressive: Used with *will be* or *shall be,* this verb tense describes an ongoing action that will continue into the future.
Example:
Correct: "The students will be studying for exams throughout the month of December."

Present perfect progressive: Used with *have been* or *has been,* this verb tense describes something that began in the past, continues into the present, and may continue into the future.
Example:
Correct: "The student has been studying hard in the hope of acing the test."

Past perfect progressive: Used with *had been,* this verb form describes an action of some duration that was completed before another past action occurred.
Example:
Correct: "Before the fire alarm rang, the student had been studying."

Future perfect progressive: Used with *will have been,* this verb form describes a future, ongoing action that will occur before a specified time.
Example:
Correct: "By the end of next year, the students will have been studying math for five years."

5.2 Study Suggestions

There are two basic ways you can study for sentence correction questions:

- **Read material that reflects standard usage.**
  One way to gain familiarity with the basic conventions of standard written English is simply to read. Suitable material will usually be found in good magazines and nonfiction books, editorials in outstanding newspapers, and the collections of essays used by many college and university writing courses.

- **Review basic rules of grammar and practice with writing exercises.**
  Begin by reviewing the grammar rules laid out in this chapter. Then, if you have school assignments (such as essays and research papers) that have been carefully evaluated for grammatical errors, it may be helpful to review the comments and corrections.

5.3 What Is Measured

Sentence correction questions test three broad aspects of language proficiency:

- **Correct expression.**
  A correct sentence is grammatically and structurally sound. It conforms to all the rules of standard written English, including noun-verb agreement, noun-pronoun agreement, pronoun consistency, pronoun case, and verb tense sequence. A correct sentence will not have dangling, misplaced, or improperly formed modifiers; unidiomatic or inconsistent expressions; or faults in parallel construction.

- **Effective expression.**
  An effective sentence expresses an idea or relationship clearly and concisely as well as grammatically. This does not mean that the choice with the fewest and simplest words is necessarily the best answer. It means that there are no superfluous words or needlessly complicated expressions in the best choice.

- **Proper diction.**
  An effective sentence also uses proper diction. (Diction refers to the standard dictionary meanings of words and the appropriateness of words in context.) In evaluating the diction of a sentence, you must be able to recognize whether the words are well chosen, accurate, and suitable for the context.

5.4 Test-Taking Strategies for Sentence Correction Questions

1. **Read the entire sentence carefully.**
    Try to understand the specific idea or relationship that the sentence should express.

2. **Evaluate the underlined passage for errors and possible corrections before reading the answer choices.**
    This strategy will help you discriminate among the answer choices. Remember, in some cases the underlined passage is correct.

3. **Read each answer choice carefully.**
    The first answer choice always repeats the underlined portion of the original sentence. Choose this answer if you think that the sentence is best as originally written, but do so *only after* examining all the other choices.

4. **Try to determine how to correct what you consider to be wrong with the original sentence.**
    Some of the answer choices may change things that are not wrong, whereas others may not change everything that is wrong.

5. **Make sure that you evaluate the sentence and the choices thoroughly.**
    Pay attention to general clarity, grammatical and idiomatic usage, economy and precision of language, and appropriateness of diction.

6. **Read the whole sentence, substituting the choice that you prefer for the underlined passage.**
    A choice may be wrong because it does not fit grammatically or structurally with the rest of the sentence. Remember that some sentences will require no correction. When the given sentence requires no correction, choose the first answer.

5.5 The Directions

These are the directions that you will see for sentence correction questions when you take the GMAT® test. If you read them carefully and understand them clearly before going to sit for the exam, you will not need to spend too much time reviewing them once you are at the test center and the exam is under way.

Sentence correction questions present a sentence, part or all of which is underlined. Beneath the sentence, you will find five ways of phrasing the underlined passage. The first answer choice repeats the original underlined passage; the other four are different. If you think the original phrasing is best, choose the first answer; otherwise choose one of the others.

This type of question tests your ability to recognize the correctness and effectiveness of expression in standard written English. In choosing your answer, follow the requirements of standard written English; that is, pay attention to grammar, choice of words, and sentence construction. Choose the answer that produces the most effective sentence; this answer should be clear and exact, without awkwardness, ambiguity, redundancy, or grammatical error.

5.6 Sentence Correction Sample Questions

Sentence correction questions present a sentence, part or all of which is underlined. Beneath the sentences, you will find five ways of phrasing the underlined passage. The first answer choice repeats the original; the other four are different. If you think the original phrasing is best, choose the first answer; otherwise choose one of the others.

This type of question tests your ability to recognize the correctness and effectiveness of expression in standard written English. In choosing your answer, follow the requirements of standard written English; that is, pay attention to grammar, choice of words, and sentence construction. Choose the answer that produces the most effective sentence; this answer should be clear and exact, without awkwardness, ambiguity, redundancy, or grammatical error.

1. Some bat caves, like honeybee hives, have residents that take on different duties such as defending the entrance, acting as sentinels and to sound a warning at the approach of danger, and scouting outside the cave for new food and roosting sites.

   (A) acting as sentinels and to sound
   (B) acting as sentinels and sounding
   (C) to act as sentinels and sound
   (D) to act as sentinels and to sound
   (E) to act as a sentinel sounding

2. However much United States voters may agree that there is waste in government and that the government as a whole spends beyond its means, it is difficult to find broad support for a movement toward a minimal state.

   (A) However much United States voters may agree that
   (B) Despite the agreement among United States voters to the fact
   (C) Although United States voters agree
   (D) Even though United States voters may agree
   (E) There is agreement among United States voters that

3. Native American burial sites dating back 5,000 years indicate that the residents of Maine at that time were part of a widespread culture of Algonquian-speaking people.

   (A) were part of a widespread culture of Algonquian-speaking people

   (B) had been part of a widespread culture of people who were Algonquian-speaking
   (C) were people who were part of a widespread culture that was Algonquian-speaking
   (D) had been people who were part of a widespread culture that was Algonquian-speaking
   (E) were a people which had been part of a widespread, Algonquian-speaking culture

4. The voluminous personal papers of Thomas Alva Edison reveal that his inventions typically sprang to life not in a flash of inspiration but evolved slowly from previous works.

   (A) sprang to life not in a flash of inspiration but evolved slowly
   (B) sprang to life not in a flash of inspiration but were slowly evolved
   (C) did not spring to life in a flash of inspiration but evolved slowly
   (D) did not spring to life in a flash of inspiration but had slowly evolved
   (E) did not spring to life in a flash of inspiration but they were slowly evolved

5. A Labor Department study states that the numbers of women employed outside the home grew by more than a thirty-five percent increase in the past decade and accounted for more than sixty-two percent of the total growth in the civilian work force.

   (A) numbers of women employed outside the home grew by more than a thirty-five percent increase

(B)   numbers of women employed outside the home grew more than thirty-five percent

(C)   numbers of women employed outside the home were raised by more than thirty-five percent

(D)   number of women employed outside the home increased by more than thirty-five percent

(E)   number of women employed outside the home was raised by more than a thirty-five percent increase

6.   From the earliest days of the tribe, kinship determined the way in which the Ojibwa society organized its labor, provided access to its resources, and defined rights and obligations involved in the distribution and consumption of those resources.

(A)   and defined rights and obligations involved in the distribution and consumption of those resources

(B)   defining rights and obligations involved in their distribution and consumption

(C)   and defined rights and obligations as they were involved in its distribution and consumption

(D)   whose rights and obligations were defined in their distribution and consumption

(E)   the distribution and consumption of them defined by rights and obligations

7.   Delighted by the reported earnings for the first quarter of the fiscal year, it was decided by the company manager to give her staff a raise.

(A)   it was decided by the company manager to give her staff a raise

(B)   the decision of the company manager was to give her staff a raise

(C)   the company manager decided to give her staff a raise

(D)   the staff was given a raise by the company manager

(E)   a raise was given to the staff by the company manager

8.   The rising of costs of data-processing operations at many financial institutions has created a growing opportunity for independent companies to provide these services more efficiently and at lower cost.

(A)   The rising of costs

(B)   Rising costs

(C)   The rising cost

(D)   Because the rising cost

(E)   Because of rising costs

9.   William H. Johnson's artistic debt to Scandinavia is evident in paintings that range from sensitive portraits of citizens in his wife's Danish home, Kerteminde, and awe-inspiring views of fjords and mountain peaks in the western and northern regions of Norway.

(A)   and

(B)   to

(C)   and to

(D)   with

(E)   in addition to

10.   Growing competitive pressures may be encouraging auditors to bend the rules in favor of clients; auditors may, for instance, allow a questionable loan to remain on the books in order to maintain a bank's profits on paper.

(A)   clients; auditors may, for instance, allow

(B)   clients, as an instance, to allow

(C)   clients, like to allow

(D)   clients, such as to be allowing

(E)   clients; which might, as an instance, be the allowing of

11.   It is well known in the supermarket industry that how items are placed on shelves and the frequency of inventory turnovers can be crucial to profits.

(A)   the frequency of inventory turnovers can be

(B)   the frequency of inventory turnovers is often

(C)   the frequency with which the inventory turns over is often

(D)   how frequently is the inventory turned over are often

(E)   how frequently the inventory turns over can be

12. Iguanas have been an important food source in Latin America since prehistoric times, and it is still prized as a game animal by the campesinos, who typically cook the meat in a heavily spiced stew.

    (A) it is still prized as a game animal
    (B) it is still prized as game animals
    (C) they are still prized as game animals
    (D) they are still prized as being a game animal
    (E) being still prized as a game animal

13. Except for a concert performance that the composer himself staged in 1911, Scott Joplin's ragtime opera "Treemonisha" was not produced until 1972, sixty-one years after its completion.

    (A) Except for a concert performance that the composer himself staged
    (B) Except for a concert performance with the composer himself staging it
    (C) Besides a concert performance being staged by the composer himself
    (D) Excepting a concert performance that the composer himself staged
    (E) With the exception of a concert performance with the staging done by the composer himself

14. From the time of its defeat by the Germans in 1940 until its liberation in 1944, France was a bitter and divided country; a kind of civil war raged in the Vichy government between those who wanted to collaborate with the Nazis with those who opposed them.

    (A) between those who wanted to collaborate with the Nazis with those who opposed
    (B) between those who wanted to collaborate with the Nazis and those who opposed
    (C) between those wanting to collaborate with the Nazis with those opposing
    (D) among those who wanted to collaborate with the Nazis and those who opposed
    (E) among those wanting to collaborate with the Nazis with those opposing

15. Chinese, the most ancient of living writing systems, consists of tens of thousands of ideographic characters, each character a miniature calligraphic composition inside its own square frame.

    (A) each character a miniature calligraphic composition inside its
    (B) all the characters a miniature calligraphic composition inside their
    (C) all the characters a miniature calligraphic composition inside its
    (D) every character a miniature calligraphic composition inside their
    (E) each character a miniature calligraphic composition inside their

16. Declining values for farm equipment and land, the collateral against which farmers borrow to get through the harvest season, is going to force many lenders to tighten or deny credit this spring.

    (A) the collateral against which farmers borrow to get through the harvest season, is
    (B) which farmers use as collateral to borrow against to get through the harvest season, is
    (C) the collateral which is borrowed against by farmers to get through the harvest season, is
    (D) which farmers use as collateral to borrow against to get through the harvest season, are
    (E) the collateral against which farmers borrow to get through the harvest season, are

17. In the mid-1960's a newly installed radar warning system mistook the rising of the moon as a massive missile attack by the Soviets.

    (A) rising of the moon as a massive missile attack by the Soviets
    (B) rising of the moon for a massive Soviet missile attack
    (C) moon rising to a massive missile attack by the Soviets
    (D) moon as it was rising for a massive Soviet missile attack
    (E) rise of the moon as a massive Soviet missile attack

18. With only 5 percent of the world's population, United States citizens consume 28 percent of its nonrenewable resources, drive more than one-third of its automobiles, and use 21 times more water per capita than Europeans do.

(A)   With
(B)   As
(C)   Being
(D)   Despite having
(E)   Although accounting for

19.   While depressed property values can hurt some large investors, they are potentially devastating for homeowners, whose equity—in many cases representing a life's savings—can plunge or even disappear.

(A)   they are potentially devastating for homeowners, whose
(B)   they can potentially devastate homeowners in that their
(C)   for homeowners they are potentially devastating, because their
(D)   for homeowners, it is potentially devastating in that their
(E)   it can potentially devastate homeowners, whose

20.   Consumers may not think of household cleaning products to be hazardous substances, but many of them can be harmful to health, especially if they are used improperly.

(A)   Consumers may not think of household cleaning products to be
(B)   Consumers may not think of household cleaning products being
(C)   A consumer may not think of their household cleaning products being
(D)   A consumer may not think of household cleaning products as
(E)   Household cleaning products may not be thought of, by consumers, as

21.   It is possible that Native Americans originally have migrated to the Western Hemisphere over a bridge of land that once existed between Siberia and Alaska.

(A)   have migrated to the Western Hemisphere over a bridge of land that once existed
(B)   were migrating to the Western Hemisphere over a bridge of land that existed once
(C)   migrated over a bridge of land to the Western Hemisphere that once existed

(D)   migrated to the Western Hemisphere over a bridge of land that once existed
(E)   were migrating to the Western Hemisphere over a bridge of land existing once

22.   In recent years cattle breeders have increasingly used crossbreeding, in part that their steers should acquire certain characteristics and partly because crossbreeding is said to provide hybrid vigor.

(A)   in part that their steers should acquire certain characteristics
(B)   in part for the acquisition of certain characteristics in their steers
(C)   partly because of their steers acquiring certain characteristics
(D)   partly because certain characteristics should be acquired by their steers
(E)   partly to acquire certain characteristics in their steers

23.   Like Auden, the language of James Merrill is chatty, arch, and conversational—given to complex syntactic flights as well as to prosaic free-verse strolls.

(A)   Like Auden, the language of James Merrill
(B)   Like Auden, James Merrill's language
(C)   Like Auden's, James Merrill's language
(D)   As with Auden, James Merrill's language
(E)   As is Auden's the language of James Merrill

24.   The period when the great painted caves at Lascaux and Altamira were occupied by Upper Paleolithic people has been established by carbon-14 dating, but what is much more difficult to determine are the reason for their decoration, the use to which primitive people put the caves, and the meaning of the magnificently depicted animals.

(A)   has been established by carbon-14 dating, but what is much more difficult to determine are
(B)   has been established by carbon-14 dating, but what is much more difficult to determine is
(C)   have been established by carbon-14 dating, but what is much more difficult to determine is
(D)   have been established by carbon-14 dating, but what is much more difficult to determine are
(E)   are established by carbon-14 dating, but that which is much more difficult to determine is

25. The Baldrick Manufacturing Company has for several years followed a policy aimed at decreasing operating costs and improving the efficiency of its distribution system.

    (A) aimed at decreasing operating costs and improving
    (B) aimed at the decreasing of operating costs and to improve
    (C) aiming at the decreasing of operating costs and improving
    (D) the aim of which is the decreasing of operating costs and improving
    (E) with the aim to decrease operating costs and to improve

26. Eating saltwater fish may significantly reduce the risk of heart attacks and also aid for sufferers of rheumatoid arthritis and asthma, according to three research studies published in the New England Journal of Medicine.

    (A) significantly reduce the risk of heart attacks and also aid for
    (B) be significant in reducing the risk of heart attacks and aid for
    (C) significantly reduce the risk of heart attacks and aid
    (D) cause a significant reduction in the risk of heart attacks and aid to
    (E) significantly reduce the risk of heart attacks as well as aiding

27. Minnesota is the only one of the contiguous forty-eight states that still has a sizable wolf population, and where this predator remains the archenemy of cattle and sheep.

    (A) that still has a sizable wolf population, and where
    (B) that still has a sizable wolf population, where
    (C) that still has a sizable population of wolves, and where
    (D) where the population of wolves is still sizable;
    (E) where there is still a sizable population of wolves and where

28. In reference to the current hostility toward smoking, smokers frequently expressed anxiety that their prospects for being hired and promoted are being stunted by their habit.

    (A) In reference to the current hostility toward smoking, smokers frequently expressed anxiety that
    (B) Referring to the current hostility toward smoking, smokers frequently expressed anxiety about
    (C) When referring to the current hostility toward smoking, smokers frequently express anxiety about
    (D) With reference to the current hostility toward smoking, smokers frequently expressed anxiety about
    (E) Referring to the current hostility toward smoking, smokers frequently express anxiety that

29. According to some economists, the July decrease in unemployment so that it was the lowest in two years suggests that the gradual improvement in the job market is continuing.

    (A) so that it was the lowest in two years
    (B) so that it was the lowest two-year rate
    (C) to what would be the lowest in two years
    (D) to a two-year low level
    (E) to the lowest level in two years

30. Thomas Eakins' powerful style and his choices of subject—the advances in modern surgery, the discipline of sport, the strains of individuals in tension with society or even with themselves—was as disturbing to his own time as it is compelling for ours.

    (A) was as disturbing to his own time as it is
    (B) were as disturbing to his own time as they are
    (C) has been as disturbing in his own time as they are
    (D) had been as disturbing in his own time as it was
    (E) have been as disturbing in his own time as

31. <u>Like Rousseau, Tolstoi rebelled</u> against the unnatural complexity of human relations in modern society.

    (A) Like Rousseau, Tolstoi rebelled
    (B) Like Rousseau, Tolstoi's rebellion was
    (C) As Rousseau, Tolstoi rebelled
    (D) As did Rousseau, Tolstoi's rebellion was
    (E) Tolstoi's rebellion, as Rousseau's, was

32. The Wallerstein study indicates that even after a decade young men and women still experience some of the effects of a divorce <u>occurring when a child</u>.

    (A) occurring when a child
    (B) occurring when children
    (C) that occurred when a child
    (D) that occurred when they were children
    (E) that has occurred as each was a child

33. Carbon-14 dating reveals that the megalithic monuments in Brittany are nearly 2,000 years <u>as old as any of their supposed</u> Mediterranean predecessors.

    (A) as old as any of their supposed
    (B) older than any of their supposed
    (C) as old as their supposed
    (D) older than any of their supposedly
    (E) as old as their supposedly

34. Lacking information about energy use, people tend to overestimate the amount of energy used by <u>equipment, such as lights, that are visible and must be turned on and off and underestimate that</u> used by unobtrusive equipment, such as water heaters.

    (A) equipment, such as lights, that are visible and must be turned on and off and underestimate that
    (B) equipment, such as lights, that are visible and must be turned on and off and underestimate it when
    (C) equipment, such as lights, that is visible and must be turned on and off and underestimate it when
    (D) visible equipment, such as lights, that must be turned on and off and underestimate that
    (E) visible equipment, such as lights, that must be turned on and off and underestimate it when

35. The rise in the Commerce Department's index of leading economic indicators <u>suggest that the economy should continue its expansion into the coming months, but that</u> the mixed performance of the index's individual components indicates that economic growth will proceed at a more moderate pace than in the first quarter of this year.

    (A) suggest that the economy should continue its expansion into the coming months, but that
    (B) suggest that the economy is to continue expansion in the coming months, but
    (C) suggests that the economy will continue its expanding in the coming months, but that
    (D) suggests that the economy is continuing to expand into the coming months, but that
    (E) suggests that the economy will continue to expand in the coming months, but

36. <u>What was as remarkable as the development of the compact disc</u> has been the use of the new technology to revitalize, in better sound than was ever before possible, some of the classic recorded performances of the pre-LP era.

    (A) What was as remarkable as the development of the compact disc
    (B) The thing that was as remarkable as developing the compact disc
    (C) No less remarkable than the development of the compact disc
    (D) Developing the compact disc has been none the less remarkable than
    (E) Development of the compact disc has been no less remarkable as

37. <u>Some buildings that were destroyed and heavily damaged in the earthquake last year were</u> constructed in violation of the city's building code.

    (A) Some buildings that were destroyed and heavily damaged in the earthquake last year were
    (B) Some buildings that were destroyed or heavily damaged in the earthquake last year had been
    (C) Some buildings that the earthquake destroyed and heavily damaged last year have been
    (D) Last year the earthquake destroyed or heavily damaged some buildings that have been
    (E) Last year some of the buildings that were destroyed or heavily damaged in the earthquake had been

38. Using a Doppler ultrasound device, fetal heartbeats can be detected by the twelfth week of pregnancy.

(A) Using a Doppler ultrasound device, fetal heartbeats can be detected by the twelfth week of pregnancy.

(B) Fetal heartbeats can be detected by the twelfth week of pregnancy, using a Doppler ultrasound device.

(C) Detecting fetal heartbeats by the twelfth week of pregnancy, a physician can use a Doppler ultrasound device.

(D) By the twelfth week of pregnancy, fetal heartbeats can be detected using a Doppler ultrasound device by a physician.

(E) Using a Doppler ultrasound device, a physician can detect fetal heartbeats by the twelfth week of pregnancy.

39. A study commissioned by the Department of Agriculture showed that if calves exercise and associated with other calves, they will require less medication and gain weight quicker than do those raised in confinement.

(A) associated with other calves, they will require less medication and gain weight quicker than do

(B) associated with other calves, they require less medication and gain weight quicker than

(C) associate with other calves, they required less medication and will gain weight quicker than do

(D) associate with other calves, they have required less medication and will gain weight more quickly than do

(E) associate with other calves, they require less medication and gain weight more quickly than

40. A recent study has found that within the past few years, many doctors had elected early retirement rather than face the threats of lawsuits and the rising costs of malpractice insurance.

(A) had elected early retirement rather than face

(B) had elected early retirement instead of facing

(C) have elected retiring early instead of facing

(D) have elected to retire early rather than facing

(E) have elected to retire early rather than face

41. The Gorton-Dodd bill requires that a bank disclose to their customers how long they will delay access to funds from deposited checks.

(A) that a bank disclose to their customers how long they will delay access to funds from deposited checks

(B) a bank to disclose to their customers how long they will delay access to funds from a deposited check

(C) that a bank disclose to its customers how long it will delay access to funds from deposited checks

(D) a bank that it should disclose to its customers how long it will delay access to funds from a deposited check

(E) that banks disclose to customers how long access to funds from their deposited check is to be delayed

42. Unlike a funded pension system, in which contributions are invested to pay future beneficiaries, a pay-as-you-go approach is the foundation of Social Security.

(A) a pay-as-you-go approach is the foundation of Social Security

(B) the foundation of Social Security is a pay-as-you-go approach

(C) the approach of Social Security is pay-as-you-go

(D) Social Security's approach is pay-as-you-go

(E) Social Security is founded on a pay-as-you-go approach

43. Although she had signed a pledge of abstinence while being an adolescent, Frances Willard was 35 years old before she chose to become a temperance activist.

(A) while being an adolescent

(B) while in adolescence

(C) at the time of her being adolescent

(D) as being in adolescence

(E) as an adolescent

44. Though the term "graphic design" may <u>suggest laying out corporate brochures and annual reports, they have come to signify widely ranging</u> work, from package designs and company logotypes to signs, book jackets, computer graphics, and film titles.

    (A) suggest laying out corporate brochures and annual reports, they have come to signify widely ranging

    (B) suggest laying out corporate brochures and annual reports, it has come to signify a wide range of

    (C) suggest corporate brochure and annual report layout, it has signified widely ranging

    (D) have suggested corporate brochure and annual report layout, it has signified a wide range of

    (E) have suggested laying out corporate brochures and annual reports, they have come to signify widely ranging

45. In contrast to large steel plants that take iron ore through all the steps needed to produce several different kinds of steel, <u>processing steel scrap into a specialized group of products has enabled small mills to put capital into new technology and remain</u> economically viable.

    (A) processing steel scrap into a specialized group of products has enabled small mills to put capital into new technology and remain

    (B) processing steel scrap into a specialized group of products has enabled small mills to put capital into new technology, remaining

    (C) the processing of steel scrap into a specialized group of products has enabled small mills to put capital into new technology, remaining

    (D) small mills, by processing steel scrap into a specialized group of products, have been able to put capital into new technology and remain

    (E) small mills, by processing steel scrap into a specialized group of products, have been able to put capital into new technology and remained

46. The psychologist William James believed that facial expressions not only provide a visible sign of an <u>emotion, actually contributing to the feeling itself</u>.

    (A) emotion, actually contributing to the feeling itself

    (B) emotion but also actually contributing to the feeling itself

    (C) emotion but also actually contribute to the feeling itself

    (D) emotion; they also actually contribute to the feeling of it

    (E) emotion; the feeling itself is also actually contributed to by them

47. The financial crash of October 1987 demonstrated that the world's capital markets are <u>integrated more closely than never before and</u> events in one part of the global village may be transmitted to the rest of the village — almost instantaneously.

    (A) integrated more closely than never before and

    (B) closely integrated more than ever before so

    (C) more closely integrated as never before while

    (D) more closely integrated than ever before and that

    (E) more than ever before closely integrated as

48. Wisconsin, Illinois, Florida, and Minnesota have begun to enforce statewide bans <u>prohibiting landfills to accept leaves, brush, and grass clippings</u>.

    (A) prohibiting landfills to accept leaves, brush, and grass clippings

    (B) prohibiting that landfills accept leaves, brush, and grass clippings

    (C) prohibiting landfills from accepting leaves, brush, and grass clippings

    (D) that leaves, brush, and grass clippings cannot be accepted in landfills

    (E) that landfills cannot accept leaves, brush, and grass clippings

49. Reporting that one of <u>its many problems had been the recent</u> extended sales slump in women's apparel, the seven-store retailer said it would start a three-month liquidation sale in all of its stores.

    (A) its many problems had been the recent
    (B) its many problems has been the recently
    (C) its many problems is the recently
    (D) their many problems is the recent
    (E) their many problems had been the recent

50. Domestic automobile manufacturers have invested millions of dollars <u>into research to develop cars more gasoline-efficient even than presently on the road.</u>

    (A) into research to develop cars more gasoline-efficient even than presently on the road
    (B) into research for developing even more gasoline-efficient cars on the road than at present
    (C) for research for cars to be developed that are more gasoline-efficient even than presently the road
    (D) in research to develop cars even more gasoline-efficient than those at present on the road
    (E) in research for developing cars that are even more gasoline-efficient than presently on the road

51. In developing new facilities for the incineration of solid wastes, we must avoid the danger of shifting environmental problems from <u>landfills polluting the water to polluting the air with incinerators.</u>

    (A) landfills polluting the water to polluting the air with incinerators
    (B) landfills polluting the water to the air being polluted with incinerators
    (C) the pollution of water by landfills to the pollution of air by incinerators
    (D) pollution of the water by landfills to incinerators that pollute the air
    (E) water that is polluted by landfills to incinerators that pollute the air

52. The winds that howl across the Great Plains not only blow away valuable topsoil, thereby reducing the potential crop yield of a tract of land, <u>and also damage or destroy</u> young plants.

    (A) and also damage or destroy
    (B) as well as damaging or destroying
    (C) but they also cause damage or destroy
    (D) but also damage or destroy
    (E) but also causing damage or destroying

53. In a 5-to-4 decision, the Supreme Court ruled <u>that two upstate New York counties owed restitution to three tribes of Oneida Indians for the unlawful seizure of</u> their ancestral lands in the eighteenth century.

    (A) that two upstate New York counties owed restitution to three tribes of Oneida Indians for the unlawful seizure of
    (B) that two upstate New York counties owed restitution to three tribes of Oneida Indians because of their unlawful seizure of
    (C) two upstate New York counties to owe restitution to three tribes of Oneida Indians for their unlawful seizure of
    (D) on two upstate New York counties that owed restitution to three tribes of Oneida Indians because they unlawfully seized
    (E) on the restitution that two upstate New York counties owed to three tribes of Oneida Indians for the unlawful seizure of

54. The extraordinary diary of William Lyon Mackenzie King, prime minister of Canada for over twenty years, revealed <u>that this most bland and circumspect of men was a mystic guided in both public and</u> private life by omens, messages received at séances, and signs from heaven.

    (A) that this most bland and circumspect of men was a mystic guided in both public and
    (B) that this most bland and circumspect of men was a mystic and also guided both in public as well as
    (C) this most bland and circumspect of men was a mystic and that he was guided in both public and
    (D) this most bland and circumspect of men was a mystic and that he was guided in both public as well as
    (E) this most bland and circumspect of men to have been a mystic and that he guided himself both in public as well as

55. In one of the most stunning reversals in the history of marketing, the Coca-Cola company in July 1985 yielded to thousands of irate consumers <u>demanding that it should</u> bring back the original Coke formula.

    (A) demanding that it should
    (B) demanding it to
    (C) and their demand to
    (D) who demanded that it
    (E) who demanded it to

56. Recently discovered fossil remains strongly suggest that the Australian egg-laying mammals of today are a branch of the main stem of mammalian evolution <u>rather than developing independently from</u> a common ancestor of mammals more than 220 million years ago.

    (A) rather than developing independently from
    (B) rather than a type that developed independently from
    (C) rather than a type whose development was independent of
    (D) instead of developing independently from
    (E) instead of a development that was independent of

57. A patient accusing a doctor of malpractice will find it difficult to prove damage <u>if there is a lack of some other doctor to testify</u> about proper medical procedures.

    (A) if there is a lack of some other doctor to testify
    (B) unless there will be another doctor to testify
    (C) without another doctor's testimony
    (D) should there be no testimony from some other doctor
    (E) lacking another doctor to testify

58. <u>A recording system was so secretly installed and operated in the Kennedy Oval Office that</u> even Theodore C. Sorensen, the White House counsel, did not know it existed.

    (A) A recording system was so secretly installed and operated in the Kennedy Oval Office that
    (B) So secret was a recording system installation and operation in the Kennedy Oval Office
    (C) It was so secret that a recording system was installed and operated in the Kennedy Oval Office
    (D) A recording system that was so secretly installed and operated in the Kennedy Oval Office
    (E) Installed and operated so secretly in the Kennedy Oval Office was a recording system that

59. <u>Neanderthals had a vocal tract that resembled those of the apes</u> and so were probably without language, a shortcoming that may explain why they were supplanted by our own species.

    (A) Neanderthals had a vocal tract that resembled those of the apes
    (B) Neanderthals had a vocal tract resembling an ape's
    (C) The vocal tracts of Neanderthals resembled an ape's
    (D) The Neanderthal's vocal tracts resembled the apes'
    (E) The vocal tracts of the Neanderthals resembled those of the apes

60. The energy source on Voyager 2 is not a nuclear reactor, in which atoms are actively broken <u>apart; rather</u> a kind of nuclear battery that uses natural radioactive decay to produce power.

    (A) apart; rather
    (B) apart, but rather
    (C) apart, but rather that of
    (D) apart, but that of
    (E) apart; it is that of

61. Archaeologists in Ireland believe that a recently discovered chalice, which dates from the eighth century, was probably buried <u>to keep from</u> being stolen by invaders.

    (A) to keep from
    (B) to keep it from
    (C) to avoid
    (D) in order that it would avoid
    (E) in order to keep from

62. Lawmakers are examining measures that would require banks to disclose all fees and account requirements in writing, <u>provide free cashing of government checks, and to create basic savings accounts to carry</u> minimal fees and require minimal initial deposits.

    (A) provide free cashing of government checks, and to create basic savings accounts to carry

    (B) provide free cashing of government checks, and creating basic savings accounts carrying

    (C) to provide free cashing of government checks, and creating basic savings accounts that carry

    (D) to provide free cashing of government checks, creating basic savings accounts to carry

    (E) to provide free cashing of government checks, and to create basic savings accounts that carry

63. <u>Certain pesticides can become ineffective if used repeatedly in the same place; one reason is suggested by the finding that there are much larger populations of pesticide-degrading microbes in soils with a relatively long history of pesticide use than in soils that are free of such chemicals.</u>

    (A) Certain pesticides can become ineffective if used repeatedly in the same place; one reason is suggested by the finding that there are much larger populations of pesticide-degrading microbes in soils with a relatively long history of pesticide use than in soils that are free of such chemicals.

    (B) If used repeatedly in the same place, one reason that certain pesticides can become ineffective is suggested by the finding that there are much larger populations of pesticide-degrading microbes in soils with a relatively long history of pesticide use than in soils that are free of such chemicals.

    (C) If used repeatedly in the same place, one reason certain pesticides can become ineffective is suggested by the finding that much larger populations of pesticide-degrading microbes are found in soils with a relatively long history of pesticide use than those that are free of such chemicals.

    (D) The finding that there are much larger populations of pesticide-degrading microbes in soils with a relatively long history of pesticide use than in soils that are free of such chemicals is suggestive of one reason, if used repeatedly in the same place, certain pesticides can become ineffective.

    (E) The finding of much larger populations of pesticide-degrading microbes in soils with a relatively long history of pesticide use than in those that are free of such chemicals suggests one reason certain pesticides can become ineffective if used repeatedly in the same place.

64. In the textbook publishing business, the second quarter is historically weak, because revenues are <u>low and marketing expenses are high as companies prepare</u> for the coming school year.

    (A) low and marketing expenses are high as companies prepare

    (B) low and their marketing expenses are high as they prepare

    (C) low with higher marketing expenses in preparation

    (D) low, while marketing expenses are higher to prepare

    (E) low, while their marketing expenses are higher in preparation

65. Parliament did not accord full refugee benefits to twelve of the recent immigrants because it believed that <u>to do it rewards</u> them for entering the country illegally.

    (A) to do it rewards

    (B) doing it rewards

    (C) to do this would reward

    (D) doing so would reward

    (E) to do it would reward

66. Many policy experts say that shifting a portion of health-benefit costs back to the workers helps to control the employer's costs, but also helps to limit medical spending by making patients more careful consumers.

    (A) helps to control the employer's costs, but also helps
    (B) helps the control of the employer's costs, and also
    (C) not only helps to control the employer's costs, but also helps
    (D) helps to control not only the employer's costs, but
    (E) not only helps to control the employer's costs, and also helps

67. Ms. Chambers is among the forecasters who predict that the rate of addition to arable lands will drop while those of loss rise.

    (A) those of loss rise
    (B) it rises for loss
    (C) those of losses rise
    (D) the rate of loss rises
    (E) there are rises for the rate of loss

68. Unlike auto insurance, the frequency of claims does not affect the premiums for personal property coverage, but if the insurance company is able to prove excessive loss due to owner negligence, it may decline to renew the policy.

    (A) Unlike auto insurance, the frequency of claims does not affect the premiums for personal property coverage
    (B) Unlike with auto insurance, the frequency of claims do not affect the premiums for personal property coverage
    (C) Unlike the frequency of claims for auto insurance, the premiums for personal property coverage are not affected by the frequency of claims
    (D) Unlike the premiums for auto insurance, the premiums for personal property coverage are not affected by the frequency of claims
    (E) Unlike with the premiums for auto insurance, the premiums for personal property coverage is not affected by the frequency of claims

69. Organized in 1966 by the Fish and Wildlife Service, the Breeding Bird Survey uses annual roadside counts along established routes for monitoring of population changes of as many as, or of more than 250 bird species, including 180 songbirds.

    (A) for monitoring of population changes of as many as, or of
    (B) to monitor population changes of as many, or
    (C) to monitor changes in the populations of
    (D) that monitors population changes of
    (E) that monitors changes in populations of as many as, or

70. Faced with an estimated $2 billion budget gap, the city's mayor proposed a nearly 17 percent reduction in the amount allocated the previous year to maintain the city's major cultural institutions and to subsidize hundreds of local arts groups.

    (A) proposed a nearly 17 percent reduction in the amount allocated the previous year to maintain the city's major cultural institutions and to subsidize
    (B) proposed a reduction from the previous year of nearly 17 percent in the amount it was allocating to maintain the city's major cultural institutions and for subsidizing
    (C) proposed to reduce, by nearly 17 percent, the amount from the previous year that was allocated for the maintenance of the city's major cultural institutions and to subsidize
    (D) has proposed a reduction from the previous year of nearly 17 percent of the amount it was allocating for maintaining the city's major cultural institutions, and to subsidize
    (E) was proposing that the amount they were allocating be reduced by nearly 17 percent from the previous year for maintaining the city's major cultural institutions and for the subsidization

71. By offering lower prices and a menu of personal communications options, such as caller identification and voice mail, the new telecommunications company has not only captured customers from other phone companies but also forced them to offer competitive prices.

    (A)   has not only captured customers from other phone companies but also forced them
    (B)   has not only captured customers from other phone companies, but it also forced them
    (C)   has not only captured customers from other phone companies but also forced these companies
    (D)   not only has captured customers from other phone companies but also these companies have been forced
    (E)   not only captured customers from other phone companies, but it also has forced them

72. The gyrfalcon, an Arctic bird of prey, has survived a close brush with extinction; its numbers are now five times greater than when the use of DDT was sharply restricted in the early 1970's.

    (A)   extinction; its numbers are now five times greater than
    (B)   extinction; its numbers are now five times more than
    (C)   extinction, their numbers now fivefold what they were
    (D)   extinction, now with fivefold the numbers they had
    (E)   extinction, now with numbers five times greater than

73. Analysts blamed May's sluggish retail sales on unexciting merchandise as well as the weather, colder and wetter than was usual in some regions, which slowed sales of barbecue grills and lawn furniture.

    (A)   colder and wetter than was usual in some regions, which slowed
    (B)   which was colder and wetter than usual in some regions, slowing
    (C)   since it was colder and wetter than usually in some regions, which slowed
    (D)   being colder and wetter than usually in some regions, slowing
    (E)   having been colder and wetter than was usual in some regions and slowed

74. The bank holds $3 billion in loans that are seriously delinquent or in such trouble that they do not expect payments when due.

    (A)   they do not expect payments when
    (B)   it does not expect payments when it is
    (C)   it does not expect payments to be made when they are
    (D)   payments are not to be expected to be paid when
    (E)   payments are not expected to be paid when they will be

75. In a recent poll, 86 percent of the public favored a Clean Air Act as strong or stronger than the present act.

    (A)   a Clean Air Act as strong or stronger than
    (B)   a Clean Air Act that is stronger, or at least so strong as,
    (C)   at least as strong a Clean Air Act as is
    (D)   a Clean Air Act as strong or stronger than is
    (E)   a Clean Air Act at least as strong as

76. State officials report that soaring rates of liability insurance have risen to force cutbacks in the operations of everything from local governments and school districts to day-care centers and recreational facilities.

    (A)   rates of liability insurance have risen to force
    (B)   rates of liability insurance are a force for
    (C)   rates for liability insurance are forcing
    (D)   rises in liability insurance rates are forcing
    (E)   liability insurance rates have risen to force

77. Each of Hemingway's wives — Hadley Richardson, Pauline Pfeiffer, Martha Gelhorn, and Mary Welsh — were strong and interesting women, very different from the often pallid women who populate his novels.

    (A)   Each of Hemingway's wives — Hadley Richardson, Pauline Pfeiffer, Martha Gelhorn, and Mary Welsh — were strong and interesting women,

(B)   Hadley Richardson, Pauline Pfeiffer, Martha Gelhorn, and Mary Welsh — each of them Hemingway's wives — were strong and interesting women,

(C)   Hemingway's wives — Hadley Richardson, Pauline Pfeiffer, Martha Gelhorn, and Mary Welsh — were all strong and interesting women,

(D)   Strong and interesting women — Hadley Richardson, Pauline Pfeiffer, Martha Gelhorn, and Mary Welsh — each a wife of Hemingway, was

(E)   Strong and interesting women — Hadley Richardson, Pauline Pfeiffer, Martha Gelhorn, and Mary Welsh — every one of Hemingway's wives were

78.   While some academicians believe that business ethics should be integrated into every business course, others say that students will take ethics seriously only if it would be taught as a separately required course.

(A)   only if it would be taught as a separately required course

(B)   only if it is taught as a separate, required course

(C)   if it is taught only as a course required separately

(D)   if it was taught only as a separate and required course

(E)   if it would only be taught as a required course, separately

79.   Scientists have observed large concentrations of heavy-metal deposits in the upper twenty centimeters of Baltic Sea sediments, which are consistent with the growth of industrial activity there.

(A)   Baltic Sea sediments, which are consistent with the growth of industrial activity there

(B)   Baltic Sea sediments, where the growth of industrial activity is consistent with these findings

(C)   Baltic Sea sediments, findings consistent with its growth of industrial activity

(D)   sediments from the Baltic Sea, findings consistent with the growth of industrial activity in the area

(E)   sediments from the Baltic Sea, consistent with the growth of industrial activity there

80.   Under a provision of the Constitution that was never applied, Congress has been required to call a convention for considering possible amendments to the document when formally asked to do it by the legislatures of two-thirds of the states.

(A)   was never applied, Congress has been required to call a convention for considering possible amendments to the document when formally asked to do it

(B)   was never applied, there has been a requirement that Congress call a convention for consideration of possible amendments to the document when asked to do it formally

(C)   was never applied, whereby Congress is required to call a convention for considering possible amendments to the document when asked to do it formally

(D)   has never been applied, whereby Congress is required to call a convention to consider possible amendments to the document when formally asked to do so

(E)   has never been applied, Congress is required to call a convention to consider possible amendments to the document when formally asked to do so

81.   The current administration, being worried over some foreign trade barriers being removed and our exports failing to increase as a result of deep cuts in the value of the dollar, has formed a group to study ways to sharpen our competitiveness.

(A)   being worried over some foreign trade barriers being removed and our exports failing

(B)   worrying over some foreign trade barriers being removed, also over the failure of our exports

(C)   worried about the removal of some foreign trade barriers and the failure of our exports

(D)   in that they were worried about the removal of some foreign trade barriers and also about the failure of our exports

(E)   because of its worry concerning the removal of some foreign trade barriers, also concerning the failure of our exports

82. Geologists believe that the warning signs for a major earthquake may include sudden fluctuations in local seismic activity, tilting, and other deformations of the Earth's crust, changing the measured strain across a fault zone and varying the electrical properties of underground rocks.

    (A) changing the measured strain across a fault zone and varying
    (B) changing measurements of the strain across a fault zone, and varying
    (C) changing the strain as measured across a fault zone, and variations of
    (D) changes in the measured strain across a fault zone, and variations in
    (E) changes in measurements of the strain across a fault zone, and variations among

83. If the proposed expenditures for gathering information abroad are reduced even further, international news reports have been and will continue to diminish in number and quality.

    (A) have been and will continue to diminish
    (B) have and will continue to diminish
    (C) will continue to diminish, as they already did,
    (D) will continue to diminish, as they have already,
    (E) will continue to diminish

84. The root systems of most flowering perennials either become too crowded, which results in loss in vigor, and spread too far outward, producing a bare center.

    (A) which results in loss in vigor, and spread
    (B) resulting in loss in vigor, or spreading
    (C) with the result of loss of vigor, or spreading
    (D) resulting in loss of vigor, or spread
    (E) with a resulting loss of vigor, and spread

85. Any medical test will sometimes fail to detect a condition when it is present and indicate that there is one when it is not.

    (A) a condition when it is present and indicate that there is one
    (B) when a condition is present and indicate that there is one
    (C) a condition when it is present and indicate that it is present

    (D) when a condition is present and indicate its presence
    (E) the presence of a condition when it is there and indicate its presence

86. Since 1986, when the Department of Labor began to allow investment officers' fees to be based on how the funds they manage perform, several corporations began paying their investment advisers a small basic fee, with a contract promising higher fees if the managers perform well.

    (A) investment officers' fees to be based on how the funds they manage perform, several corporations began
    (B) investment officers' fees to be based on the performance of the funds they manage, several corporations began
    (C) that fees of investment officers be based on how the funds they manage perform, several corporations have begun
    (D) fees of investment officers to be based on the performance of the funds they manage, several corporations have begun
    (E) that investment officers' fees be based on the performance of the funds they manage, several corporations began

87. The diet of the ordinary Greek in classical times was largely vegetarian — vegetables, fresh cheese, oatmeal, and meal cakes, and meat rarely.

    (A) and meat rarely
    (B) and meat was rare
    (C) with meat as rare
    (D) meat a rarity
    (E) with meat as a rarity

88. Down-zoning, zoning that typically results in the reduction of housing density, allows for more open space in areas where little water or services exist.

    (A) little water or services exist
    (B) little water or services exists
    (C) few services and little water exists
    (D) there is little water or services available
    (E) there are few services and little available water

89. Those who come to church with a predisposition to religious belief will be happy in an auditorium or even a storefront, and there is no doubt that religion is sometimes better served by adapted spaces of this kind instead of by some of the buildings actually designed for it.

   (A) adapted spaces of this kind instead of by some of the buildings actually designed for it
   (B) adapted spaces like these rather than some of the buildings actually designed for them
   (C) these adapted spaces instead of by some of the buildings actually designed for it
   (D) such adapted spaces rather than by some of the buildings actually designed for them
   (E) such adapted spaces than by some of the buildings actually designed for it

90. The concept of the grand jury dates from the twelfth century, when Henry II of England ordered panels of common citizens should prepare lists of who were their communities' suspected criminals.

   (A) should prepare lists of who were their communities' suspected criminals
   (B) would do the preparation of lists of their communities' suspected criminals
   (C) preparing lists of suspected criminals in their communities
   (D) the preparing of a list of suspected criminals in their communities
   (E) to prepare lists of suspected criminals in their communities

91. In theory, international civil servants at the United Nations are prohibited from continuing to draw salaries from their own governments; in practice, however, some governments merely substitute living allowances for their employees' paychecks, assigned by them to the United Nations.

   (A) for their employees' paychecks, assigned by them
   (B) for the paychecks of their employees who have been assigned
   (C) for the paychecks of their employees, having been assigned
   (D) in place of their employees' paychecks, for those of them assigned
   (E) in place of the paychecks of their employees to have been assigned by them

92. According to a study by the Carnegie Foundation for the Advancement of Teaching, companies in the United States are providing job training and general education for nearly eight million people, about equivalent to the enrollment of the nation's four-year colleges and universities.

   (A) equivalent to the enrollment of
   (B) the equivalent of those enrolled in
   (C) equal to those who are enrolled in
   (D) as many as the enrollment of
   (E) as many as are enrolled in

93. Intar, the oldest Hispanic theater company in New York, has moved away from the Spanish classics and now it draws on the works both of contemporary Hispanic authors who live abroad and of those in the United States.

   (A) now it draws on the works both of contemporary Hispanic authors who live abroad and of those
   (B) now draws on the works of contemporary Hispanic authors, both those who live abroad and those who live
   (C) it draws on the works of contemporary Hispanic authors now, both those living abroad and who live
   (D) draws now on the works both of contemporary Hispanic authors living abroad and who are living
   (E) draws on the works now of both contemporary Hispanic authors living abroad and those

94. Last year, land values in most parts of the pinelands rose almost so fast, and in some parts even faster than what they did outside the pinelands.

   (A) so fast, and in some parts even faster than what they did
   (B) so fast, and in some parts even faster than, those
   (C) as fast, and in some parts even faster than, those
   (D) as fast as, and in some parts even faster than, those
   (E) as fast as, and in some parts even faster than what they did

95. If Dr. Wade was right, any apparent connection of the eating of highly processed foods and excelling at sports is purely coincidental.

    (A) If Dr. Wade was right, any apparent connection of the eating of
    (B) Should Dr. Wade be right, any apparent connection of eating
    (C) If Dr. Wade is right, any connection that is apparent between eating of
    (D) If Dr. Wade is right, any apparent connection between eating
    (E) Should Dr. Wade have been right, any connection apparent between eating

96. The commission proposed that funding for the park's development, which could be open to the public early next year, is obtained through a local bond issue.

    (A) that funding for the park's development, which could be open to the public early next year, is
    (B) that funding for development of the park, which could be open to the public early next year, be
    (C) funding for the development of the park, perhaps open to the public early next year, to be
    (D) funds for the park's development, perhaps open to the public early next year, be
    (E) development funding for the park, which could be open to the public early next year, is to be

97. Seismologists studying the earthquake that struck northern California in October 1989 are still investigating some of its mysteries: the unexpected power of the seismic waves, the upward thrust that threw one man straight into the air, and the strange electromagnetic signals detected hours before the temblor.

    (A) the upward thrust that threw one man straight into the air, and the strange electromagnetic signals detected hours before the temblor
    (B) the upward thrust that threw one man straight into the air, and strange electromagnetic signals were detected hours before the temblor
    (C) the upward thrust threw one man straight into the air, and hours before the temblor strange electromagnetic signals were detected
    (D) one man was thrown straight into the air by the upward thrust, and hours before the temblor strange electromagnetic signals were detected
    (E) one man who was thrown straight into the air by the upward thrust, and strange electromagnetic signals that were detected hours before the temblor

98. Two new studies indicate that many people become obese more due to the fact that their bodies burn calories too slowly than overeating.

    (A) due to the fact that their bodies burn calories too slowly than overeating
    (B) due to their bodies burning calories too slowly than to eating too much
    (C) because their bodies burn calories too slowly than that they are overeaters
    (D) because their bodies burn calories too slowly than because they eat too much
    (E) because of their bodies burning calories too slowly than because of their eating too much

99. Judge Bonham denied a motion to allow members of the jury to go home at the end of each day instead of to confine them to a hotel.

    (A) to allow members of the jury to go home at the end of each day instead of to confine them to
    (B) that would have allowed members of the jury to go home at the end of each day instead of confined to
    (C) under which members of the jury are allowed to go home at the end of each day instead of confining them in
    (D) that would allow members of the jury to go home at the end of each day rather than confinement in
    (E) to allow members of the jury to go home at the end of each day rather than be confined to

100. Proponents of artificial intelligence say they will be able to make computers that can understand English and other human languages, recognize objects, and reason as an expert does—computers that will be used to diagnose equipment breakdowns, deciding whether to authorize a loan, or other purposes such as these.

    (A) as an expert does—computers that will be used to diagnose equipment breakdowns, deciding whether to authorize a loan, or other purposes such as these
    (B) as an expert does, which may be used for purposes such as diagnosing equipment breakdowns or deciding whether to authorize a loan
    (C) like an expert—computers that will be used for such purposes as diagnosing equipment breakdowns or deciding whether to authorize a loan
    (D) like an expert, the use of which would be for purposes like the diagnosis of equipment breakdowns or the decision whether or not a loan should be authorized
    (E) like an expert, to be used to diagnose equipment breakdowns, deciding whether to authorize a loan or not, or the like

101. Unlike the United States, where farmers can usually depend on rain or snow all year long, the rains in most parts of Sri Lanka are concentrated in the monsoon months, June to September, and the skies are generally clear for the rest of the year.

    (A) Unlike the United States, where farmers can usually depend on rain or snow all year long, the rains in most parts of Sri Lanka
    (B) Unlike the United States farmers who can usually depend on rain or snow all year long, the rains in most parts of Sri Lanka
    (C) Unlike those of the United States, where farmers can usually depend on rain or snow all year long, most parts of Sri Lanka's rains
    (D) In comparison with the United States, whose farmers can usually depend on rain or snow all year long, the rains in most parts of Sri Lanka
    (E) In the United States, farmers can usually depend on rain or snow all year long, but in most parts of Sri Lanka the rains

102. Although Napoleon's army entered Russia with far more supplies than they had in their previous campaigns, it had provisions for only twenty-four days.

    (A) they had in their previous campaigns
    (B) their previous campaigns had had
    (C) they had for any previous campaign
    (D) in their previous campaigns
    (E) for any previous campaign

103. After the Civil War, contemporaries of Harriet Tubman's maintained that she has all of the qualities of a great leader: coolness in the face of danger, an excellent sense of strategy, and an ability to plan in minute detail.

    (A) Tubman's maintained that she has
    (B) Tubman's maintain that she had
    (C) Tubman's have maintained that she had
    (D) Tubman maintained that she had
    (E) Tubman had maintained that she has

104. The Federalist papers, a strong defense of the United States Constitution and important as a body of work in political science as well, represents the handiwork of three different authors.

    (A) and important as a body of work in political science as well, represents
    (B) as well as an important body of work in political science, represent
    (C) and also a body of work of importance in political science is representing
    (D) an important body of work in political science and has been representative of
    (E) and as political science an important body of work too, represent

105. As business grows more complex, students <u>majoring in specialized areas like those of finance and marketing have been becoming increasingly</u> successful in the job market.

   (A) majoring in specialized areas like those of finance and marketing have been becoming increasingly
   (B) who major in such specialized areas as finance and marketing are becoming more and more
   (C) who majored in specialized areas such as those of finance and marketing are being increasingly
   (D) who major in specialized areas like those of finance and marketing have been becoming more and more
   (E) having majored in such specialized areas as finance and marketing are being increasingly

106. Inuits of the Bering Sea were <u>in isolation from contact with Europeans longer than</u> Aleuts or Inuits of the North Pacific and northern Alaska.

   (A) in isolation from contact with Europeans longer than
   (B) isolated from contact with Europeans longer than
   (C) in isolation from contact with Europeans longer than were
   (D) isolated from contact with Europeans longer than were
   (E) in isolation and without contacts with Europeans longer than

107. The physical structure of the human eye enables it to sense light of wavelengths up to 0.0005 millimeters; <u>infrared radiation, however, is invisible because its wavelength—0.1 millimeters—is too long to be registered by the eye.</u>

   (A) infrared radiation, however, is invisible because its wavelength—0.1 millimeters—is too long to be registered by the eye
   (B) however, the wavelength of infrared radiation—0.1 millimeters—is too long to be registered by the eye making it invisible
   (C) infrared radiation, however, is invisible because its wavelength—0.1 millimeters—is too long for the eye to register it
   (D) however, because the wavelength of infrared radiation is 0.1 millimeters, it is too long for the eye to register and thus invisible
   (E) however, infrared radiation has a wavelength of 0.1 millimeters that is too long for the eye to register, thus making it invisible

108. <u>As well as heat and light, the Sun is the source of a continuous stream</u> of atomic particles known as the solar wind.

   (A) As well as heat and light, the Sun is the source of a continuous stream
   (B) Besides heat and light, also the Sun is the source of a continuous stream
   (C) Besides heat and light, the Sun is also the source of a continuous streaming
   (D) The Sun is the source not only of heat and light, but also of a continuous stream
   (E) The Sun is the source of not only heat and light but, as well, of a continuous streaming

109. Bluegrass musician Bill Monroe, whose repertory, views on musical collaboration, and vocal style <u>were influential on generations of bluegrass artists, was also an inspiration to many musicians, that included Elvis Presley and Jerry Garcia, whose music differed significantly from</u> his own.

   (A) were influential on generations of bluegrass artists, was also an inspiration to many musicians, that included Elvis Presley and Jerry Garcia, whose music differed significantly from
   (B) influenced generations of bluegrass artists, also inspired many musicians, including Elvis Presley and Jerry Garcia, whose music differed significantly from
   (C) was influential to generations of bluegrass artists, was also inspirational to many musicians, that included Elvis Presley and Jerry Garcia, whose music was different significantly in comparison to
   (D) was influential to generations of bluegrass artists, also inspired many musicians, who included Elvis Presley and Jerry Garcia, the music of whom differed significantly when compared to

(E) were an influence on generations of
bluegrass artists, was also an inspiration
to many musicians, including Elvis Presley
and Jerry Garcia, whose music was
significantly different from that of

110. The nephew of Pliny the Elder wrote the only
eyewitness account of the great eruption of
Vesuvius in two letters to the historian Tacitus.

(A) The nephew of Pliny the Elder wrote the only
eyewitness account of the great eruption
of Vesuvius in two letters to the historian
Tacitus.
(B) To the historian Tacitus, the nephew of Pliny
the Elder wrote two letters, being the only
eyewitness accounts of the great eruption
of Vesuvius.
(C) The only eyewitness account is in two letters
by the nephew of Pliny the Elder writing
to the historian Tacitus an account of the
great eruption of Vesuvius.
(D) Writing the only eyewitness account, Pliny
the Elder's nephew accounted for the great
eruption of Vesuvius in two letters to the
historian Tacitus.
(E) In two letters to the historian Tacitus, the
nephew of Pliny the Elder wrote the only
eyewitness account of the great eruption
of Vesuvius.

111. Being a United States citizen since 1988 and born
in Calcutta in 1940, author Bharati Mukherjee has
lived in England and Canada, and first came to the
United States in 1961 to study at the Iowa Writers'
Workshop.

(A) Being a United States citizen since 1988 and
born in Calcutta in 1940, author Bharati
Mukherjee has
(B) Having been a United States citizen since
1988, she was born in Calcutta in 1940;
author Bharati Mukherjee
(C) Born in Calcutta in 1940, author Bharati
Mukherjee became a United States citizen
in 1988; she has
(D) Being born in Calcutta in 1940 and having
been a United States citizen since 1988,
author Bharati Mukherjee

(E) Having been born in Calcutta in 1940 and being
a United States citizen since 1988, author
Bharati Mukherjee

112. Initiated five centuries after Europeans arrived in
the New World on Columbus Day 1992, Project SETI
pledged a $100 million investment in the search for
extraterrestrial intelligence.

(A) Initiated five centuries after Europeans arrived in
the New World on Columbus Day 1992, Project
SETI pledged a $100 million investment in the
search for extraterrestrial intelligence.
(B) Initiated on Columbus Day 1992, five centuries after
Europeans arrived in the New World, a $100
million investment in the search for extraterrestrial
intelligence was pledged by Project SETI.
(C) Initiated on Columbus Day 1992, five centuries
after Europeans arrived in the New World,
Project SETI pledged a $100 million investment
in the search for extraterrestrial intelligence.
(D) Pledging a $100 million investment in the search for
extraterrestrial intelligence, the initiation of Project
SETI five centuries after Europeans arrived in the
New World on Columbus Day 1992.
(E) Pledging a $100 million investment in the search
for extraterrestrial intelligence five centuries
after Europeans arrived in the New World, on
Columbus Day 1992, the initiation of Project
SETI took place.

113. In A.D. 391, resulting from the destruction of the
largest library of the ancient world at Alexandria, later
generations lost all but the Iliad and Odyssey among
Greek epics, most of the poetry of Pindar and Sappho,
and dozens of plays by Aeschylus and Euripides.

(A) resulting from the destruction of the largest
library of the ancient world at Alexandria,
(B) the destroying of the largest library of the
ancient world at Alexandria resulted and
(C) because of the result of the destruction of
the library at Alexandria, the largest of the
ancient world,
(D) as a result of the destruction of the library at
Alexandria, the largest of the ancient world,
(E) Alexandria's largest library of the ancient world
was destroyed, and the result was

5.7 Sentence Correction Answer Key

1.	B	32.	D	63.	A	94.	D
2.	A	33.	B	64.	A	95.	D
3.	A	34.	D	65.	D	96.	B
4.	C	35.	E	66.	C	97.	A
5.	D	36.	C	67.	D	98.	D
6.	A	37.	B	68.	D	99.	E
7.	C	38.	E	69.	C	100.	C
8.	C	39.	E	70.	A	101.	E
9.	B	40.	E	71.	C	102.	E
10.	A	41.	C	72.	A	103.	D
11.	E	42.	E	73.	B	104.	B
12.	C	43.	E	74.	C	105.	B
13.	A	44.	B	75.	E	106.	D
14.	B	45.	D	76.	C	107.	A
15.	A	46.	C	77.	C	108.	D
16.	E	47.	D	78.	B	109.	B
17.	B	48.	C	79.	D	110.	E
18.	E	49.	A	80.	E	111.	C
19.	A	50.	D	81.	C	112.	C
20.	D	51.	C	82.	D	113.	D
21.	D	52.	D	83.	E		
22.	E	53.	A	84.	D		
23.	C	54.	A	85.	C		
24.	B	55.	D	86.	D		
25.	A	56.	B	87.	E		
26.	C	57.	C	88.	E		
27.	E	58.	A	89.	E		
28.	E	59.	B	90.	E		
29.	E	60.	B	91.	B		
30.	B	61.	B	92.	E		
31.	A	62.	E	93.	B		

5.8 Sentence Correction Answer Explanations

The following discussion of sentence correction is intended to familiarize you with the most efficient and effective approaches to these kinds of questions. The particular questions in this chapter are generally representative of the kinds of sentence correction questions you will encounter on the GMAT®.

1. Some bat caves, like honeybee hives, have residents that take on different duties such as defending the entrance, <u>acting as sentinels and to sound</u> a warning at the approach of danger, and scouting outside the cave for new food and roosting sites.

    (A) acting as sentinels and to sound
    (B) acting as sentinels and sounding
    (C) to act as sentinels and sound
    (D) to act as sentinels and to sound
    (E) to act as a sentinel sounding

    Parallelism + Agreement

    The original sentence has an error in parallel structure. It starts by using the −ing (participial) form to list the bats' duties. *Defending*, *acting*, and *scouting* all use the same −ing form. The phrase *to sound* uses the to- (infinitive) form, and so it is not parallel. The word *sounding* is required in this sentence.

    A   *To sound* is not parallel to *defending*, *acting*, and *scouting*.
    B   **Correct.** This sentence has *sounding*, which properly parallels *defending*, *acting*, and *scouting*.
    C   *To act* and *sound* are not parallel to *defending* and *scouting*.
    D   *To act* and *to sound* are not parallel to *defending* and *scouting*.
    E   Introduces agreement error (*a sentinel*); *to act* is not parallel to *scouting*.

    The correct answer is B.

2. <u>However much United States voters may agree that</u> there is waste in government and that the government as a whole spends beyond its means, it is difficult to find broad support for a movement toward a minimal state.

    (A) However much United States voters may agree that
    (B) Despite the agreement among United States voters to the fact
    (C) Although United States voters agree
    (D) Even though United States voters may agree
    (E) There is agreement among United States voters that

    Parallelism + Grammatical construction

    In this correctly written sentence, parallel subordinate clauses are followed by a main clause. These parallel subordinate clauses are both introduced by *that*: *that there is...* and *that the government....*

    A   **Correct.** In this sentence, the repetition of *that* to introduce two subordinate clauses makes the construction parallel and correct.
    B   *That* is omitted; the sense of the sentence is changed by the omission of *may*; *agreement... to the fact* is awkward.
    C   *That* is omitted; the sense of the sentence is changed by the omission of *may*.
    D   *That* is omitted.
    E   Using two independent clauses separated only by a comma creates a run-on sentence; the sense of the sentence is changed by the omission of *may*.

    The correct answer is A.

3. Native American burial sites dating back 5,000 years indicate that the residents of Maine at that time were part of a widespread culture of Algonquian-speaking people.

(A) were part of a widespread culture of Algonquian-speaking people
(B) had been part of a widespread culture of people who were Algonquian-speaking
(C) were people who were part of a widespread culture that was Algonquian-speaking
(D) had been people who were part of a widespread culture that was Algonquian-speaking
(E) were a people which had been part of a widespread, Algonquian-speaking culture

Verb form + Rhetorical construction

The original sentence contains no errors. Each alternative introduces an error, adds unnecessary words, or changes the meaning of the original sentence.

A **Correct.** The original sentence uses the correct verb tense (*were*) to indicate an ongoing action in the past; the phrasing is concise and clear.
B *Had been* is an incorrect verb tense, suggesting that the Native Americans were no longer part of the culture; wordy.
C *Algonquian-speaking* should refer to *people*, not *culture*; wordy.
D *Had been* is an incorrect verb tense, suggesting that the Native Americans were no longer part of the culture; wordy and imprecise.
E *Were* and *had been* are inconsistent verb tenses; *which* is not the proper pronoun for *people*; wordy and imprecise.

The correct answer is A.

4. The voluminous personal papers of Thomas Alva Edison reveal that his inventions typically sprang to life not in a flash of inspiration but evolved slowly from previous works.

(A) sprang to life not in a flash of inspiration but evolved slowly
(B) sprang to life not in a flash of inspiration but were slowly evolved
(C) did not spring to life in a flash of inspiration but evolved slowly
(D) did not spring to life in a flash of inspiration but had slowly evolved
(E) did not spring to life in a flash of inspiration but they were slowly evolved

Parallelism + Idiom

The construction *not… but* shows a contrast. The words following *not* must be parallel in construction to the words following *but*. In the original sentence *not* is followed by a prepositional phrase (*in a flash of inspiration*); *but* is followed by a verb (*evolved*). To make the two contrasting elements parallel, *not* should be followed by a verb rather than a phrase.

A Construction following *not* is not parallel to the construction following *but*.
B Construction following *not* is not parallel to the construction following *but*; the passive voice *were evolved* is incorrect.
C **Correct.** In this sentence, *not* is followed by the verb *spring* just as *but* is followed by the verb *evolved*.
D *Had evolved* introduces an incorrect verb tense.
E Construction following *not* is not parallel to the construction following *but*.

The correct answer is C.

5.	A Labor Department study states that the <u>numbers of women employed outside the home grew by more than a thirty-five percent increase</u> in the past decade and accounted for more than sixty-two percent of the total growth in the civilian work force.

(A)	numbers of women employed outside the home grew by more than a thirty-five percent increase

(B)	numbers of women employed outside the home grew more than thirty-five percent

(C)	numbers of women employed outside the home were raised by more than thirty-five percent

(D)	number of women employed outside the home increased by more than thirty-five percent

(E)	number of women employed outside the home was raised by more than a thirty-five percent increase

Diction + Rhetorical construction

The sentence misuses the word *numbers* and contains the redundant word *increase*. The plural *numbers* means a large crowd or multitude, while the singular *number* refers to a specific quantity of individuals. The count of women here should be expressed as *the number*. The noun *increase* repeats the meaning already present in the verb *grew*; only one of the two words is necessary to the sentence.

A	*Numbers* should be *number*; *grew* and *increase* repeat the same idea.
B	*Numbers* should be the singular *number*.
C	*Numbers* should be *number*; the passive voice verb *were raised by* is unclear and wordy.
D	**Correct.** In this sentence, *number* correctly replaces *numbers*, and redundancy is eliminated with the use of the verb *increased*.
E	Passive voice verb *were raised by* is unclear and wordy; *increase* is redundant.

The correct answer is D.

6.	From the earliest days of the tribe, kinship determined the way in which the Ojibwa society organized its labor, provided access to its resources, <u>and defined rights and obligations involved in the distribution and consumption of those resources.</u>

(A)	and defined rights and obligations involved in the distribution and consumption of those resources

(B)	defining rights and obligations involved in their distribution and consumption

(C)	and defined rights and obligations as they were involved in its distribution and consumption

(D)	whose rights and obligations were defined in their distribution and consumption

(E)	the distribution and consumption of them defined by rights and obligations

Parallelism

This correctly written sentence uses a series of three parallel constructions to describe how the Ojibwa society *organized…, provided…, and defined…* The three verbs match each other, an example of correct parallelism.

A	**Correct.** The three verbs are parallel in this sentence.
B	*Defining* is not parallel to *organized* and *provided.*
C	*As they were* is wordy and imprecise; *its* has no clear referent.
D	*Whose rights and obligations* illogically refers to *resources.*
E	This construction breaks the parallel structure and is illogical and ungrammatical.

The correct answer is A.

7.	Delighted by the reported earnings for the first quarter of the fiscal year, <u>it was decided by the company manager to give her staff a raise.</u>

(A)	it was decided by the company manager to give her staff a raise

(B)	the decision of the company manager was to give her staff a raise

(C)	the company manager decided to give her staff a raise

(D)	the staff was given a raise by the company manager

(E)	a raise was given to the staff by the company manager

Logical predication + Verb form

Who was *delighted*? The *company manager* was *delighted*. The long modifying phrase that introduces the sentence describes a person, not *it*; the delighted person must be the subject of the sentence. Correcting the modification error also changes the construction from passive voice, *it was decided by x*, to active voice, *x decided*; the active voice is generally preferred.

A   The modifier illogically describes *it*, not the *company manager*; wordy.

B   The modifier illogically describes *the decision*; wordy.

C   **Correct.** The modifying phrase correctly modifies the *company manager*; using the active voice creates a better sentence.

D   The modifier describes *the staff* rather than *the company manager*; wordy.

E   The modifier illogically describes *a raise*; the passive voice is wordy.

The correct answer is C.

8.   The rising of costs of data-processing operations at many financial institutions has created a growing opportunity for independent companies to provide these services more efficiently and at lower cost.

(A)   The rising of costs
(B)   Rising costs
(C)   The rising cost
(D)   Because the rising cost
(E)   Because of rising costs

Idiom + Agreement

The rising of costs is wordy and awkward. The correct idiom is the more concise *the rising cost*. The main verb of the sentence, *has created*, requires a singular subject to maintain subject-verb agreement.

A   *The rising of costs* is not the correct idiom.

B   *Rising costs* does not agree with singular verb, *has created*.

C   **Correct.** *The rising cost* is the correct idiom, and it agrees with the singular verb in this sentence.

D   *Because* introduces a subordinate clause, creating a sentence fragment.

E   *Because* introduces a subordinate clause, creating a sentence fragment.

The correct answer is C.

9   William H. Johnson's artistic debt to Scandinavia is evident in paintings that range from sensitive portraits of citizens in his wife's Danish home, Kerteminde, <u>and</u> awe-inspiring views of fjords and mountain peaks in the western and northern regions of Norway.

(A)   and
(B)   to
(C)   and to
(D)   with
(E)   in addition to

Idiom

The correct idiom is *range from x to y*. In this sentence, the correct idiom is *paintings that range from sensitive portraits… to awe-inspiring views*.

A   *And* does not complete the idiomatic expression correctly.

B   **Correct.** In this sentence, *to* correctly completes the idiomatic construction *range from x to y*.

C   *And to* does not complete the idiomatic expression correctly.

D   *With* does not complete the idiomatic expression correctly.

E   *In addition to* does not complete the idiomatic expression correctly.

The correct answer is B.

10. Growing competitive pressures may be encouraging auditors to bend the rules in favor of <u>clients; auditors may, for instance, allow</u> a questionable loan to remain on the books in order to maintain a bank's profits on paper.

    (A) clients; auditors may, for instance, allow
    (B) clients, as an instance, to allow
    (C) clients, like to allow
    (D) clients, such as to be allowing
    (E) clients; which might, as an instance, be the allowing of

Grammatical construction

This sentence correctly joins two independent clauses with a semicolon. The first clause makes a generalization; the second clause gives a particular example that supports the generalization.

A **Correct.** This sentence correctly has two independent clauses with linked ideas joined with a semicolon.

B In trying to condense two main clauses into one, this construction produces an ungrammatical sequence of words with no clear meaning.

C The preposition *like* should not be used to introduce the example *to allow*, as is done here; it would be proper to use the comparative preposition *like* when making a comparison between two nouns.

D *Such as to be allowing* is not a correct idiomatic expression.

E Wordy, incorrect construction results in a sentence fragment.

The correct answer is A.

11. It is well known in the supermarket industry that how items are placed on shelves and <u>the frequency of inventory turnovers can be</u> crucial to profits.

    (A) the frequency of inventory turnovers can be
    (B) the frequency of inventory turnovers is often
    (C) the frequency with which the inventory turns over is often
    (D) how frequently is the inventory turned over are often
    (E) how frequently the inventory turns over can be

Parallelism

Two activities are considered *crucial*, and those two activities should appear as grammatically parallel elements in the sentence. The first is *how items are placed on shelves*, so the second should be *how frequently the inventory turns over*.

A *The frequency…* is not parallel to *how items….*

B *The frequency…* is not parallel to *how items…*; *is* does not agree with the compound subject.

C *The frequency… over* is lengthy, wordy, and not parallel; *is* does not agree with the compound subject.

D *Is the inventory* is not parallel to *items are placed.*

E **Correct.** In this sentence, the two clauses, *how items are placed on shelves* and *how frequently the inventory turns over,* are parallel.

The correct answer is E.

12. Iguanas have been an important food source in Latin America since prehistoric times, and <u>it is still prized as a game animal</u> by the campesinos, who typically cook the meat in a heavily spiced stew.

    (A) it is still prized as a game animal
    (B) it is still prized as game animals
    (C) they are still prized as game animals
    (D) they are still prized as being a game animal
    (E) being still prized as a game animal

Agreement

The pronouns and nouns that refer to the plural noun *iguanas* must be plural, as should the verb following the (corrected) pronoun in the second clause. Thus, the sentence should read: *Iguanas… they are still prized as game animals.*

A *It is* and *a game animal* do not agree with *iguanas.*

B *It is* does not agree with *iguanas* or *game animals.*

C **Correct.** In this sentence, *they are* and *game animals* properly agree with *iguanas.*

D *A game animal* does not agree with *iguanas*; *being* is unnecessary and awkward.

E *A game animal* does not agree with *iguanas*; the second independent clause requires a subject and a verb, not the participle *being.*

The correct answer is C.

13. Except for a concert performance that the composer himself staged in 1911, Scott Joplin's ragtime opera "Treemonisha" was not produced until 1972, sixty-one years after its completion.

(A) Except for a concert performance that the composer himself staged

(B) Except for a concert performance with the composer himself staging it

(C) Besides a concert performance being staged by the composer himself

(D) Excepting a concert performance that the composer himself staged

(E) With the exception of a concert performance with the staging done by the composer himself

Idiom + Rhetorical construction

This sentence requires attention to idiom and to conciseness. *Except for* is correctly followed by a noun, *concert performance*; *that the composer staged himself* is a clause that clearly and concisely describes the performance.

A **Correct.** In this sentence, the correct idiom is used in a clear and concise expression.

B *With… it* is an ungrammatical construction; *staging* suggests ongoing action rather than action completed in 1911.

C *Being staged* suggests ongoing rather than completed action; the passive voice is wordy and awkward.

D *Excepting* usually appears in negative constructions; it is not the correct idiom in this sentence.

E This sentence is awkward and wordy.

The correct answer is A.

14. From the time of its defeat by the Germans in 1940 until its liberation in 1944, France was a bitter and divided country; a kind of civil war raged in the Vichy government between those who wanted to collaborate with the Nazis with those who opposed them.

(A) between those who wanted to collaborate with the Nazis with those who opposed

(B) between those who wanted to collaborate with the Nazis and those who opposed

(C) between those wanting to collaborate with the Nazis with those opposing

(D) among those who wanted to collaborate with the Nazis and those who opposed

(E) among those wanting to collaborate with the Nazis with those opposing

Idiom

This sentence depends on the idiomatic construction *between x and y*. In this sentence, *between x with y* violates the idiom. *Among* is used only when more than two elements are involved; *between* is needed for the two elements here.

A *Between those… with those* is not the correct idiom.

B **Correct.** *Between those… and those* is the correct idiom for this sentence.

C *Between those… with those* is not the correct idiom.

D *Among* is used only when more than two elements are involved.

E *Between* is used for two elements; *among* is used for more than two elements.

The correct answer is B.

15. Chinese, the most ancient of living writing systems, consists of tens of thousands of ideographic characters, <u>each character a miniature calligraphic composition inside its</u> own square frame.

    (A) each character a miniature calligraphic composition inside its
    (B) all the characters a miniature calligraphic composition inside their
    (C) all the characters a miniature calligraphic composition inside its
    (D) every character a miniature calligraphic composition inside their
    (E) each character a miniature calligraphic composition inside their

Agreement

The underlined part of the original sentence acts as a modifier, or a phrase in apposition, describing Chinese ideographic characters. The modifier correctly uses the singular for all three terms: *character*, *composition*, and *its* all agree.

A **Correct.** In this sentence, the nouns *character* and *composition* and the pronoun *its* agree.
B *Characters* and *their* are plural, but *composition* is singular.
C While *characters* is plural, *composition* and *its* are singular.
D *Character* and *composition* are singular, but *their* is plural.
E *Character* and *composition* are singular, but *their* is plural.

The correct answer is A.

16. Declining values for farm equipment and land, <u>the collateral against which farmers borrow to get through the harvest season, is</u> going to force many lenders to tighten or deny credit this spring.

    (A) the collateral against which farmers borrow to get through the harvest season, is
    (B) which farmers use as collateral to borrow against to get through the harvest season, is
    (C) the collateral which is borrowed against by farmers to get through the harvest season, is
    (D) which farmers use as collateral to borrow against to get through the harvest season, are
    (E) the collateral against which farmers borrow to get through the harvest season, are

Agreement

Because a lengthy construction appears between the subject and the verb, it may be hard to see at first that the plural subject *values* does not agree with the singular verb *is*. *Values* requires *are*.

A Singular verb *is* does not agree with the plural subject *values*.
B *Is* does not agree with *values*; the clause is awkward and redundant.
C *Is* does not agree with *values*; the clause is awkward and wordy.
D *Use as collateral to borrow against* is redundant; the wording is awkward.
E **Correct.** In this sentence, the plural subject *values* agrees with the plural verb *are*.

The correct answer is E.

17. In the mid-1960's a newly installed radar warning system mistook the <u>rising of the moon as a massive missile attack by the Soviets</u>.

    (A) rising of the moon as a massive missile attack by the Soviets
    (B) rising of the moon for a massive Soviet missile attack
    (C) moon rising to a massive missile attack by the Soviets
    (D) moon as it was rising for a massive Soviet missile attack
    (E) rise of the moon as a massive Soviet missile attack

Idiom

This sentence depends on the correct use of the idiom *to mistake x for y*; *x* and *y* must be parallel. The sentence should read: the system *mistook the rising of the moon (x) for a massive missile attack (y)*. For a more concise expression of *y*, the phrase *by the Soviets* may be condensed to the adjective *Soviet*, placed before *missile attack*.

A The correct idiom calls for the verb *mistook* to be followed by *for*, not *as*.

B **Correct.** This sentence uses the correct idiom, *mistook x for y*; a more concise adjective replaces the modifying phrase.

C Use of *rising* as a participle following *moon* is confusing; it could be misread as *rising to a massive Soviet missile attack*.

D *As it was rising* is wordy and could be misread *rising for a massive... attack*.

E *Rise of the moon* is awkward; correct idiom calls for the verb *mistook* to be followed by *for*, not *as*.

The correct answer is B.

18. <u>With</u> only 5 percent of the world's population, United States citizens consume 28 percent of its nonrenewable resources, drive more than one-third of its automobiles, and use 21 times more water per capita than Europeans do.

(A) With
(B) As
(C) Being
(D) Despite having
(E) Although accounting for

Idiom

This sentence contrasts the small percent of population with the large percent of consumption. The contrast should be evident from the first word, showing the relationship of the information in the opening phrase to that in the main clause. *With* does not show contrast. *Although accounting for* prepares readers to expect a contrast.

A *With* does not suggest contrast; its suggestion of possession is illogical here.

B *As* is a conjunction that introduces a clause; *as* cannot introduce a phrase.

C *Being* does not show contrast and is awkward.

D *Despite having* modifies *citizens*; citizens are the population; they cannot *have* it.

E **Correct.** In this sentence, *although accounting for* shows contrast and relates logically to *citizens*.

The correct answer is E.

19. While depressed property values can hurt some large investors, <u>they are potentially devastating for homeowners, whose</u> equity—in many cases representing a life's savings—can plunge or even disappear.

(A) they are potentially devastating for homeowners, whose
(B) they can potentially devastate homeowners in that their
(C) for homeowners they are potentially devastating, because their
(D) for homeowners, it is potentially devastating in that their
(E) it can potentially devastate homeowners, whose

Rhetorical construction + Agreement

This sentence is correct and concise. *They* clearly refers to *property values*, and *whose* refers to *homeowners*.

A **Correct.** The relationship between nouns and pronouns is correct in this sentence; the expression is concise and clear.

B *Can potentially* is redundant; *in that their* is wordy, awkward, and ambiguous.

C *Their* appears to refer to *they* (*property values*) rather than to *homeowners*.

D *It* does not agree with *property values*; *in that their* is wordy and awkward.

E *It* does not agree with *property values*; *can potentially* is redundant.

The correct answer is A.

20. <u>Consumers may not think of household cleaning products to be</u> hazardous substances, but many of them can be harmful to health, especially if they are used improperly.

(A) Consumers may not think of household cleaning products to be
(B) Consumers may not think of household cleaning products being
(C) A consumer may not think of their household cleaning products being
(D) A consumer may not think of household cleaning products as
(E) Household cleaning products may not be thought of, by consumers, as

Idiom

The sentence uses an idiom that is correctly expressed as *to think of x as y*. The use of *to be* is incorrect.

A   *To be* is incorrect in the idiom *to think of x as y*.

B   *Being* is incorrect in the idiom *to think of x as y*.

C   *Being* is incorrect in the idiom *to think of x as*; *their* does not agree with *a consumer*.

D   **Correct.** This sentence uses the idiom correctly: *think of household products as*.

E   Passive-voice construction is awkward and wordy.

The correct answer is D.

21. It is possible that Native Americans originally <u>have migrated to the Western Hemisphere over a bridge of land that once existed</u> between Siberia and Alaska.

(A)   have migrated to the Western Hemisphere over a bridge of land that once existed

(B)   were migrating to the Western Hemisphere over a bridge of land that existed once

(C)   migrated over a bridge of land to the Western Hemisphere that once existed

(D)   migrated to the Western Hemisphere over a bridge of land that once existed

(E)   were migrating to the Western Hemisphere over a bridge of land existing once

Verb form + Logical predication

The simple past tense, used to describe an action completed in the past, is required in speaking of Native American migration to the Western Hemisphere.

A   The present-perfect verb *have migrated* implies that the migration is continuing into the present.

B   The verb *were migrating* improperly describes a continuing action in the past; the adverb *once* should precede the verb *existed*.

C   The modifying phrase *that once existed* logically refers to the bridge of land, not the Western Hemisphere, which fortunately for many

continues to exist. This phrase must be placed immediately following the word or word group that it modifies.

D   **Correct.** This sentence uses the correct verb tense, *migrated*, to describe an action completed in the past; the order of the prepositional phrases makes the meaning clear and logical.

E   The verb *were migrating* is incorrect, and the phrase *existing once* is imprecise.

The correct answer is D.

22. In recent years cattle breeders have increasingly used crossbreeding, <u>in part that their steers should acquire certain characteristics</u> and partly because crossbreeding is said to provide hybrid vigor.

(A)   in part that their steers should acquire certain characteristics

(B)   in part for the acquisition of certain characteristics in their steers

(C)   partly because of their steers acquiring certain characteristics

(D)   partly because certain characteristics should be acquired by their steers

(E)   partly to acquire certain characteristics in their steers

Parallelism + Rhetorical construction

The sentence gives two reasons that cattle breeders use crossbreeding; these reasons should be introduced in parallel ways with the word *partly*. The infinitive *to acquire* clearly and concisely conveys the purpose of the crossbreeding.

A   *In part* should be *partly*; use of relative clause is ungrammatical.

B   *In part* should be *partly*; wordy and awkward use of prepositional phrases.

C   *Because of* suggests that crossbreeding has occurred because the steers have already acquired certain characteristics.

D   Passive voice *should be acquired by* is awkward and illogical.

E   **Correct.** In this sentence, the word *partly* is used to introduce both reasons; the phrase *to acquire certain characteristics* is clear and concise.

The correct answer is E.

23. <u>Like Auden, the language of James Merrill</u> is chatty, arch, and conversational—given to complex syntactic flights as well as to prosaic free-verse strolls.

   (A)   Like Auden, the language of James Merrill
   (B)   Like Auden, James Merrill's language
   (C)   Like Auden's, James Merrill's language
   (D)   As with Auden, James Merrill's language
   (E)   As is Auden's the language of James Merrill

Logical predication + Diction

The intent of the sentence is to compare the *language* used by the two authors; both write in a *chatty, arch, and conversational* way. Using the phrase *like Auden's* to begin the comparison creates a concise statement, and the parallel construction of *Merrill's* also reduces wordiness and enhances clarity. Since the possessive *Auden's* matches the possessive *Merrill's*, the word *language* is not needed following the word *Auden's*.

A   *Auden* is illogically compared to *language*.
B   *Auden* is illogically compared to *language*.
C   **Correct.** This sentence states the comparison correctly and concisely, making it clear that Auden's language is being compared with Merrill's language.
D   *Auden* is illogically compared to *language*.
E   The sentence attempts to compare Auden's language with Merrill's, but the introductory *as is* is incorrect and the meaning is garbled.

The correct answer is C.

24. The period when the great painted caves at Lascaux and Altamira were occupied by Upper Paleolithic people <u>has been established by carbon-14 dating, but what is much more difficult to determine are</u> the reason for their decoration, the use to which primitive people put the caves, and the meaning of the magnificently depicted animals.

   (A)   has been established by carbon-14 dating, but what is much more difficult to determine are
   (B)   has been established by carbon-14 dating, but what is much more difficult to determine is
   (C)   have been established by carbon-14 dating, but what is much more difficult to determine is
   (D)   have been established by carbon-14 dating, but what is much more difficult to determine are
   (E)   are established by carbon-14 dating, but that which is much more difficult to determine is

Agreement

The singular subject of the first independent clause is *the period*; the singular subject of the second independent clause is *what is much more difficult to determine*. These singular subjects require the singular verbs *has* and *is*. In this sentence, the second verb, *are*, is incorrect.

A   *Are* does not agree with *what is much more difficult to determine*.
B   **Correct.** In this sentence, both verbs are singular and therefore correct.
C   *Have been established* does not agree with *the period*.
D   *Have been established* does not agree with *the period*; *are* does not agree with *what is much more difficult to determine*.
E   *Are established* does not agree with *the period*; this verb should be in the present perfect tense to express action completed in the past; *that which* construction is ungrammatical.

The correct answer is B.

25. The Baldrick Manufacturing Company has for several years followed a policy <u>aimed at decreasing operating costs and improving</u> the efficiency of its distribution system.

   (A)   aimed at decreasing operating costs and improving
   (B)   aimed at the decreasing of operating costs and to improve
   (C)   aiming at the decreasing of operating costs and improving
   (D)   the aim of which is the decreasing of operating costs and improving
   (E)   with the aim to decrease operating costs and to improve

Parallelism

This correct sentence uses the grammatically parallel elements *decreasing* and *improving* to describe the two aims of the company's policy.

A **Correct.** *Decreasing* and *improving* are grammatically parallel; *aimed at* is a correct and concise expression.

B *The decreasing* and *to improve* are not parallel.

C Using *the* before *decreasing* creates a gerund, which is not parallel to the participle *improving.*

D *The aim of which* is awkward and wordy; *the decreasing* is not parallel to *improving.*

E *With the aim to* is not the correct idiom; the correct idiom is *with the aim of* followed by an –ing form such as *decreasing.*

The correct answer is A.

26. Eating saltwater fish may <u>significantly reduce the risk of heart attacks and also aid for</u> sufferers of rheumatoid arthritis and asthma, according to three research studies published in the New England Journal of Medicine.

    (A) significantly reduce the risk of heart attacks and also aid for

    (B) be significant in reducing the risk of heart attacks and aid for

    (C) significantly reduce the risk of heart attacks and aid

    (D) cause a significant reduction in the risk of heart attacks and aid to

    (E) significantly reduce the risk of heart attacks as well as aiding

Diction + Parallelism

The word *aid* can be a noun or a verb; here it should be a verb that is parallel to the verb *reduce.* If *aid* were a noun, it would parallel *risk* and so would mean illogically that eating fish reduces *aid for sufferers* as well as *the risk of heart attacks.*

A *Aid for* seems to be a noun, parallel to the noun *risk,* indicating that *eating saltwater fish* reduces *aid for sufferers.*

B *Aid for* seems to be a noun, parallel to the noun *risk,* indicating that *eating saltwater fish* reduces *aid for sufferers.*

C **Correct.** In this sentence, *aid* is used as a verb, parallel to the verb *reduce. Sufferers* is the direct object of aid; no preposition is needed.

D *Aid to* is incorrectly used as a noun, suggesting that *eating saltwater fish* reduces

aid for sufferers.

E While this sentence is not incorrect, it lacks the parallel structure found in the correct answer.

The correct answer is C.

27. Minnesota is the only one of the contiguous forty-eight states <u>that still has a sizable wolf population, and where</u> this predator remains the archenemy of cattle and sheep.

    (A) that still has a sizable wolf population, and where

    (B) that still has a sizable wolf population, where

    (C) that still has a sizable population of wolves, and where

    (D) where the population of wolves is still sizable;

    (E) where there is still a sizable population of wolves and where

Parallelism

The sentence is making two points about Minnesota, but one point is introduced by *that* and the other is introduced by *where.* The same word should be used to introduce each point; either *that… and that* or *where… and where.*

A *That still has… and where* are not parallel.

B In this construction, the *where* clause modifies *wolf population* rather than *Minnesota.*

C *That still has… and where* are not parallel.

D While grammatically correct, this sentence needs a conjunction to show the logical relationship between the two independent clauses rather than the semi-colon that implies their equality.

E **Correct.** The use of *where… and where* creates two parallel clauses that clearly modify *Minnesota.*

The correct answer is E.

28. In reference to the current hostility toward smoking, smokers frequently expressed anxiety that their prospects for being hired and promoted are being stunted by their habit.

   (A) In reference to the current hostility toward smoking, smokers frequently expressed anxiety that

   (B) Referring to the current hostility toward smoking, smokers frequently expressed anxiety about

   (C) When referring to the current hostility toward smoking, smokers frequently express anxiety about

   (D) With reference to the current hostility toward smoking, smokers frequently expressed anxiety about

   (E) Referring to the current hostility toward smoking, smokers frequently express anxiety that

Verb form + Grammatical construction

The phrase *the current hostility* and the verb *are being stunted* indicate that the sentence concerns the present time. Therefore, the past-tense verb *expressed* should instead be the present-tense *express*.

A *Expressed* should be *express*.

B *Expressed* should be *express*; the preposition *about* cannot be used to introduce the clause *prospects... are being stunted*; a conjunction such as *that* is required.

C The preposition *about* cannot be used to introduce a clause; a conjunction such as *that* is required.

D *Expressed* should be *express*; the preposition *about* cannot be used to introduce a clause; a conjunction such as *that* is required.

E **Correct.** In this sentence, the verb is the correct present-tense *express*; the conjunction *that* correctly links *anxiety* with the clause that modifies it.

The correct answer is E.

29. According to some economists, the July decrease in unemployment so that it was the lowest in two years suggests that the gradual improvement in the job market is continuing.

   (A) so that it was the lowest in two years
   (B) so that it was the lowest two-year rate
   (C) to what would be the lowest in two years
   (D) to a two-year low level
   (E) to the lowest level in two years

Idiom + Grammatical construction

In this sentence, *decrease* is used as a noun and cannot grammatically be modified by the adverbial *so that*. The simple prepositional phrase *to the lowest level in two years* is a precise, concise alternative.

A The use of *so that it was* after a noun is ungrammatical; *it* could refer to either *decrease* or *unemployment*.

B The use of *so that it was* after a noun is ungrammatical; *it* could refer to either *decrease* or *unemployment*; the word *rate* is unclear.

C The conditional *would* should not be used to state a fact; *lowest* should be followed by a noun such as *level*.

D The meaning of *to a two-year low level* is unclear, and the phrase is unidiomatic.

E **Correct.** This sentence uses a clear, simple phrase that conveys an unambiguous meaning.

The correct answer is E.

30. Thomas Eakins' powerful style and his choices of subject—the advances in modern surgery, the discipline of sport, the strains of individuals in tension with society or even with themselves—<u>was as disturbing to his own time as it is</u> compelling for ours.

    (A) was as disturbing to his own time as it is
    (B) were as disturbing to his own time as they are
    (C) has been as disturbing in his own time as they are
    (D) had been as disturbing in his own time as it was
    (E) have been as disturbing in his own time as

    Agreement

    The compound subject of this sentence, *style and choices*, is followed by singular verbs, *was* and *is*, and a singular pronoun, *it*. The compound subject requires the plural verbs *were* and *are* and the plural pronoun *they*.

    A The verbs and pronoun are singular, but the subject is plural.
    B **Correct.** Verbs (*were, are*) and pronoun (*they*) agree with the plural subject in this sentence.
    C *Has been* is singular; it illogically indicates that Eakins' time continues today.
    D *Had been* indicates an anterior time; *it was* is singular and the wrong tense.
    E *Have been* illogically indicates that Eakins' time continues into the present day.

    The correct answer is B.

31. <u>Like Rousseau, Tolstoi rebelled</u> against the unnatural complexity of human relations in modern society.

    (A) Like Rousseau, Tolstoi rebelled
    (B) Like Rousseau, Tolstoi's rebellion was
    (C) As Rousseau, Tolstoi rebelled
    (D) As did Rousseau, Tolstoi's rebellion was
    (E) Tolstoi's rebellion, as Rousseau's, was

    Diction

    The preposition *like* correctly compares two equal nouns, in this case, two writers. The comparison must be between two equal elements; it cannot be between a person and an event. The original sentence is direct, clear, and concise.

    A **Correct.** The two writers are compared clearly and succinctly in this sentence.
    B *Tolstoi's rebellion* rather than *Tolstoi* is compared to *Rousseau*.
    C *As* is a conjunction that introduces clauses, not phrases or nouns.
    D *Tolstoi's rebellion* is compared to *Rousseau*; to be correct, this construction would have to be *as did Rousseau, Tolstoi rebelled*, but this is a wordy alternative.
    E *Tolstoi's rebellion… was against* is awkward and wordy; *Tolstoi rebelled against* is more direct.

    The correct answer is A.

32. The Wallerstein study indicates that even after a decade young men and women still experience some of the effects of a divorce <u>occurring when a child</u>.

    (A) occurring when a child
    (B) occurring when children
    (C) that occurred when a child
    (D) that occurred when they were children
    (E) that has occurred as each was a child

    Logical predication + Agreement

    The original sentence has two problems. (1) The phrasing implies that the young men and women had divorced in childhood. (2) The word *child* does not agree with the antecedent *men and women*.

    A *Child* does not agree with *men and women*; also, incorrect clause.
    B This choice does not correct logic or agreement errors.
    C *Child* does not agree with *men and women*.
    D **Correct.** This sentence corrects both problems by making it clear that the divorce took place when the men and women were children and by using *they* and *children* to agree with *men and women*.
    E *Each* does not agree with *men and women*; also, incorrect verb tense.

    The correct answer is D.

33. Carbon-14 dating reveals that the megalithic monuments in Brittany are nearly 2,000 years <u>as old as any of their supposed</u> Mediterranean predecessors.

    (A) as old as any of their supposed
    (B) older than any of their supposed
    (C) as old as their supposed
    (D) older than any of their supposedly
    (E) as old as their supposedly

Logical predication + Diction

The original sentence has two problems. (1) Comparisons must be logical and easy to follow. The Brittany monuments are logically older than the Mediterranean ones. Therefore, the appropriate comparison uses the phrase *older than*, not *as old as*. (2) Adjectives, not adverbs, modify nouns. The phrase *Mediterranean predecessors* requires the adjective *supposed*.

A Suggests two sets of megaliths are equally old, not that one is older
B **Correct.** This sentence makes the proper comparison and uses the adjective *supposed*.
C Suggests two sets of megaliths are equally old, not that one is older
D Makes correct comparison; adverb *supposedly* used instead of adjective *supposed*
E Suggests two sets of megaliths are equally old, not that one is older

The correct answer is B.

34. Lacking information about energy use, people tend to overestimate the amount of energy used by <u>equipment, such as lights, that are visible and must be turned on and off and underestimate that</u> used by unobtrusive equipment, such as water heaters.

    (A) equipment, such as lights, that are visible and must be turned on and off and underestimate that
    (B) equipment, such as lights, that are visible and must be turned on and off and underestimate it when
    (C) equipment, such as lights, that is visible and must be turned on and off and underestimate it when
    (D) visible equipment, such as lights, that must be turned on and off and underestimate that
    (E) visible equipment, such as lights, that must be turned on and off and underestimate it when

Parallelism + Agreement

This sentence has errors in parallelism and in subject verb agreement. The clause *that are visible* is not parallel to the adjective *unobtrusive*. Two kinds of equipment are being contrasted, *visible* and *unobtrusive*, so to be parallel (and concise) each adjective should appear directly before the noun it modifies, *equipment*. The noun *equipment* is singular and requires a singular verb.

A *That are visible* is not parallel to *unobtrusive*; error in subject-verb agreement between *equipment* and *are*.
B *Such as lights* is not parallel to *unobtrusive*; the singular noun *equipment* requires a singular verb; *it when used by* is not parallel to *the amount... used by*.
C *Such as lights* is not parallel to *unobtrusive*; *it when used by* is not parallel to *the amount... used by*.
D **Correct.** In this sentence, the two adjectives *visible* and *unobtrusive* are parallel, and placing *visible* before *equipment* eliminates the verb and solves the agreement problem. The construction *overestimate the amount of energy used by... and... underestimate that used by* provides parallel structure.
E *Such as lights* is not parallel to *unobtrusive*; *it when used by* is not parallel to *the amount... used by*.

The correct answer is D.

35. The rise in the Commerce Department's index of leading economic indicators <u>suggest that the economy should continue its expansion into the coming months, but that</u> the mixed performance of the index's individual components indicates that economic growth will proceed at a more moderate pace than in the first quarter of this year.

    (A) suggest that the economy should continue its expansion into the coming months, but that
    (B) suggest that the economy is to continue expansion in the coming months, but
    (C) suggests that the economy will continue its expanding in the coming months, but that
    (D) suggests that the economy is continuing to expand into the coming months, but that
    (E) suggests that the economy will continue to expand in the coming months, but

    ### Agreement + Grammatical construction + Verb form

    The singular subject *the rise* requires the singular verb *suggests*, not the plural *suggest*. This sentence is best composed of a main clause followed by a subordinate clause, the coordinating conjunction *but*, and then another main clause followed by a subordinate clause. When *that* is repeated after *but*, this structure is lost and a grammatically incorrect one put in its place. The second half of the sentence uses the future tense *will proceed*, so the first half should use *will continue*, the future tense reinforced by the phrase *in the coming months*. The usage *to expand* is the most clear and concise of the alternatives.

    A   *Suggest* does not agree with *the rise*; *that* should be omitted to create a main clause; the verb should be future tense *will continue*.
    B   *Suggest* does not agree with *the rise*; the verb should be future tense *will continue*.
    C   *Suggest* does not agree with *the rise*; use of *that* results in a subordinate clause when a main clause is required; *its expanding* is awkward.
    D   *That* used after *but* results in an incomplete grammatical construction; the verb should be future tense *will continue*.
    E   **Correct.** This sentence is complete and correct with the subject and verb in agreement and the verbs correctly using the future tense.

    The correct answer is E.

36. <u>What was as remarkable as the development of the compact disc</u> has been the use of the new technology to revitalize, in better sound than was ever before possible, some of the classic recorded performances of the pre-LP era.

    (A) What was as remarkable as the development of the compact disc
    (B) The thing that was as remarkable as developing the compact disc
    (C) No less remarkable than the development of the compact disc
    (D) Developing the compact disc has been none the less remarkable than
    (E) Development of the compact disc has been no less remarkable as

    ### Parallelism + Rhetorical construction

    This sentence compares *the development of the compact disc* with *the use of the new technology*; these two phrases must use parallel grammatical structures to make the comparison clear. Unnecessary words disrupt the parallelism and clutter the meaning; they must be omitted. The correct idiom for comparison must be used.

    A   *What was* is awkward and unnecessary; construction uses a verb tense that does not agree with *has been*.
    B   *The thing that was* is wordy and unnecessary, and it introduces a verb tense that does not agree with *has been*.
    C   **Correct.** *No less remarkable than* is the clearest, most concise, and idiomatically correct way for this sentence to introduce the comparison between *the development* and *the use*.
    D   *Developing* is not parallel to *the use*; *nonetheless* followed by *than* is not a correct idiom for comparison.
    E   Without its article, *development* is not parallel to *the use*; *no less... as* is not a correct idiom for comparison.

    The correct answer is C.

37. <u>Some buildings that were destroyed and heavily damaged in the earthquake last year were</u> constructed in violation of the city's building code.

(A) Some buildings that were destroyed and heavily damaged in the earthquake last year were

(B) Some buildings that were destroyed or heavily damaged in the earthquake last year had been

(C) Some buildings that the earthquake destroyed and heavily damaged last year have been

(D) Last year the earthquake destroyed or heavily damaged some buildings that have been

(E) Last year some of the buildings that were destroyed or heavily damaged in the earthquake had been

Logical predication + Verb form

The buildings cannot be both *destroyed* and *heavily damaged* at the same time; they must be one *or* the other. This sentence requires two verb tenses: the simple past, *were*, for the earthquake occurring last year; and the past perfect, *had been*, for the time prior to that when the buildings were constructed.

A The buildings are illogically said to be both *destroyed* and *damaged*; the verb tense indicates the buildings were constructed at the same time they were damaged or destroyed.

B Correct. This sentence properly states that the buildings were either destroyed *or* damaged and clarifies they *had been constructed* before the earthquake struck.

C Buildings cannot be both destroyed *and* damaged; the verb tense makes it seem that they were constructed after the earthquake.

D The verb tense indicates that the buildings *have been constructed* since the earthquake.

E This structure indicates that construction of the buildings, rather than the earthquake, occurred *last year*.

The correct answer is B.

38. <u>Using a Doppler ultrasound device, fetal heartbeats can be detected by the twelfth week of pregnancy.</u>

(A) Using a Doppler ultrasound device, fetal heartbeats can be detected by the twelfth week of pregnancy.

(B) Fetal heartbeats can be detected by the twelfth week of pregnancy, using a Doppler ultrasound device.

(C) Detecting fetal heartbeats by the twelfth week of pregnancy, a physician can use a Doppler ultrasound device.

(D) By the twelfth week of pregnancy, fetal heartbeats can be detected using a Doppler ultrasound device by a physician.

(E) Using a Doppler ultrasound device, a physician can detect fetal heartbeats by the twelfth week of pregnancy.

Logical predication

Using a Doppler ultrasound device is a modifying phrase; the noun it modifies must follow immediately after it. Who is using the device? Clearly a physician is using the device, but this sentence illogically says that *fetal heartbeats* are using the device.

A The phrase incorrectly modifies *fetal heartbeats*.

B The modifying phrase has no referent.

C This sentence suggests that a physician first detects heartbeats and then uses the device.

D The passive voice construction is unnecessary, wordy, and incorrect (*by a physician* must follow *detected*).

E Correct. This sentence uses the more concise active voice, and the phrase correctly modifies *a physician*.

The correct answer is E.

39. A study commissioned by the Department of Agriculture showed that if calves exercise and <u>associated with other calves, they will require less medication and gain weight quicker than do</u> those raised in confinement.

(A) associated with other calves, they will require less medication and gain weight quicker than do

(B) associated with other calves, they require less medication and gain weight quicker than

(C)   associate with other calves, they required less
      medication and will gain weight quicker than do

(D)   associate with other calves, they have
      required less medication and will gain
      weight more quickly than do

(E)   associate with other calves, they require less
      medication and gain weight more quickly
      than

Verb form + Diction

The first and last verbs in the series of verbs
that describe the calves are in the present tense,
so the two in the middle should be as well:
the calves *exercise… associate… require… gain
weight*. Adverbs, not adjectives, describe how an
action is carried out. These calves gain weight
more quickly, not *quicker*, than other calves.
The comparison is between *calves* and *those*
(referring to another set of calves); the verb *do*
ungrammatically interrupts the comparison and
should be eliminated.

A   *Associated* and *will require* do not match
    exercise and *gain*; the adjective *quicker* should
    be the adverb *more quickly*; *do* must be
    omitted.
B   *Associated* is in the past rather than the
    present tense; *quicker* is used in place of the
    correct *more quickly*.
C   *Required* and *will gain* are not in the present
    tense; *quicker* is used in place of the correct
    more quickly; *do* must be omitted.
D   *Have required* and *will gain* should be in the
    present tense; *do* must be omitted.
E   **Correct.** In this sentence, the verbs are
    all in the present tense; an adverb correctly
    modifies the verb phrase; the comparison is
    logical and grammatically correct.

The correct answer is E.

40.   A recent study has found that within the past few
      years, many doctors had elected early retirement
      rather than face the threats of lawsuits and the
      rising costs of malpractice insurance.

(A)   had elected early retirement rather than face
(B)   had elected early retirement instead of facing
(C)   have elected retiring early instead of facing
(D)   have elected to retire early rather than facing
(E)   have elected to retire early rather than face

Verb form + Parallelism

For action that started in the past and continues
into the present, it is correct to use the present
perfect tense: *has found, have elected*. When
a choice is presented using the *rather than*
construction—*the doctors have chosen x rather than
y*—the *x* and the *y* must be parallel. In this case,
the doctors have chosen *to retire* rather than (*to
understood*) *face*. *To* does not need to be repeated
in order to maintain parallelism because it is
understood.

A   *Had elected* shows an action completed in the
    past; *early retirement* is not parallel to *face*.
B   *Had elected* shows an action completed in the
    past; *retirement* and *facing* are not parallel.
C   *Have elected* must be followed by an infinitive.
D   *Facing* and *to retire early* are not parallel.
E   **Correct.** In this sentence, *have elected* shows
    action continuing into the present; *to retire*
    and (*to* understood) *face* are parallel.

The correct answer is E.

41.   The Gorton-Dodd bill requires that a bank disclose
      to their customers how long they will delay access
      to funds from deposited checks.

(A)   that a bank disclose to their customers how
      long they will delay access to funds from
      deposited checks

(B)   a bank to disclose to their customers how
      long they will delay access to funds from a
      deposited check

(C)   that a bank disclose to its customers how
      long it will delay access to funds from
      deposited checks

(D)   a bank that it should disclose to its customers
      how long it will delay access to funds from
      a deposited check

(E)   that banks disclose to customers how long
      access to funds from their deposited check
      is to be delayed

Agreement

A bank is singular and must be followed by the singular pronouns *its* and *it* rather than the plural pronouns *their* and *they*.

A   *Their* and *they* do not agree with *a bank*.

B   *Their* and *they* do not agree with *a bank*; the singular *check* is illogical since customers do not share one check.

C   **Correct.** In this sentence, the pronouns *its* and *it* agree with *a bank*, and *deposited checks* is a logical fit with *customers*.

D   *Requires a bank that is should* is not a grammatical construction; the singular *check* is illogical since the customers do not share one check.

E   The passive voice *is to be delayed* conceals the bank's role in delaying access; the singular *check* with the plural *their* is illogical.

The correct answer is C.

42.   Unlike a funded pension system, in which contributions are invested to pay future beneficiaries, <u>a pay-as-you-go approach is the foundation of Social Security</u>.

   (A)   a pay-as-you-go approach is the foundation of Social Security

   (B)   the foundation of Social Security is a pay-as-you-go approach

   (C)   the approach of Social Security is pay-as-you-go

   (D)   Social Security's approach is pay-as-you-go

   (E)   Social Security is founded on a pay-as-you-go approach

Logical predication

This sentence contrasts two systems, *a funded pension system* and *Social Security*. The sentence must be structured so that the contrast is logical and grammatical. After the first (*funded pension*) system is introduced and described, the second (*Social Security*) system must be introduced. The original sentence makes the mistake of contrasting *a funded pension system* with *a pay-as-you-go approach*.

A   *A funded pension system* is contrasted with an *approach* rather than with *Social Security*.

B   *A funded pension system* is contrasted with *the foundation* rather than with *Social Security*.

C   *A funded pension system* is contrasted with *the approach* rather than with *Social Security*.

D   *A funded pension system* is contrasted with *Social Security's approach* rather than with *Social Security*.

E   **Correct.** The two systems are contrasted in a logical, grammatical way in this sentence.

The correct answer is E.

43.   Although she had signed a pledge of abstinence <u>while being an adolescent</u>, Frances Willard was 35 years old before she chose to become a temperance activist.

   (A)   while being an adolescent

   (B)   while in adolescence

   (C)   at the time of her being adolescent

   (D)   as being in adolescence

   (E)   as an adolescent

Idiom

This sentence must use the correct idiom to describe a stage of Frances Willard's life as concisely as possible. *While being an adolescent* is awkward and wordy; *as an adolescent* is concise and clear. *As an adolescent* is a correct idiomatic expression, while all the other choices are not.

A   *While being an adolescent* is not an accepted idiomatic expression.

B   *While in adolescence* is not the correct idiom for this sentence.

C   *At the time of her being adolescent* is awkward and wordy.

D   *As being in adolescence* is not an accepted idiomatic expression.

E   **Correct.** This sentence uses the concise and idiomatically correct expression *as an adolescent*.

The correct answer is E.

44.   Though the term "graphic design" may <u>suggest laying out corporate brochures and annual reports, they have come to signify widely ranging</u> work, from package designs and company logotypes to signs, book jackets, computer graphics, and film titles.

(A) suggest laying out corporate brochures and annual reports, they have come to signify widely ranging

(B) suggest laying out corporate brochures and annual reports, it has come to signify a wide range of

(C) suggest corporate brochure and annual report layout, it has signified widely ranging

(D) have suggested corporate brochure and annual report layout, it has signified a wide range of

(E) have suggested laying out corporate brochures and annual reports, they have come to signify widely ranging

Agreement + Diction

The subject of the sentence is the singular noun *term,* which must be followed by the singular *it has* rather than the plural *they have. Widely ranging* could describe a conversation that moves from one topic to another; in this context, it is incorrect because the work does not move from one place to another. *A wide range of work* shows that the work consists of many different kinds of projects.

A *They have* does not agree with *term; widely ranging work* is imprecise.

B **Correct.** In this sentence, *it has* agrees with *term;* the phrase *a wide range of work* suggests a variety of projects.

C *Has come to signify* means that it still signifies, but *has signified* suggests a completed action and thus alters the meaning; *widely ranging work* is imprecise.

D *Have suggested* does not agree with *term;* the verb tenses suggest a completed situation rather than an ongoing one.

E *Have suggested* and *they have* do not agree with *term; widely ranging work* is imprecise.

The correct answer is B.

45. In contrast to large steel plants that take iron ore through all the steps needed to produce several different kinds of steel, <u>processing steel scrap into a specialized group of products has enabled small mills to put capital into new technology and remain</u> economically viable.

(A) processing steel scrap into a specialized group of products has enabled small mills to put capital into new technology and remain

(B) processing steel scrap into a specialized group of products has enabled small mills to put capital into new technology, remaining

(C) the processing of steel scrap into a specialized group of products has enabled small mills to put capital into new technology, remaining

(D) small mills, by processing steel scrap into a specialized group of products, have been able to put capital into new technology and remain

(E) small mills, by processing steel scrap into a specialized group of products, have been able to put capital into new technology and remained

Logical predication

This sentence contrasts *large steel plants* with *small mills.* Since the first half of the sentence begins with *in contrast to large steel plants,* the second half should begin with *small mills* to make the contrast immediately obvious and thus easy to understand.

A *Large steel plants* should be contrasted with *small mills,* not with *processing steel scrap.*

B *Large steel plants* appear to be contrasted with *processing steel scrap* rather than *small mills; remaining* and *to put* are not parallel.

C *Large steel plants* appear to be contrasted with *the processing of steel scrap; remaining* and *to put* are not parallel.

D **Correct.** In this sentence, *large steel plants* are clearly contrasted with *small mills,* and *to put* is parallel with (*to* understood) *remain.*

E *Remained* violates the parallelism with *to put* and changes the meaning of the sentence.

The correct answer is D.

46. The psychologist William James believed that facial expressions not only provide a visible sign of an <u>emotion, actually contributing to the feeling itself.</u>

    (A) emotion, actually contributing to the feeling itself
    (B) emotion but also actually contributing to the feeling itself
    (C) emotion but also actually contribute to the feeling itself
    (D) emotion; they also actually contribute to the feeling of it
    (E) emotion; the feeling itself is also actually contributed to by them

Idiom

This sentence should depend on the correlative construction *not only x… but also y*, where *x* and *y* are parallel. However, the faulty construction in the original sentence does not properly include the second element, *but also,* and so produces a sentence fragment. James says that facial expressions have two effects: they provide a sign of emotion and they contribute to emotion. Thus, in this sentence, *not only* should be followed by (*x*) *provide a visible sign of emotion,* and *but also* should be followed by (*y*) *actually contribute to the feeling itself.*

A The *not only… but also* construction is violated, creating a sentence fragment.
B *But also actually contributing* is not parallel to *not only provide*; because *contributing* is a participle and not a verb, the result is a sentence fragment.
C **Correct.** The *not only… but also* construction is parallel, resulting in a complete sentence.
D The *not only* construction requires *but also* to finish it; the use of the semicolon in this construction is incorrect; *the feeling of it* is awkward and wordy.
E Use of the semicolon in the *not only… but also* construction is not correct; the passive voice *was contributed to* is awkward and not parallel to *provide.*

The correct answer is C.

47. The financial crash of October 1987 demonstrated that the world's capital markets are <u>integrated more closely than never before and</u> events in one part of the global village may be transmitted to the rest of the village — almost instantaneously.

    (A) integrated more closely than never before and
    (B) closely integrated more than ever before so
    (C) more closely integrated as never before while
    (D) more closely integrated than ever before and that
    (E) more than ever before closely integrated as

Parallelism + Idiom

The 1987 crash demonstrated two truths: *that the world's capital markets are integrated…* and *that events… may be transmitted.* Because these two truths must be presented in grammatically parallel structure, *that* must be added to the second clause. The correct idiom is *more than ever*, not *more than never*.

A Second subordinate clause must begin with *that*; *more than never* is incorrect.
B Moving *more* distorts the meaning; *so* is not parallel to *that*.
C *More… as never before* is not correct; *while* is not parallel to *that*.
D **Correct.** In this sentence, the two clauses are parallel, each beginning with *that*, and they are correctly joined with the conjunction *and*; the correct idiom is used.
E This word sequence is incoherent; *as* is not parallel to *that*.

The correct answer is D.

48. Wisconsin, Illinois, Florida, and Minnesota have begun to enforce statewide bans prohibiting landfills to accept leaves, brush, and grass clippings.

    (A) prohibiting landfills to accept leaves, brush, and grass clippings
    (B) prohibiting that landfills accept leaves, brush, and grass clippings
    (C) prohibiting landfills from accepting leaves, brush, and grass clippings
    (D) that leaves, brush, and grass clippings cannot be accepted in landfills
    (E) that landfills cannot accept leaves, brush, and grass clippings

Idiom

This sentence misuses the idiomatic construction *prohibits x from doing y*; an alternative construction with the same meaning is *forbids x to do y*. The verb from the first construction, *prohibits*, is incorrectly joined with the infinitive form required in the second construction, *to accept*. The correct statement is *prohibiting landfills from accepting*.

A *Prohibiting… to accept* is not the correct idiom.
B *Prohibiting that… accept* is not the correct idiom.
C **Correct.** *Prohibiting… from accepting* is the correct idiom to use in this sentence.
D *Bans that… cannot be accepted* is not a correct idiom; *cannot* following *bans* is not logical.
E *Bans that… cannot accept* is an incorrect idiom; *cannot* following *bans* is illogical.

The correct answer is C.

49. Reporting that one of its many problems had been the recent extended sales slump in women's apparel, the seven-store retailer said it would start a three-month liquidation sale in all of its stores.

    (A) its many problems had been the recent
    (B) its many problems has been the recently
    (C) its many problems is the recently
    (D) their many problems is the recent
    (E) their many problems had been the recent

Agreement + Verb form + Logical predication

The correct use of pronoun reference, verb tense, and modifier make the sentence clear and easy to understand. The singular possessive pronoun *its* refers to the singular noun *retailer*. The past perfect verb *had been* indicates action completed before the action in the simple past tense *said*. The adjective *recent* modifies *extended sales slump*.

A **Correct.** *Its* agrees with *retailers*; the past perfect *had been* indicates action prior to the simple past *said*; *recent* modifies *extended sales slump*.
B *Has been* indicates ongoing, not completed, action; the adverb *recently* modifies only the adjective *extended*, distorting meaning.
C *Is* shows present, rather than completed, action; the adverb *recently* modifies only the adjective *extended*, distorting meaning.
D *Their* does not agree with *retailer*; *is* shows present, rather than completed, action.
E The plural *their* does not agree with the singular *retailer*.

The correct answer is A.

50. Domestic automobile manufacturers have invested millions of dollars into research to develop cars more gasoline-efficient even than presently on the road.

    (A) into research to develop cars more gasoline-efficient even than presently on the road
    (B) into research for developing even more gasoline-efficient cars on the road than at present
    (C) for research for cars to be developed that are more gasoline-efficient even than presently the road
    (D) in research to develop cars even more gasoline-efficient than those at present on the road
    (E) in research for developing cars that are even more gasoline-efficient than presently on the road

    Comparison + Logical predication

    The construction for comparison is *more x than y*; *x* and *y* must be grammatically parallel. This sentence suffers from faulty parallelism when it compares *more gas-efficient (cars)* to *presently on the road*. To be parallel, *gas-efficient (cars)* should be compared to *those* that are *at present on the road*. *Even* modifies *more gas-efficient*, not *than*. *Invested in* is the correct idiom rather than *invested into* or *invested for*.

    A *Presently on the road* is not parallel to *gas-efficient (cars)*; *even* incorrectly modifies *than*.
    B *Research* must be followed by *to develop*, not *for developing*; the two elements being compared are not parallel.
    C *Invested for research for cars* is awkward and idiomatically incorrect; the comparison is illogical and ungrammatical.
    D **Correct.** *Invested in* is the correct idiom; *those* is parallel to *gas-efficient (cars)*; *even* modifies *more gas-efficient*.
    E *Research* must be followed by *to develop*, not *for developing*; *presently on the road* is not parallel to *gas-efficient (cars)*.

    The correct answer is D.

51. In developing new facilities for the incineration of solid wastes, we must avoid the danger of shifting environmental problems from landfills polluting the water to polluting the air with incinerators.

    (A) landfills polluting the water to polluting the air with incinerators
    (B) landfills polluting the water to the air being polluted with incinerators
    (C) the pollution of water by landfills to the pollution of air by incinerators
    (D) pollution of the water by landfills to incinerators that pollute the air
    (E) water that is polluted by landfills to incinerators that pollute the air

    Parallelism

    When the construction is *from x to y*, *x* and *y* must be grammatically parallel. In this case, *x* and *y* are the two environment problems: *x = the pollution of water by landfills* and *y = the pollution of air by incinerators*. Starting the parallel phrases with *the pollution* emphasizes the similarity of the problem; each of the other elements, *of water/of air* and *by landfills/by incinerators*, emphasizes difference.

    A Lack of parallelism makes these two phrases difficult to understand.
    B *Landfills polluting…* is not parallel to *the air being…* .
    C **Correct.** The correct use of parallel structure clarifies the meaning of the sentence.
    D *Pollution of…* is not parallel to *incinerators that…* .
    E *Water that is polluted…* is not parallel to *incinerators that pollute…* .

    The correct answer is C.

52. The winds that howl across the Great Plains not only blow away valuable topsoil, thereby reducing the potential crop yield of a tract of land, and also damage or destroy young plants.

    (A)   and also damage or destroy
    (B)   as well as damaging or destroying
    (C)   but they also cause damage or destroy
    (D)   but also damage or destroy
    (E)   but also causing damage or destroying

Idiom

This sentence uses the construction *not only x but also y*; *x* and *y* must be grammatically parallel. In this sentence, *not only* appears directly before the first verb, so *but also* should appear immediately before the second set of verbs. *The winds… not only blow… but also damage or destroy*.

A   *And also* is not the correct idiom; *not only* is followed by *but also* or *also*.
B   *As well as* does not complete *not only*; *damaging or destroying* are not parallel to *blow*.
C   The subject (*they*) does not need to be repeated; *cause damage* is not parallel to *blow* and would require the preposition *to* before *young plants*.
D   Correct. In this sentence, *not only* is properly followed by *but also*, and *damage or destroy* is parallel to *blow*.
E   *Causing damage or destroying* is not parallel to *blow*.

The correct answer is D.

53. In a 5-to-4 decision, the Supreme Court ruled that two upstate New York counties owed restitution to three tribes of Oneida Indians for the unlawful seizure of their ancestral lands in the eighteenth century.

    (A)   that two upstate New York counties owed restitution to three tribes of Oneida Indians for the unlawful seizure of
    (B)   that two upstate New York counties owed restitution to three tribes of Oneida Indians because of their unlawful seizure of
    (C)   two upstate New York counties to owe restitution to three tribes of Oneida Indians for their unlawful seizure of
    (D)   on two upstate New York counties that owed restitution to three tribes of Oneida Indians because they unlawfully seized
    (E)   on the restitution that two upstate New York counties owed to three tribes of Oneida Indians for the unlawful seizure of

Idiom + Rhetorical construction

The underlined part of the sentence correctly introduces a subordinate clause with *that* to identify the Supreme Court's ruling. The idiomatic expression *owed restitution to x for y* is also correctly used.

A   Correct. This sentence properly uses a subordinate clause introduced by *that*; the correct idiom is used.
B   *Owed restitution to x because of y* is not the correct idiom; the pronoun reference *their* is ambiguous.
C   *That* is omitted, resulting in an awkward construction; the pronoun reference *their* is ambiguous.
D   *Ruled on… that* begins an awkward construction; the pronoun reference *they* is ambiguous.
E   *Ruled on… that* begins an awkward and imprecise construction.

The correct answer is A.

54. The extraordinary diary of William Lyon Mackenzie King, prime minister of Canada for over twenty years, revealed that this most bland and circumspect of men was a mystic guided in both public and private life by omens, messages received at séances, and signs from heaven.

   (A) that this most bland and circumspect of men was a mystic guided in both public and
   (B) that this most bland and circumspect of men was a mystic and also guided both in public as well as
   (C) this most bland and circumspect of men was a mystic and that he was guided in both public and
   (D) this most bland and circumspect of men was a mystic and that he was guided in both public as well as
   (E) this most bland and circumspect of men to have been a mystic and that he guided himself both in public as well as

Rhetorical construction + Idiom

The underlined portion of the sentence correctly uses a subordinate clause to describe King. *Guided* correctly modifies *mystic*, and parallel adjectives follow the *both... and* construction.

A Correct. The underlined clause in this sentence is grammatically and idiomatically correct.
B *Guided* should modify *mystic*, not be separated from it; *both in... as well as* is not a correct construction.
C Making a second subordinate clause (*that he was guided...*) incorrectly separates a single idea into two parts.
D The second subordinate clause separates a single idea, *a mystic guided in...*, into two parts; *as well as* incorrectly follows *both in*.
E The subordinate clause requires a verb, *was*, not an infinitive (*to have been*); the two clauses should be condensed to one; *as well as* incorrectly follows *both in*.

The correct answer is A.

55. In one of the most stunning reversals in the history of marketing, the Coca-Cola company in July 1985 yielded to thousands of irate consumers demanding that it should bring back the original Coke formula.

   (A) demanding that it should
   (B) demanding it to
   (C) and their demand to
   (D) who demanded that it
   (E) who demanded it to

Verb form + Grammatical construction

The use of the subjunctive is relatively infrequent in English; this sentence is an instance when it must be used. When a *that* clause follows a verb such as ask, recommend, request, or *demand*, the subjunctive (formed from the base form of the verb, such as *be* or *bring*) is used in the clause. Thus, the correct use of the subjunctive here is *consumers who demanded that it bring... .*

A The construction requires the subjunctive; the use of *should* is incorrect.
B *Demanding it to bring* is not a grammatically correct construction.
C Using both *consumers* and *their demand* is redundant.
D Correct. In this sentence, the subjunctive *bring* correctly follows *demanded that it*.
E *Demanded it to bring* is not a grammatically correct construction.

The correct answer is D.

56. Recently discovered fossil remains strongly suggest that the Australian egg-laying mammals of today are a branch of the main stem of mammalian evolution rather than developing independently from a common ancestor of mammals more than 220 million years ago.

    (A) rather than developing independently from
    (B) rather than a type that developed independently from
    (C) rather than a type whose development was independent of
    (D) instead of developing independently from
    (E) instead of a development that was independent of

    Idiom + Parallelism

    The original point is that the mammals mentioned are thought to be an offshoot of *the main stem of mammalian evolution* and not a descendent of *a common ancestor of* [all] *mammals.* This sentence makes a contrast using the construction *x rather than y* or *x instead of y*; *x* and *y* must be parallel in either case. The mammals are (*x*) *a branch* rather than (*y*); here *y* should consist of an article and a noun to match *a branch.* The second half of the contrast may be rewritten *a type that developed independently from* to complete the parallel construction. The idiom *independently from* is different in meaning from the idiom *independent of*; the logic of this sentence requires the use of *independently from.*

    A *Developing independently from* is not parallel to *a branch.*
    B **Correct.** This idiomatically correct sentence properly uses *a type* in parallel to *a branch.*
    C Verb *developed* is preferable to the awkward relative clause using the noun *development*; *independent of* distorts the original meaning.
    D *Developing independently from* is not parallel to *a branch.*
    E While *a development* may appear to parallel *a branch*, the logic of the sentence is contradicted by the meaning of this usage, and the verb *developed* is preferable to the noun *development*; *independent of* distorts the original meaning.

    The correct answer is B.

57. A patient accusing a doctor of malpractice will find it difficult to prove damage if there is a lack of some other doctor to testify about proper medical procedures.

    (A) if there is a lack of some other doctor to testify
    (B) unless there will be another doctor to testify
    (C) without another doctor's testimony
    (D) should there be no testimony from some other doctor
    (E) lacking another doctor to testify

    Rhetorical construction + Idiom

    The underlined clause is wordy and awkward; *lack of some other doctor* is not a correct idiomatic expression. This clause must be replaced by a more concise construction. *If there is a lack of* can be replaced by the preposition *without*; *some other doctor* is better expressed as *another doctor*; and *testimony* can be substituted for *to testify.* The result, *without another doctor's testimony*, clearly expresses in four words what the original statement poorly conveyed in eleven.

    A Clause is wordy and awkward; *lack of some other doctor* is not idiomatic.
    B Construction *y will happen unless x happens first* requires the present tense following the *unless* clause, rather than the future tense used here.
    C **Correct.** This sentence uses a phrase that is clear and concise.
    D This alternative is awkward and wordy.
    E *Lacking* illogically and incorrectly modifies *damage.*

    The correct answer is C.

58. <u>A recording system was so secretly installed and operated in the Kennedy Oval Office that</u> even Theodore C. Sorensen, the White House counsel, did not know it existed.

(A) A recording system was so secretly installed and operated in the Kennedy Oval Office that
(B) So secret was a recording system installation and operation in the Kennedy Oval Office
(C) It was so secret that a recording system was installed and operated in the Kennedy Oval Office
(D) A recording system that was so secretly installed and operated in the Kennedy Oval Office
(E) Installed and operated so secretly in the Kennedy Oval Office was a recording system that

Idiom + Agreement

This sentence correctly uses the idiomatic construction *so x that y*: the system was *so secretly installed* (x) *that even… Sorensen… did not know* (y) *that it existed*. The pronoun *it* clearly refers to *a recording system*.

A **Correct.** In this sentence, both pronoun reference and idiomatic construction (*so x that y*) are clear and correct.
B *So* must be followed by *that*; inverting the word order makes the pronoun reference ambiguous.
C *It was* is unnecessary; *that* is required before *even Theodore C. Sorensen…*; the pronoun reference is ambiguous.
D This construction results in a sentence fragment.
E The inverted word order does not grammatically fit into the rest of the sentence.

The correct answer is A.

59. Neanderthals had a vocal tract that resembled those of the apes and so were probably without language, a shortcoming that may explain why they were supplanted by our own species.

(A) Neanderthals had a vocal tract that resembled those of the apes
(B) Neanderthals had a vocal tract resembling an ape's
(C) The vocal tracts of Neanderthals resembled an ape's
(D) The Neanderthal's vocal tracts resembled the apes'
(E) The vocal tracts of the Neanderthals resembled those of the apes

Agreement + Grammatical construction

In the underlined portion of the sentence, the plural pronoun *those* does not agree with its singular referent, *a vocal tract*. To correct this error, the clause *that resembled those of the apes* may be rewritten as a phrase using the singular, *resembling an ape's*. In this case, *ape's vocal tract* is understood.

A *Those* does not agree with *vocal tract*; relative clause is wordy and unnecessary.
B **Correct.** In this concise sentence, the singular *an ape's* (*vocal tract* understood) agrees with *a vocal tract*.
C *Neanderthals* must be the subject of the second verb, *were*; *vocal tracts… were probably without language* is illogical; *tracts* is compared to *an ape's* (*tract*).
D *Vocal tracts* cannot logically be the subject of the second verb; *Neanderthal's* is singular but *vocal tracts* is plural.
E Making *vocal tracts* the subject here also makes it the illogical subject of *were probably without language*.

The correct answer is B.

60. The energy source on Voyager 2 is not a nuclear reactor, in which atoms are actively broken apart; rather a kind of nuclear battery that uses natural radioactive decay to produce power.

    (A) apart; rather
    (B) apart, but rather
    (C) apart, but rather that of
    (D) apart, but that of
    (E) apart; it is that of

Grammatical construction

This sentence focuses on a contrast by using the construction *not x, but rather y*; *x* and *y* are parallel. In this sentence *not x* (*a nuclear reactor*), should be followed by *but rather y* (*a kind of nuclear battery*). A comma, not a semicolon, should separate the two parallel parts of the contrast; using a semicolon results in a sentence fragment unless a subject and verb are provided in the construction.

A Using a semicolon results in a sentence fragment; *not x* should be balanced by *but rather y*.
B **Correct.** In this sentence, the contrast is clearly drawn in the correct construction *not a nuclear reactor... , but rather a kind of nuclear battery*.
C *That of* has no referent and results in an illogical, ungrammatical construction.
D *Rather* should be included to emphasize contrast; *that of* has no referent.
E No word is used to indicate contrast; *that of* has no referent.

The correct answer is B.

61. Archaeologists in Ireland believe that a recently discovered chalice, which dates from the eighth century, was probably buried to keep from being stolen by invaders.

    (A) to keep from
    (B) to keep it from
    (C) to avoid
    (D) in order that it would avoid
    (E) in order to keep from

Grammatical construction

The phrase *to keep from being stolen* is incomplete; the reader does not know what might be stolen. Inserting a pronoun makes it clear to the reader that it is the chalice that might be stolen.

A Pronoun *it* is needed for clarity.
B **Correct.** The sentence is clarified by inserting the word *it*, which refers back to *chalice*.
C Pronoun *it* is needed for clarity; this suggests the chalice acts to prevent its own theft.
D Pronoun *it* is needed for clarity; this suggests the chalice acts to prevent its own theft; *in order that it would* is wordy.
E Pronoun *it* is needed for clarity.

The correct answer is B.

62. Lawmakers are examining measures that would require banks to disclose all fees and account requirements in writing, provide free cashing of government checks, and to create basic savings accounts to carry minimal fees and require minimal initial deposits.

    (A) provide free cashing of government checks, and to create basic savings accounts to carry
    (B) provide free cashing of government checks, and creating basic savings accounts carrying
    (C) to provide free cashing of government checks, and creating basic savings accounts that carry
    (D) to provide free cashing of government checks, creating basic savings accounts to carry
    (E) to provide free cashing of government checks, and to create basic savings accounts that carry

Parallelism

The sentence uses parallel structure to describe what new legislation would require banks to do. The first requirement is written as *to disclose*; the other two requirements must be parallel in form. In this case, the other two requirements can be given as either *to provide... to create* or *provide... create*, with the *to* understood. In addition, using the same infinitive form for a different purpose in *to carry* is potentially confusing; using *that carry* is a clearer construction.

A   *Provide* and *to create* are not parallel.
B   *Provide* and *creating* are not parallel.
C   *Creating* is not parallel with *to provide.*
D   *To provide* and *creating* are not parallel in form; leaving out the word *and* makes *creating* appear to modify *checks.*
E   **Correct.** Parallelism is maintained in this sentence by following *to disclose* with *to create* and *to provide.* In this setting, the form *that carry* is more readily understood than *to carry.*

The correct answer is E.

63.   Certain pesticides can become ineffective if used repeatedly in the same place; one reason is suggested by the finding that there are much larger populations of pesticide-degrading microbes in soils with a relatively long history of pesticide use than in soils that are free of such chemicals.

(A)   Certain pesticides can become ineffective if used repeatedly in the same place; one reason is suggested by the finding that there are much larger populations of pesticide-degrading microbes in soils with a relatively long history of pesticide use than in soils that are free of such chemicals.

(B)   If used repeatedly in the same place, one reason that certain pesticides can become ineffective is suggested by the finding that there are much larger populations of pesticide-degrading microbes in soils with a relatively long history of pesticide use than in soils that are free of such chemicals.

(C)   If used repeatedly in the same place, one reason certain pesticides can become ineffective is suggested by the finding that much larger populations of pesticide-degrading microbes are found in soils with a relatively long history of pesticide use than those that are free of such chemicals.

(D)   The finding that there are much larger populations of pesticide-degrading microbes in soils with a relatively long history of pesticide use than in soils that are free of such chemicals is suggestive of one reason, if used repeatedly in the same place, certain pesticides can become ineffective.

(E)   The finding of much larger populations of pesticide-degrading microbes in soils with a relatively long history of pesticide use than in those that are free of such chemicals suggests one reason certain pesticides can become ineffective if used repeatedly in the same place.

Logical predication

The sentence is correctly constructed; it has two independent clauses connected by a semicolon. *If used repeatedly in the same place* clearly and correctly modifies *certain pesticides.*

A   **Correct.** The sentence is correctly constructed; the modifier *if used repeatedly in the same place* is correctly placed.
B   *If used repeatedly in the same place* modifies *one reason* when it should modify *certain pesticides.*
C   *If used repeatedly in the same place* modifies *one reason* when it should modify *certain pesticides*; the relative clause following *reason* should be introduced by *that.*
D   *If used repeatedly in the same place* ambiguously modifies *one reason* when it should clearly modify *certain pesticides.*
E   The comparison *the finding of much larger populations… than in those that* is improperly constructed so that the meaning of *the finding*, or the research result, is distorted into that of the discovery; the relative clause following *reason* should be introduced by *that.*

The correct answer is A.

64. In the textbook publishing business, the second quarter is historically weak, because revenues are <u>low and marketing expenses are high as companies prepare</u> for the coming school year.

    (A) low and marketing expenses are high as companies prepare
    (B) low and their marketing expenses are high as they prepare
    (C) low with higher marketing expenses in preparation
    (D) low, while marketing expenses are higher to prepare
    (E) low, while their marketing expenses are higher in preparation

Parallelism + Idiom

This sentence is correctly written. It uses parallel structure to give two reasons why textbook publishers have weak second quarters: revenues *are low* and expenses *are high*. The construction *as companies prepare for the coming school year* is clear, as opposed to the awkward constructions using the ambiguous plural pronouns *they* and *their*.

A **Correct.** This sentence uses the parallel forms *are low… are high* and employs the unambiguous *companies* as the subject of *prepare*.
B *Their* seems illogically to refer to *revenues*; subject of *prepare* is the ambiguous *they*.
C *Higher* is not parallel to *low*, and it is illogical since no comparison is being made.
D *Higher* is not parallel to *low* and is illogical since no comparison is being made; awkward and illogical infinitive construction.
E *Higher* is not parallel to *low* and is illogical since no comparison is being made; *their* has no clear referent.

The correct answer is A.

65. Parliament did not accord full refugee benefits to twelve of the recent immigrants because it believed that <u>to do it rewards</u> them for entering the country illegally.

    (A) to do it rewards
    (B) doing it rewards
    (C) to do this would reward
    (D) doing so would reward
    (E) to do it would reward

Grammatical construction + Verb form

The problem in the underlined section is how to refer back to the verb *accord*. It is a grammatical error to use a pronoun such as *it* or *this* to make the reference. The adverb *so* can correctly be used to refer back to the verb. The verb *rewards* is incorrectly in the indicative mood, the mood used to state a fact; in the context of a hypothetical action, the conditional *would reward* is more appropriate.

A Pronoun *it* cannot be used to refer back to the verb *accord*; *rewards* should be *would reward*.
B Pronoun *it* cannot be used to refer back to the verb *accord*; *rewards* should be *would reward*.
C Pronoun *this* cannot be used to refer back to the verb *accord*.
D **Correct.** The adverb *so* is correctly used to refer back to the verb *accord*; the conditional *would reward* is appropriate in referring to something contrary to fact.
E Pronoun *it* cannot be used to refer back to the verb *accord*.

The correct answer is D.

66. Many policy experts say that shifting a portion of health-benefit costs back to the workers <u>helps to control the employer's costs, but also helps</u> to limit medical spending by making patients more careful consumers.

    (A) helps to control the employer's costs, but also helps
    (B) helps the control of the employer's costs, and also
    (C) not only helps to control the employer's costs, but also helps
    (D) helps to control not only the employer's costs, but
    (E) not only helps to control the employer's costs, and also helps

Idiom + Parallelism

The correlative pair *not only... but also* can be used to describe the two effects: *not only helps to control... but also helps to limit.* These effects should be grammatically and logically parallel. It is incorrect to use *but also* by itself. Alternatively, the two effects, stated in parallel ways, could simply be linked by *and also.*

A *But also* must be used as part of the correlative pair *not only... but also.*

B *Helps the control of* is awkward and is not parallel to the effect *to limit.*

C **Correct.** This sentence uses the *not only... but also* construction correctly and expresses the two effects in parallel ways.

D *Also* is required in the *not only... but also* construction; *not only* should precede *helps.*

E The *not only... but also* construction requires the phrase *but also*, rather than *and also.*

The correct answer is C.

---

67. Ms. Chambers is among the forecasters who predict that the rate of addition to arable lands will drop while <u>those of loss rise</u>.

(A) those of loss rise
(B) it rises for loss
(C) those of losses rise
(D) the rate of loss rises
(E) there are rises for the rate of loss

Logical predication + Parallelism

The forecaster is making predictions about two different rates. The forecast changes in the rates can be compared using the construction *the rate of x will drop while the rate of y rises*; *x* and *y* should be parallel.

A There is no referent for *those.*

B *It* refers *to the rate of addition*, creating a nonsensical statement.

C There is no referent for *those*; *of losses* should be singular to parallel *of addition.*

D **Correct.** This sentence uses a construction that clearly states the predicted changes in the rates; the rates are expressed in parallel ways.

E *There are rises for* is wordy and unidiomatic.

The correct answer is D.

---

68. <u>Unlike auto insurance, the frequency of claims does not affect the premiums for personal property coverage</u>, but if the insurance company is able to prove excessive loss due to owner negligence, it may decline to renew the policy.

(A) Unlike auto insurance, the frequency of claims does not affect the premiums for personal property coverage

(B) Unlike with auto insurance, the frequency of claims do not affect the premiums for personal property coverage

(C) Unlike the frequency of claims for auto insurance, the premiums for personal property coverage are not affected by the frequency of claims

(D) Unlike the premiums for auto insurance, the premiums for personal property coverage are not affected by the frequency of claims

(E) Unlike with the premiums for auto insurance, the premiums for personal property coverage is not affected by the frequency of claims

Logical predication + Agreement

The point of this sentence is to contrast premiums for auto insurance and premiums for personal property insurance, but the sentence has been written so that *auto insurance* is contrasted with *the frequency of claims.* The correct contrast is between *the premiums for auto insurance* and *the premiums for personal property coverage.*

A *Auto insurance* is illogically contrasted with *the frequency of claims.*

B *Unlike with* is an incorrect idiom; *auto insurance* is contrasted with *the frequency of claims*; the singular subject *frequency* does not agree with the plural verb *do.*

C *The frequency of claims* is contrasted with *the premiums for personal property coverage*

D **Correct.** The contrast between *the premiums for auto insurance* and *the premiums for personal property coverage* is clearly and correctly stated in this sentence.

E *Unlike with* is an incorrect idiom; the plural subject *premiums* does not agree with the singular verb *is not affected.*

The correct answer is D.

69. Organized in 1966 by the Fish and Wildlife Service, the Breeding Bird Survey uses annual roadside counts along established routes <u>for monitoring of population changes of as many as, or of</u> more than 250 bird species, including 180 songbirds.

    (A) for monitoring of population changes of as many as, or of
    (B) to monitor population changes of as many, or
    (C) to monitor changes in the populations of
    (D) that monitors population changes of
    (E) that monitors changes in populations of as many as, or

    Idiom + Rhetorical construction

    Several changes will help make this awkward, wordy sentence easier to understand. A statement of purpose can be introduced by *in order to x*; the *in order* may be omitted and the purpose given with the concise *to monitor. Changes in the populations of* is clearer than *population changes of. Of as many as, or of* is wordy and should be eliminated.

    A *For monitoring of* should be *to monitor*; *of as many as, or of* is wordy.
    B *Of as many, or* is wordy.
    C **Correct.** This sentence uses *to monitor* to introduce a clear statement of purpose; *changes in the populations of* is precise; wordiness has been eliminated.
    D *That* has no referent.
    E *That* has no referent; *of as many as, or* is wordy.

    The correct answer is C.

70. Faced with an estimated $2 billion budget gap, the city's mayor <u>proposed a nearly 17 percent reduction in the amount allocated the previous year to maintain the city's major cultural institutions and to subsidize</u> hundreds of local arts groups.

    (A) proposed a nearly 17 percent reduction in the amount allocated the previous year to maintain the city's major cultural institutions and to subsidize

    (B) proposed a reduction from the previous year of nearly 17 percent in the amount it was allocating to maintain the city's major cultural institutions and for subsidizing
    (C) proposed to reduce, by nearly 17 percent, the amount from the previous year that was allocated for the maintenance of the city's major cultural institutions and to subsidize
    (D) has proposed a reduction from the previous year of nearly 17 percent of the amount it was allocating for maintaining the city's major cultural institutions, and to subsidize
    (E) was proposing that the amount they were allocating be reduced by nearly 17 percent from the previous year for maintaining the city's major cultural institutions and for the subsidization

    Parallelism + Grammar

    The original sentence contains no errors. Each alternative introduces an error or adds unnecessary words. The sentence must use parallel construction *to maintain* and *to subsidize* to show clearly the two areas where the 17 percent reduction in funds will be applied. In addition, the *17 percent reduction* should be closely followed by *the amount allocated the previous year* to clarify what is being reduced by 17 percent.

    A **Correct.** The sentence uses parallel construction and a well-placed modifier.
    B *To maintain* and *for subsidizing* are not parallel; imprecise, with unclear antecedent for *it*.
    C *For the maintenance* and *to subsidize* are not parallel; wordy.
    D *For maintaining* and *to subsidize* are not parallel; unclear whether only one budget is being reduced to subsidize the other activity; imprecise, with unclear antecedent for *it*.
    E *Maintaining* and *the subsidization* are not parallel; unclear whether one activity's budget is being reduced to maintain or subsidize the other activity; imprecise, with unclear antecedent for *they*.

    The correct answer is A.

71. By offering lower prices and a menu of personal communications options, such as caller identification and voice mail, the new telecommunications company has not only captured customers from other phone companies but also forced them to offer competitive prices.

    (A) has not only captured customers from other phone companies but also forced them
    (B) has not only captured customers from other phone companies, but it also forced them
    (C) has not only captured customers from other phone companies but also forced these companies
    (D) not only has captured customers from other phone companies but also these companies have been forced
    (E) not only captured customers from other phone companies, but it also has forced them

Parallelism + Pronoun reference

The sentence intends to show the effect of the new telecommunications company on the other phone companies. In the original sentence, the antecedent of the pronoun *them* is unclear; it may refer to *companies* or to *customers*. If it refers to *customers*, the sentence structure illogically has the new company forcing customers to offer competitive prices.

A   Pronoun reference is unclear.
B   Pronoun reference is unclear; redundant use of *it*.
C   **Correct.** The verbs are parallel in this sentence, and *these companies* is clearly the object of the verb *forced*.
D   Sentence does not maintain parallelism, unnecessarily changing from active voice (*has captured*) to passive voice (*have been forced*).
E   Pronoun reference is unclear; *captured* and *has forced* are not parallel in verb tense; redundant use of *it*.

The correct answer is C.

72. The gyrfalcon, an Arctic bird of prey, has survived a close brush with extinction; its numbers are now five times greater than when the use of DDT was sharply restricted in the early 1970's.

    (A) extinction; its numbers are now five times greater than
    (B) extinction; its numbers are now five times more than
    (C) extinction, their numbers now fivefold what they were
    (D) extinction, now with fivefold the numbers they had
    (E) extinction, now with numbers five times greater than

Agreement + Structure

The original sentence contains no errors. Each alternative introduces an error or changes the meaning of the original sentence. The semicolon correctly connects the closely related ideas in the two independent clauses. The *gyrfalcon* is the antecedent for *its* in the second phrase.

A   **Correct.** The original sentence correctly uses a singular pronoun, *its*, to refer to the singular antecedent *gyrfalcon*, and it properly uses the construction *its numbers are... greater than*.
B   The use of *more* instead of *greater* inappropriately implies there are now more numbers, rather than more gyrfalcons.
C   The pronoun *their* is plural and incorrect since the antecedent *gyrfalcon* is singular.
D   The pronoun *they* is plural and incorrect since the antecedent *gyrfalcon* is singular; comma usage introduces a confusing phrase seeming to modify *extinction*.
E   Comma usage introduces a confusing phrase seeming to modify *extinction*.

The correct answer is A.

73. Analysts blamed May's sluggish retail sales on unexciting merchandise as well as the weather, <u>colder and wetter than was usual in some regions, which slowed</u> sales of barbecue grills and lawn furniture.

    (A) colder and wetter than was usual in some regions, which slowed
    (B) which was colder and wetter than usual in some regions, slowing
    (C) since it was colder and wetter than usually in some regions, which slowed
    (D) being colder and wetter than usually in some regions, slowing
    (E) having been colder and wetter than was usual in some regions and slowed

Referents + Grammar

The sentence must clearly indicate that the inclement weather had slowed retail sales. Relative pronouns, such as *which,* should follow as closely as possible the nouns to which they refer. The adjective *usual,* rather than the adverb *usually,* is required when modifying a noun. The usage *wetter than usual* is correct and concise.

A Insertion of *was* is unnecessary; referent of *which* is unclear because *regions,* not *weather,* is the nearest noun.
B **Correct.** This sentence is concise, correct, and idiomatic, and *which* has a clear referent, *the weather.*
C With the linking verb *was,* the adjective *usual* is needed in place of the adverb *usually* to complete the meaning of the verb (*it was… usual*); referent of *which* is unclear because *regions,* not *weather,* is the nearest noun.
D *Being colder* does not refer to *weather* as clearly as *which* does; the adjective *usual* should be used to modify the noun *weather* instead of the adverb *usually.*
E *Having been colder* does not refer to *weather* as clearly as *which* does; insertion of *was* is unnecessary; also, fails to maintain parallelism in verb tense (*having been* and *slowed*).

The correct answer is B.

74. The bank holds $3 billion in loans that are seriously delinquent or in such trouble that <u>they do not expect payments when</u> due.

    (A) they do not expect payments when
    (B) it does not expect payments when it is
    (C) it does not expect payments to be made when they are
    (D) payments are not to be expected to be paid when
    (E) payments are not expected to be paid when they will be

Agreement + Logical predication + Verb form

The plural pronoun *they* cannot be used to refer to the singular noun *bank.* The structure of *they do not expect payments when due* is awkward and unclear.

A *Bank* requires the singular pronoun *it,* not the plural pronoun *they;* structure of *when due* creates ambiguity in meaning.
B *Payments* is a plural noun so the singular *it is* is incorrect.
C **Correct.** In this correct sentence, pronouns and their referents agree, as do subjects and their verbs. The addition of the modifying phrase *to be made* clarifies the meaning of the sentence.
D Since the passive voice adds no meaningful contribution here, its use should be avoided; *payments… to be paid* is redundant; *are not to be* incorrectly shifts the action to the future.
E Since the passive voice adds no meaningful contribution here, its use should be avoided; *payments… to be paid* is redundant; *will be* incorrectly shifts the action to the future.

The correct answer is C.

75. In a recent poll, 86 percent of the public favored <u>a Clean Air Act as strong or stronger than</u> the present act.

    (A) a Clean Air Act as strong or stronger than
    (B) a Clean Air Act that is stronger, or at least so strong as,
    (C) at least as strong a Clean Air Act as is
    (D) a Clean Air Act as strong or stronger than is
    (E) a Clean Air Act at least as strong as

    Idiom

    This sentence depends on the comparative construction *as x as*. The public wants as act *as strong as* or *stronger than* the present act. The second *as* is omitted in this sentence, leaving the incomplete and incoherent construction *as strong the present act*. The lengthy, awkward comparison *as strong as or stronger than* can be more concisely expressed by *at least as strong as*.

    A *As strong* must be followed by *as*.
    B *Stronger* requires *than*; *so strong as* is not a correct idiom.
    C Two nouns (*Clean Air Act, present act*) must be compared; the verb *is* violates parallelism
    D *As strong* must be followed by *as*; the verb *is* is unnecessary and incorrect.
    E **Correct.** In this sentence, *at least as strong as* concisely and correctly expresses the comparison.

    The correct answer is E.

76. State officials report that soaring <u>rates of liability insurance have risen to force</u> cutbacks in the operations of everything from local governments and school districts to day-care centers and recreational facilities.

    (A) rates of liability insurance have risen to force
    (B) rates of liability insurance are a force for
    (C) rates for liability insurance are forcing
    (D) rises in liability insurance rates are forcing
    (E) liability insurance rates have risen to force

    Rhetorical construction + Verb form + Idiom

    This sentence does not clearly present its main point. It should be revised to eliminate redundancy, clarify cause-and-effect relationships, and use the word *rates* correctly. The adjective *soaring* and the verb form *have risen* express the same idea, so the verb should be omitted and replaced with *are forcing*, which shows clearly what the *soaring rates* are doing. Moreover, the present progressive verb tense (*are forcing*) indicates this is an ongoing problem. When *rate* means a *price charged*, it is followed by the preposition *for*.

    A *For* should be used following *rates*, not *of*; redundant verb form *have risen*.
    B *For* should be used following *rates*, not *of*; the wordy construction *are a force for* is not as clear as the more concise *are forcing*.
    C **Correct.** The sentence is concise and uses the correct preposition following *rates*, and the present progressive verb tense properly reveals an ongoing situation.
    D *Rises* repeats the idea already expressed in the adjective *soaring*.
    E *Have risen* repeats the idea expressed in the adjective *soaring*.

    The correct answer is C.

77. Each of Hemingway's wives — Hadley Richardson, Pauline Pfeiffer, Martha Gelhorn, and Mary Welsh — were strong and interesting women, very different from the often pallid women who populate his novels.

    (A) Each of Hemingway's wives — Hadley Richardson, Pauline Pfeiffer, Martha Gelhorn, and Mary Welsh — were strong and interesting women,
    (B) Hadley Richardson, Pauline Pfeiffer, Martha Gelhorn, and Mary Welsh — each of them Hemingway's wives — were strong and interesting women,
    (C) Hemingway's wives — Hadley Richardson, Pauline Pfeiffer, Martha Gelhorn, and Mary Welsh — were all strong and interesting women,
    (D) Strong and interesting women — Hadley Richardson, Pauline Pfeiffer, Martha Gelhorn, and Mary Welsh — each a wife of Hemingway, was
    (E) Strong and interesting women — Hadley Richardson, Pauline Pfeiffer, Martha Gelhorn, and Mary Welsh — every one of Hemingway's wives were

Agreement

The list that comes between the singular subject *each* and the plural verb *were* may distract attention from the lack of agreement. Replacing the singular pronoun *each* with the plural noun *wives* both corrects the agreement error and makes the sentence slightly more concise. In addition, the use of the plural is then consistent in the sentence: *wives... strong and interesting women... pallid women.*

A *Each* does not agree with the plural verb *were*.
B *Each of them Hemingway's wives* is illogical since *each* was *a wife*, not *wives*.
C **Correct.** In this sentence, the plural subject *wives* matches the plural verb *were*.
D *Women* does not agree with *was*; the awkward changes in sentence construction obscure the meaning.
E *Every one* is singular and does not agree with *women* or *were*; the construction is awkward and unclear.

The correct answer is C.

78. While some academicians believe that business ethics should be integrated into every business course, others say that students will take ethics seriously only if it would be taught as a separately required course.

    (A) only if it would be taught as a separately required course
    (B) only if it is taught as a separate, required course
    (C) if it is taught only as a course required separately
    (D) if it was taught only as a separate and required course
    (E) if it would only be taught as a required course, separately

Grammatical construction + Verb form

Conditional constructions require specific verb tenses. For a present condition, like this debate between academicians, the subordinate clause introduced by *if* uses the present indicative, and the main clause uses the future tense: *if x happens, then y will happen.* The order of the two clauses may be reversed, as is the case here: *y will happen only if x happens first.* The *y* clause is *students will take...*, so the *x* clause must be *only if it is taught...* Logically, the *course* is to be both *separate* and *required*, so the two adjectives should equally modify the noun and thus be separated by a comma: *separate, required course.*

A The verb tense in the *if* clause is incorrect; the adverb *separately* should be the adjective *separate*.
B **Correct.** This sentence has the correct verb tense, and the two adjectives equally modify the noun.
C *Only* must precede *if*; a course required separately is unclear.
D Incorrect verb tense in the *if* clause; *only* must precede *if*.
E Incorrect verb tense in the *if* clause; *only* must precede *if*; the adverb *separately* should be the adjective *separate* and should precede the noun.

The correct answer is B.

79. Scientists have observed large concentrations of heavy-metal deposits in the upper twenty centimeters of Baltic Sea sediments, which are consistent with the growth of industrial activity there.

(A)   Baltic Sea sediments, which are consistent with the growth of industrial activity there

(B)   Baltic Sea sediments, where the growth of industrial activity is consistent with these findings

(C)   Baltic Sea sediments, findings consistent with its growth of industrial activity

(D)   sediments from the Baltic Sea, findings consistent with the growth of industrial activity in the area

(E)   sediments from the Baltic Sea, consistent with the growth of industrial activity there

Grammatical construction + Logical predication

This ambiguous sentence can be clarified by asking a series of questions: The *deposits* are in *the upper twenty centimeters of* what? Of the *sediments*, not of the *Baltic Sea*, so it is clearer to place *sediments* directly after *centimeters*. As the sentence is written, *which* seems to refer back to the whole previous clause. Substituting a noun, *findings*, makes the reference clear. Where has the growth of industrial activity taken place? *There* is too vague and makes it seem that the industry is taking place in the sediments. Replacing *there* with the more specific *in the area* solves this problem.

A   *Baltic Sea sediments* is hard to understand; *which* has no logical referent; *there* is too vague.

B   *Baltic Sea sediments* is hard to understand; *where* has no logical referent.

C   *Baltic Sea sediments* is hard to understand; *its* does not have a referent.

D   Correct. This sentence is logical and clear. *Sediments from the Baltic Sea* is a clear reference; *findings* refers back to the scientists' observations; *in this area* identifies a place more specifically.

E   The phrase beginning with *consistent* illogically describes the Baltic Sea.

The correct answer is D.

80.   Under a provision of the Constitution that <u>was never applied, Congress has been required to call a convention for considering possible amendments to the document when formally asked to do it</u> by the legislatures of two-thirds of the states.

(A)   was never applied, Congress has been required to call a convention for considering possible amendments to the document when formally asked to do it

(B)   was never applied, there has been a requirement that Congress call a convention for consideration of possible amendments to the document when asked to do it formally

(C)   was never applied, whereby Congress is required to call a convention for considering possible amendments to the document when asked to do it formally

(D)   has never been applied, whereby Congress is required to call a convention to consider possible amendments to the document when formally asked to do so

(E)   has never been applied, Congress is required to call a convention to consider possible amendments to the document when formally asked to do so

Verb form + Idiom + Logical predication

The meaning of this sentence is distorted by the use of incorrect verb tenses. The provisions of the Constitution, created in 1789, remain in force today. The present perfect tense *has been applied* is used for action that began in the past and continues into the present. Since the provisions currently apply, the present tense is needed for the next verb: *Congress is required...* The idiom is *call... to consider*, not *call... for considering*. Finally, the pronoun *it* ungrammatically refers back to the entire expression regarding what Congress is required to do and should be replaced by *to do so*, which more clearly and correctly refers to what Congress must do.

A   The verb tenses are incorrect; *call for considering* should be *call to consider*; *it* has no clear referent.

B   The verb tenses are incorrect; the idiom *call to consider* is violated; *it* has no clear referent; wordy.

C   The first verb tense is incorrect; *whereby* introduces a sentence fragment; the idiom *call to consider* is violated; *it* has no clear referent.

D   *Whereby* introduces a sentence fragment.

E   Correct. In this sentence, the verb tenses indicate that the provisions are in effect; the correct idiom is used; *to do so* correctly refers to what Congress is required to do.

The correct answer is E.

81. The current administration, <u>being worried over some foreign trade barriers being removed and our exports failing</u> to increase as a result of deep cuts in the value of the dollar, has formed a group to study ways to sharpen our competitiveness.

    (A) being worried over some foreign trade barriers being removed and our exports failing
    (B) worrying over some foreign trade barriers being removed, also over the failure of our exports
    (C) worried about the removal of some foreign trade barriers and the failure of our exports
    (D) in that they were worried about the removal of some foreign trade barriers and also about the failure of our exports
    (E) because of its worry concerning the removal of some foreign trade barriers, also concerning the failure of our exports

Parallelism + Rhetorical construction

The underlined part of the sentence begins a phrase describing *administration*. A modifying phrase that interrupts a sentence must be as concise as possible; *being* (which is often unnecessary in sentences) makes an awkward start to an unnecessarily wordy phrase. *Worried* is used as an adjective to describe *administration* and is a good way to begin the phrase; the correct idiom is *worried about* rather than *worried over*. *Some trade barriers being removed* and *our exports failing* need to be stated in concise, parallel expressions: *the removal of some trade barriers* is parallel to *the failure of our exports*.

A *Being* introduces a wordy phrase; the two objects of worry should be parallel; not idiomatically correct.
B The two objects of worry are not parallel; wordy; not idiomatic.
C **Correct.** In this sentence, *worried* begins a clear, concise, and correctly parallel phrase describing the *administration*.
D *In that* begins a wordy construction; *they* does not agree with the singular *administration*.
E *Because* introduces an unnecessarily wordy phrase; the two objects of worry are not equal and parallel.

The correct answer is C.

82. Geologists believe that the warning signs for a major earthquake may include sudden fluctuations in local seismic activity, tilting and other deformations of the Earth's crust, <u>changing the measured strain across a fault zone and varying</u> the electrical properties of underground rocks.

    (A) changing the measured strain across a fault zone and varying
    (B) changing measurements of the strain across a fault zone, and varying
    (C) changing the strain as measured across a fault zone, and variations of
    (D) changes in the measured strain across a fault zone, and variations in
    (E) changes in measurements of the strain across a fault zone, and variations among

Parallelism

This sentence uses four phrases to describe the *warning signs* for an earthquake. These phrases should be parallel. The first sign is *sudden fluctuations in local seismic activity*; the second is *tilting and other deformations of the Earth's crust*. *Tilting* in this case is used as a noun, just as *deformations* and *fluctuations* are nouns. The first two signs are parallel. The third and fourth warning signs resemble *tilting* in the –*ing* form, but they are not parallel because they are used as verbs rather than as nouns: *changing… the strain*; *varying… the properties*. To make the latter two signs parallel, nouns must replace verbs: *changes in… variations in*.

A *Changing* and *varying* are used as verbs and so are not parallel to the nouns *fluctuations* and *tilting*.
B The four signs are not parallel; the substitution of *measurements of the strain* distorts meaning.
C *Changing* is used as a verb and so does not parallel the nouns *fluctuations, tilting*, and *variations*.
D **Correct.** In this sentence, the four nouns—*fluctuations, tilting, changes, variations*—are parallel, and the meaning of *the measured strain* is not distorted.
E This sentence says that the *measurements* indicate an earthquake when the measured *strain* is the warning sign.

The correct answer is D.

83. If the proposed expenditures for gathering information abroad are reduced even further, international news reports have been and will continue to diminish in number and quality.

    (A) have been and will continue to diminish
    (B) have and will continue to diminish
    (C) will continue to diminish, as they already did,
    (D) will continue to diminish, as they have already,
    (E) will continue to diminish

Verb form + Grammatical construction

This sentence is based on the conditional construction *if x happens, then y will happen*. In this case, *x* is *proposed expenditures* and the present-tense verb is *are reduced*; *y* is *news reports*, but the verb is incorrect. The construction calls for a verb in the future tense, *will continue to diminish*.

A *Have been* is the wrong verb tense; the construction is also not grammatical.
B *Have* is the wrong verb tense; the construction is also not grammatical.
C *As they already did* is awkward and redundant; *continue* expresses this idea.
D *As they have already* is awkward and redundant; *continue* expresses this idea.
E **Correct.** *Will continue to diminish* provides the correct future-tense verb for the conditional construction in this sentence.

The correct answer is E.

84. The root systems of most flowering perennials either become too crowded, which results in loss in vigor, and spread too far outward, producing a bare center.

    (A) which results in loss in vigor, and spread
    (B) resulting in loss in vigor, or spreading
    (C) with the result of loss of vigor, or spreading
    (D) resulting in loss of vigor, or spread
    (E) with a resulting loss of vigor, and spread

Idiom + Parallelism

This sentence has two problems. It uses the construction *either x or y; x* and *y* must be grammatically parallel. In this case, *and spread* must be *or spread*. The second problem is the use of a relative clause (*which... vigor*) when a descriptive phrase is required. *Which* is a pronoun and must refer to a noun preceding it, but here it refers vaguely to the whole clause that precedes it, creating a grammatically incorrect construction. A phrase must be used instead: *resulting in loss of vigor*.

A *Either* is incorrectly followed by *and*; *which* has no clear referent.
B *Or spreading* is not parallel to *either become*.
C *With the result of* is wordy; *or spreading* is not parallel to *either become*.
D **Correct.** The phrase *resulting in loss of vigor* concisely modifies the first clause; the either/or construction is correct and parallel in this sentence.
E *Either* is incorrectly followed by *and*; *with a resulting loss* is wordy.

The correct answer is D.

85. Any medical test will sometimes fail to detect <u>a condition when it is present and indicate that there is one</u> when it is not.

    (A) a condition when it is present and indicate that there is one
    (B) when a condition is present and indicate that there is one
    (C) a condition when it is present and indicate that it is present
    (D) when a condition is present and indicate its presence
    (E) the presence of a condition when it is there and indicate its presence

Grammatical construction

In this sentence the pronoun *it* does not always refer to *condition*, and, for the sake of clarity and correctness, it must. *Detect a condition when it is present* is correct and should be followed by a corresponding construction: *indicate that it is present when it is not.* The construction of *there is one* leaves *it* without a referent.

A   *There is one* leaves *it* in the final clause without a referent.
B   *Detect a condition* is more precise because it emphasizes the condition itself; *there is one* leaves *it* without a referent.
C   **Correct.** The three uses of the pronoun *it* refer clearly to *condition*, and the two parts of the sentence correspond.
D   *When a condition is present* emphasizes the time of the detection rather than the condition itself; the final *it* has no referent.
E   *Presence* illogically repeats the same idea as *when it is there*; the final *it* has no referent.

The correct answer is C.

86. Since 1986, when the Department of Labor began to allow <u>investment officers' fees to be based on how the funds they manage perform, several corporations began</u> paying their investment advisers a small basic fee, with a contract promising higher fees if the managers perform well.

    (A) investment officers' fees to be based on how the funds they manage perform, several corporations began
    (B) investment officers' fees to be based on the performance of the funds they manage, several corporations began
    (C) that fees of investment officers be based on how the funds they manage perform, several corporations have begun
    (D) fees of investment officers to be based on the performance of the funds they manage, several corporations have begun
    (E) that investment officers' fees be based on the performance of the funds they manage, several corporations began

Verb form + Logical predication

Since 1986 indicates action begun in the past and continuing into the present, and the form of the verb must show that continuity, as the present perfect tense does: since 1986, corporations *have begun*. The pronoun *they* lacks a referent. While *they* would seem to refer to *investment officers'*, grammatically it cannot because *investment officers'* is a possessive modifying *fees*, rather than a plural noun standing by itself. The sentence needs to be revised so that *investment officers* is a plural noun.

A   *Have begun* should replace *began*; *they* has no referent.
B   *Have begun* should replace *began*; *they* has no referent.
C   *Allow that... be based on* is not a correct idiom; it should be *allow... to be based on.*
D   **Correct.** Substituting *fees of investment officers* in this sentence allows the pronoun *they* to refer to the *officers*; *have begun* properly indicates a continuing situation.
E   *Allow that... be based on* is an incorrect idiom; *they* has no referent; *began* does not indicate the continuity necessary after *since 1986.*

The correct answer is D.

87. The diet of the ordinary Greek in classical times was largely vegetarian — vegetables, fresh cheese, oatmeal, and meal cakes, <u>and meat rarely</u>.

    (A) and meat rarely
    (B) and meat was rare
    (C) with meat as rare
    (D) meat a rarity
    (E) with meat as a rarity

Logical predication

The main clause establishes that *the diet… was largely vegetarian*; the list details the foods of the *vegetarian* diet. *Meat* cannot be considered as a part of this list. The diet was *largely*, not wholly, vegetarian, and the final phrase about *meat* functions as a further explanation of the main clause: *the diet… was largely vegetarian… with meat as a rarity*.

A *And meat rarely* is not a grammatical construction that explains the main clause.
B *And meat was rare* could mean that meat was scarce or that it was not well done.
C *With meat as rare* is not a correct idiomatic construction.
D *Meat a rarity* requires a word such as *with* to link it to the main clause.
E **Correct.** *With meat as a rarity* is a grammatically correct expression that further explains the main clause of this sentence.

The correct answer is E.

88. Down-zoning, zoning that typically results in the reduction of housing density, allows for more open space in areas where <u>little water or services exist</u>.

    (A) little water or services exist
    (B) little water or services exists
    (C) few services and little water exists
    (D) there is little water or services available
    (E) there are few services and little available water

Diction + Agreement

In this sentence, the adjective *little* correctly modifies the noun *water* because *water* is not a countable quantity. However, the noun *services* is a countable quantity and must be modified by *few*, not by *little*. Logically, the areas described would suffer from both *little water* and *few services* at the same time, so the correct conjunction is *and*, not *or*. This compound subject requires a plural verb.

A *Services* should be modified by *few*, not *little*.
B Singular verb *exists* does not agree with the plural subject *services*; when a compound subject is joined by *or*, the verb agrees with the closer subject.
C When a compound subject consists of two distinct units joined by the conjunction *and*, the verb must be plural.
D *Little* cannot modify *services*.
E **Correct.** In this sentence, *few* correctly modifies *services*; *and* correctly joins *services* and *water*.

The correct answer is E.

89. Those who come to church with a predisposition to religious belief will be happy in an auditorium or even a storefront, and there is no doubt that religion is sometimes better served by <u>adapted spaces of this kind instead of by some of the buildings actually designed for it</u>.

    (A) adapted spaces of this kind instead of by some of the buildings actually designed for it
    (B) adapted spaces like these rather than some of the buildings actually designed for them
    (C) these adapted spaces instead of by some of the buildings actually designed for it
    (D) such adapted spaces rather than by some of the buildings actually designed for them
    (E) such adapted spaces than by some of the buildings actually designed for it

Idiom + Rhetorical construction

This comparison depends on the idiomatic construction *better served by x than by y*, so this sentence should be: *better served by adapted spaces… than by some… buildings.* *Such* is more concise than *of this kind* and clearly refers to places such as auditoriums and storefronts.

A *Better served by x* cannot be completed by *instead of by y*; *of this kind* is wordy.
B *Better served by x* cannot be completed by *rather than y*; *like these* is clumsy; pronoun *them* does not agree with *religion*.
C *Better served by x* cannot be completed by *instead of by y*; *these* limits the *adapted spaces* too specifically to the auditorium and the storefront.
D *Better served by x* cannot be completed by *rather than y*; pronoun *them* does not agree with *religion*.
E **Correct.** The correct idiomatic construction is used in this sentence; *such* more concisely replaces *of this kind*; *it* agrees with *religion*.

The correct answer is E.

90. The concept of the grand jury dates from the twelfth century, when Henry II of England ordered panels of common citizens <u>should prepare lists of who were their communities' suspected criminals</u>.

    (A) should prepare lists of who were their communities' suspected criminals
    (B) would do the preparation of lists of their communities' suspected criminals
    (C) preparing lists of suspected criminals in their communities
    (D) the preparing of a list of suspected criminals in their communities
    (E) to prepare lists of suspected criminals in their communities

Grammatical construction

The sentence fails to use the familiar idiomatic construction *ordered x to do y*. The awkward *who were* should be omitted. A list should be followed by the elements that compose it, so *lists* here should be followed by *of suspected criminals*, preventing the possible misreading of *lists of communities*.

A *Ordered* should be followed by *to prepare*; *who were* is awkward and unnecessary; *lists* should be followed by *suspected criminals*.
B *Ordered* is followed by *would do* rather than *to prepare*; *do the preparation* is wordy; *lists* should be followed by *suspected criminals*.
C *Ordered* is followed by *preparing* rather than *to prepare*.
D *Ordered* is followed by *the preparing of* rather than *to prepare*.
E **Correct.** In this sentence, *ordered* is correctly followed by *to prepare*, *lists* is immediately followed by *of suspected criminals*, and placing *in their communities* at the end prevents misreading.

The correct answer is E.

91. In theory, international civil servants at the United Nations are prohibited from continuing to draw salaries from their own governments; in practice, however, some governments merely substitute living allowances for their employees' paychecks, assigned by them to the United Nations.

    (A) for their employees' paychecks, assigned by them
    (B) for the paychecks of their employees who have been assigned
    (C) for the paychecks of their employees, having been assigned
    (D) in place of their employees' paychecks, for those of them assigned
    (E) in place of the paychecks of their employees to have been assigned by them

    Logical predication

    It is difficult to tell which parts of this sentence go together because of errors and confusion in the underlined portion. *Living allowances* is the counterpart of *paychecks*, so it is better to say governments… *substitute living allowances for the paychecks of their employees* because it makes the substitution clearer. This change also makes it easier to correct the modification error that appears in the phrase *assigned by them*, which incorrectly modifies *paychecks* rather than *employees*. The modifying clause *who have been assigned* clearly describes *employees* and fits into the remaining part of the sentence, *to the United Nations*.

    A *Paychecks* should balance *living allowances*; *assigned by them* incorrectly and illogically modifies *paychecks*.
    B **Correct.** In this sentence, the substitution is clearer when *paychecks* is separated from *employees*; the relative clause clearly modifies *employees*.
    C The sentence uses present-tense verbs; *having been assigned* casts doubt on whether the employees are still assigned to the United Nations.
    D The correct construction is *substitutes x for y*, not *substitutes x in place of y*; the construction following *paychecks* is wordy and awkward.
    E The correct construction is *substitutes x for y*, not *substitutes x in place of y*; the construction following *employees* is wordy and awkward.

    The correct answer is B.

92. According to a study by the Carnegie Foundation for the Advancement of Teaching, companies in the United States are providing job training and general education for nearly eight million people, about equivalent to the enrollment of the nation's four-year colleges and universities.

    (A) equivalent to the enrollment of
    (B) the equivalent of those enrolled in
    (C) equal to those who are enrolled in
    (D) as many as the enrollment of
    (E) as many as are enrolled in

    Diction + Logical predication

    This sentence compares two groups of people. The best phrase to use for a comparison of two countable quantities (such as people) is *as many as*. *Equivalent* is incorrect because its meaning is much broader; it is not limited to number only, which is the focus of this sentence. The number of *people* in job training should be compared to the number of *people* in colleges, but the original sentence mistakenly compares *people* to *enrollment*.

    A *Equivalent* is too broad and vague a term for comparing groups of people; the groups being compared must be parallel, but *enrollment* is not parallel to *people*.
    B *The equivalent* is too broad and vague a term for comparing groups of people.
    C *Equal* is generally used for uncountable quantities, such as *equal justice*, not countable quantities, such as people; its meaning is too broad for this context.
    D *People* are incorrectly compared with *enrollment* rather than with other *people*.
    E **Correct.** In this sentence, *as many as* compares countable quantities; *people* are compared with *people*, the understood subject of *are enrolled*.

    The correct answer is E.

93. Intar, the oldest Hispanic theater company in New York, has moved away from the Spanish classics and now it draws on the works both of contemporary Hispanic authors who live abroad and of those in the United States.

    (A) now it draws on the works both of contemporary Hispanic authors who live abroad and of those
    (B) now draws on the works of contemporary Hispanic authors, both those who live abroad and those who live
    (C) it draws on the works of contemporary Hispanic authors now, both those living abroad and who live
    (D) draws now on the works both of contemporary Hispanic authors living abroad and who are living
    (E) draws on the works now of both contemporary Hispanic authors living abroad and those

Grammatical construction + Idiom + Parallelism

As the subject of the main clause, Intar should be followed by the compound verbs *has moved away* and *draws on*. The pronoun *it* before the second verb results in an ungrammatical construction; removing the pronoun removes the error. The construction *both x and y*, where *x* and *y* are parallel, is used incorrectly when the wrong two elements are linked; *of contemporary Hispanic authors* is not parallel to *of those in the United States*. The company *draws on the works of contemporary Hispanic authors* who live in two different places. *Those who live abroad* is parallel to *those who live in the United States*.

A The use of *it* creates an ungrammatical construction; the elements following *both... and* are not parallel.
B Correct. In this sentence, Intar is the subject of *draws on*; parallel constructions follow *both... and*.
C *It* creates an ungrammatical construction; *those living abroad* is not parallel to *who live*.
D The construction following *both* is not parallel to the construction following *and*

E *Now* modifies the verb and should precede it; the parallelism of the *both... and* construction is violated.

The correct answer is B.

94. Last year, land values in most parts of the pinelands rose almost so fast, and in some parts even faster than what they did outside the pinelands.

    (A) so fast, and in some parts even faster than what they did
    (B) so fast, and in some parts even faster than, those
    (C) as fast, and in some parts even faster than, those
    (D) as fast as, and in some parts even faster than, those
    (E) as fast as, and in some parts even faster than what they did

Idiom + Parallelism

This sentence says *x* rose *almost so fast y*, which is not a correct idiomatic construction; *x* rose *almost as fast as y* is the correct idiom for this comparison. The two elements being compared, *x* and *y*, must be parallel, but the noun *land values* (*x*) is not parallel to *what they did* (*y*), a clause that results in an ungrammatical construction. *Land values* in the pinelands (*x*) must be compared with *those* (the pronoun correctly replacing *land values*) outside the pinelands (*y*).

A *So fast* is used instead of *as fast as*; *what they did* is not parallel to *land values*.
B *So fast* is not the correct idiom for comparison.
C *As fast* must be followed by *as* in this comparison.
D Correct. *As fast as* is the correct comparative conjunction used in this sentence; *those* is parallel to *land values*.
E *What they did* is not parallel to *land values*.

The correct answer is D.

95. If Dr. Wade was right, any apparent connection of the eating of highly processed foods and excelling at sports is purely coincidental.

   (A) If Dr. Wade was right, any apparent connection of the eating of
   (B) Should Dr. Wade be right, any apparent connection of eating
   (C) If Dr. Wade is right, any connection that is apparent between eating of
   (D) If Dr. Wade is right, any apparent connection between eating
   (E) Should Dr. Wade have been right, any connection apparent between eating

Verb form + Idiom + Parallelism

The verb in the main clause is present tense (*is*), but the subordinate clause uses the simple past tense *was* when no change in time is indicated; both verbs should be present tense. This sentence also uses the idiomatic construction *connection between x and y*; *x* and *y* must be parallel. Thus, *connection* must be followed by *between* rather than *of*, and *the eating of* (*x*) must be made parallel to *excelling at* (*y*). *The eating* is a gerund, or noun form, but *eating* is a participle and thus parallel to the participle *excelling*.

A The two verbs, *was* and *is*, do not agree in tense; *connection* must be followed by *between*; *the eating of* is not parallel to *excelling*.
B *Should be* cannot be followed by a present-tense verb; *connection of* is the incorrect idiom.
C *Apparent connection* is preferable to the wordy *connection that is apparent*.
D **Correct.** In this sentence, the verb is present tense, and the correct idiom is used; *eating* is also parallel to *excelling*.
E *Should have been* cannot be followed by a present-tense verb; *apparent* should precede *connection* rather than follow it.

The correct answer is D.

96. The commission proposed that funding for the park's development, which could be open to the public early next year, is obtained through a local bond issue.

   (A) that funding for the park's development, which could be open to the public early next year, is
   (B) that funding for development of the park, which could be open to the public early next year, be
   (C) funding for the development of the park, perhaps open to the public early next year, to be
   (D) funds for the park's development, perhaps open to the public early next year, be
   (E) development funding for the park, which could be open to the public early next year, is to be

Logical predication + Verb form

Which modifies the noun that precedes it; in this sentence, the clause beginning *which* illogically refers to *development* rather than the *park*. This error can be corrected by substituting *development of the park* (*which* follows *park*) for *park's development* (*which* follows *development*). When a verb such as recommend, request, or *propose* is used in the main clause, the verb following *that* in the subordinate clause is subjunctive (*be*) rather than indicative (*is*).

A *Which* modifies *development* instead of *park*; *be* is required, not *is*.
B **Correct.** In this sentence, *which* clearly modifies *park*; the subjunctive *be* correctly follows *proposed that*.
C *That* is omitted when it is necessary; *be* is required, not the infinitive *to be*.
D *That* is omitted when it is necessary; the phrase modifies *development*, not *park*.
E *Development funding* distorts meaning; *be* is required, not *is to be*.

The correct answer is B.

97. Seismologists studying the earthquake that struck northern California in October 1989 are still investigating some of its mysteries: the unexpected power of the seismic waves, the upward thrust that threw one man straight into the air, and the strange electromagnetic signals detected hours before the temblor.

    (A) the upward thrust that threw one man straight into the air, and the strange electromagnetic signals detected hours before the temblor
    (B) the upward thrust that threw one man straight into the air, and strange electromagnetic signals were detected hours before the temblor
    (C) the upward thrust threw one man straight into the air, and hours before the temblor strange electromagnetic signals were detected
    (D) one man was thrown straight into the air by the upward thrust, and hours before the temblor strange electromagnetic signals were detected
    (E) one man who was thrown straight into the air by the upward thrust, and strange electromagnetic signals that were detected hours before the temblor

    Parallelism

    Some of the earthquake's *mysteries* are described in a series of three correctly parallel elements: (1) *the unexpected power…* , (2) *the upward thrust…* , and (3) *the strange electromagnetic signals…* . Each of the three elements begins with an article (*the*), a modifier, and a noun. This parallelism is crucial, but each mystery is allowed the further modification most appropriate to it, whether a prepositional phrase (1), a clause (2) or a participial phrase (3).

    A **Correct.** This sentence correctly provides a parallel series of three mysteries.
    B *The* is omitted before *strange*; the verb *were detected* makes the last element not parallel to the previous two.
    C Because they use complete independent clauses, the last two elements are not parallel to the first.
    D The constructions beginning *one man* and *hours before* are not parallel to the construction beginning *the unexpected power*.
    E The grammatical constructions describing the mysteries are not parallel.

    The correct answer is A.

98. Two new studies indicate that many people become obese more due to the fact that their bodies burn calories too slowly than overeating.

    (A) due to the fact that their bodies burn calories too slowly than overeating
    (B) due to their bodies burning calories too slowly than to eating too much
    (C) because their bodies burn calories too slowly than that they are overeaters
    (D) because their bodies burn calories too slowly than because they eat too much
    (E) because of their bodies burning calories too slowly than because of their eating too much

    Comparison + Parallelism + Phetorical construction

    To compare two explanations for weight gain, this sentence uses the construction *more x than y*; *x* and *y* must be parallel. Here, *x* is *due to the fact that their bodies burn calories too slowly* and *y* is *overeating*. *Due to the fact that* uses five words to say what *because* does in one; *because* is a better choice to introduce both elements. The single-word *y* can be made parallel to the clause *x* by introducing a subject, verb, and adverb: *because they eat too much*.

    A *Due to the fact that* is wordy and awkward; the two parts of the comparison are not parallel.
    B *Due to* is not the correct idiom; the two parts of the comparison are not parallel.
    C *That* has no referent; the two parts of the comparison are not parallel.
    D **Correct.** In this sentence, the two parts of the comparison are parallel and concise.
    E This alternative, though parallel, is awkward and wordy; *bodies* must be *bodies'* because the possessive case is required before a gerund.

    The correct answer is D.

99. Judge Bonham denied a motion <u>to allow members of the jury to go home at the end of each day instead of to</u> confine them to a hotel.

   (A) to allow members of the jury to go home at the end of each day instead of to confine them to
   (B) that would have allowed members of the jury to go home at the end of each day instead of confined to
   (C) under which members of the jury are allowed to go home at the end of each day instead of confining them in
   (D) that would allow members of the jury to go home at the end of each day rather than confinement in
   (E) to allow members of the jury to go home at the end of each day rather than be confined to

Parallelism + Idiom

The logic of this sentence has two possible options for the *members of the jury*: they can go home or be confined to a hotel. The first option is expressed using the infinitive *to go home*, the second option should use the parallel form (*to* understood) *be confined*. Since the *members of the jury* are not doing the confining themselves, the passive form must be used. The construction *(x) instead of (y)*, when *x* and *y* are infinitives, is clumsy; the idiomatic construction *(x) rather than (y)* is better here. Both constructions require *x* and *y* to be parallel.

A The passive form *to be confined* is required, since the jurors are not confining themselves.
B The infinitive form *to be confined* is required, rather than the past participle; awkward and wordy.
C *Members of the jury* are the illogical object in *confining them*; *confining* is not parallel to *to go home*.
D The noun *confinement* is not parallel to *to go home*.
E **Correct.** *Be confined to* uses the infinitive form just as *to go home* does; the *to* before *be confined* is understood and does not need to be repeated. The *(x) rather than (y)* construction is appropriately used in this sentence.

The correct answer is E.

100. Proponents of artificial intelligence say they will be able to make computers that can understand English and other human languages, recognize objects, and reason <u>as an expert does—computers that will be used to diagnose equipment breakdowns, deciding whether to authorize a loan, or other purposes such as these.</u>

   (A) as an expert does—computers that will be used to diagnose equipment breakdowns, deciding whether to authorize a loan, or other purposes such as these
   (B) as an expert does, which may be used for purposes such as diagnosing equipment breakdowns or deciding whether to authorize a loan
   (C) like an expert—computers that will be used for such purposes as diagnosing equipment breakdowns or deciding whether to authorize a loan
   (D) like an expert, the use of which would be for purposes like the diagnosis of equipment breakdowns or the decision whether or not a loan should be authorized
   (E) like an expert, to be used to diagnose equipment breakdowns, deciding whether to authorize a loan or not, or the like

Parallelism + Rhetorical construction

The sentence presents three functions of intelligent computers, but these functions (*to diagnose…, deciding…, or other purposes*) are not written in parallel ways. Moreover, the final function is vague. Turning this final function into an introductory statement and using parallel forms for the two elements *diagnosing* and *deciding* creates a stronger sentence. Either the clause, *as an expert does*, or the prepositional phrase, *like an expert*, is correct and idiomatic in this sentence.

A The series *to diagnose…, deciding…, or other purposes* should be expressed in parallel ways.
B *Which* has no clear referent.
C **Correct.** Moving *for such purposes as* to an introductory position strengthens the sentence; *diagnosing* and *deciding* are parallel.
D *To diagnose* and *deciding* are not parallel; *the use of which would be for purposes like* is wordy and awkward; *which* has no clear referent.
E *To be used, deciding*, and *or the like* are not parallel.

The correct answer is C.

101. Unlike the United States, where farmers can usually depend on rain or snow all year long, the rains in most parts of Sri Lanka are concentrated in the monsoon months, June to September, and the skies are generally clear for the rest of the year.

    (A) Unlike the United States, where farmers can usually depend on rain or snow all year long, the rains in most parts of Sri Lanka

    (B) Unlike the United States farmers who can usually depend on rain or snow all year long, the rains in most parts of Sri Lanka

    (C) Unlike those of the United States, where farmers can usually depend on rain or snow all year long, most parts of Sri Lanka's rains

    (D) In comparison with the United States, whose farmers can usually depend on rain or snow all year long, the rains in most parts of Sri Lanka

    (E) In the United States, farmers can usually depend on rain or snow all year long, but in most parts of Sri Lanka the rains

Logical predication

The intent of the sentence is to compare seasonal rainfall patterns in the United States and Sri Lanka. There are many ways to set up such comparisons: *unlike x, y; in comparison with x, y; compared to x, y*, and so on. The *x* and *y* being compared must be grammatically and logically parallel. An alternative way of stating the comparison is the use of two independent clauses connected by *but*. The original sentence compares *the United States* to *rains in most parts of Sri Lanka*; this illogical comparison cannot convey the writer's intention.

A   Illogically compares *the United States* to *rains in most parts of Sri Lanka*.
B   Comparing *United States farmers* to *the rains in most parts of Sri Lanka* is not logical.
C   The sentence awkwardly and illogically seems to be comparing most parts of the United States with *most parts of Sri Lanka's rains*.
D   This sentence compares *the United States* and *the rains*; it is not a logical comparison.

E   **Correct.** This sentence uses two independent clauses to make the comparison. The first clause describes conditions in the United States, and the second clause describes conditions in Sri Lanka. The comparison is clear and logical.

The correct answer is E.

102. Although Napoleon's army entered Russia with far more supplies than they had in their previous campaigns, it had provisions for only twenty-four days.

    (A) they had in their previous campaigns
    (B) their previous campaigns had had
    (C) they had for any previous campaign
    (D) in their previous campaigns
    (E) for any previous campaign

Agreement + Verb form

The sentence incorrectly uses the plural pronouns *they* and *their* to refer back to the singular noun *army*. The verb tense would need to be the past perfect *had had* rather than the simple past *had* because this action occurs before the action in the main clause. In the context of *supplies for a campaign*, the preposition *for* is preferable to the preposition *in*. In cases such as this, where the sentence has multiple errors, it is often helpful to look among the answer choices for an alternate construction.

A   Pronouns referring to the noun army should be *it* and *its*, not *they* and *their*; the verb should be *had had*.
B   *Their* does not agree with the singular noun *army*.
C   *They* does not agree with the singular noun *army*; the verb should be *had had*.
D   The proposition used should be *for*, not *in*; *their* should be *its* to agree with *army*.
E   **Correct.** This simple construction avoids the problems of pronoun agreement and verb tense; it is clear, correct, and concise.

The correct answer is E.

103. After the Civil War, contemporaries of Harriet Tubman's maintained that she has all of the qualities of a great leader: coolness in the face of danger, an excellent sense of strategy, and an ability to plan in minute detail.

    (A) Tubman's maintained that she has
    (B) Tubman's maintain that she had
    (C) Tubman's have maintained that she had
    (D) Tubman maintained that she had
    (E) Tubman had maintained that she has

Idiom + Verb form

The apostrophe in a possessive noun such as *Tubman's* indicates that the word *of* has been omitted. It is correct to write *Tubman's* or *of Tubman*; it is incorrect to write *of Tubman's*. The verbs *maintained* and *had* describe actions that were completed in the past and occurred at about the same time. Since Tubman died long ago, she *had*, not *has*, the qualities of great leader. Her contemporaries were people who lived at the same time as Tubman; the simple past should be used to describe their actions.

A   *Of Harriet Tubman's* is an incorrect possessive; *has* should be the simple past tense *had*.
B   *Of Harriet Tubman's* is an incorrect possessive.
C   *Of Harriet Tubman's* is an incorrect possessive; *have maintained* should be simple past tense *maintained*.
D Correct. In this sentence, the possessive is properly expressed with the phrase *of Tubman*; *maintained* and *had* both use the simple past tense.
E   Simple past tense should be used for both verbs.

The correct answer is D.

104. The Federalist papers, a strong defense of the United States Constitution and important as a body of work in political science as well, represents the handiwork of three different authors.

    (A) and important as a body of work in political science as well, represents
    (B) as well as an important body of work in political science, represent
    (C) and also a body of work of importance in political science is representing
    (D) an important body of work in political science and has been representative of
    (E) and as political science an important body of work too, represent

Agreement + Parallelism

The subject of this sentence is *the Federalist papers*; this plural subject requires the plural verb *represent*. The subject is followed by a long modifying phrase set off by commas; both elements of the phrase should be parallel. Thus, *important as a body of work* should be revised so that is parallel to *a strong defense*.

A   *Represents* does not agree with *the Federalist papers*; *important as a body of work* is not parallel to *a strong defense*.
B Correct. The plural verb *represent* agrees with the plural subject; *an important body of work* is parallel to *a strong defense*.
C   The present progressive *is representing* does not agree with the plural subject and wrongly suggests a developing situation; *a body of work of importance in political science* is wordy and awkward; the closing comma of the pair is omitted.
D   Omission of *and* is incorrect; *has been representative of* does not agree with the plural subject, uses an incorrect tense, and introduces an awkward construction.
E   The inverted word order is awkward and is not parallel to *a strong defense*.

The correct answer is B.

105. As business grows more complex, students <u>majoring in specialized areas like those of finance and marketing have been becoming increasingly</u> successful in the job market.

    (A) majoring in specialized areas like those of finance and marketing have been becoming increasingly
    (B) who major in such specialized areas as finance and marketing are becoming more and more
    (C) who majored in specialized areas such as those of finance and marketing are being increasingly
    (D) who major in specialized areas like those of finance and marketing have been becoming more and more
    (E) having majored in such specialized areas as finance and marketing are being increasingly

Verb form + Idiom

The subordinate clause *as business grows more complex* uses the present tense verb *grows* to describe an ongoing situation. The main clause describes an effect of this growing complexity; the verbs in the main clause should also use present-tense verbs. The present perfect progressive *have been becoming* is incorrect. The correct way to introduce examples is with the phrase *such as*, rather than with the word *like*.

A *Like* should be replaced by *such as*; *have been becoming* is an incorrect verb tense.
B **Correct.** In this sentence, *major* and *are becoming* are present-tense verbs; *such as* is the correct form for introducing examples.
C *Majored* is a past-tense verb; *those of* is unnecessary and wordy; *becoming* is preferable to *being* for describing an unfolding pattern of events.
D *Like* should be replaced by *such as*; *those of* is unnecessary and wordy; *have been becoming* is an incorrect verb tense.
E *Having majored* is an awkward past participle; *becoming* is preferable to *being* for describing an unfolding pattern of events.

The correct answer is B.

106. Inuits of the Bering Sea were <u>in isolation from contact with Europeans longer than</u> Aleuts or Inuits of the North Pacific and northern Alaska.

    (A) in isolation from contact with Europeans longer than
    (B) isolated from contact with Europeans longer than
    (C) in isolation from contact with Europeans longer than were
    (D) isolated from contact with Europeans longer than were
    (E) in isolation and without contacts with Europeans longer than

Idiom + Logical predication

The construction *in isolation from* is awkward; the idiomatic way to express this idea is *isolated from*. The comparison is ambiguous; it could mean the Bering Sea Inuits were isolated from Europeans longer than they were isolated from Aleuts and other Inuits or that they were isolated from Europeans longer than Aleuts and other Inuits were isolated from Europeans. Adding *were* after *than* will solve this problem.

A *In isolation from* is not the correct idiom; the comparison is ambiguous.
B The comparison is ambiguous.
C *In isolation from* is not the correct idiom.
D **Correct.** The idiom *isolated from* is correctly used in this sentence; the comparison is clear and unambiguous.
E *In isolation... with* is incorrect and confusing; the comparison is ambiguous.

The correct answer is D.

107. The physical structure of the human eye enables it to sense light of wavelengths up to 0.0005 millimeters; infrared radiation, however, is invisible because its wavelength—0.1 millimeters—is too long to be registered by the eye.

   (A) infrared radiation, however, is invisible because its wavelength—0.1 millimeters—is too long to be registered by the eye
   (B) however, the wavelength of infrared radiation—0.1 millimeters—is too long to be registered by the eye making it invisible
   (C) infrared radiation, however, is invisible because its wavelength—0.1 millimeters—is too long for the eye to register it
   (D) however, because the wavelength of infrared radiation is 0.1 millimeters, it is too long for the eye to register and thus invisible
   (E) however, infrared radiation has a wavelength of 0.1 millimeters that is too long for the eye to register, thus making it invisible

Grammatical construction + Logical predication

This sentence requires attention to clear references and appropriate modification. Here *its* clearly refers to *infrared radiation*; it is the *radiation* that is *invisible,* and the *wavelength* that is *too long.*

A **Correct.** This sentence clearly and grammatically explains why infrared radiation is invisible.
B *Making it invisible* modifies *eye,* rather than *wavelength.*
C *It* is ambiguous and lacks a clear referent.
D *It* is imprecise; *thus invisible* modifies *wavelength,* rather than *infrared radiation.*
E Using a restrictive clause introduced by *that* suggests that not all wavelengths of *0.1 millimeters* are *too long for the eye to register; it* is ambiguous and lacks a clear referent.

The correct answer is A.

108. As well as heat and light, the Sun is the source of a continuous stream of atomic particles known as the solar wind.

   (A) As well as heat and light, the Sun is the source of a continuous stream
   (B) Besides heat and light, also the Sun is the source of a continuous stream
   (C) Besides heat and light, the Sun is also the source of a continuous streaming
   (D) The Sun is the source not only of heat and light, but also of a continuous stream
   (E) The Sun is the source of not only heat and light but, as well, of a continuous streaming

Idiom + Logical predication + Rhetorical construction

The underlined section must be revised to eliminate modification errors and to clarify meaning by using parallel construction. *As well as heat and light* cannot logically modify the Sun, as grammar requires; the sentence seems to suggest that heat, light and the Sun are the source of the solar wind. The sentence can be improved by employing the construction *not only (x)… but also (y); x* and *y* should be parallel.

A *As well as heat and light* is misplaced and confusing.
B *Besides heat and light* is confusing; the word order of *also the Sun* is awkward.
C *Besides heat and light* is confusing; *streaming* should be the more straightforward *stream.*
D **Correct.** This sentence uses the *not only… but also* construction to solve the modification error; *of heat and light* is parallel to *of a continuous stream.*
E *As well* is incorrect in the *not only… but also* construction; *heat and light* is not parallel to *of a continuous streaming; streaming* should be the more straightforward *stream.*

The correct answer is D.

109. Bluegrass musician Bill Monroe, whose repertory, views on musical collaboration, and vocal style <u>were influential on generations of bluegrass artists, was also an inspiration to many musicians, that included Elvis Presley and Jerry Garcia, whose music differed significantly from</u> his own.

    (A) were influential on generations of bluegrass artists, was also an inspiration to many musicians, that included Elvis Presley and Jerry Garcia, whose music differed significantly from
    (B) influenced generations of bluegrass artists, also inspired many musicians, including Elvis Presley and Jerry Garcia, whose music differed significantly from
    (C) was influential to generations of bluegrass artists, was also inspirational to many musicians, that included Elvis Presley and Jerry Garcia, whose music was different significantly in comparison to
    (D) was influential to generations of bluegrass artists, also inspired many musicians, who included Elvis Presley and Jerry Garcia, the music of whom differed significantly when compared to
    (E) were an influence on generations of bluegrass artists, was also an inspiration to many musicians, including Elvis Presley and Jerry Garcia, whose music was significantly different from that of

Verb tense + Diction + Grammar

The original sentence logically intends to explain that Monroe's work influenced generations of artists in his own musical field and that he inspired many musicians in other musical fields. Who or what influenced or inspired whom must be more clearly stated. Additionally, the original sentence lacks precision, being overly wordy and using phrases that are not idiomatic. Concise and consistent verb forms, as well as the use of subordinate phrases rather than clauses, improve the precision of the sentence.

A The phrase *were influential on* is wordy and is not idiomatic; use of verb forms *were* (the predicate of *repertory, views,* and *style*) and *was* (the predicate of *Monroe*) is confusing; incorrect use of *that* rather than *who* to refer *musicians.*

B **Correct.** The use of the concise verb forms of *influenced* and *inspired* simplifies and clarifies the sentence. The concise use of *including* avoids the pronoun error and unnecessary wordiness.

C The subject-verb agreement in *repertory, views,* and *style… was* (compound subject with singular verb) is incorrect; unnecessary wordiness in *was influential to* and in *different… in comparison to*; incorrect use of *that* rather than *who* to refer *musicians.*

D The subject-verb agreement in *repertory, views,* and *style… was* (compound subject with singular verb) is incorrect; unnecessary wordiness in *was influential to* and in *when compared to*; *the music of whom* is cumbersome and stilted.

E The phrase *were an influence on* is wordy and not idiomatic; phrases *was an inspiration to* and *was significantly different* are unnecessarily wordy; the phrase *from that of* is unclear and confusing.

The correct answer is B.

110. <u>The nephew of Pliny the Elder wrote the only eyewitness account of the great eruption of Vesuvius in two letters to the historian Tacitus.</u>

    (A) The nephew of Pliny the Elder wrote the only eyewitness account of the great eruption of Vesuvius in two letters to the historian Tacitus.
    (B) To the historian Tacitus, the nephew of Pliny the Elder wrote two letters, being the only eyewitness accounts of the great eruption of Vesuvius.
    (C) The only eyewitness account is in two letters by the nephew of Pliny the Elder writing to the historian Tacitus an account of the great eruption of Vesuvius.
    (D) Writing the only eyewitness account, Pliny the Elder's nephew accounted for the great eruption of Vesuvius in two letters to the historian Tacitus.
    (E) In two letters to the historian Tacitus, the nephew of Pliny the Elder wrote the only eyewitness account of the great eruption of Vesuvius.

Logical predication + Rhetorical construction

The challenge in this sentence lies in the correct placement of a prepositional phrase. In the original version, the placement of *in two letters to the historian Tacitus* suggests that Vesuvius erupted in the letters themselves. Placing the phrase at the beginning of the sentence solves the problem.

A The sentence suggests that the eruption of Vesuvius took place in the letters themselves.

B Beginning the sentence with *to the historian Tacitus* is clumsy and unclear; the verb phrase *being…* seems illogically to modify *the nephew*, creating with the use of the unnecessary *being* the awkward suggestion that *the nephew* was *the eyewitness accounts*.

C The sentence's meaning is unclear due to an extended sequence of prepositional phrases.

D *An account* is a narrative record; *to account for* means to be the cause of; using both words in the same sentence is confusing and here suggests that the nephew caused the eruption; the sentence also suggests that the eruption of Vesuvius took place in the letters themselves.

E **Correct.** The placement of the prepositional phrase at the beginning of the sentence clarifies the meaning of the sentence; the construction of the rest of the sentence is straightforward.

The correct answer is E.

111. Being a United States citizen since 1988 and born in Calcutta in 1940, author Bharati Mukherjee has lived in England and Canada, and first came to the United States in 1961 to study at the Iowa Writers' Workshop.

    (A) Being a United States citizen since 1988 and born in Calcutta in 1940, author Bharati Mukherjee has

    (B) Having been a United States citizen since 1988, she was born in Calcutta in 1940; author Bharati Mukherjee

    (C) Born in Calcutta in 1940, author Bharati Mukherjee became a United States citizen in 1988; she has

    (D) Being born in Calcutta in 1940 and having been a United States citizen since 1988, author Bharati Mukherjee

    (E) Having been born in Calcutta in 1940 and being a United States citizen since 1988, author Bharati Mukherjee

Grammatical construction + Rhetorical construction

To be logical, the underlined portion of this sentence must use chronological order; to be clear, it must omit wordy or awkward phrasing. *Born in Calcutta in 1940* is a logically and grammatically correct way to begin the sentence, and this modifying phrase must be immediately followed by the noun it modifies, *author Bharati Mukherjee*. *Being… since* is an awkward, wordy construction better replaced by the more direct *became a United States citizen in 1988*. Since the original phrase (*being…*) has been made into a main clause with this change, a semicolon should separate it from the second main clause beginning *she has lived*.

A The phrases are expressed in an illogical and ungrammatical sequence.

B *Having been* suggests that the citizenship came chronologically before the birth; the author's name must be used before the pronoun.

C **Correct.** In this sentence, the sequence of events is expressed logically, grammatically, and concisely in each independent clause.

D Progressive verb forms *being born* and *having been* illogically suggest continuous action and fail to establish a logical time sequence; wordy and awkward.

E Progressive verb forms *having been born* and *being* illogically suggest continuous action and fail to establish a logical time sequence; wordy and awkward.

The correct answer is C.

112. Initiated five centuries after Europeans arrived in the New World on Columbus Day 1992, Project SETI pledged a $100 million investment in the search for extraterrestrial intelligence.

    (A) Initiated five centuries after Europeans arrived in the New World on Columbus Day 1992, Project SETI pledged a $100 million investment in the search for extraterrestrial intelligence.

    (B) Initiated on Columbus Day 1992, five centuries after Europeans arrived in the New World, a $100 million investment in the search for extraterrestrial intelligence was pledged by Project SETI.

(C)   Initiated on Columbus Day 1992, five centuries after Europeans arrived in the New World, Project SETI pledged a $100 million investment in the search for extraterrestrial intelligence.

(D)   Pledging a $100 million investment in the search for extraterrestrial intelligence, the initiation of Project SETI five centuries after Europeans arrived in the New World on Columbus Day 1992.

(E)   Pledging a $100 million investment in the search for extraterrestrial intelligence five centuries after Europeans arrived in the New World, on Columbus Day 1992, the initiation of Project SETI took place.

Logical predication

The original sentence becomes illogical when phrases do not modify what they are intended to modify. This sentence mistakenly says that *Europeans arrived in the New World on Columbus Day 1992*. It also says that Project SETI was *initiated five centuries after… Columbus Day 1992*. To make the modifiers grammatically and logically correct, the sentence may be revised: *Initiated on Columbus Day 1992, five centuries after Europeans arrived in the New World, Project SETI….*

A   Project SETI cannot have been *initiated five centuries after… 1992*, nor did Europeans first arrive in 1992.

B   *Initiated…* modifies *$100 million investment* instead of *Project SETI*.

C   **Correct.** The modifiers are grammatically and logically correct in this sentence.

D   *Pledging…* incorrectly modifies *the initiation*; this alternative is a sentence fragment.

E   *Pledging…* incorrectly modifies *the initiation*; Europeans appear to have arrived on Columbus Day 1992; the construction is awkward, unbalanced, and imprecise.

The correct answer is C.

113.   In A.D. 391, resulting from the destruction of the largest library of the ancient world at Alexandria, later generations lost all but the Iliad and Odyssey among Greek epics, most of the poetry of Pindar and Sappho, and dozens of plays by Aeschylus and Euripides.

(A)   resulting from the destruction of the largest library of the ancient world at Alexandria,

(B)   the destroying of the largest library of the ancient world at Alexandria resulted and

(C)   because of the result of the destruction of the library at Alexandria, the largest of the ancient world,

(D)   as a result of the destruction of the library at Alexandria, the largest of the ancient world,

(E)   Alexandria's largest library of the ancient world was destroyed, and the result was

Logical predication + Idiom

Because it is introduced by a participle, the phrase that begins *resulting from* illogically modifies *later generations*. Substituting the idiom *as a result of* for *resulting from* corrects this error. *The largest library of the ancient world at Alexandria* is both cumbersome and ambiguous because it suggests that the *ancient world* was located *at* (and only at) *Alexandria*. This problem is best corrected by breaking the series of phrases into two distinct parts: *the library at Alexandria, the largest of the ancient world.* Here, the second phrase clearly modifies the first.

A   *Resulting from* illogically modifies *later generations*; the series of prepositional phrases is confusing and ambiguous.

B   *The destroying of* is wordy, awkward, and, when followed by *resulted*, ungrammatical; *and* creates a second main clause, which would need to be appropriately punctuated with a comma before *and*.

C   *Because of the result of* is redundant.

D   **Correct.** *As a result of* begins the phrase clearly and correctly in this sentence; the *library* rather than the *ancient world* is properly located *at Alexandria*; the *largest of the ancient world* correctly modifies *library*.

E   *Alexandria's largest library of the ancient world* is an illogical reference; *the result was* must be followed by *that*.

The correct answer is D.

Appendix A Percentile Ranking Tables

Table 1 Percentages of Examinees Tested from January 2003 through December 2005 (including Repeaters) Who Scored Below Specified Verbal Scores			
Verbal Scaled Score	Percentage Below	Verbal Scaled Score	Percentage Below
46–60	99	26	43
45	98	25	38
43-44	97	24	36
42	95	23	31
41	93	22	29
40	90	21	25
39	88	20	21
38	85	19	17
37	83	18	16
36	80	17	13
35	76	16	10
34	71	15	8
33	69	14	7
32	66	13	5
31	61	12	4
30	59	11	3
29	56	10	2
28	51	7–9	1
27	45	0–6	0

Number of Candidates = 622,975
Mean = 27.3
Standard deviation = 9.0

Table 2
Percentages of Examinees Tested from January 2003 through December 2005 (including Repeaters) Who Scored Below Specified Quantitative Scores

Quantitative Scaled Score	Percentage Below	Quantitative Scaled Score	Percentage Below
51–60	99	30	31
50	95	29	27
49	90	28	25
48	86	27	21
47	82	26	20
46	80	25	17
45	78	24	15
44	73	23	13
43	71	22	11
42	67	21	10
41	64	20	8
40	62	19	7
39	58	18	6
38	56	17	5
37	53	16	4
36	49	15	4
35	45	14	3
34	43	13	2
33	41	11-12	2
32	37	7–10	1
31	33	0–6	0

Number of Candidates = 622,975
Mean = 35
Standard deviation = 10.5

Table 3
Percentages of Examinees Tested from January 2003 through December 2005 (including Repeaters) Who Scored Below Specified Total Scores

Total Scaled Score	Percentage Below	Total Scaled Score	Percentage Below
760–800	99	500	39
750	98	490	36
740	98	480	33
730	97	470	31
720	96	460	27
710	94	450	24
700	92	440	22
690	91	430	20
680	89	420	18
670	88	410	16
660	86	400	14
650	83	390	12
640	80	380	11
630	78	370	10
620	76	360	8
610	73	350	7
600	70	340	6
590	67	330	5
580	64	320	4
570	61	300-310	3
560	58	290	2
550	54	280	2
540	51	270	2
530	47	260	2
520	45	230-250	1
510	42	200–220	0

Number of Candidates = 622,975
Mean = 526.6
Standard deviation = 117

Table 4 Percentages of Examinees Tested from January 2002 through December 2004 (including Repeaters) Who Scored Below Specified AWA Scores	
AWA Scaled Score	Percentage Below
6.0	95
5.5	87
5.0	73
4.5	55
4.1	34
3.5	18
3.0	8
2.5	4
2.0	3
1.5	3
1.0	3
0.5	2
0.0	0

Number of Candidates = 622,975
Mean = 4.1
Standard deviation = 1.1

Appendix B Extra Answer Sheets

Reading Comprehension Extra Answer Sheet

1.	32.	63.	94.
2.	33.	64.	95.
3.	34.	65.	96.
4.	35.	66.	97.
5.	36.	67.	98.
6.	37.	68.	99.
7.	38.	69.	100.
8.	39.	70.	101.
9.	40.	71.	102.
10.	41.	72.	103.
11.	42.	73.	104.
12.	43.	74.	105.
13.	44.	75.	
14.	45.	76.	
15.	46.	77.	
16.	47.	78.	
17.	48.	79.	
18.	49.	80.	
19.	50.	81.	
20.	51.	82.	
21.	52.	83.	
22.	53.	84.	
23.	54.	85.	
24.	55.	86.	
25.	56.	87.	
26.	57.	88.	
27.	58.	89.	
28.	59.	90.	
29.	60.	91.	
30.	61.	92.	
31.	62.	93.	

Reading Comprehension Extra Answer Sheet

1.	32.	63.	94.
2.	33.	64.	95.
3.	34.	65.	96.
4.	35.	66.	97.
5.	36.	67.	98.
6.	37.	68.	99.
7.	38.	69.	100.
8.	39.	70.	101.
9.	40.	71.	102.
10.	41.	72.	103.
11.	42.	73.	104.
12.	43.	74.	105.
13.	44.	75.	
14.	45.	76.	
15.	46.	77.	
16.	47.	78.	
17.	48.	79.	
18.	49.	80.	
19.	50.	81.	
20.	51.	82.	
21.	52.	83.	
22.	53.	84.	
23.	54.	85.	
24.	55.	86.	
25.	56.	87.	
26.	57.	88.	
27.	58.	89.	
28.	59.	90.	
29.	60.	91.	
30.	61.	92.	
31.	62.	93.	

Reading Comprehension Extra Answer Sheet

1.	32.	63.	94.
2.	33.	64.	95.
3.	34.	65.	96.
4.	35.	66.	97.
5.	36.	67.	98.
6.	37.	68.	99.
7.	38.	69.	100.
8.	39.	70.	101.
9.	40.	71.	102.
10.	41.	72.	103.
11.	42.	73.	104.
12.	43.	74.	105.
13.	44.	75.	
14.	45.	76.	
15.	46.	77.	
16.	47.	78.	
17.	48.	79.	
18.	49.	80.	
19.	50.	81.	
20.	51.	82.	
21.	52.	83.	
22.	53.	84.	
23.	54.	85.	
24.	55.	86.	
25.	56.	87.	
26.	57.	88.	
27.	58.	89.	
28.	59.	90.	
29.	60.	91.	
30.	61.	92.	
31.	62.	93.	

Reading Comprehension Extra Answer Sheet

1.	32.	63.	94.
2.	33.	64.	95.
3.	34.	65.	96.
4.	35.	66.	97.
5.	36.	67.	98.
6.	37.	68.	99.
7.	38.	69.	100.
8.	39.	70.	101.
9.	40.	71.	102.
10.	41.	72.	103.
11.	42.	73.	104.
12.	43.	74.	105.
13.	44.	75.	
14.	45.	76.	
15.	46.	77.	
16.	47.	78.	
17.	48.	79.	
18.	49.	80.	
19.	50.	81.	
20.	51.	82.	
21.	52.	83.	
22.	53.	84.	
23.	54.	85.	
24.	55.	86.	
25.	56.	87.	
26.	57.	88.	
27.	58.	89.	
28.	59.	90.	
29.	60.	91.	
30.	61.	92.	
31.	62.	93.	

Critical Reasoning Extra Answer Sheet

1.	32.	63.	94.
2.	33.	64.	95.
3.	34.	65.	96.
4.	35.	66.	97.
5.	36.	67.	98.
6.	37.	68.	99.
7.	38.	69.	100.
8.	39.	70.	101.
9.	40.	71.	102.
10.	41.	72.	103.
11.	42.	73.	104.
12.	43.	74.	105.
13.	44.	75.	106.
14.	45.	76.	107.
15.	46.	77.	108.
16.	47.	78.	109.
17.	48.	79.	110.
18.	49.	80.	111.
19.	50.	81.	112.
20.	51.	82.	113.
21.	52.	83.	114.
22.	53.	84.	115.
23.	54.	85.	116.
24.	55.	86.	117.
25.	56.	87.	118.
26.	57.	88.	119.
27.	58.	89.	120.
28.	59.	90.	121.
29.	60.	91.	122.
30.	61.	92.	123.
31.	62.	93.	124.

Critical Reasoning Extra Answer Sheet

1.	32.	63.	94.
2.	33.	64.	95.
3.	34.	65.	96.
4.	35.	66.	97.
5.	36.	67.	98.
6.	37.	68.	99.
7.	38.	69.	100.
8.	39.	70.	101.
9.	40.	71.	102.
10.	41.	72.	103.
11.	42.	73.	104.
12.	43.	74.	105.
13.	44.	75.	106.
14.	45.	76.	107.
15.	46.	77.	108.
16.	47.	78.	109.
17.	48.	79.	110.
18.	49.	80.	111.
19.	50.	81.	112.
20.	51.	82.	113.
21.	52.	83.	114.
22.	53.	84.	115.
23.	54.	85.	116.
24.	55.	86.	117.
25.	56.	87.	118.
26.	57.	88.	119.
27.	58.	89.	120.
28.	59.	90.	121.
29.	60.	91.	122.
30.	61.	92.	123.
31.	62.	93.	124.

Critical Reasoning Extra Answer Sheet

1.	32.	63.	94.
2.	33.	64.	95.
3.	34.	65.	96.
4.	35.	66.	97.
5.	36.	67.	98.
6.	37.	68.	99.
7.	38.	69.	100.
8.	39.	70.	101.
9.	40.	71.	102.
10.	41.	72.	103.
11.	42.	73.	104.
12.	43.	74.	105.
13.	44.	75.	106.
14.	45.	76.	107.
15.	46.	77.	108.
16.	47.	78.	109.
17.	48.	79.	110.
18.	49.	80.	111.
19.	50.	81.	112.
20.	51.	82.	113.
21.	52.	83.	114.
22.	53.	84.	115.
23.	54.	85.	116.
24.	55.	86.	117.
25.	56.	87.	118.
26.	57.	88.	119.
27.	58.	89.	120.
28.	59.	90.	121.
29.	60.	91.	122.
30.	61.	92.	123.
31.	62.	93.	124.

Second Attempt

Critical Reasoning Extra Answer Sheet

1.	32.	63.	94.
2.	33.	64.	95.
3.	34.	65.	96.
4.	35.	66.	97.
5.	36.	67.	98.
6.	37.	68.	99.
7.	38.	69.	100.
8.	39.	70.	101.
9.	40.	71.	102.
10.	41.	72.	103.
11.	42.	73.	104.
12.	43.	74.	105.
13.	44.	75.	106.
14.	45.	76.	107.
15.	46.	77.	108.
16.	47.	78.	109.
17.	48.	79.	110.
18.	49.	✓ 80. D X	111.
19.	50.	✓ 81. E	112.
20.	51.	✓ 82. C	113.
21.	52.	83.	114.
22.	53.	84.	115.
23.	54.	85.	116.
24.	55.	86.	117.
25.	56.	87.	118.
26.	57.	88.	119.
27.	58.	89.	120.
28.	59.	90.	121.
29.	60.	91.	122.
30.	61.	92.	123.
31.	62.	93.	124.

Sentence Correction Extra Answer Sheet

1.	32.	63.	94.
2.	33.	64.	95.
3.	34.	65.	96.
4.	35.	66.	97.
5.	36.	67.	98.
6.	37.	68.	99.
7.	38.	69.	100.
8.	39.	70.	101.
9.	40.	71.	102.
10.	41.	72.	103.
11.	42.	73.	104.
12.	43.	74.	105.
13.	44.	75.	106.
14.	45.	76.	107.
15.	46.	77.	108.
16.	47.	78.	109.
17.	48.	79.	110.
18.	49.	80.	111.
19.	50.	81.	112.
20.	51.	82.	113.
21.	52.	83.	
22.	53.	84.	
23.	54.	85.	
24.	55.	86.	
25.	56.	87.	
26.	57.	88.	
27.	58.	89.	
28.	59.	90.	
29.	60.	91.	
30.	61.	92.	
31.	62.	93.	

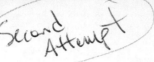
Second Attempt

Sentence Correction Extra Answer Sheet

1.	32.	63.	94. D ✓
2.	33.	64.	95. D ✓
3.	34.	65.	96. B ✓
4.	35.	66.	97. A ✓
5.	36.	67.	98. D ✓
6.	37.	68.	x 99. A x
7.	38.	69.	100. C ✓
8.	39.	70.	101. E ✓
9.	40.	71.	102. E ✓
10.	41.	72.	103. D ✓
11.	42.	73.	104. B ✓
12.	43.	74.	105. B ✓
13.	44.	75.	106. D ✓
14.	45.	76.	107. A ✓
15.	46.	77.	108. D ✓
16.	47.	78.	109. B ✓
17.	48.	79.	110. E ✓
18.	49.	80.	111. C ✓
19.	50.	81.	112. C ✓
20.	51.	82.	113. D ✓
21.	52.	83.	
22.	53.	84.	
23.	54.	85.	
24.	55.	86.	
25.	56.	87.	
26.	57.	88.	
27.	58.	89.	
28.	59.	90.	
29.	60.	91.	
30.	61.	92. E ✓	
31.	62.	93. B ✓	

Sentence Correction Extra Answer Sheet

1.	32.	63.	94.
2.	33.	64.	95.
3.	34.	65.	96.
4.	35.	66.	97.
5.	36.	67.	98.
6.	37.	68.	99.
7.	38.	69.	100.
8.	39.	70.	101.
9.	40.	71.	102.
10.	41.	72.	103.
11.	42.	73.	104.
12.	43.	74.	105.
13.	44.	75.	106.
14.	45.	76.	107.
15.	46.	77.	108.
16.	47.	78.	109.
17.	48.	79.	110.
18.	49.	80.	111.
19.	50.	81.	112.
20.	51.	82.	113.
21.	52.	83.	
22.	53.	84.	
23.	54.	85.	
24.	55.	86.	
25.	56.	87.	
26.	57.	88.	
27.	58.	89.	
28.	59.	90.	
29.	60.	91.	
30.	61.	92.	
31.	62.	93.	

Sentence Correction Extra Answer Sheet

1. B ✓
2. A ✓
3. A ✓
4. (B) ✗
5. D ✓
6. A ✓
7. C ✓
8. C ✓
9. B
10. A
11. E
12. (B) ✗
13. A
14. B
15. A
16. (D) ✗
17. B
18. (D) ✗
19. A ✓
20. D ✓
21. D
22. C ✗
23. C ✓
24. B ✓
25. (A) ✓
26. C ✓
27. (A) ✗
28. (C) ✗
29. E ✓
30. (C) ✗
31. A ✓

32. D ✓
33. B ✓
34. (E) ✗
35. E ✓
36. C ✓
37. B ✓
38. E ✓
39. E ✓
40. (C) ✗
41. C ✓
42. (A) ✗
43. E ✓
44. (D) ✗
45. D ✓
46. C ✓
47. D ✓
48. C ✓
49. A ✓
50. D ✓
51. C ✓
52. D ✓
53. (B) ✗
54. (C) ✗
55. (E)
56. B ✓
57. C ✓
58. A ✓
59. (A)
60. B ✓
61. B ✓
62. E ✓

63. A ✓
64. A ✓
65. D ✓
66. C ✓
67. D ✓
68. D ✓
69. C ✓
70. (C)
71. C ✓
72. B
73. B ✓
74. C ✓
75. E
76. B
77. C
78. E
✓ 79. D
✓ 80. (E) whereby ?
✓ 81. C
✓ 82. D
✓ 83. E
✗ 84. (B)
✓ 85. C
✓ 86. D
✗ 87. (A) → ?
✗ 88. (C) ✓
✓ 89. E
✓ 90. E
✓ 91. B
✗ 92. (B) ✻
✓ 93. B

✗ (94. A)
✓ 95. D
✓ 96. B
✓ 97. A
✓ 98. D
✗ (99. A)
✓ 100. C
✓ 101. E
✗ (102. D)
✓ 103. D
✓ 104. B
✗ (105. A → B)
✗ (106. B → D)
✓ 107. A
✓? 108. D
✓ 109. B
✗ (110. A → E)
✓ 111. C ?
✓ 112. C
✓ 113. D